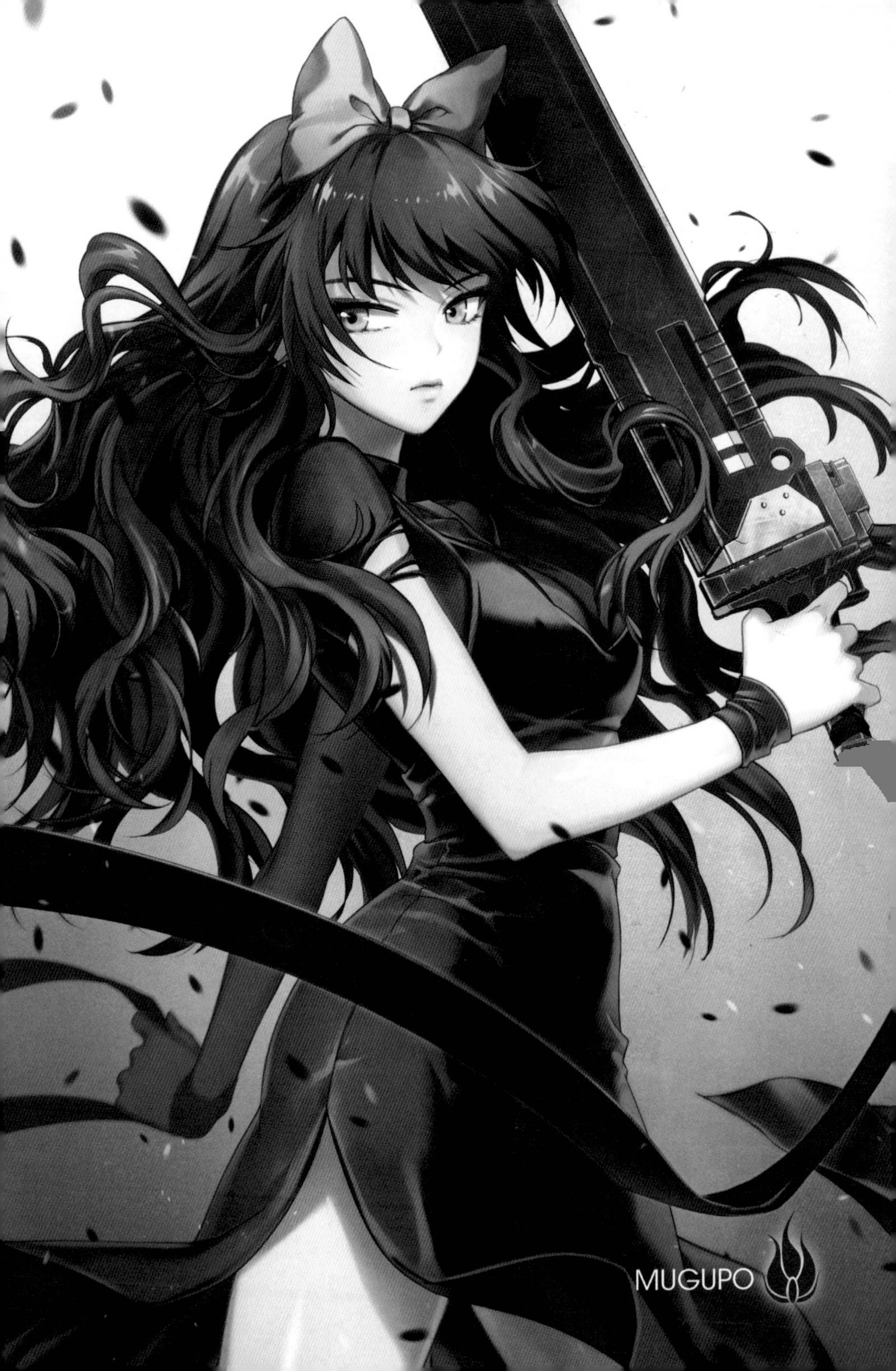
MUGUPO

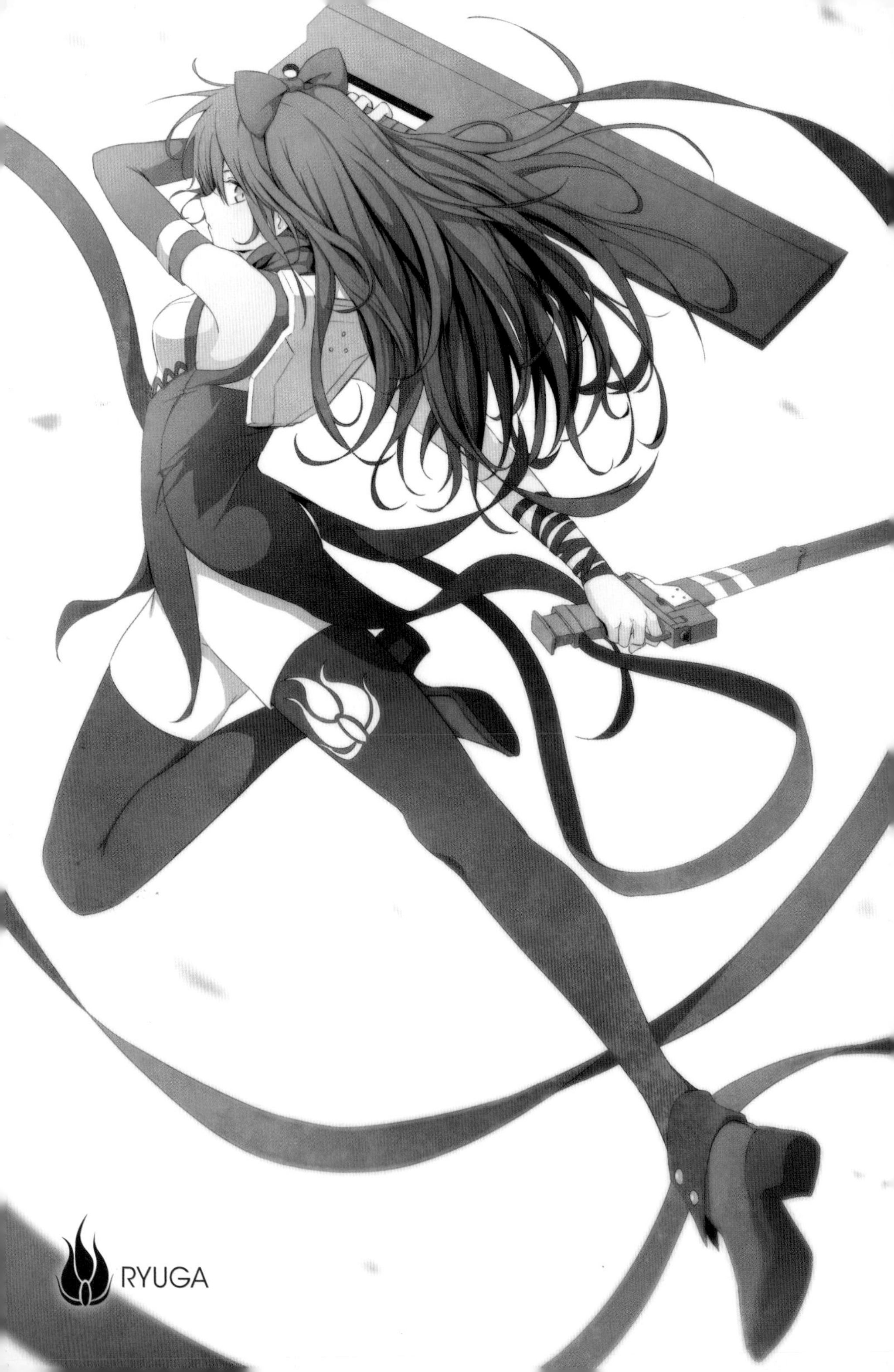
RYUGA

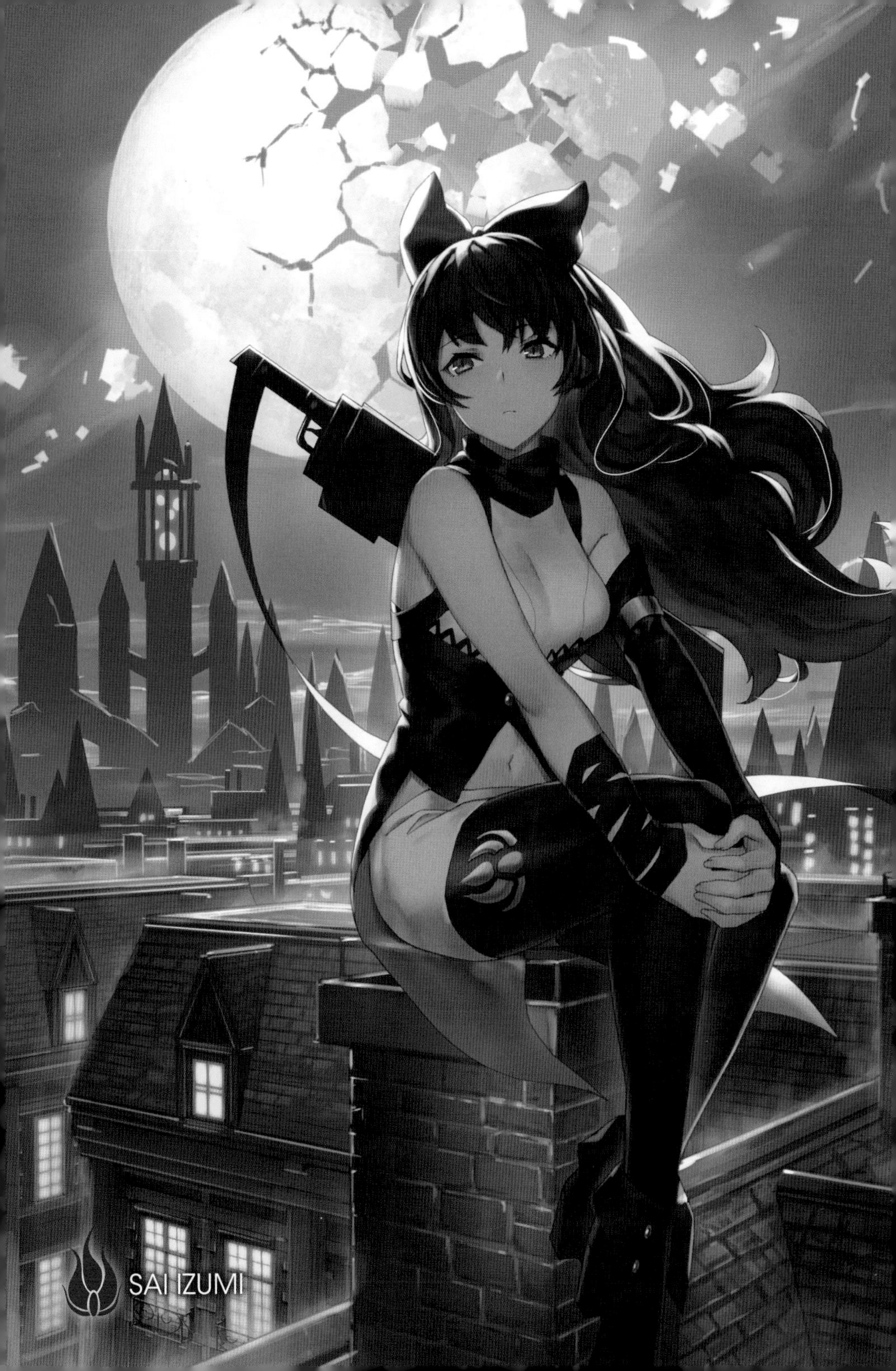
SAI IZUMI

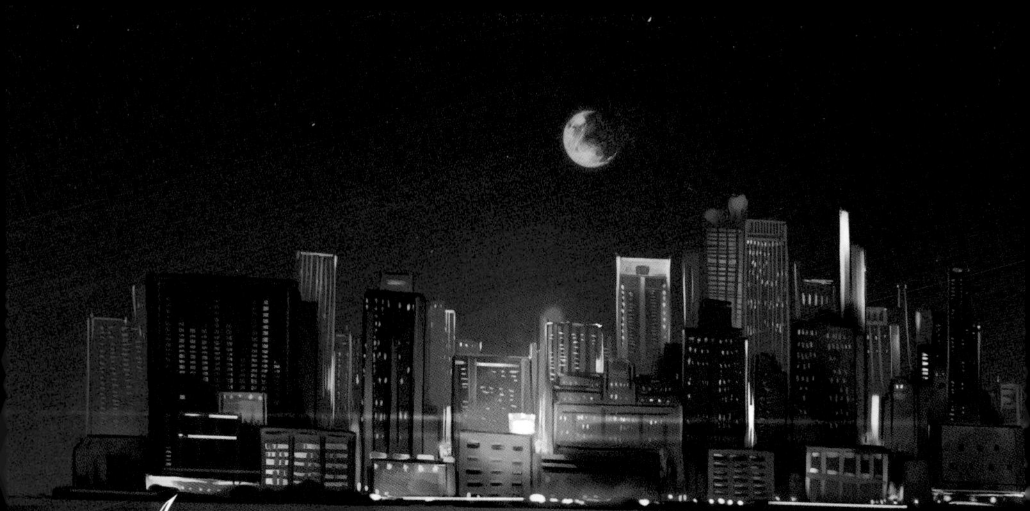

Intruder: Black Cat

Ritsu Hayami

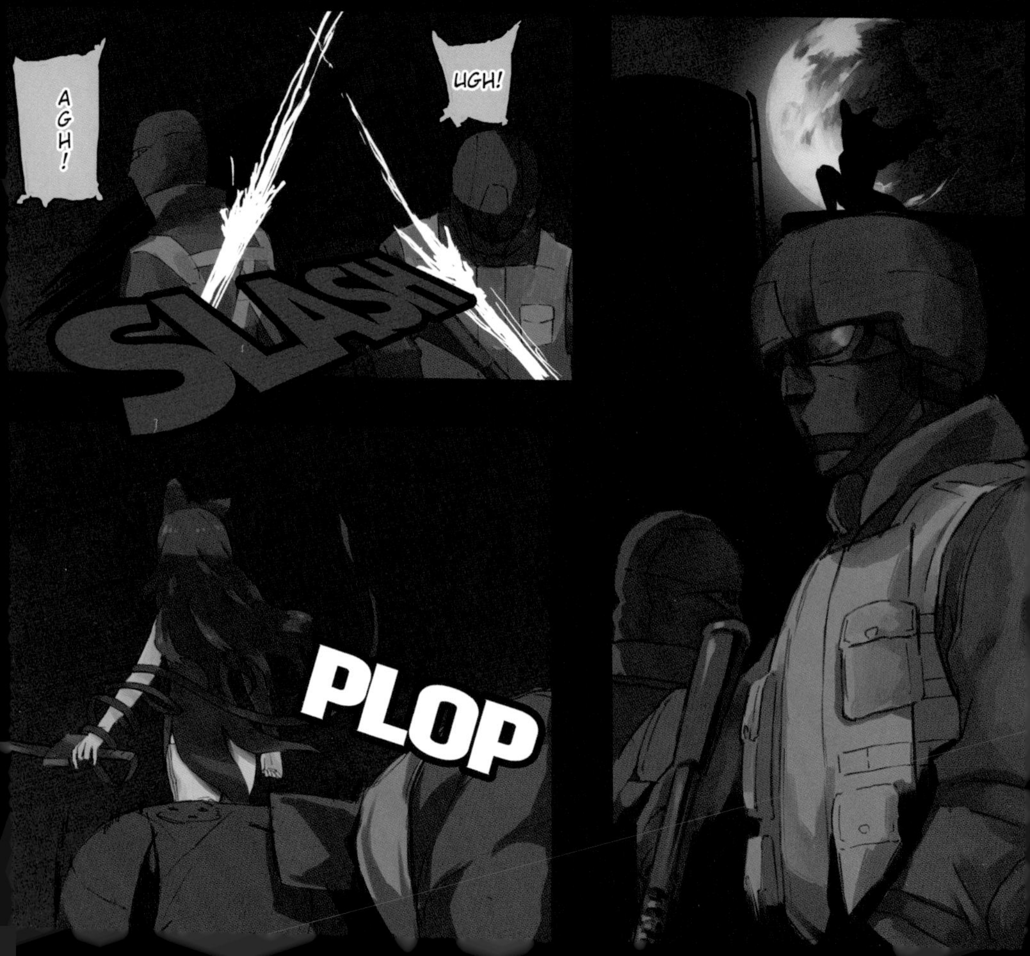
UGH!
AGH!
SLASH
PLOP

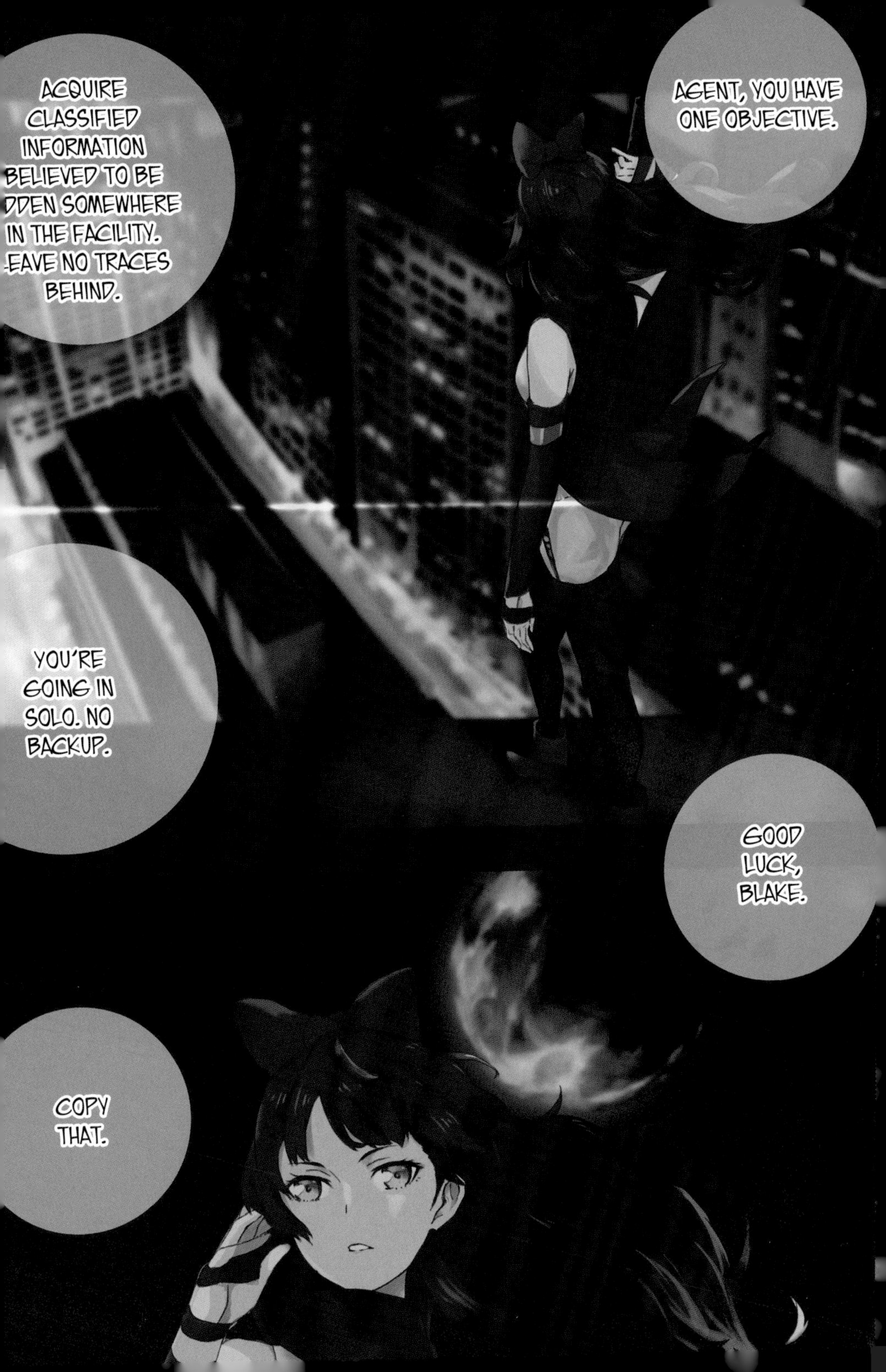
AGENT, YOU HAVE ONE OBJECTIVE.
ACQUIRE CLASSIFIED INFORMATION BELIEVED TO BE DDEN SOMEWHERE IN THE FACILITY. EAVE NO TRACES BEHIND.
YOU'RE GOING IN SOLO. NO BACKUP.
GOOD LUCK, BLAKE.
COPY THAT.

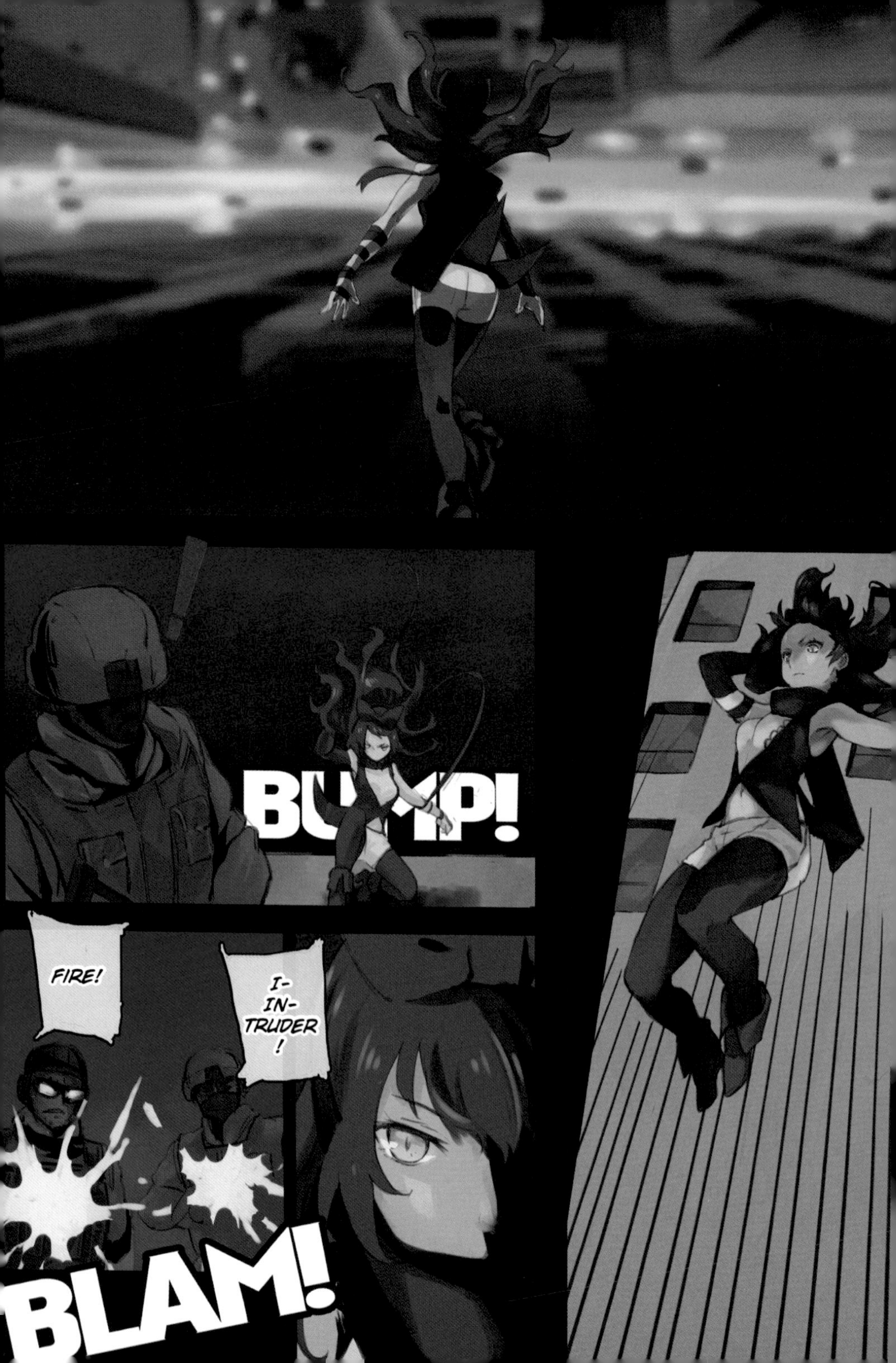
BUMP!
I- IN- TRUDER !
FIRE!
BLAM!

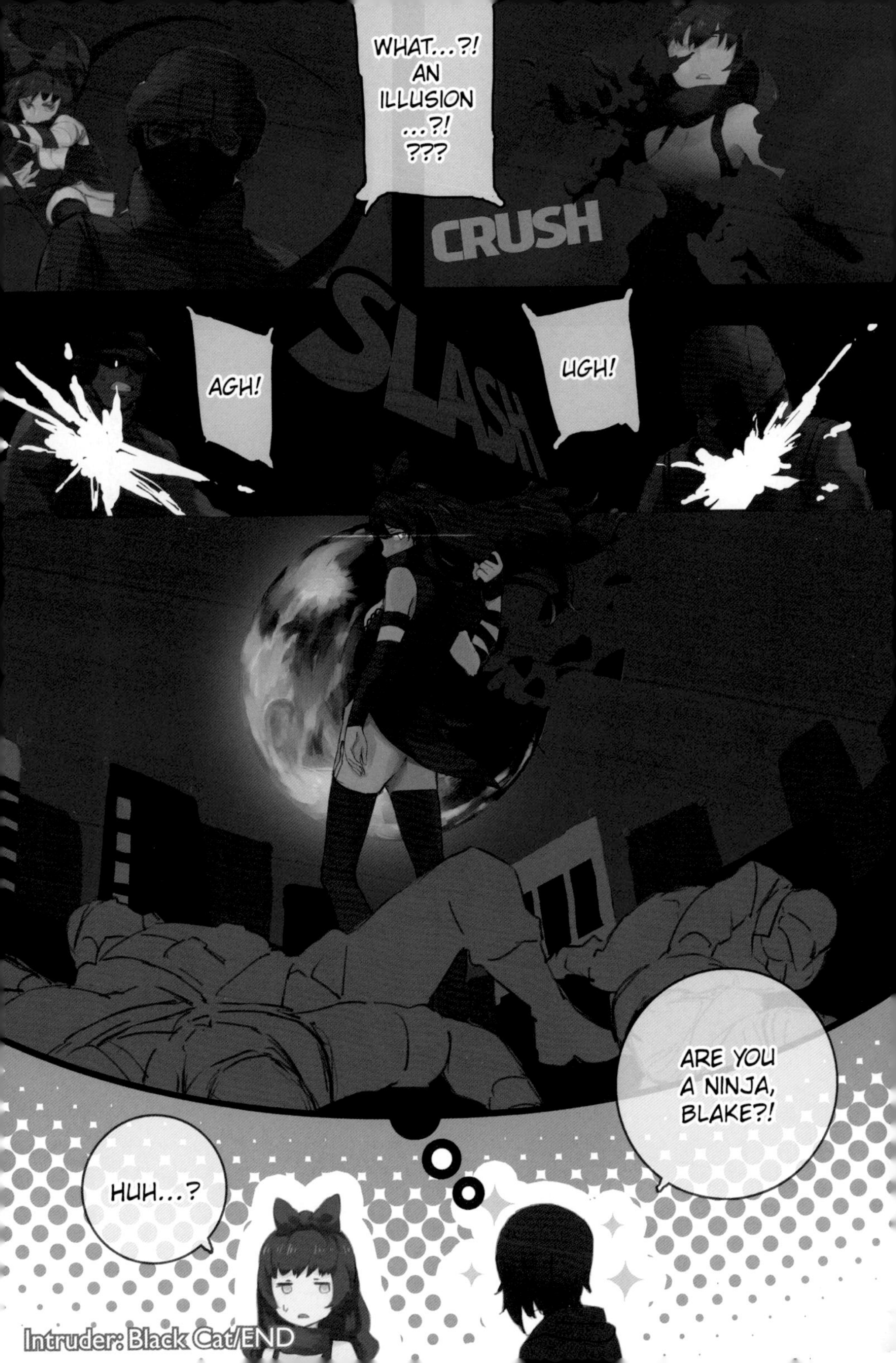
CRUSH
WHAT...?! AN ILLUSION ...?! ???
UGH!
SLASH
AGH!
ARE YOU A NINJA, BLAKE?!
HUH...?
Intruder: Black Cat/END

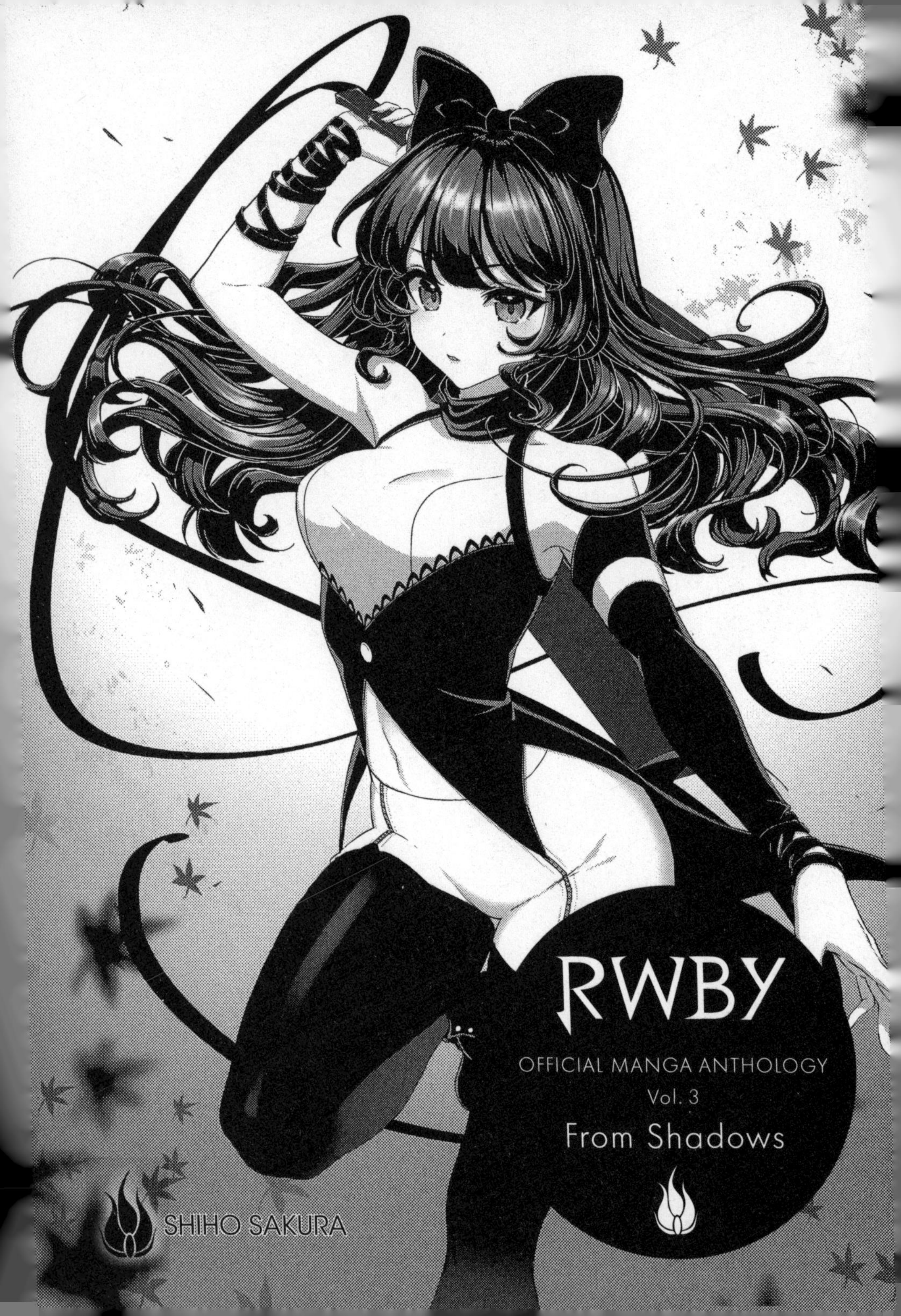
RWBY
OFFICIAL MANGA ANTHOLOGY
Vol. 3
From Shadows
SHIHO SAKURA

RWBY

OFFICIAL MANGA ANTHOLOGY 3

From Shadows

CONTENTS

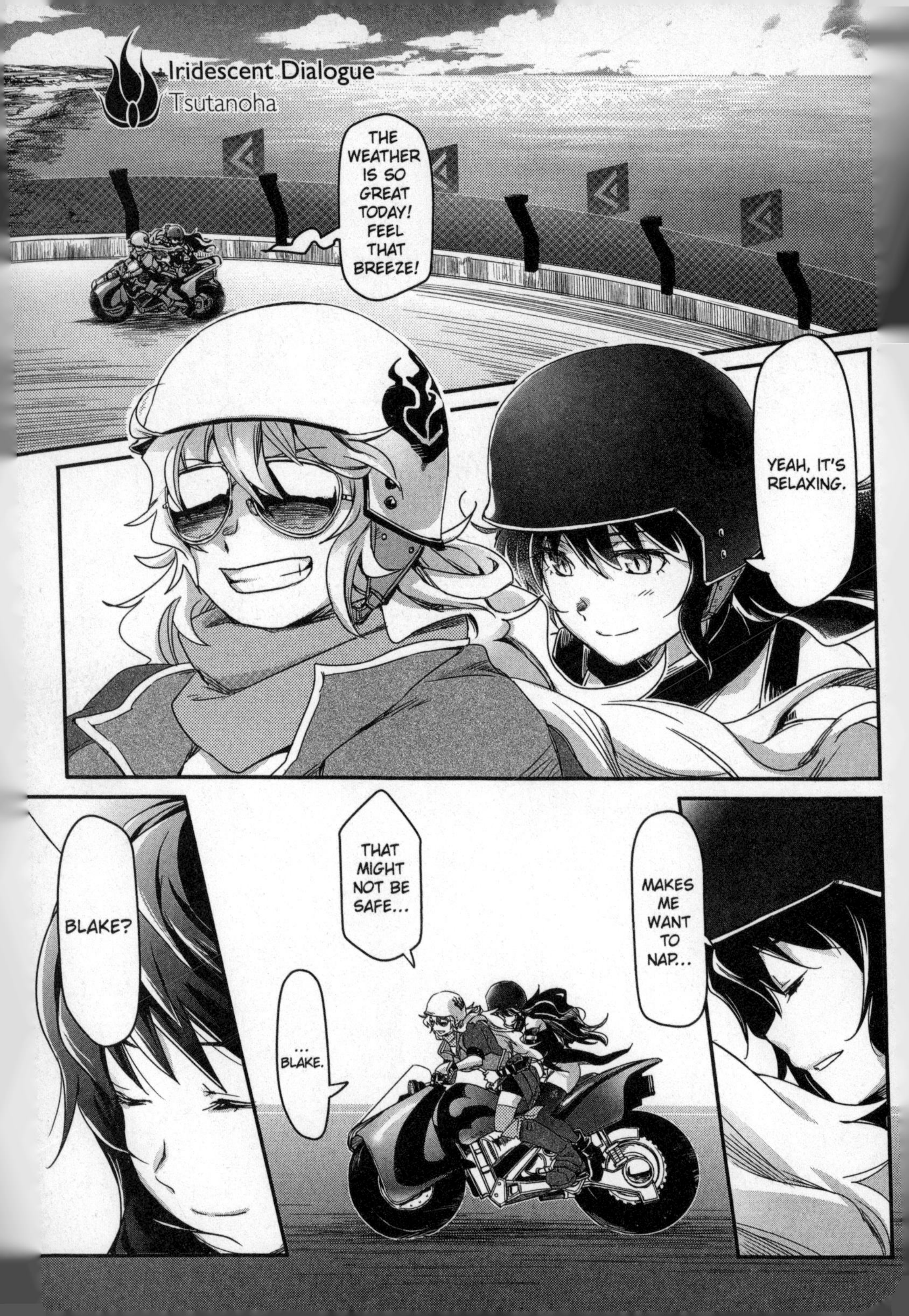
Iridescent Dialogue
Tsutanoha
THE WEATHER IS SO GREAT TODAY! FEEL THAT BREEZE!
YEAH, IT'S RELAXING.
MAKES ME WANT TO NAP...
THAT MIGHT NOT BE SAFE...
... BLAKE.
BLAKE?

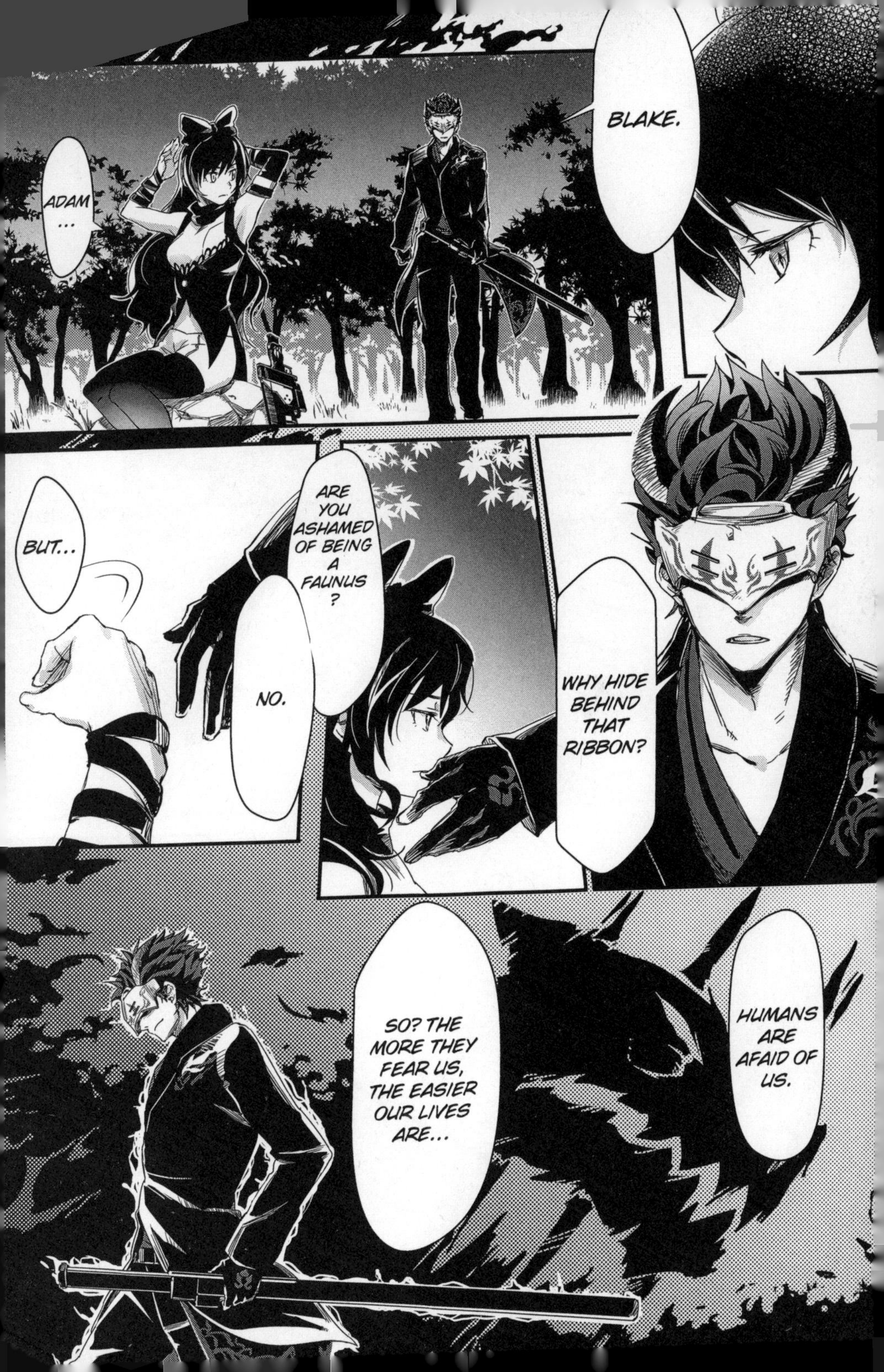
BLAKE.
ADAM ...
WHY HIDE BEHIND THAT RIBBON?
ARE YOU ASHAMED OF BEING A FAUNUS?
NO.
BUT...
HUMANS ARE AFAID OF US.
SO? THE MORE THEY FEAR US, THE EASIER OUR LIVES ARE...

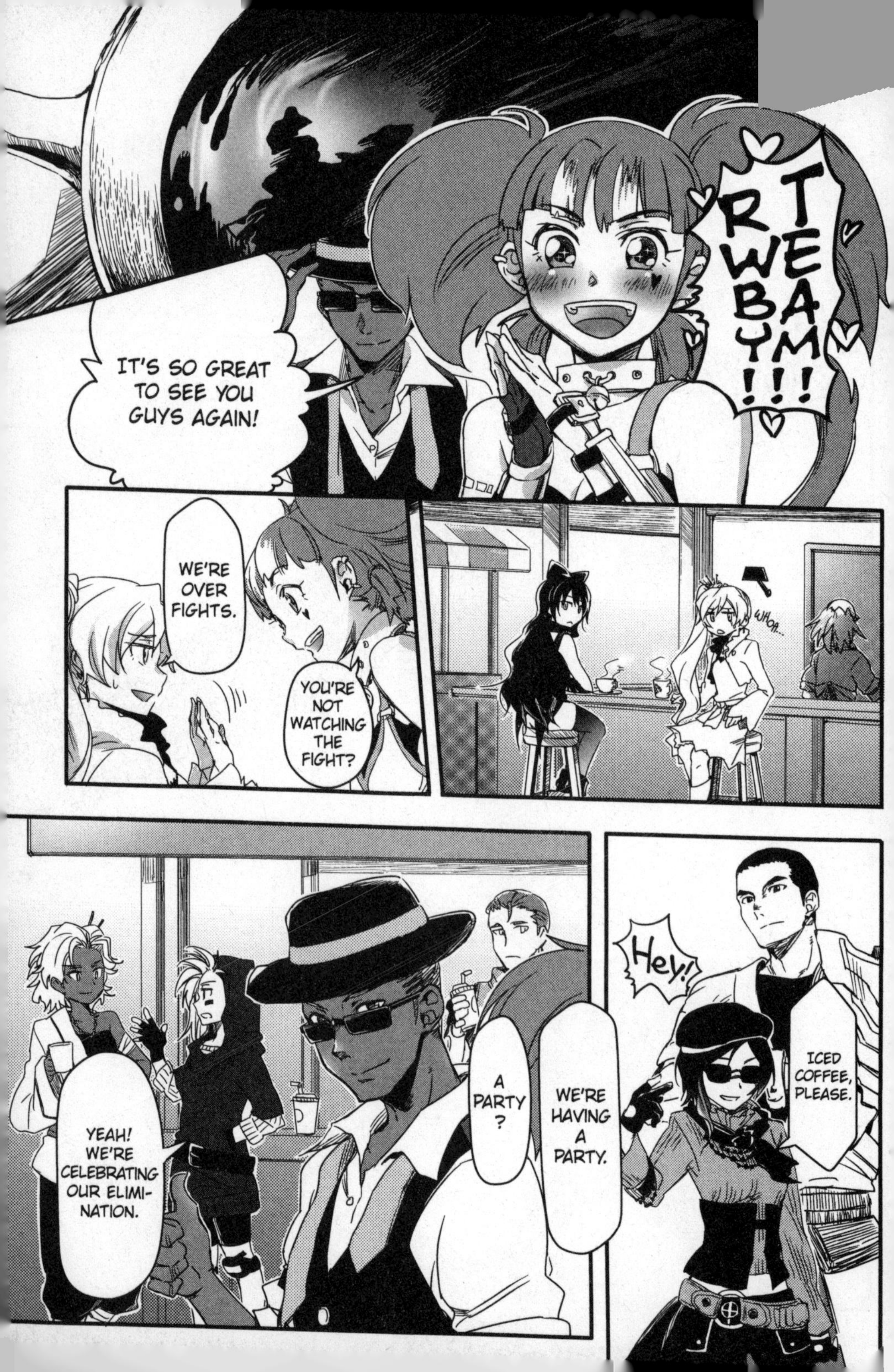
TEAM RWBY!!!
IT'S SO GREAT TO SEE YOU GUYS AGAIN!
WHOA...
YOU'RE NOT WATCHING THE FIGHT?
WE'RE OVER FIGHTS.
Hey!
ICED COFFEE, PLEASE.
WE'RE HAVING A PARTY.
A PARTY?
YEAH! WE'RE CELEBRATING OUR ELIMINATION.

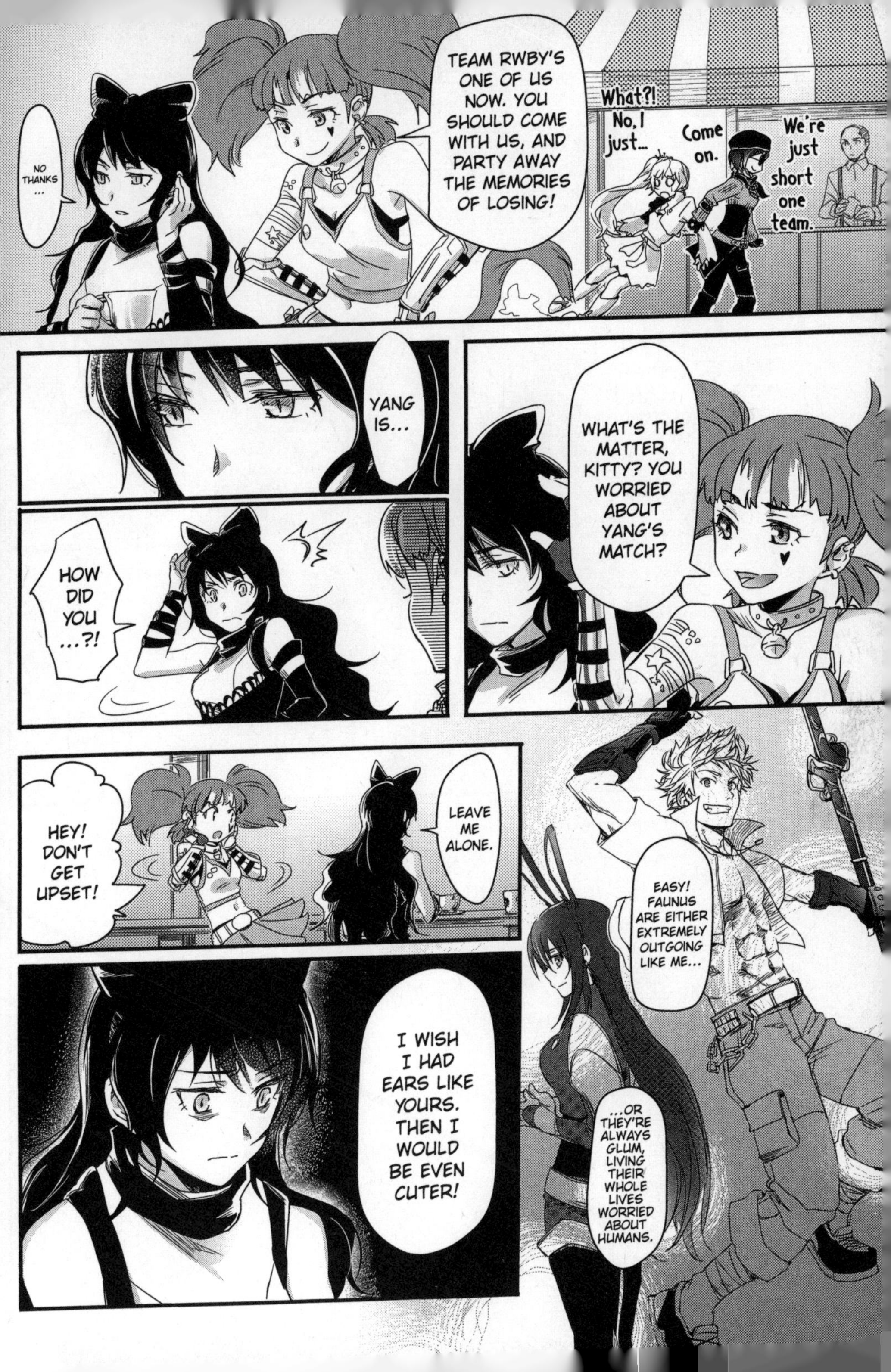
We're just short one team.
Come on.
What?! No, I just...
TEAM RWBY'S ONE OF US NOW. YOU SHOULD COME WITH US, AND PARTY AWAY THE MEMORIES OF LOSING!
NO THANKS ...
WHAT'S THE MATTER, KITTY? YOU WORRIED ABOUT YANG'S MATCH?
YANG IS...
HOW DID YOU ...?!
EASY! FAUNUS ARE EITHER EXTREMELY OUTGOING LIKE ME...
...OR THEY'RE ALWAYS GLUM, LIVING THEIR WHOLE LIVES WORRIED ABOUT HUMANS.
LEAVE ME ALONE.
HEY! DON'T GET UPSET!
I WISH I HAD EARS LIKE YOURS. THEN I WOULD BE EVEN CUTER!

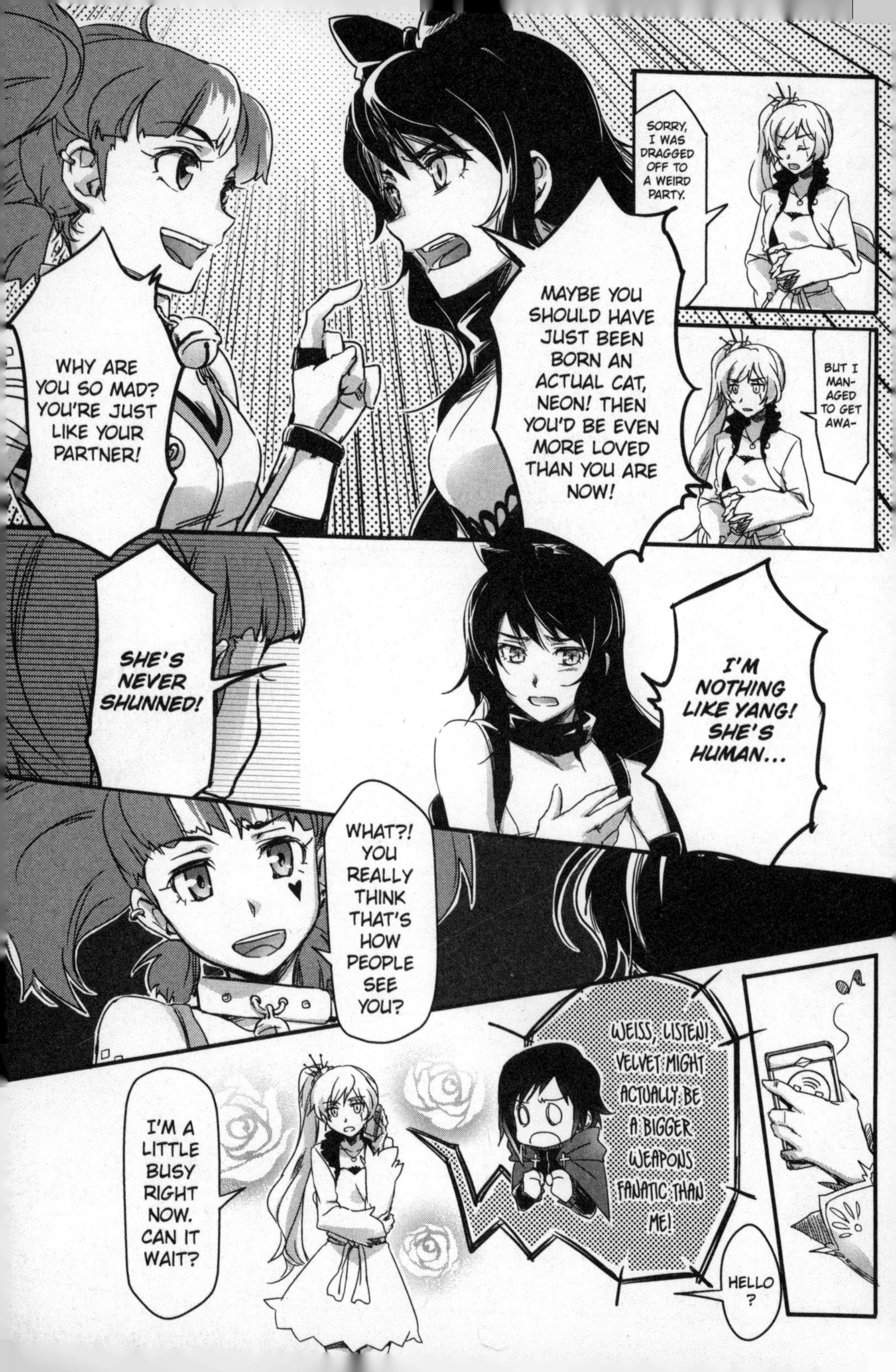
SORRY, I WAS DRAGGED OFF TO A WEIRD PARTY.
BUT I MAN-AGED TO GET AWA-
MAYBE YOU SHOULD HAVE JUST BEEN BORN AN ACTUAL CAT, NEON! THEN YOU'D BE EVEN MORE LOVED THAN YOU ARE NOW!
WHY ARE YOU SO MAD? YOU'RE JUST LIKE YOUR PARTNER!
I'M NOTHING LIKE YANG! SHE'S HUMAN...
SHE'S NEVER SHUNNED!
WHAT?! YOU REALLY THINK THAT'S HOW PEOPLE SEE YOU?
HELLO ?
WEISS, LISTEN! VELVET MIGHT ACTUALLY BE A BIGGER WEAPONS FANATIC THAN ME!
I'M A LITTLE BUSY RIGHT NOW. CAN IT WAIT?

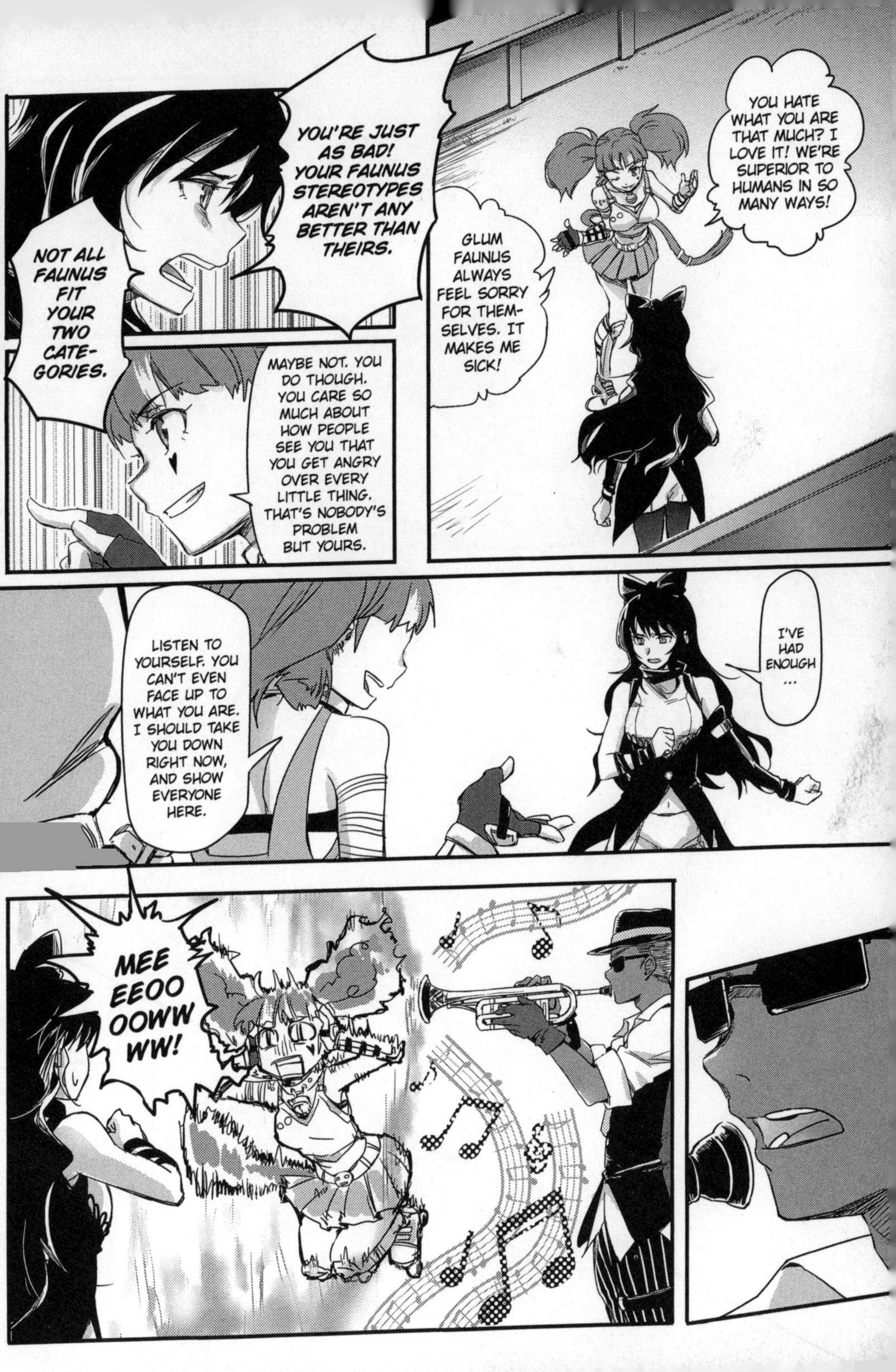
YOU HATE WHAT YOU ARE THAT MUCH? I LOVE IT! WE'RE SUPERIOR TO HUMANS IN SO MANY WAYS!
GLUM FAUNUS ALWAYS FEEL SORRY FOR THEMSELVES. IT MAKES ME SICK!
YOU'RE JUST AS BAD! YOUR FAUNUS STEREOTYPES AREN'T ANY BETTER THAN THEIRS.
NOT ALL FAUNUS FIT YOUR TWO CATEGORIES.
MAYBE NOT. YOU DO THOUGH. YOU CARE SO MUCH ABOUT HOW PEOPLE SEE YOU THAT YOU GET ANGRY OVER EVERY LITTLE THING. THAT'S NOBODY'S PROBLEM BUT YOURS.
I'VE HAD ENOUGH...
LISTEN TO YOURSELF. YOU CAN'T EVEN FACE UP TO WHAT YOU ARE. I SHOULD TAKE YOU DOWN RIGHT NOW, AND SHOW EVERYONE HERE.
MEEEEOOOOWWWW!

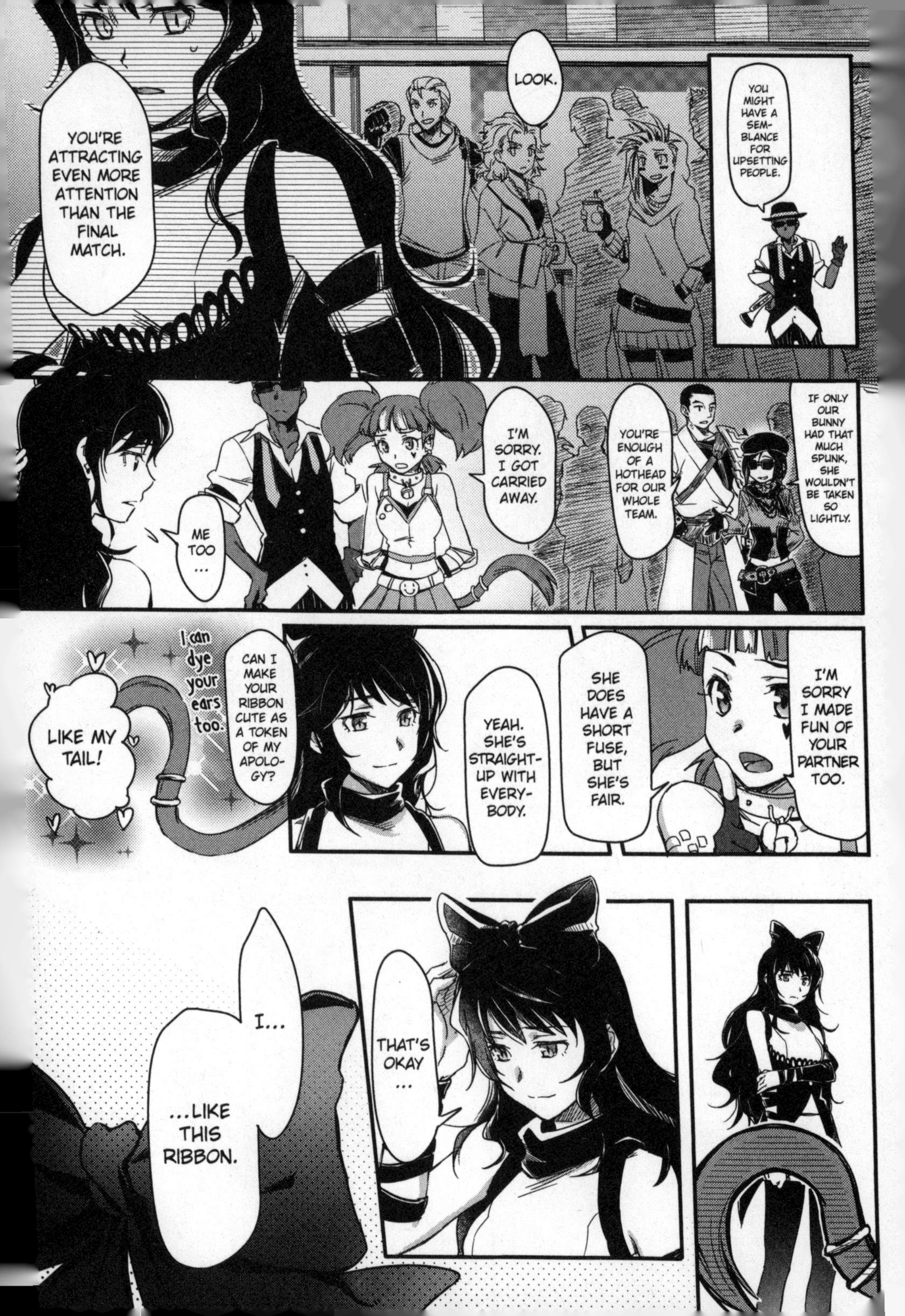
YOU MIGHT HAVE A SEMBLANCE FOR UPSETTING PEOPLE.
LOOK.
YOU'RE ATTRACTING EVEN MORE ATTENTION THAN THE FINAL MATCH.
IF ONLY OUR BUNNY HAD THAT MUCH SPUNK, SHE WOULDN'T BE TAKEN SO LIGHTLY.
YOU'RE ENOUGH OF A HOTHEAD FOR OUR WHOLE TEAM.
I'M SORRY. I GOT CARRIED AWAY.
ME TOO...
I'M SORRY I MADE FUN OF YOUR PARTNER TOO.
SHE DOES HAVE A SHORT FUSE, BUT SHE'S FAIR.
YEAH. SHE'S STRAIGHT-UP WITH EVERYBODY.
CAN I MAKE YOUR RIBBON CUTE AS A TOKEN OF MY APOLOGY?
I can dye your ears too.
LIKE MY TAIL!
THAT'S OKAY...
I...
...LIKE THIS RIBBON.

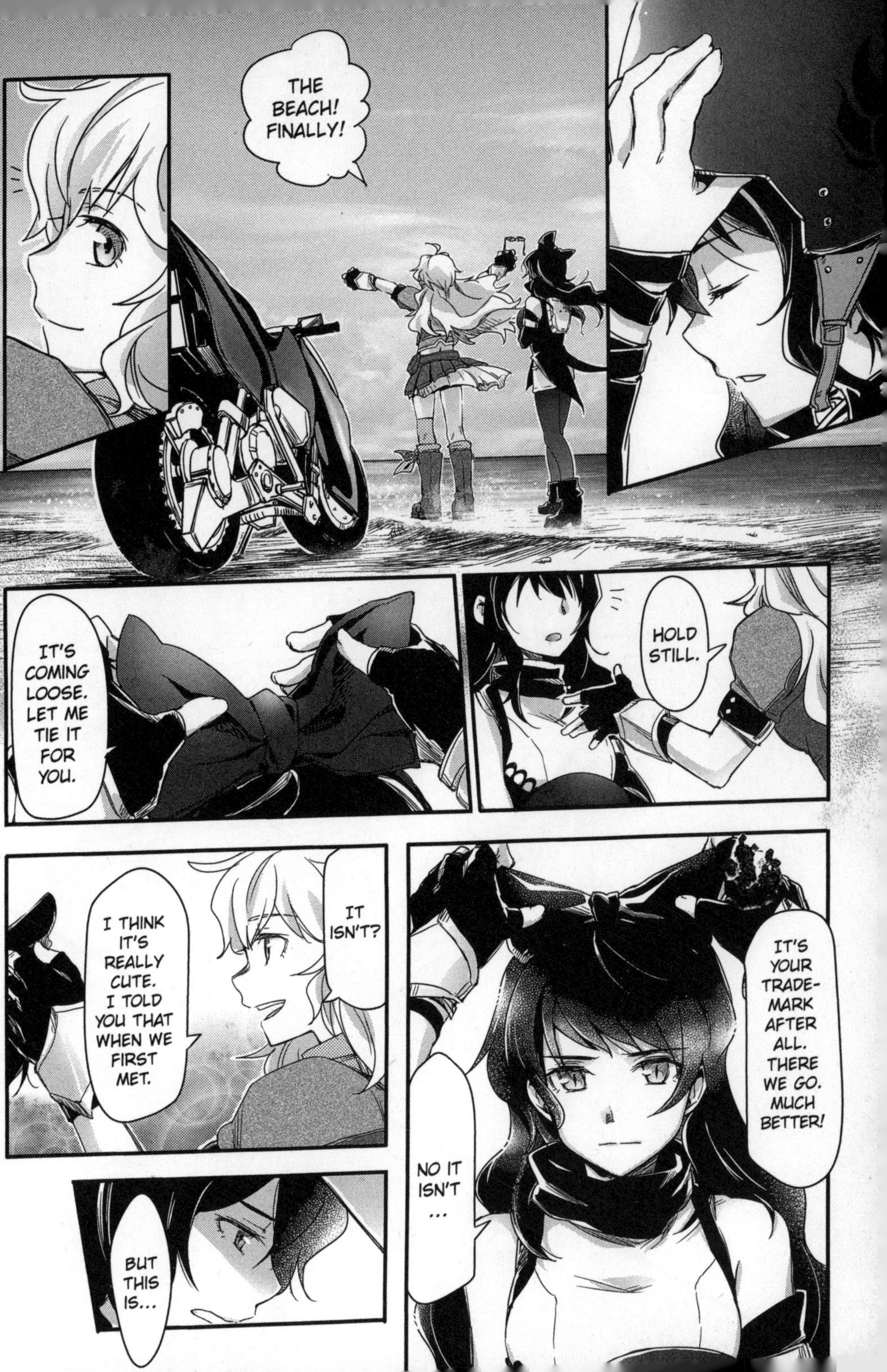
THE BEACH! FINALLY!
HOLD STILL.
IT'S COMING LOOSE. LET ME TIE IT FOR YOU.
IT'S YOUR TRADE-MARK AFTER ALL. THERE WE GO. MUCH BETTER!
NO IT ISN'T ...
IT ISN'T?
I THINK IT'S REALLY CUTE. I TOLD YOU THAT WHEN WE FIRST MET.
BUT THIS IS...

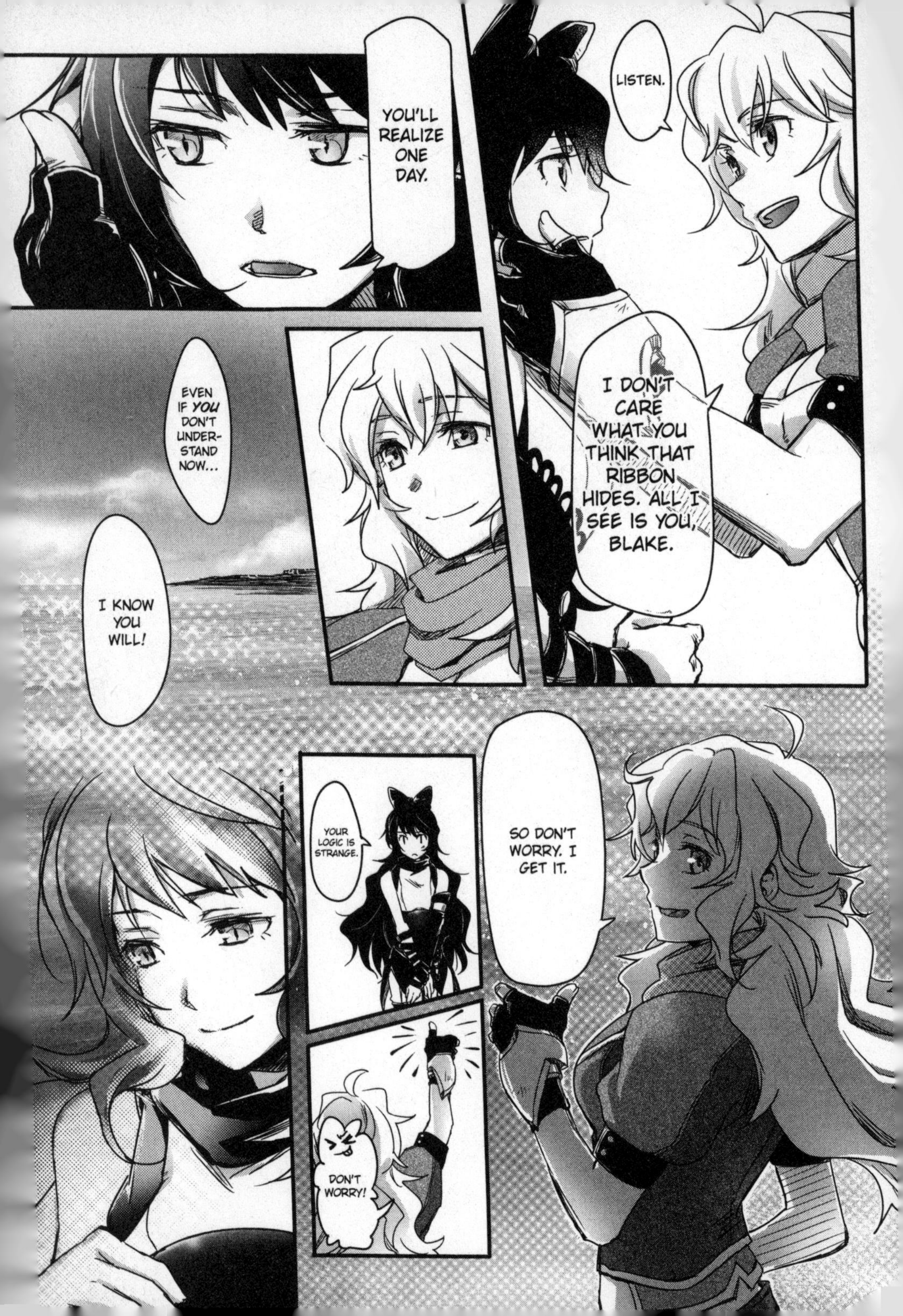
LISTEN.
I DON'T CARE WHAT YOU THINK THAT RIBBON HIDES. ALL I SEE IS YOU, BLAKE.
YOU'LL REALIZE ONE DAY.
EVEN IF *YOU* DON'T UNDER-STAND NOW...
I KNOW YOU WILL!
SO DON'T WORRY. I GET IT.
YOUR LOGIC IS STRANGE.
DON'T WORRY!

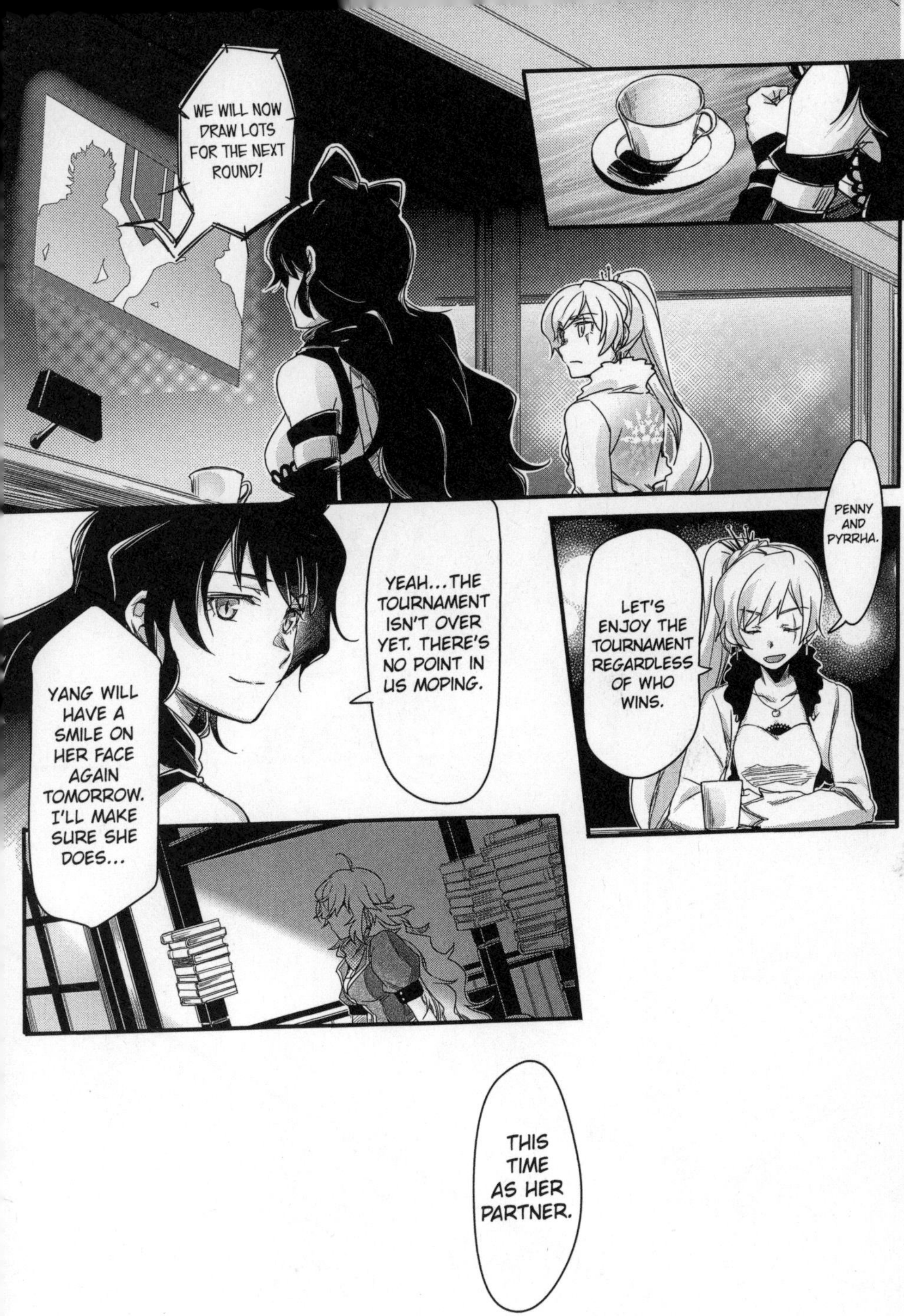
WE WILL NOW DRAW LOTS FOR THE NEXT ROUND!
PENNY AND PYRRHA.
LET'S ENJOY THE TOURNAMENT REGARDLESS OF WHO WINS.
YEAH...THE TOURNAMENT ISN'T OVER YET. THERE'S NO POINT IN US MOPING.
YANG WILL HAVE A SMILE ON HER FACE AGAIN TOMORROW. I'LL MAKE SURE SHE DOES...
THIS TIME AS HER PARTNER.

Iridescent Dialogue/END

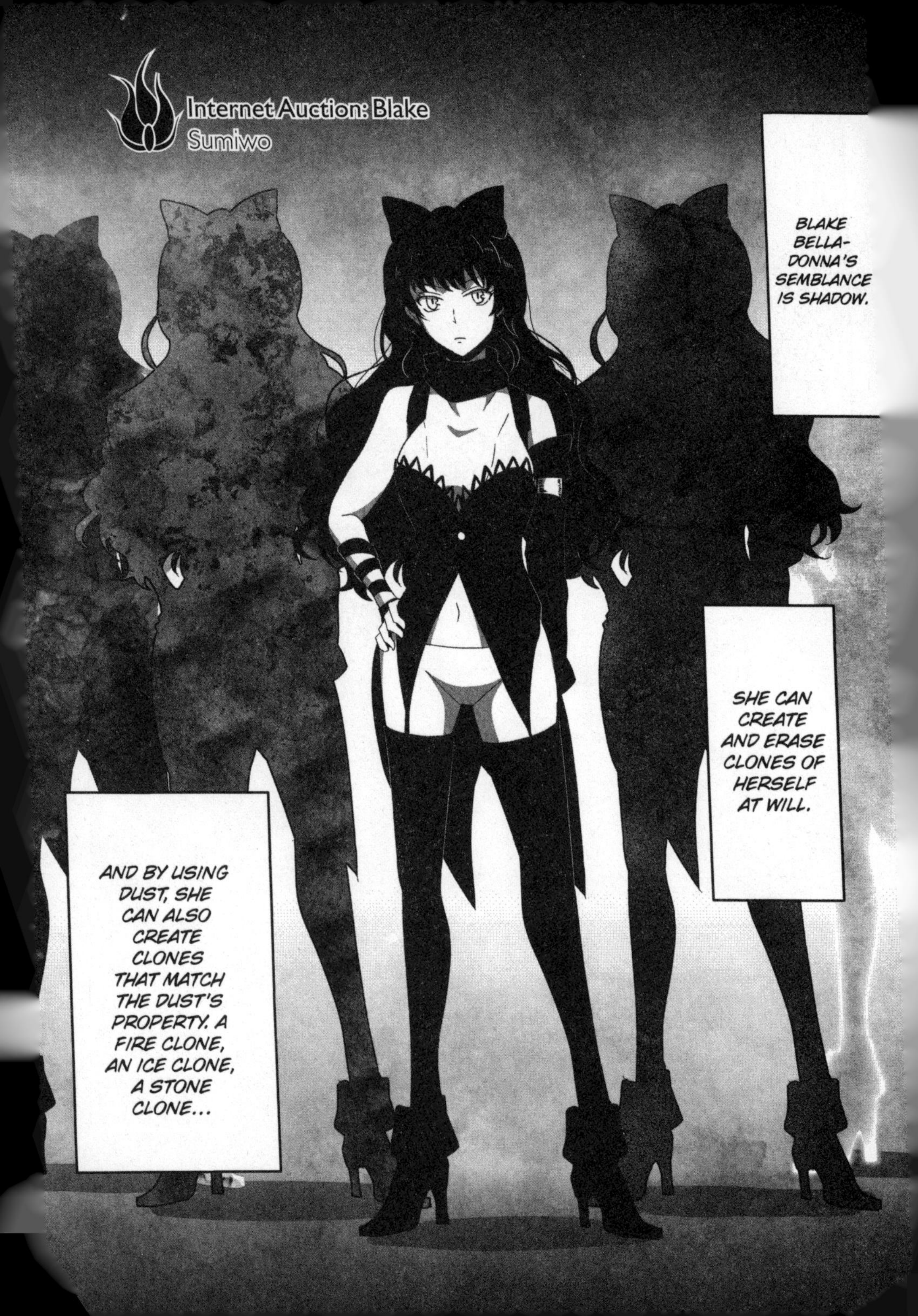
Internet Auction: Blake
Sumiwo
BLAKE BELLADONNA'S SEMBLANCE IS SHADOW.
SHE CAN CREATE AND ERASE CLONES OF HERSELF AT WILL.
AND BY USING DUST, SHE CAN ALSO CREATE CLONES THAT MATCH THE DUST'S PROPERTY. A FIRE CLONE, AN ICE CLONE, A STONE CLONE...

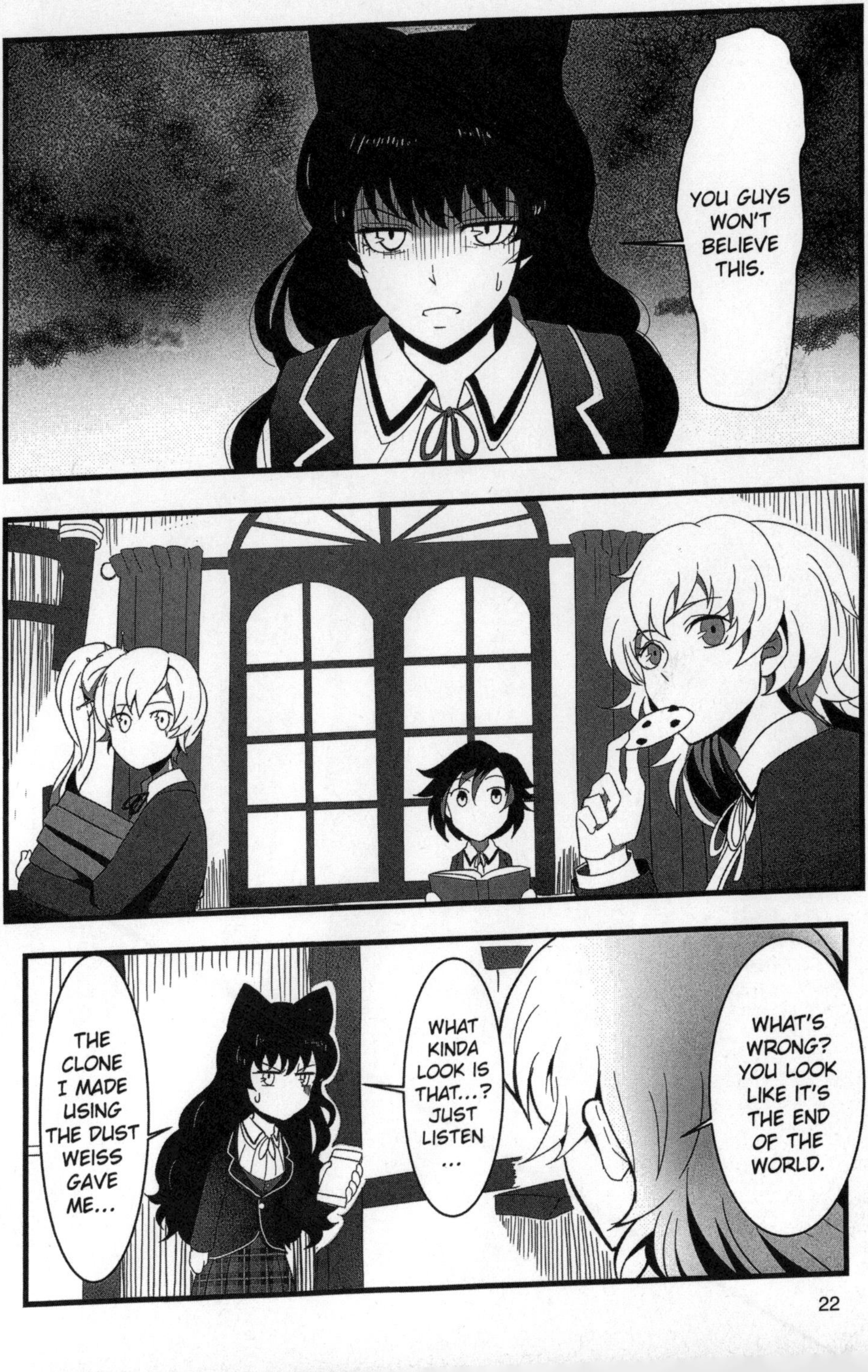
YOU GUYS WON'T BELIEVE THIS.
WHAT'S WRONG? YOU LOOK LIKE IT'S THE END OF THE WORLD.
WHAT KINDA LOOK IS THAT...? JUST LISTEN ...
THE CLONE I MADE USING THE DUST WEISS GAVE ME...

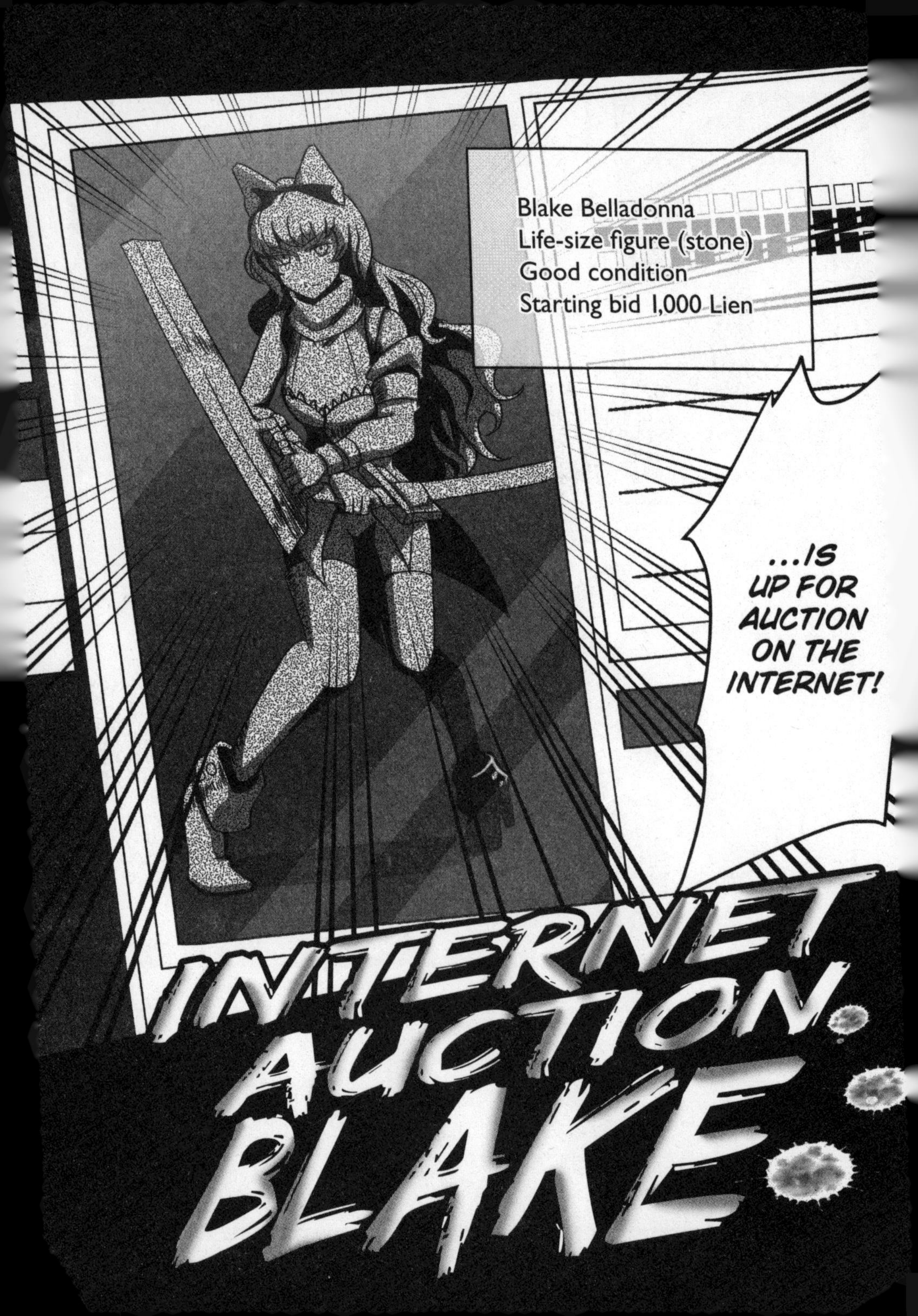
Blake Belladonna
Life-size figure (stone)
Good condition
Starting bid 1,000 Lien
...IS UP FOR AUCTION ON THE INTERNET!
INTERNET AUCTION BLAKE

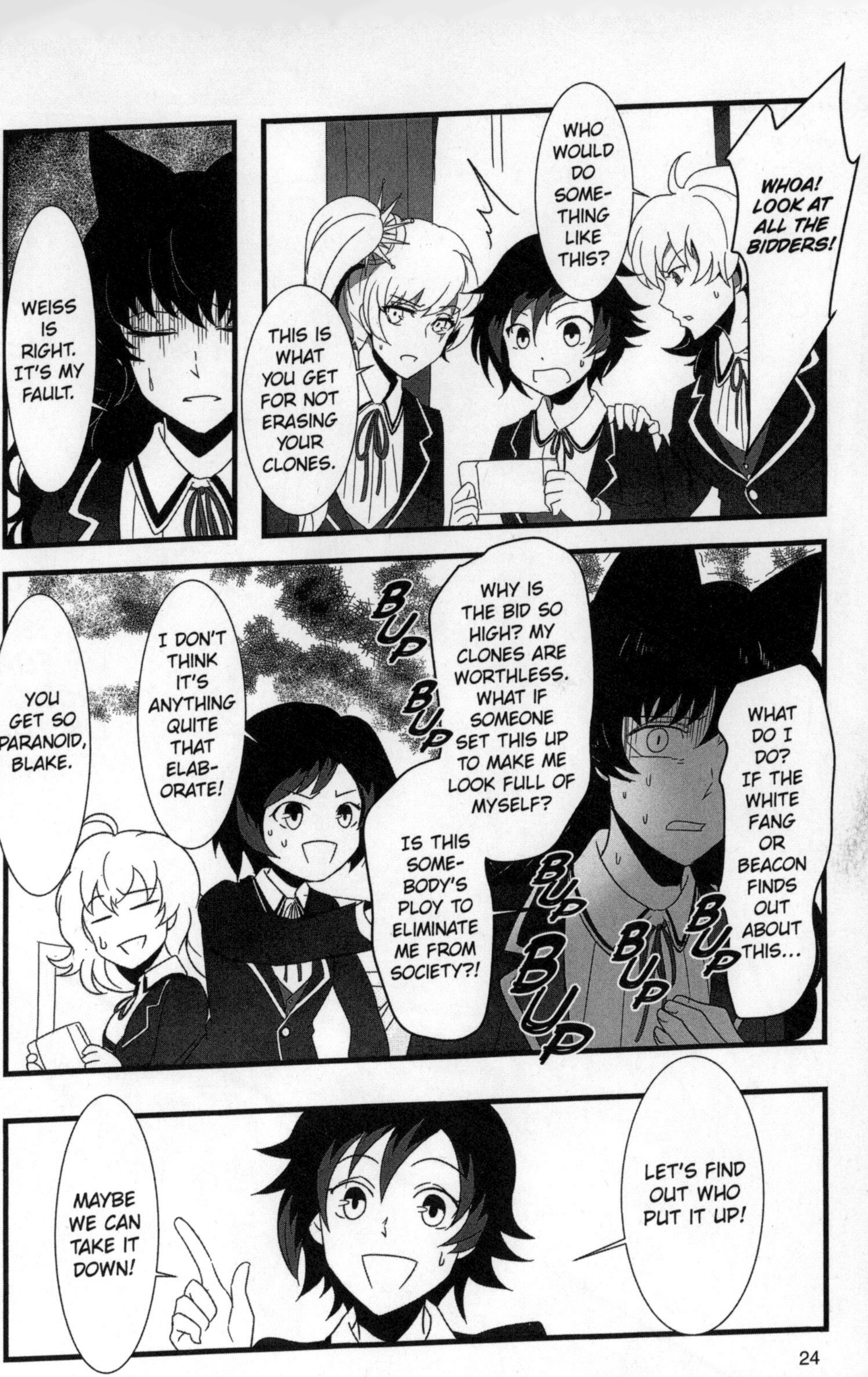
WHOA! LOOK AT ALL THE BIDDERS!
WHO WOULD DO SOME-THING LIKE THIS?
THIS IS WHAT YOU GET FOR NOT ERASING YOUR CLONES.
WEISS IS RIGHT. IT'S MY FAULT.
WHAT DO I DO? IF THE WHITE FANG OR BEACON FINDS OUT ABOUT THIS...
BUP BUP BUP BUP
BUP BUP
WHY IS THE BID SO HIGH? MY CLONES ARE WORTHLESS. WHAT IF SOMEONE SET THIS UP TO MAKE ME LOOK FULL OF MYSELF?
IS THIS SOME-BODY'S PLOY TO ELIMINATE ME FROM SOCIETY?!
BUP BUP
I DON'T THINK IT'S ANYTHING QUITE THAT ELAB-ORATE!
YOU GET SO PARANOID, BLAKE.
LET'S FIND OUT WHO PUT IT UP!
MAYBE WE CAN TAKE IT DOWN!

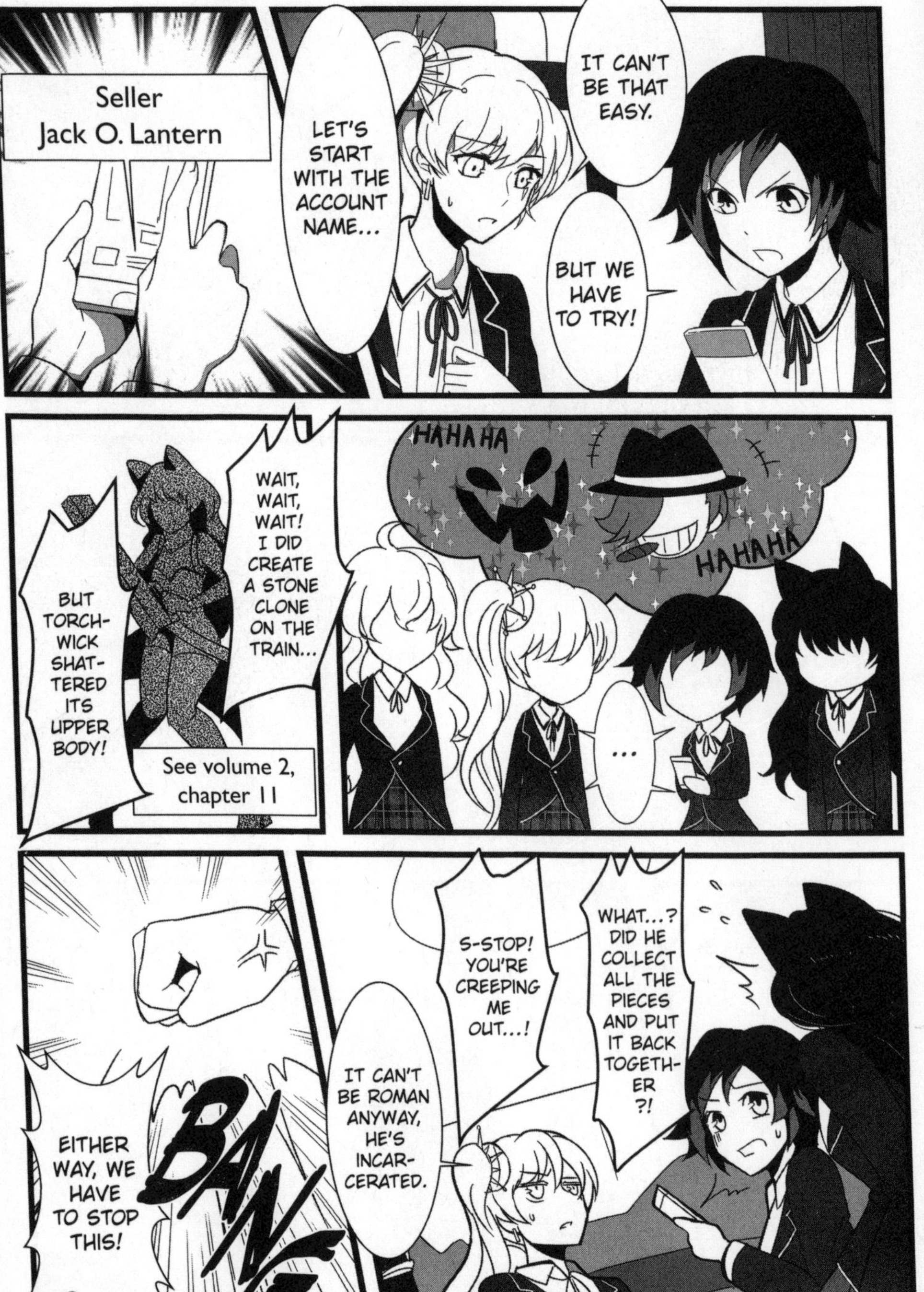
IT CAN'T BE THAT EASY.
LET'S START WITH THE ACCOUNT NAME...
BUT WE HAVE TO TRY!
Seller
Jack O. Lantern
HAHAHA
HAHAHA
...
WAIT, WAIT, WAIT! I DID CREATE A STONE CLONE ON THE TRAIN...
BUT TORCH-WICK SHAT-TERED ITS UPPER BODY!
See volume 2, chapter 11
WHAT...? DID HE COLLECT ALL THE PIECES AND PUT IT BACK TOGETH-ER?!
S-STOP! YOU'RE CREEPING ME OUT...!
IT CAN'T BE ROMAN ANYWAY, HE'S INCAR-CERATED.
EITHER WAY, WE HAVE TO STOP THIS!
BANG

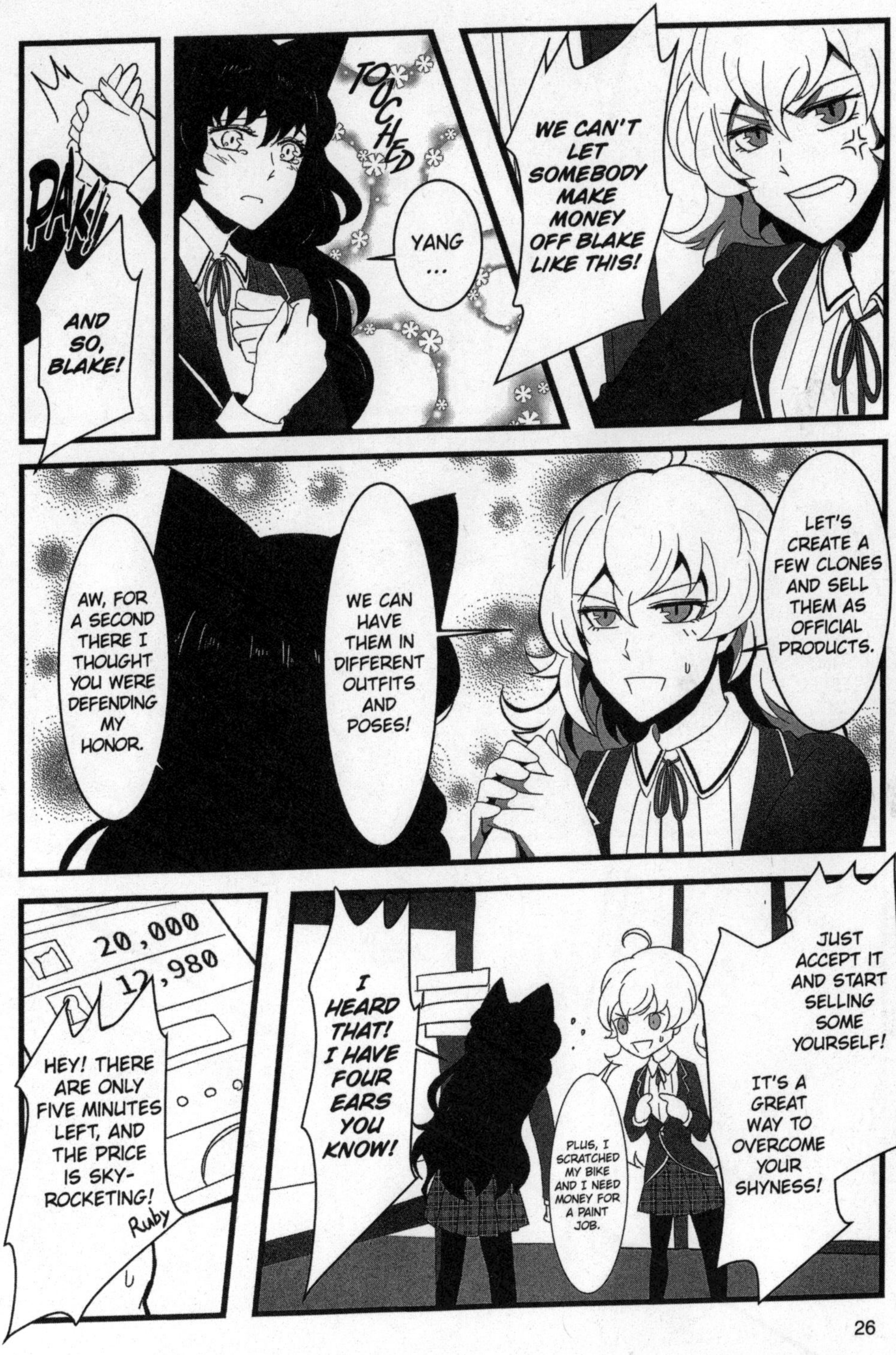
WE CAN'T LET SOMEBODY MAKE MONEY OFF BLAKE LIKE THIS!
TOUCHED
YANG ...
PAK!
AND SO, BLAKE!
LET'S CREATE A FEW CLONES AND SELL THEM AS OFFICIAL PRODUCTS.
WE CAN HAVE THEM IN DIFFERENT OUTFITS AND POSES!
AW, FOR A SECOND THERE I THOUGHT YOU WERE DEFENDING MY HONOR.
JUST ACCEPT IT AND START SELLING SOME YOURSELF!
IT'S A GREAT WAY TO OVERCOME YOUR SHYNESS!
PLUS, I SCRATCHED MY BIKE AND I NEED MONEY FOR A PAINT JOB.
I HEARD THAT! I HAVE FOUR EARS YOU KNOW!
20,000
12,980
HEY! THERE ARE ONLY FIVE MINUTES LEFT, AND THE PRICE IS SKY-ROCKETING!
Ruby

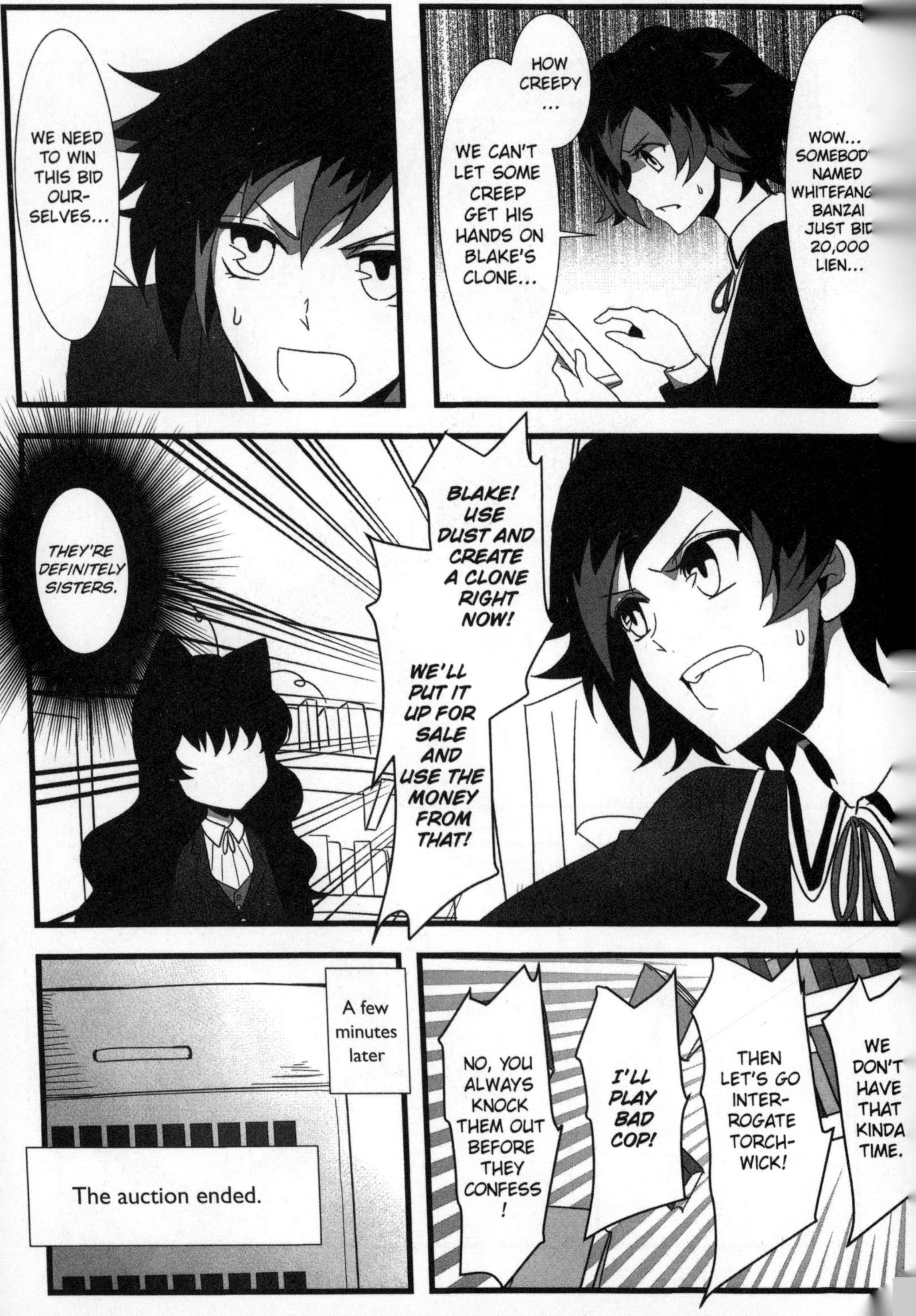
WOW... SOMEBOD NAMED WHITEFANG BANZAI JUST BID 20,000 LIEN...
HOW CREEPY ...
WE CAN'T LET SOME CREEP GET HIS HANDS ON BLAKE'S CLONE...
WE NEED TO WIN THIS BID OUR-SELVES...
BLAKE! USE DUST AND CREATE A CLONE RIGHT NOW!
WE'LL PUT IT UP FOR SALE AND USE THE MONEY FROM THAT!
THEY'RE DEFINITELY SISTERS.
WE DON'T HAVE THAT KINDA TIME.
THEN LET'S GO INTER-ROGATE TORCH-WICK!
I'LL PLAY BAD COP!
NO, YOU ALWAYS KNOCK THEM OUT BEFORE THEY CONFESS !
A few minutes later
The auction ended.

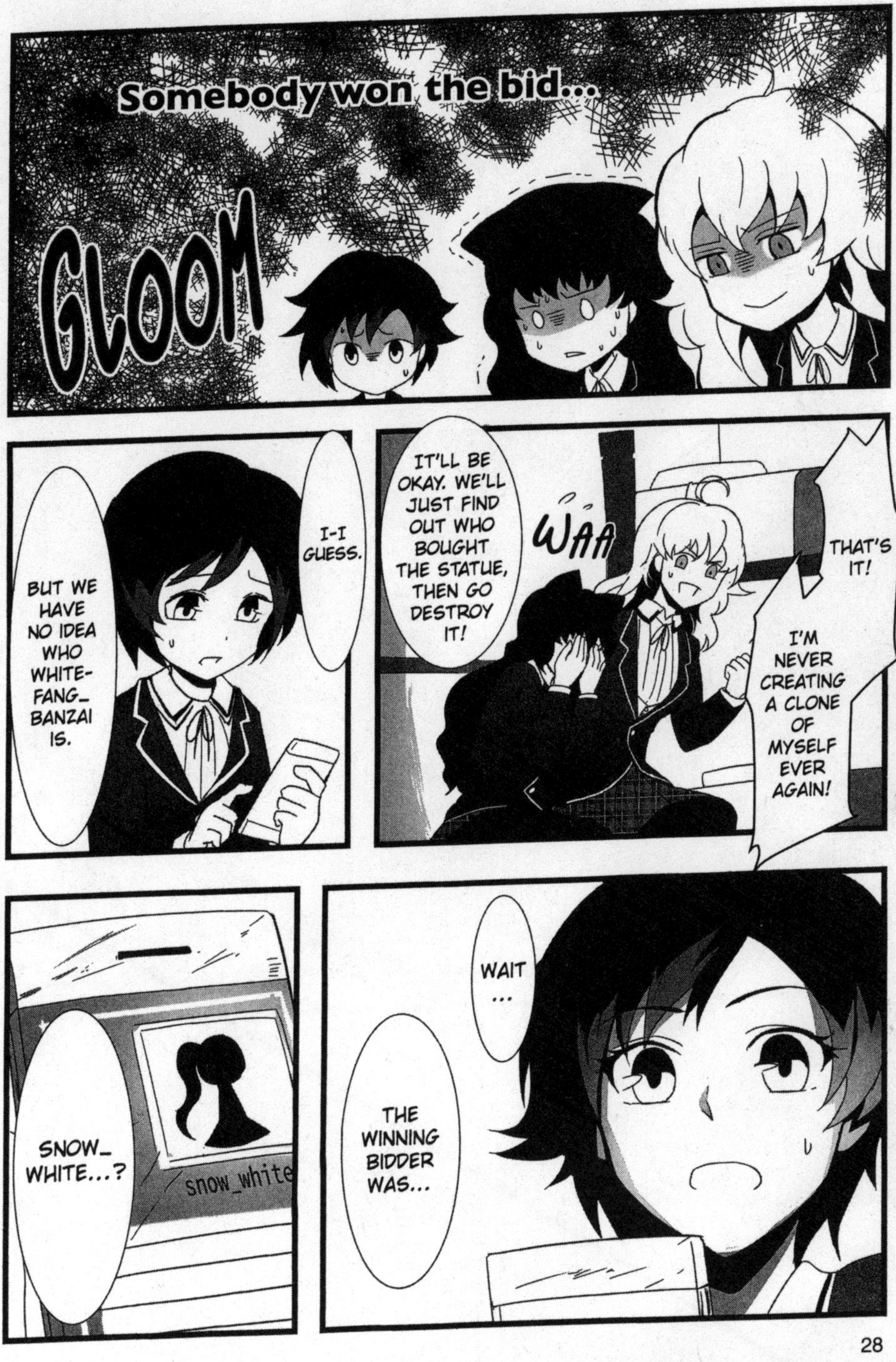
Somebody won the bid...
GLOOM
THAT'S IT!
I'M NEVER CREATING A CLONE OF MYSELF EVER AGAIN!
WAA
IT'LL BE OKAY. WE'LL JUST FIND OUT WHO BOUGHT THE STATUE, THEN GO DESTROY IT!
I-I GUESS.
BUT WE HAVE NO IDEA WHO WHITE-FANG_BANZAI IS.
WAIT...
THE WINNING BIDDER WAS...
snow_white
SNOW_WHITE...?

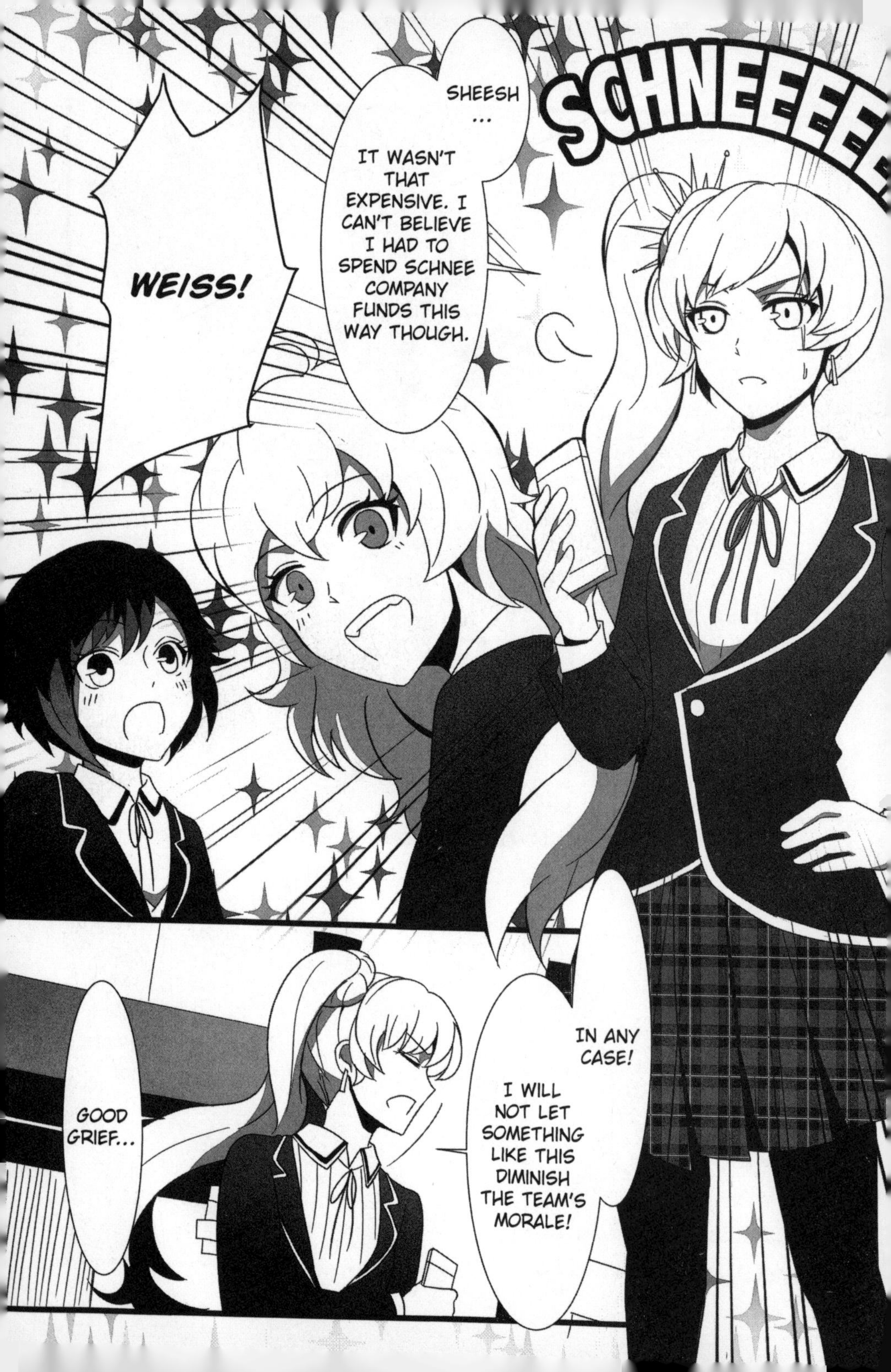
SCHNEEEEE
SHEESH ... IT WASN'T THAT EXPENSIVE. I CAN'T BELIEVE I HAD TO SPEND SCHNEE COMPANY FUNDS THIS WAY THOUGH.
WEISS!
IN ANY CASE! I WILL NOT LET SOMETHING LIKE THIS DIMINISH THE TEAM'S MORALE!
GOOD GRIEF...

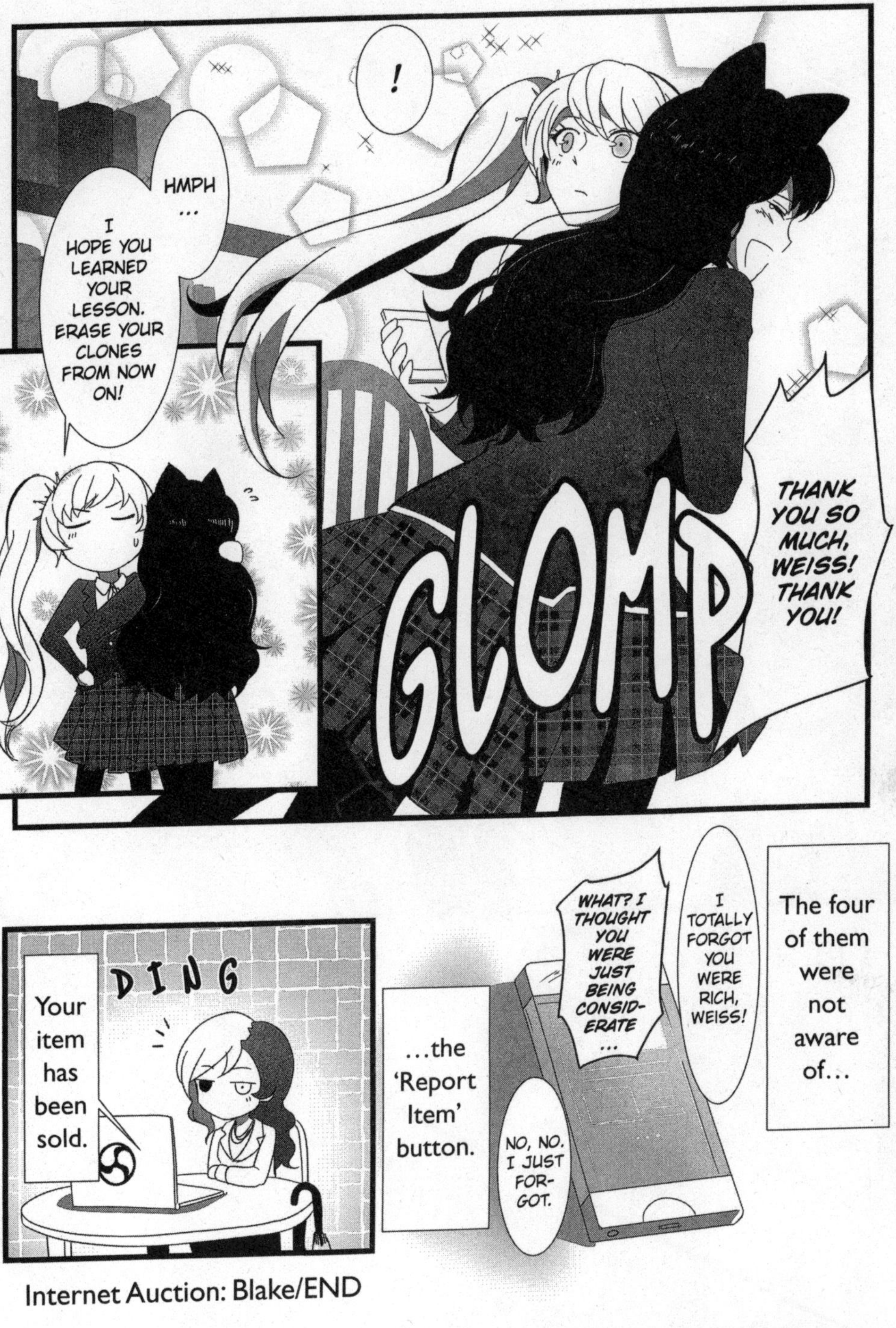
!
THANK YOU SO MUCH, WEISS! THANK YOU!
GLOMP
HMPH...
I HOPE YOU LEARNED YOUR LESSON. ERASE YOUR CLONES FROM NOW ON!
The four of them were not aware of…
I TOTALLY FORGOT YOU WERE RICH, WEISS!
WHAT? I THOUGHT YOU WERE JUST BEING CONSIDERATE…
NO, NO. I JUST FORGOT.
…the 'Report Item' button.
DING
Your item has been sold.

Internet Auction: Blake/END

RWBY
OFFICIAL MANGA ANTHOLOGY
Volume 3

From Shadows

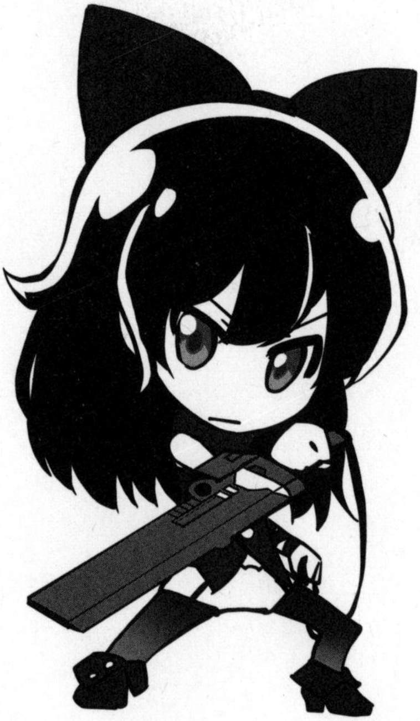

METEO

RWBY
OFFICIAL MANGA ANTHOLOGY
Volume 3

From Shadows

The Monster

monorobu

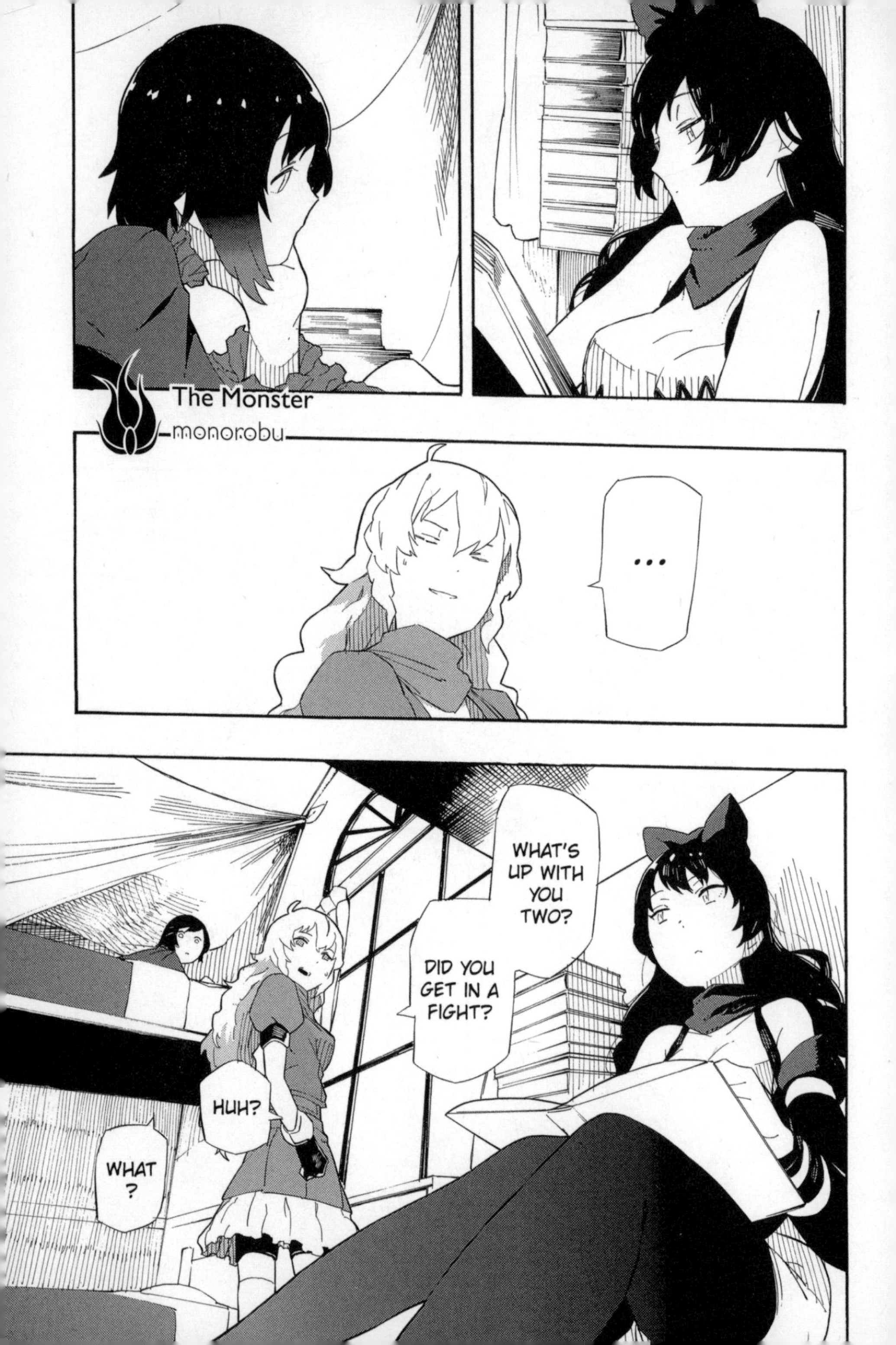
...
WHAT'S UP WITH YOU TWO?
DID YOU GET IN A FIGHT?
HUH?
WHAT?

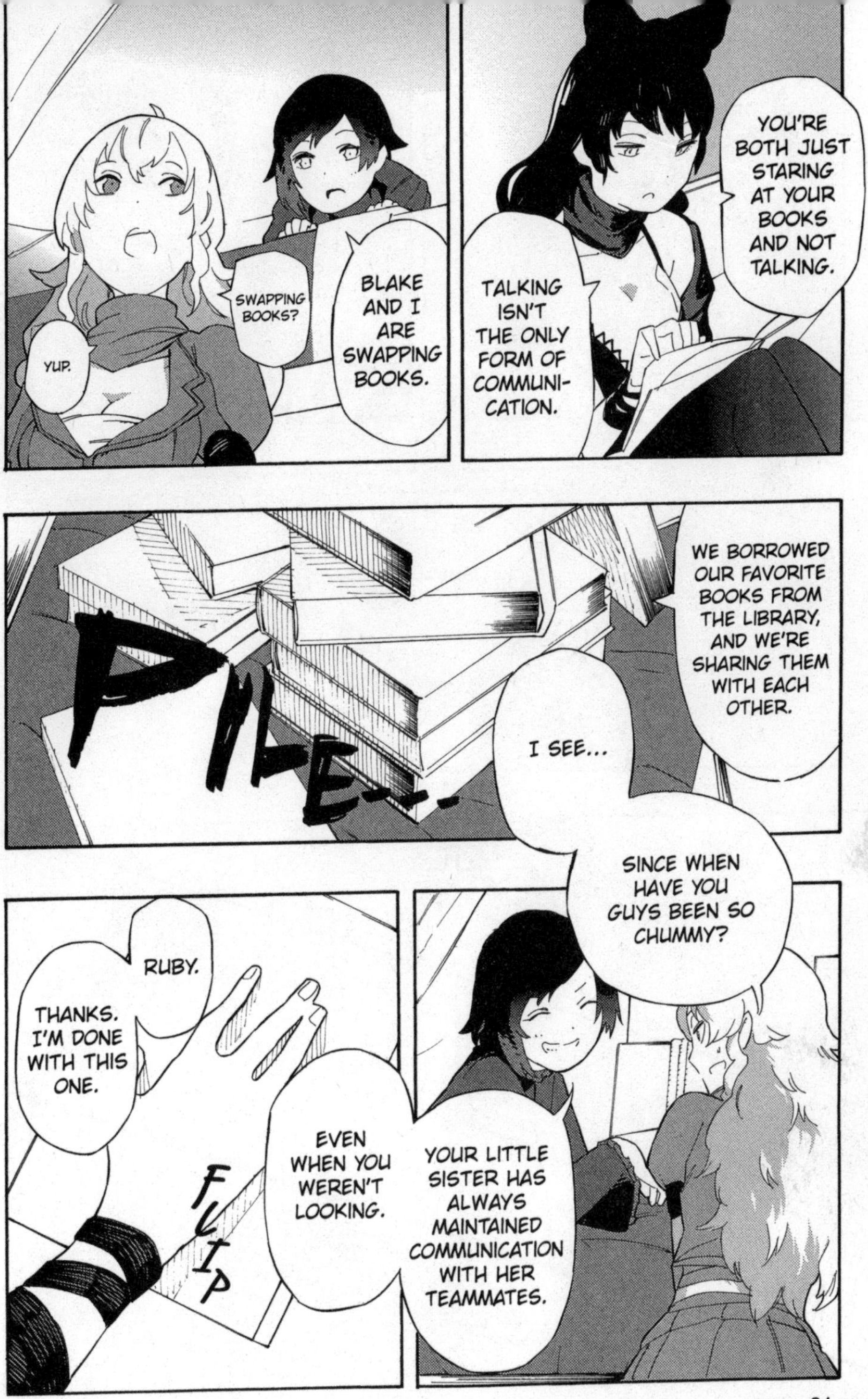
YOU'RE BOTH JUST STARING AT YOUR BOOKS AND NOT TALKING.
TALKING ISN'T THE ONLY FORM OF COMMUNI-CATION.
BLAKE AND I ARE SWAPPING BOOKS.
SWAPPING BOOKS?
YUP.
WE BORROWED OUR FAVORITE BOOKS FROM THE LIBRARY, AND WE'RE SHARING THEM WITH EACH OTHER.
PILE...
I SEE...
SINCE WHEN HAVE YOU GUYS BEEN SO CHUMMY?
YOUR LITTLE SISTER HAS ALWAYS MAINTAINED COMMUNICATION WITH HER TEAMMATES.
EVEN WHEN YOU WEREN'T LOOKING.
RUBY.
THANKS. I'M DONE WITH THIS ONE.
FLIP

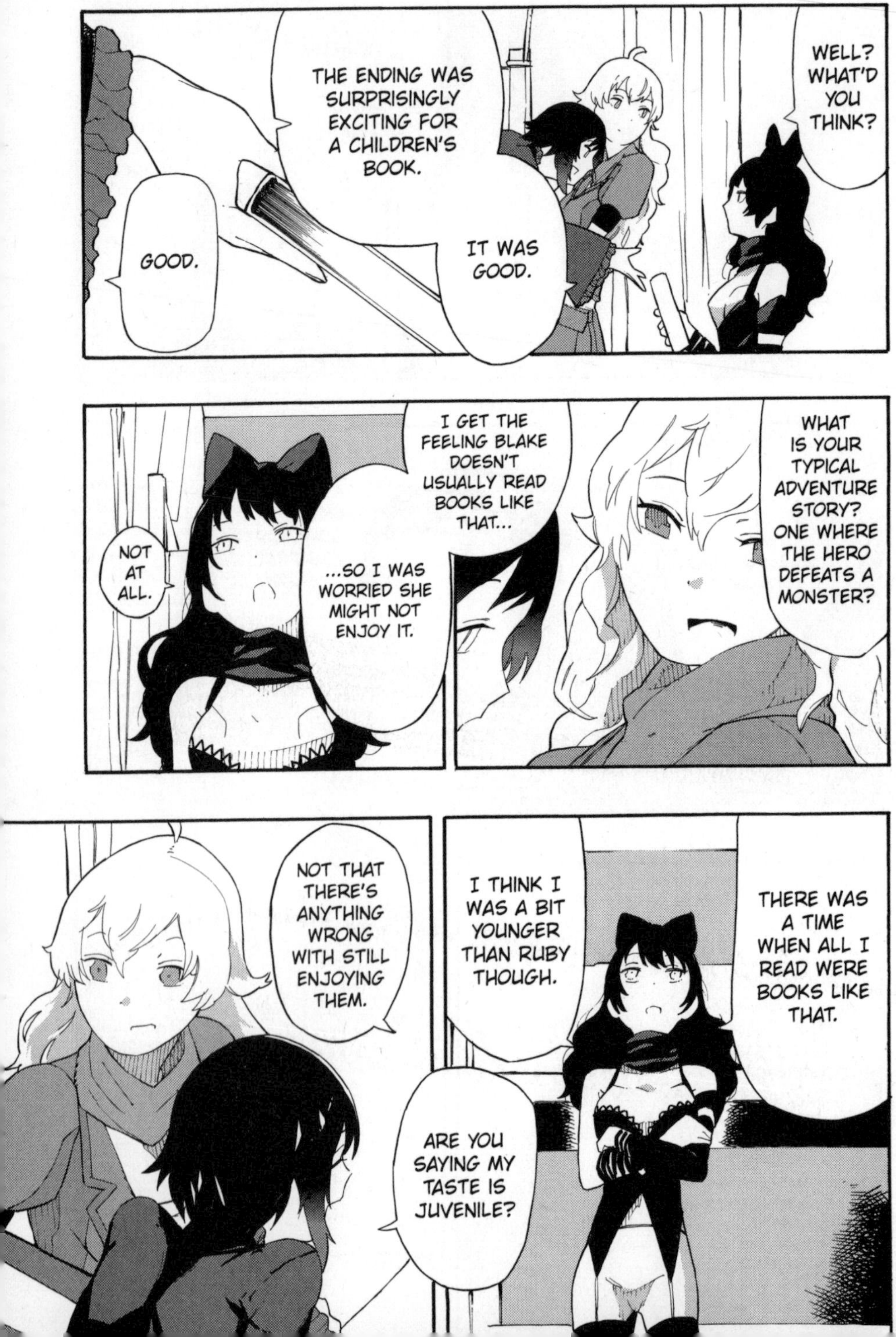
WELL? WHAT'D YOU THINK?
THE ENDING WAS SURPRISINGLY EXCITING FOR A CHILDREN'S BOOK.
IT WAS GOOD.
GOOD.
WHAT IS YOUR TYPICAL ADVENTURE STORY? ONE WHERE THE HERO DEFEATS A MONSTER?
I GET THE FEELING BLAKE DOESN'T USUALLY READ BOOKS LIKE THAT...
...SO I WAS WORRIED SHE MIGHT NOT ENJOY IT.
NOT AT ALL.
THERE WAS A TIME WHEN ALL I READ WERE BOOKS LIKE THAT.
I THINK I WAS A BIT YOUNGER THAN RUBY THOUGH.
ARE YOU SAYING MY TASTE IS JUVENILE?
NOT THAT THERE'S ANYTHING WRONG WITH STILL ENJOYING THEM.

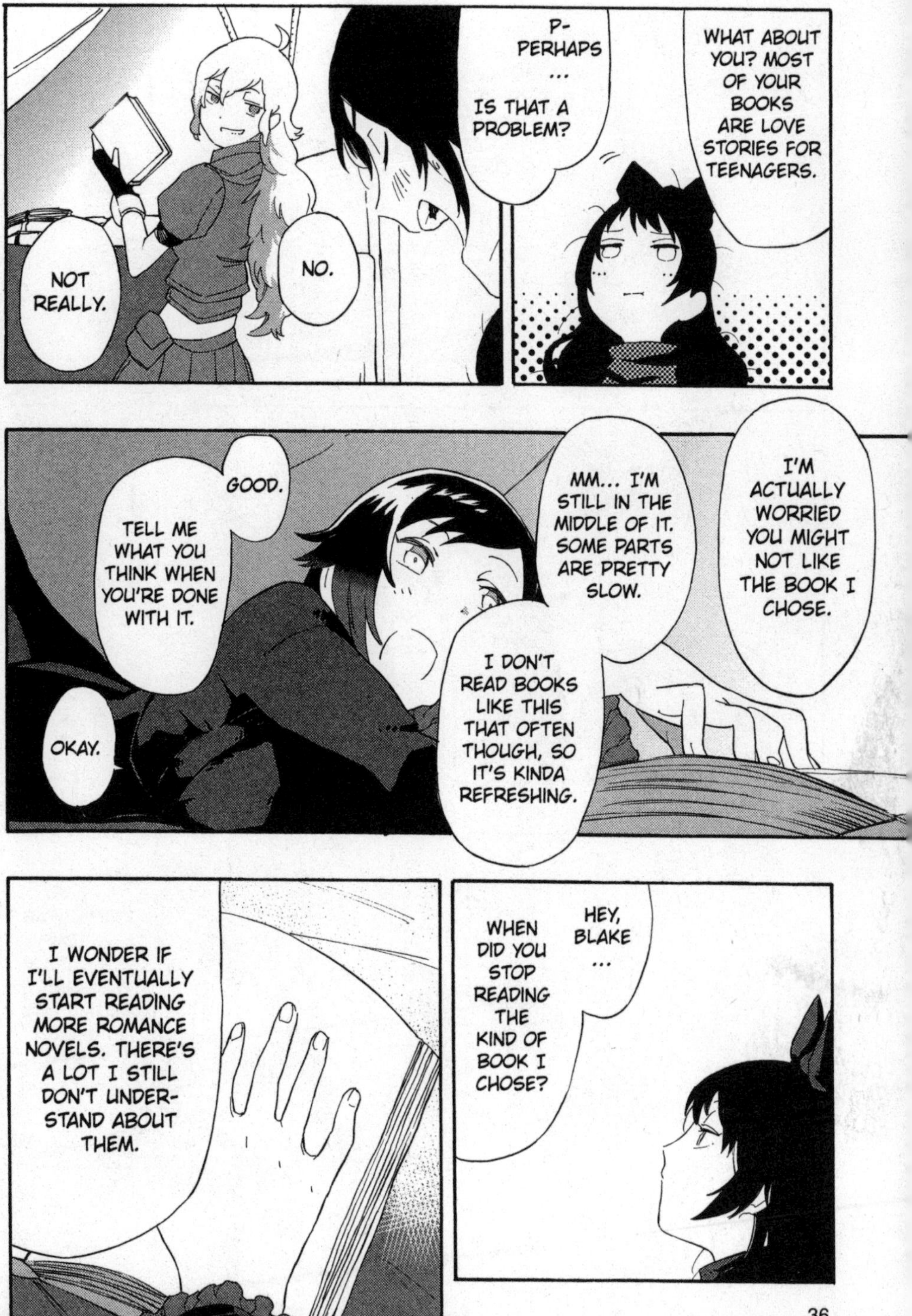
WHAT ABOUT YOU? MOST OF YOUR BOOKS ARE LOVE STORIES FOR TEENAGERS.
P- PERHAPS ...
IS THAT A PROBLEM?
NO.
NOT REALLY.
I'M ACTUALLY WORRIED YOU MIGHT NOT LIKE THE BOOK I CHOSE.
MM... I'M STILL IN THE MIDDLE OF IT. SOME PARTS ARE PRETTY SLOW.
I DON'T READ BOOKS LIKE THIS THAT OFTEN THOUGH, SO IT'S KINDA REFRESHING.
GOOD.
TELL ME WHAT YOU THINK WHEN YOU'RE DONE WITH IT.
OKAY.
HEY, BLAKE ...
WHEN DID YOU STOP READING THE KIND OF BOOK I CHOSE?
I WONDER IF I'LL EVENTUALLY START READING MORE ROMANCE NOVELS. THERE'S A LOT I STILL DON'T UNDER-STAND ABOUT THEM.

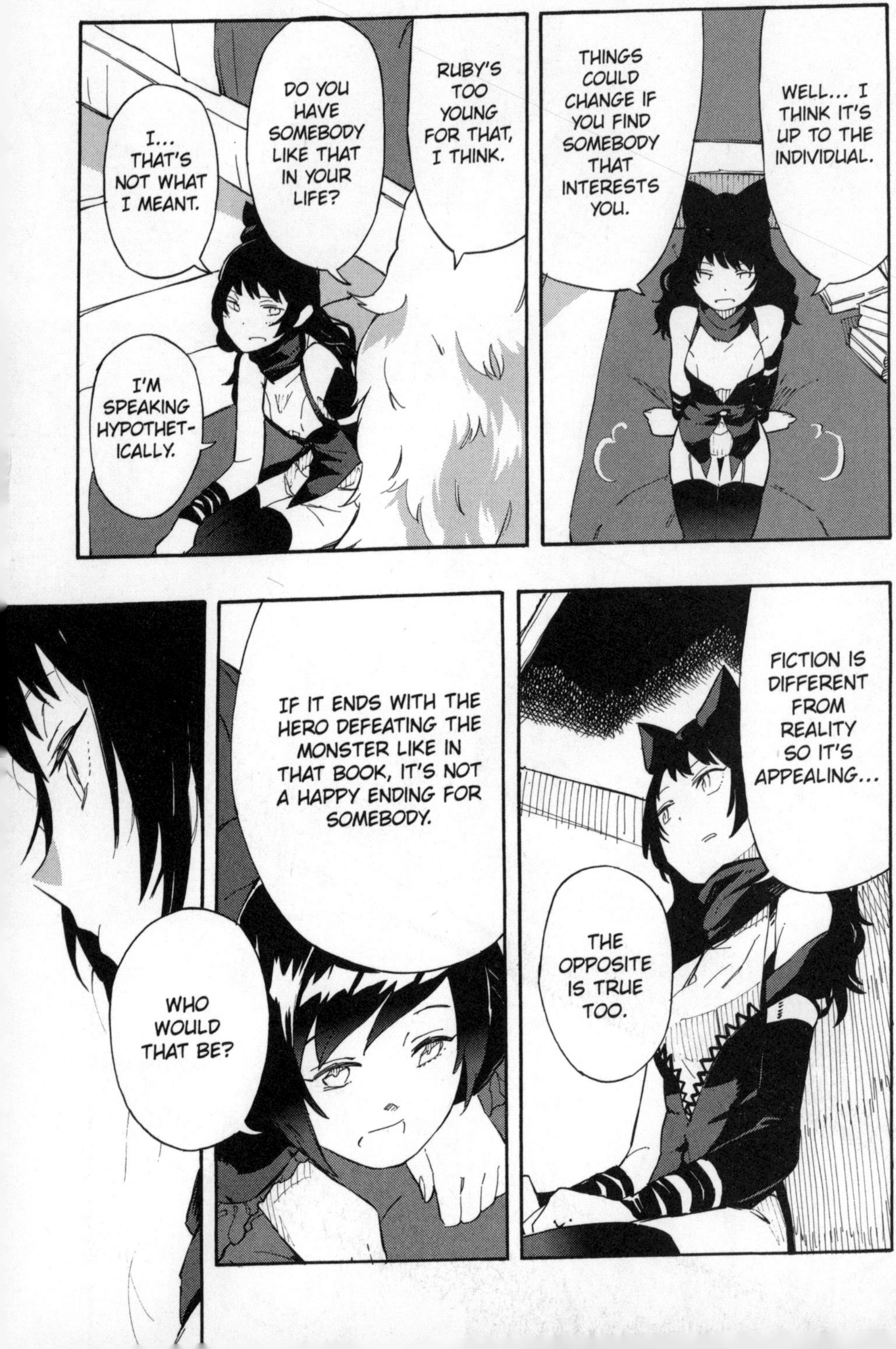
WELL... I THINK IT'S UP TO THE INDIVIDUAL.
THINGS COULD CHANGE IF YOU FIND SOMEBODY THAT INTERESTS YOU.
RUBY'S TOO YOUNG FOR THAT, I THINK.
DO YOU HAVE SOMEBODY LIKE THAT IN YOUR LIFE?
I... THAT'S NOT WHAT I MEANT.
I'M SPEAKING HYPOTHET-ICALLY.
FICTION IS DIFFERENT FROM REALITY SO IT'S APPEALING...
THE OPPOSITE IS TRUE TOO.
IF IT ENDS WITH THE HERO DEFEATING THE MONSTER LIKE IN THAT BOOK, IT'S NOT A HAPPY ENDING FOR SOMEBODY.
WHO WOULD THAT BE?

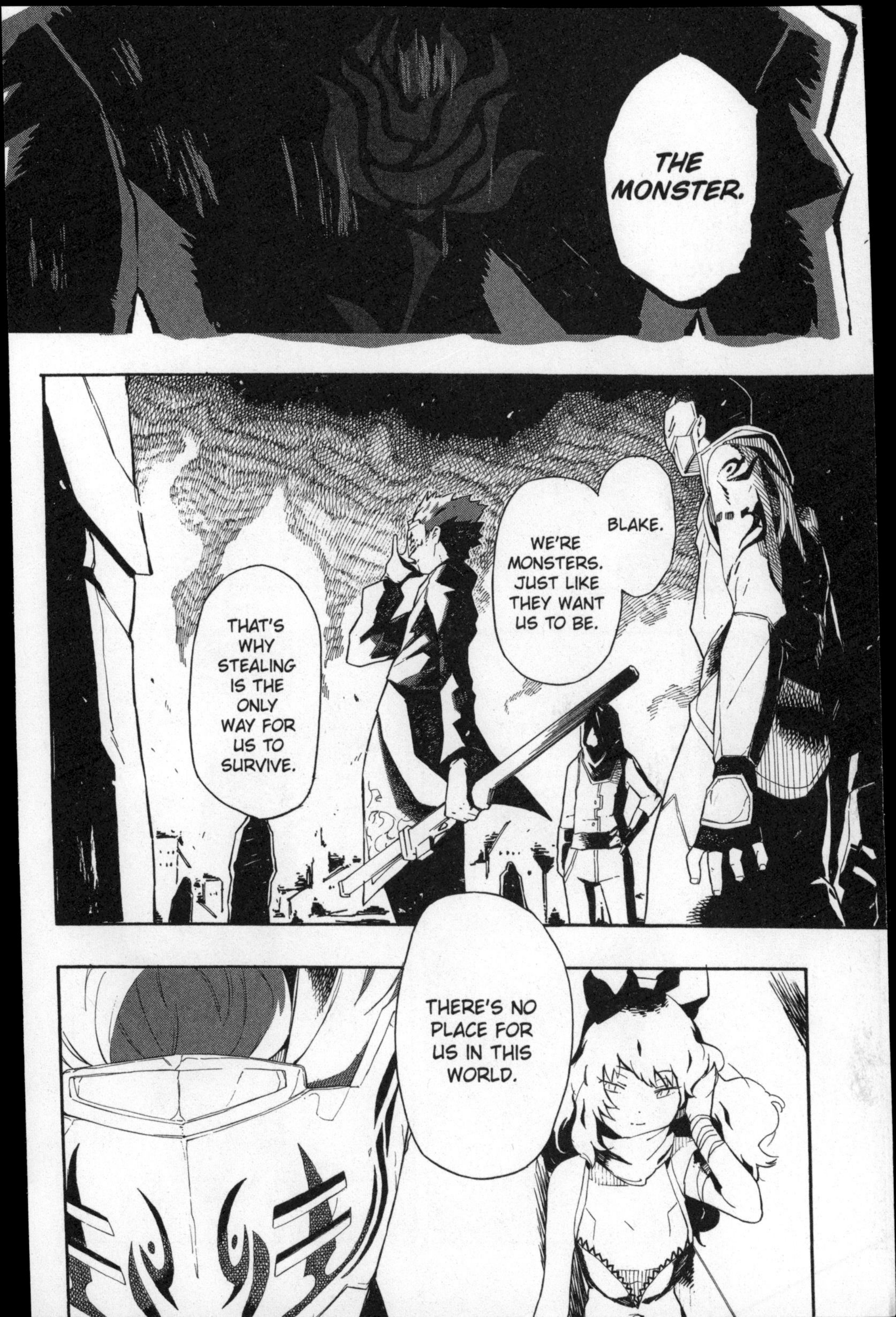
THE MONSTER.
BLAKE.
WE'RE MONSTERS. JUST LIKE THEY WANT US TO BE.
THAT'S WHY STEALING IS THE ONLY WAY FOR US TO SURVIVE.
THERE'S NO PLACE FOR US IN THIS WORLD.

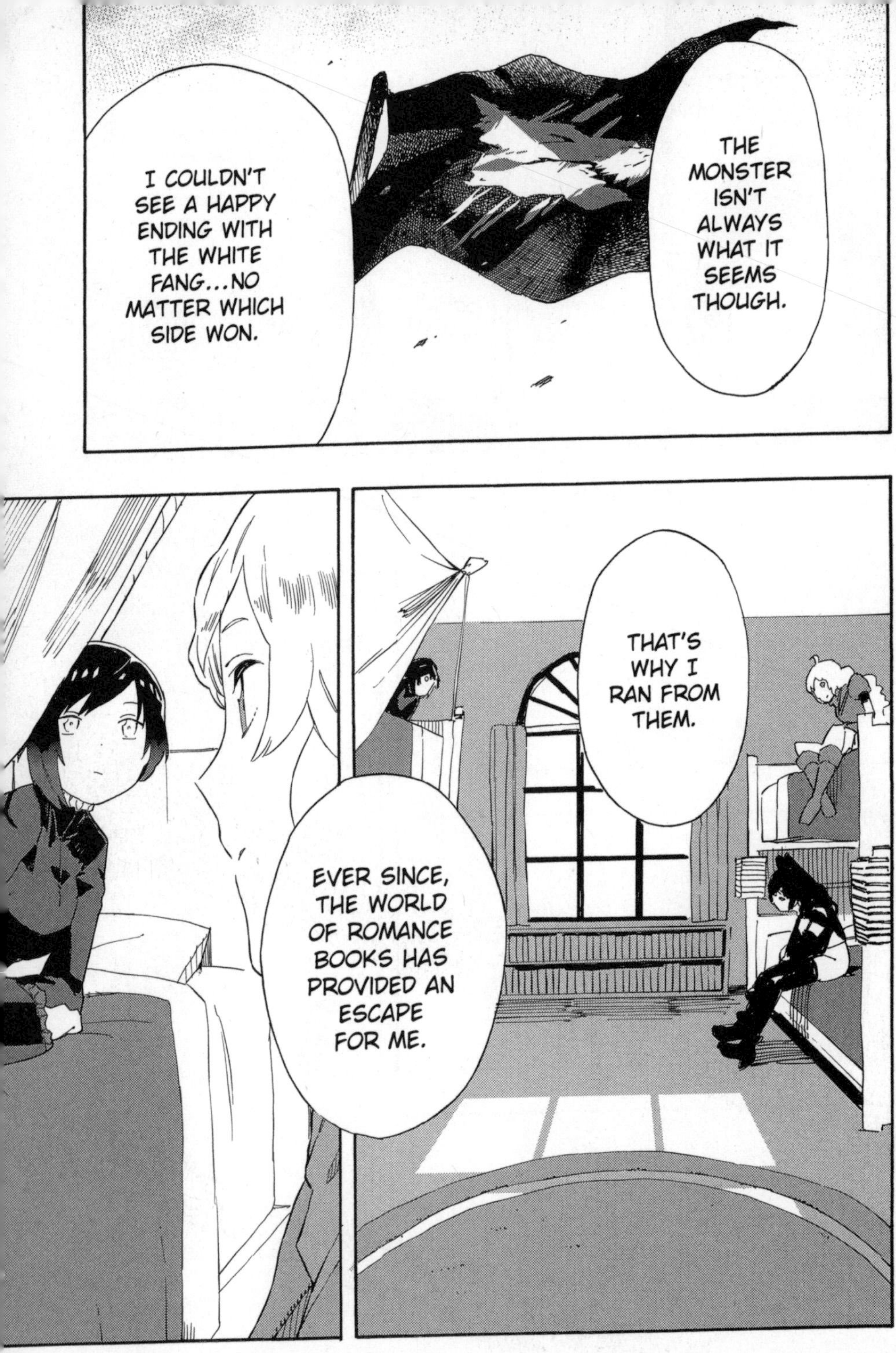
THE MONSTER ISN'T ALWAYS WHAT IT SEEMS THOUGH.
I COULDN'T SEE A HAPPY ENDING WITH THE WHITE FANG...NO MATTER WHICH SIDE WON.
THAT'S WHY I RAN FROM THEM.
EVER SINCE, THE WORLD OF ROMANCE BOOKS HAS PROVIDED AN ESCAPE FOR ME.

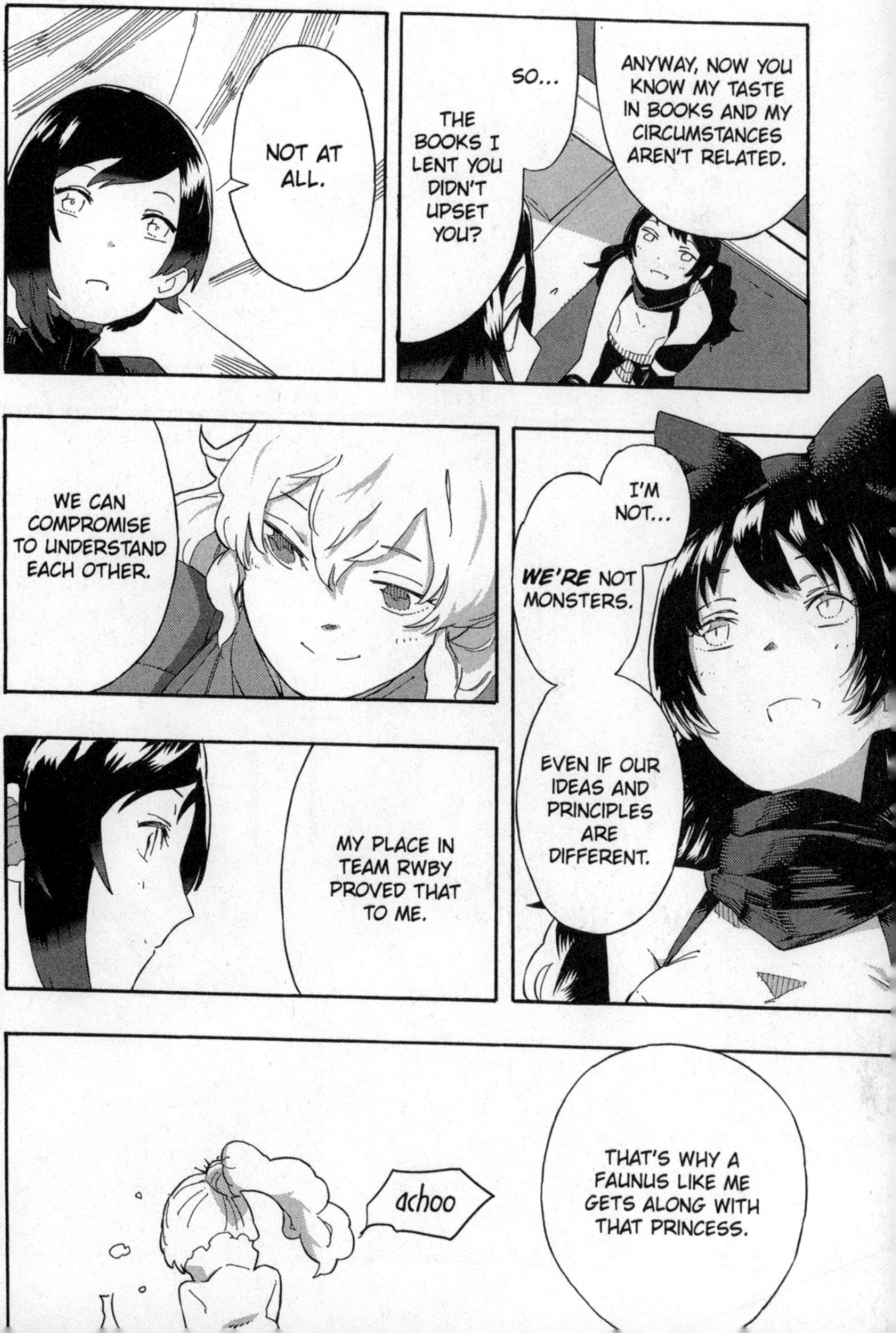
ANYWAY, NOW YOU KNOW MY TASTE IN BOOKS AND MY CIRCUMSTANCES AREN'T RELATED.
SO...
THE BOOKS I LENT YOU DIDN'T UPSET YOU?
NOT AT ALL.
I'M NOT...
WE'RE NOT MONSTERS.
EVEN IF OUR IDEAS AND PRINCIPLES ARE DIFFERENT.
WE CAN COMPROMISE TO UNDERSTAND EACH OTHER.
MY PLACE IN TEAM RWBY PROVED THAT TO ME.
THAT'S WHY A FAUNUS LIKE ME GETS ALONG WITH THAT PRINCESS.
achoo

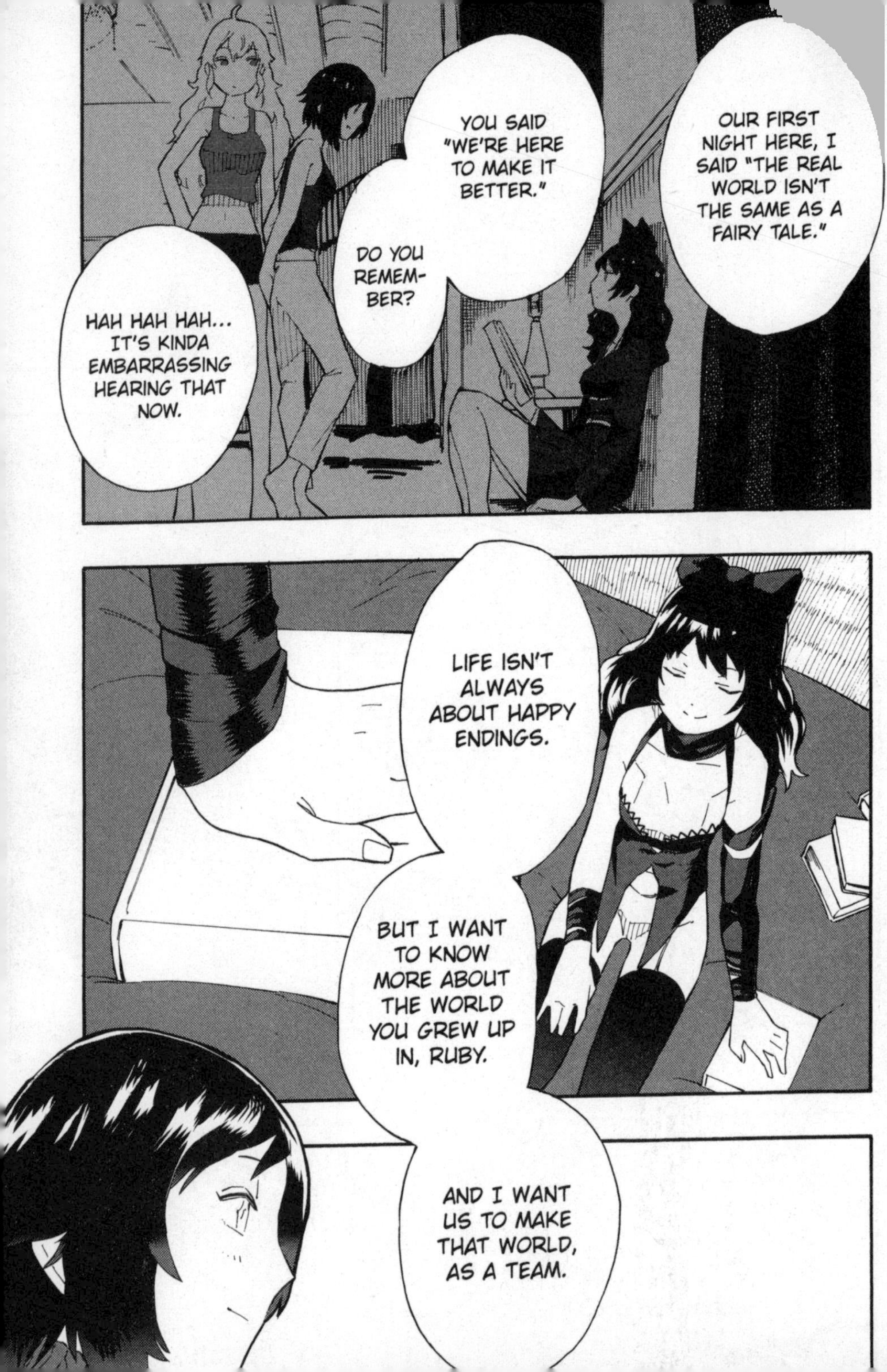
OUR FIRST NIGHT HERE, I SAID "THE REAL WORLD ISN'T THE SAME AS A FAIRY TALE."
YOU SAID "WE'RE HERE TO MAKE IT BETTER."
DO YOU REMEMBER?
HAH HAH HAH... IT'S KINDA EMBARRASSING HEARING THAT NOW.
LIFE ISN'T ALWAYS ABOUT HAPPY ENDINGS.
BUT I WANT TO KNOW MORE ABOUT THE WORLD YOU GREW UP IN, RUBY.
AND I WANT US TO MAKE THAT WORLD, AS A TEAM.

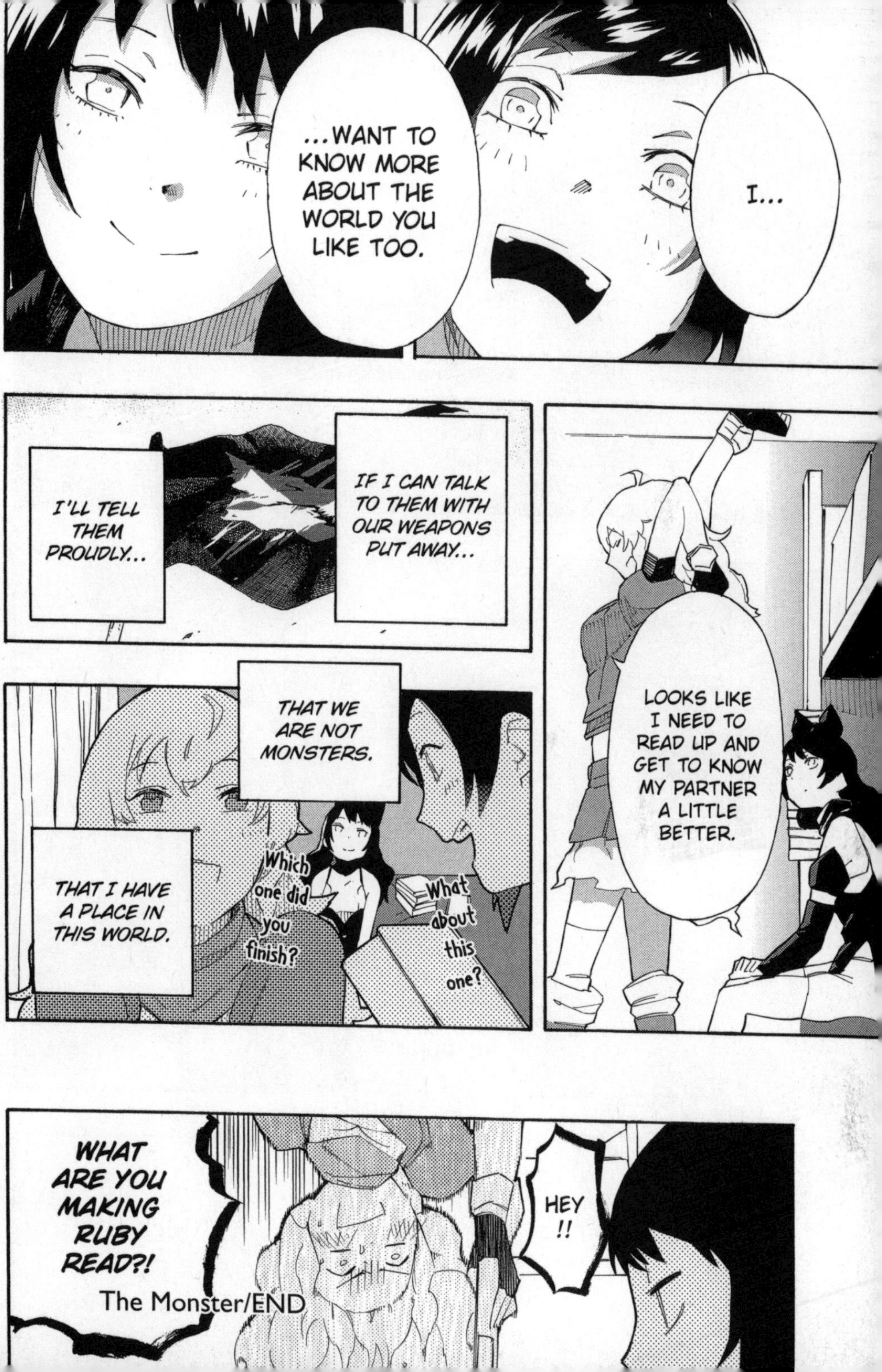
I...
...WANT TO KNOW MORE ABOUT THE WORLD YOU LIKE TOO.
LOOKS LIKE I NEED TO READ UP AND GET TO KNOW MY PARTNER A LITTLE BETTER.
IF I CAN TALK TO THEM WITH OUR WEAPONS PUT AWAY...
I'LL TELL THEM PROUDLY...
THAT WE ARE NOT MONSTERS.
What about this one?
Which one did you finish?
THAT I HAVE A PLACE IN THIS WORLD.
HEY !!
WHAT ARE YOU MAKING RUBY READ?!
The Monster/END

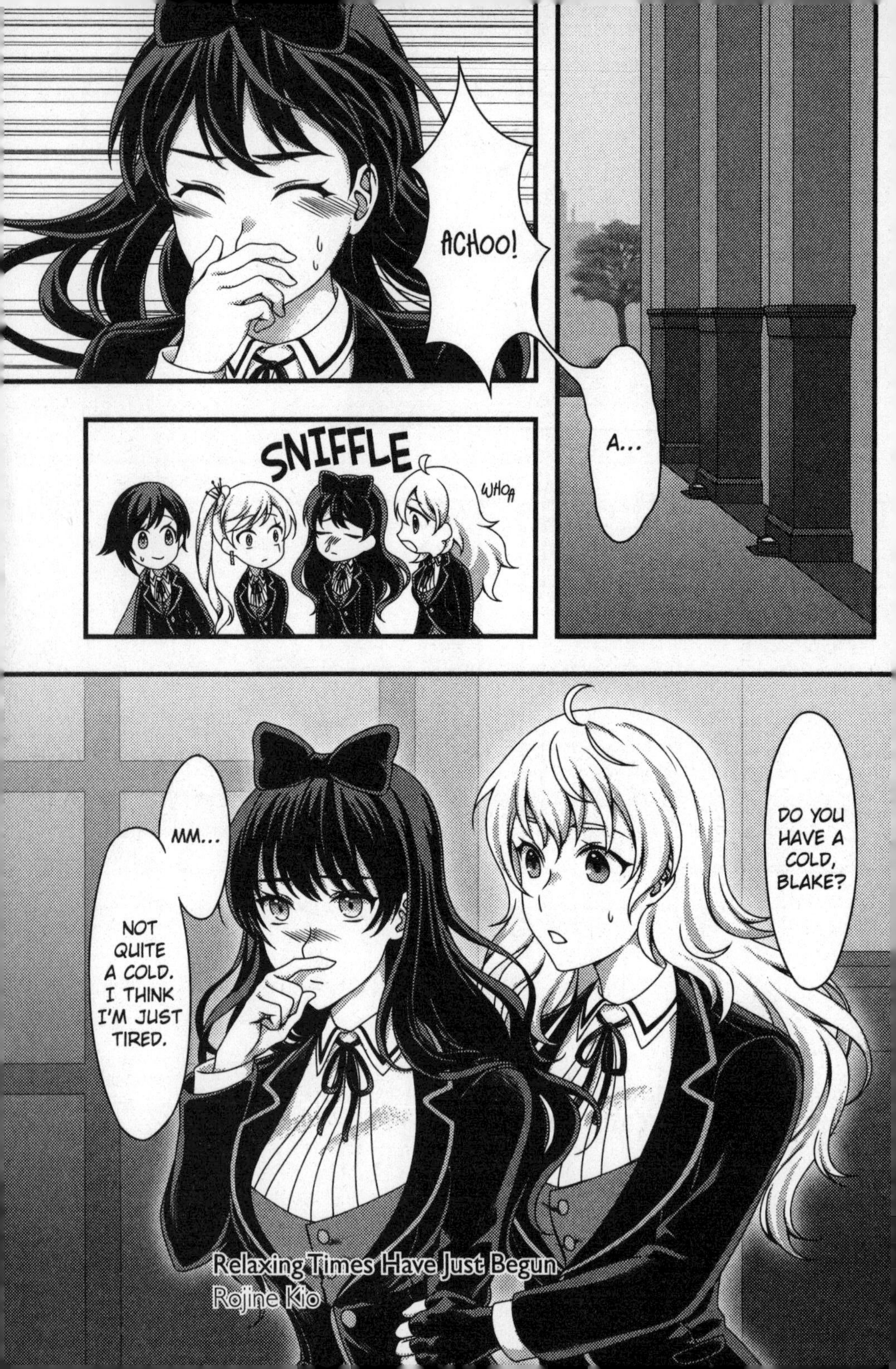
A...
ACHOO!
SNIFFLE
WHOA
DO YOU HAVE A COLD, BLAKE?
MM...
NOT QUITE A COLD. I THINK I'M JUST TIRED.
Relaxing Times Have Just Begun
Rojine Kio

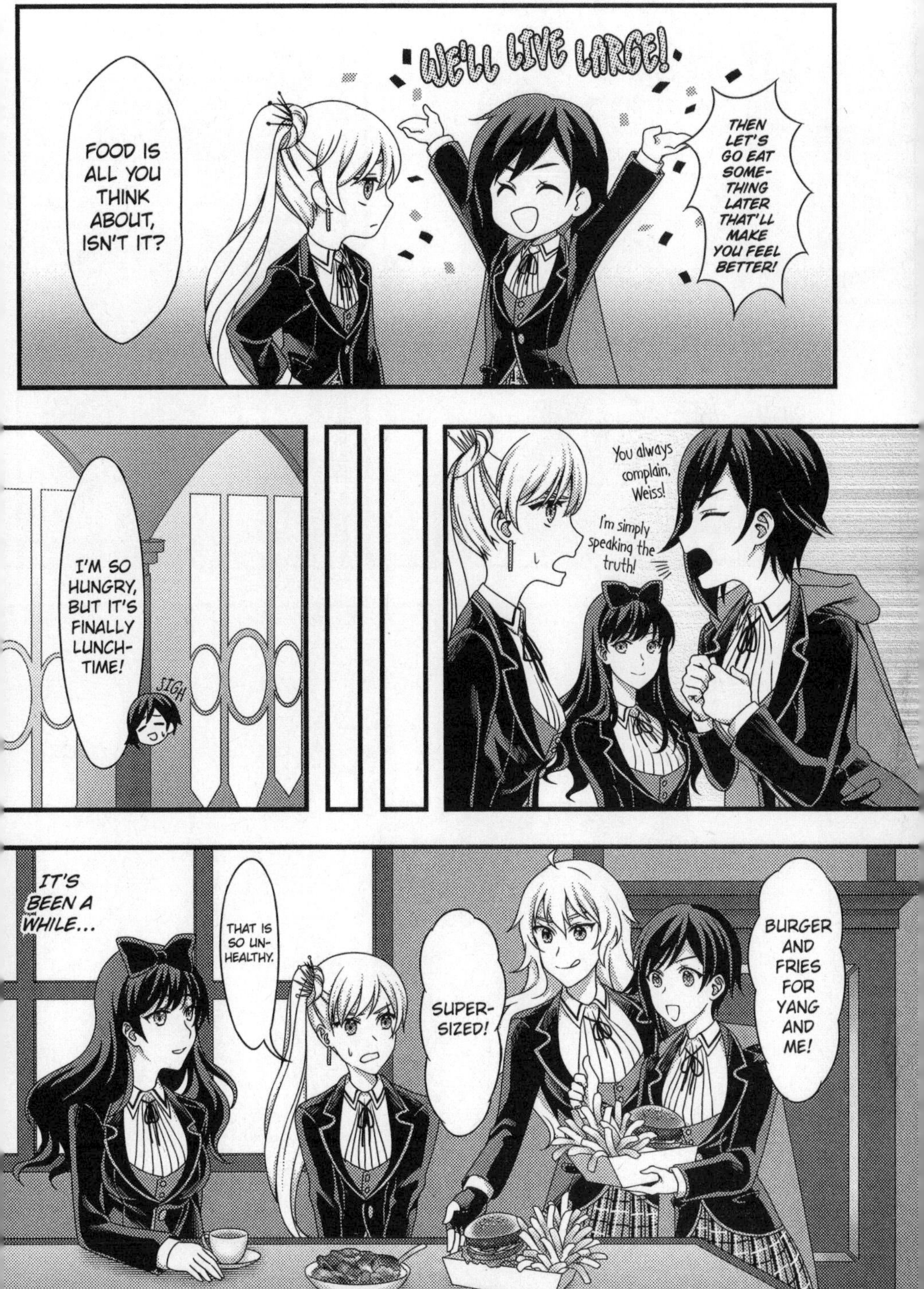
THEN LET'S GO EAT SOMETHING LATER THAT'LL MAKE YOU FEEL BETTER!
WE'LL LIVE LARGE!
FOOD IS ALL YOU THINK ABOUT, ISN'T IT?
You always complain, Weiss!
I'm simply speaking the truth!
I'M SO HUNGRY, BUT IT'S FINALLY LUNCH-TIME!
SIGH
BURGER AND FRIES FOR YANG AND ME!
SUPER-SIZED!
THAT IS SO UN-HEALTHY.
IT'S BEEN A WHILE...

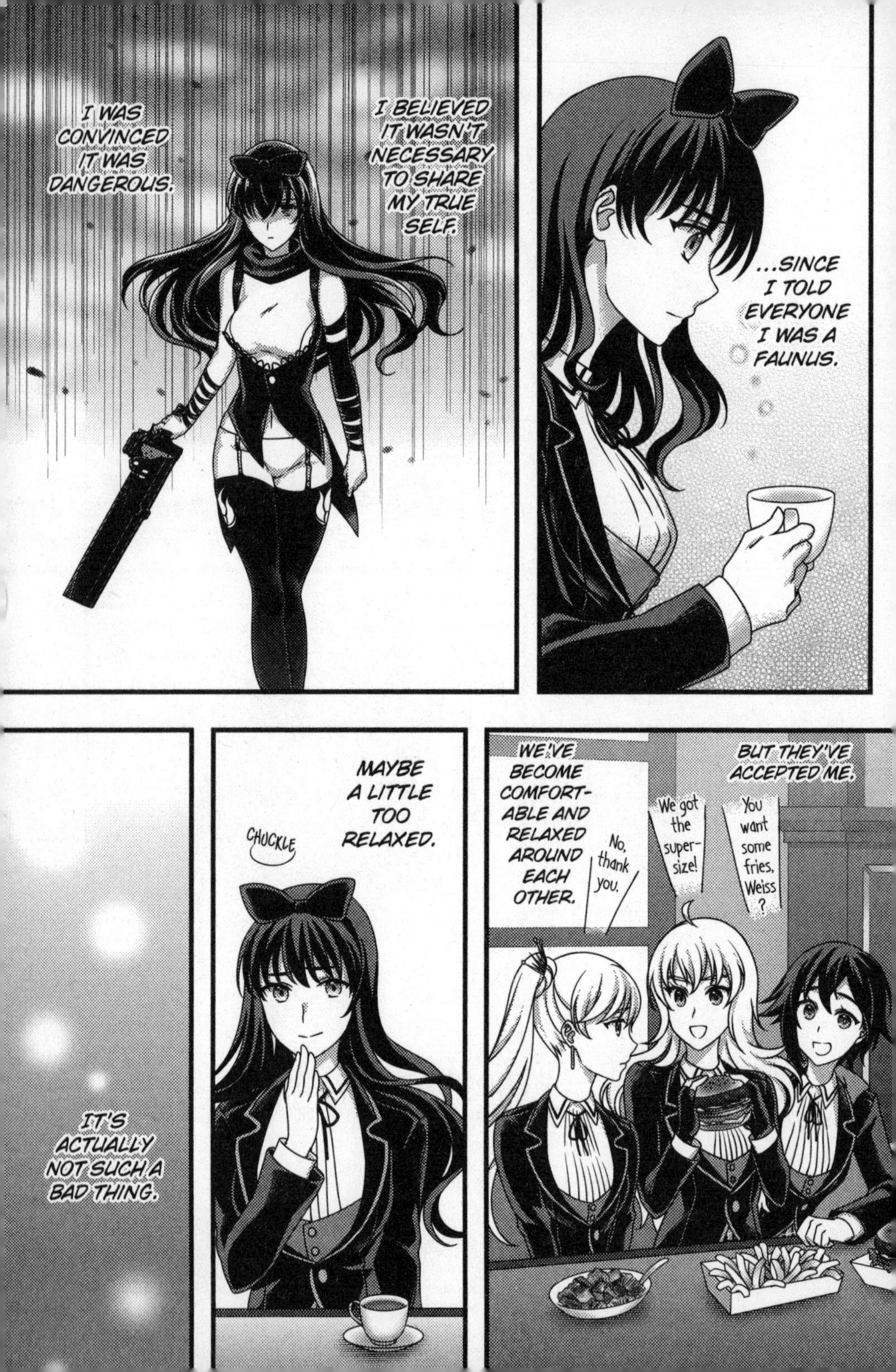
...SINCE I TOLD EVERYONE I WAS A FAUNUS.
I BELIEVED IT WASN'T NECESSARY TO SHARE MY TRUE SELF.
I WAS CONVINCED IT WAS DANGEROUS.
BUT THEY'VE ACCEPTED ME.
You want some fries, Weiss?
We got the super-size!
No, thank you.
WE'VE BECOME COMFORTABLE AND RELAXED AROUND EACH OTHER.
MAYBE A LITTLE TOO RELAXED.
CHUCKLE
IT'S ACTUALLY NOT SUCH A BAD THING.

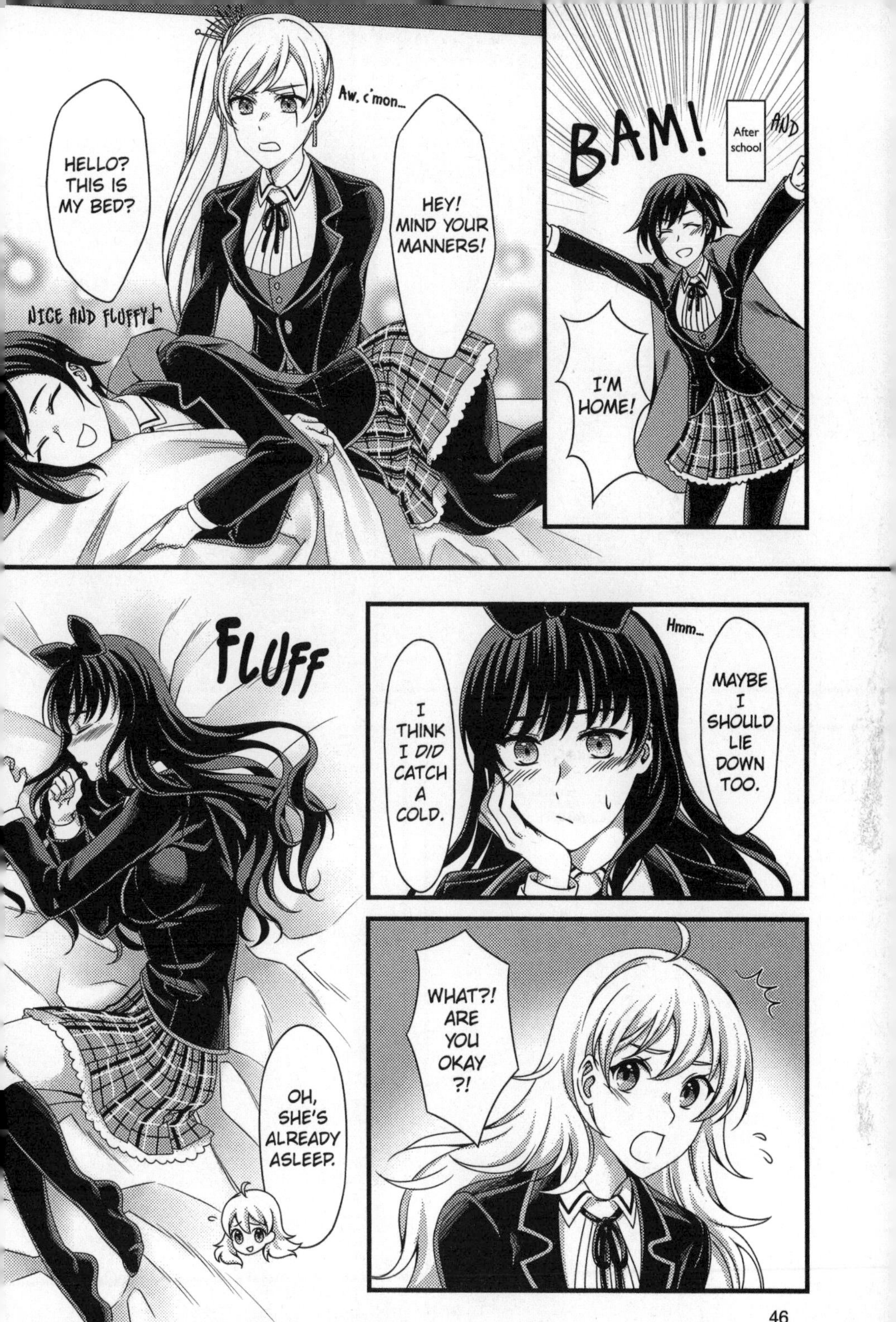
BAM!
After school
AND
I'M HOME!
Aw, c'mon...
HEY! MIND YOUR MANNERS!
HELLO? THIS IS MY BED?
NICE AND FLUFFY♪
Hmm...
MAYBE I SHOULD LIE DOWN TOO.
I THINK I *DID* CATCH A COLD.
WHAT?! ARE YOU OKAY?!
FLUFF
OH, SHE'S ALREADY ASLEEP.

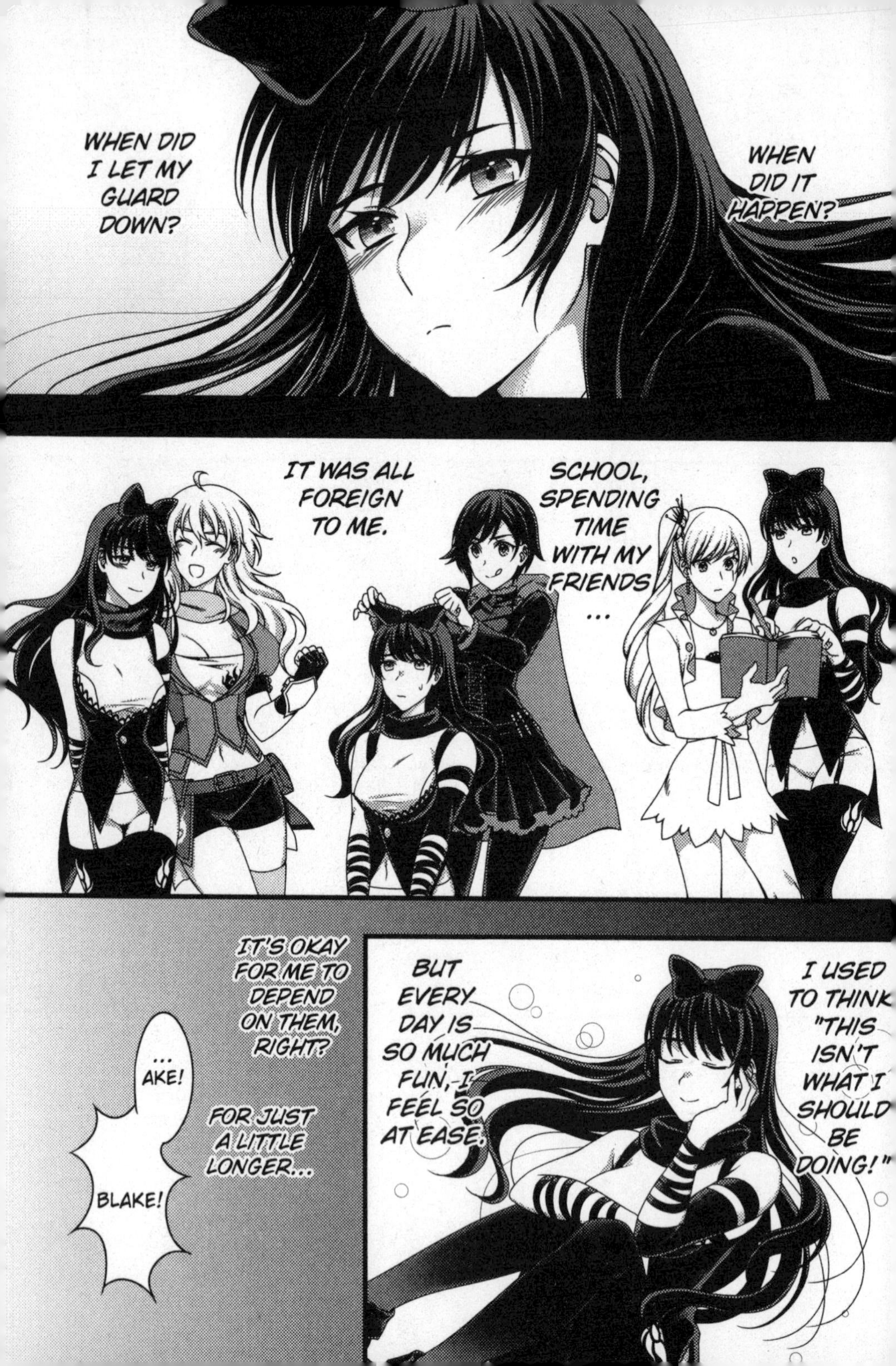
WHEN DID IT HAPPEN?
WHEN DID I LET MY GUARD DOWN?
SCHOOL, SPENDING TIME WITH MY FRIENDS...
IT WAS ALL FOREIGN TO ME.
I USED TO THINK "THIS ISN'T WHAT I SHOULD BE DOING!"
BUT EVERY DAY IS SO MUCH FUN, I FEEL SO AT EASE.
IT'S OKAY FOR ME TO DEPEND ON THEM, RIGHT?
...AKE!
FOR JUST A LITTLE LONGER...
BLAKE!

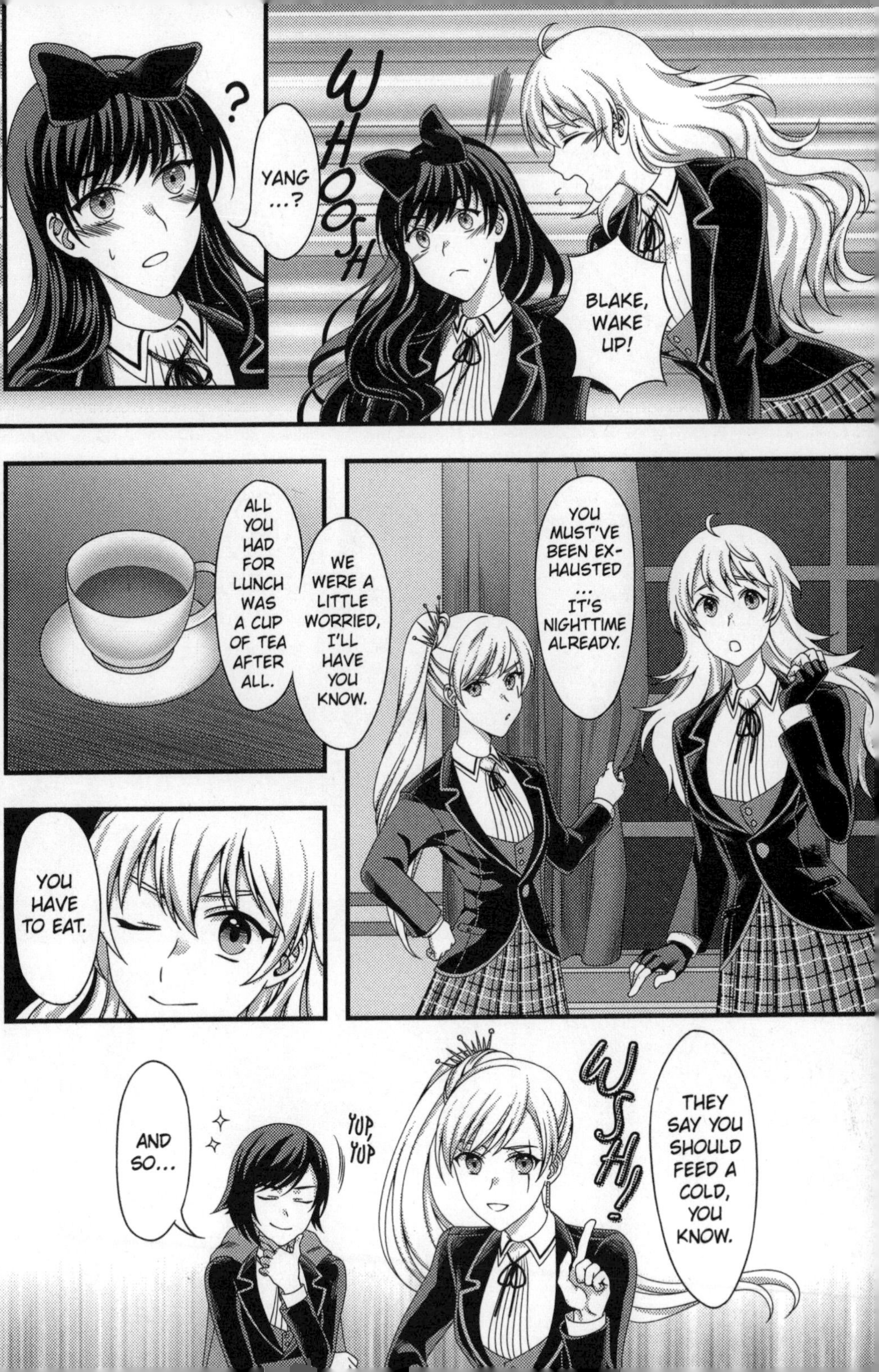
WHOOSH
BLAKE, WAKE UP!
?
YANG ...?
YOU MUST'VE BEEN EX-HAUSTED ... IT'S NIGHTTIME ALREADY.
WE WERE A LITTLE WORRIED, I'LL HAVE YOU KNOW.
ALL YOU HAD FOR LUNCH WAS A CUP OF TEA AFTER ALL.
YOU HAVE TO EAT.
THEY SAY YOU SHOULD FEED A COLD, YOU KNOW.
WSH!
YUP, YUP
AND SO...

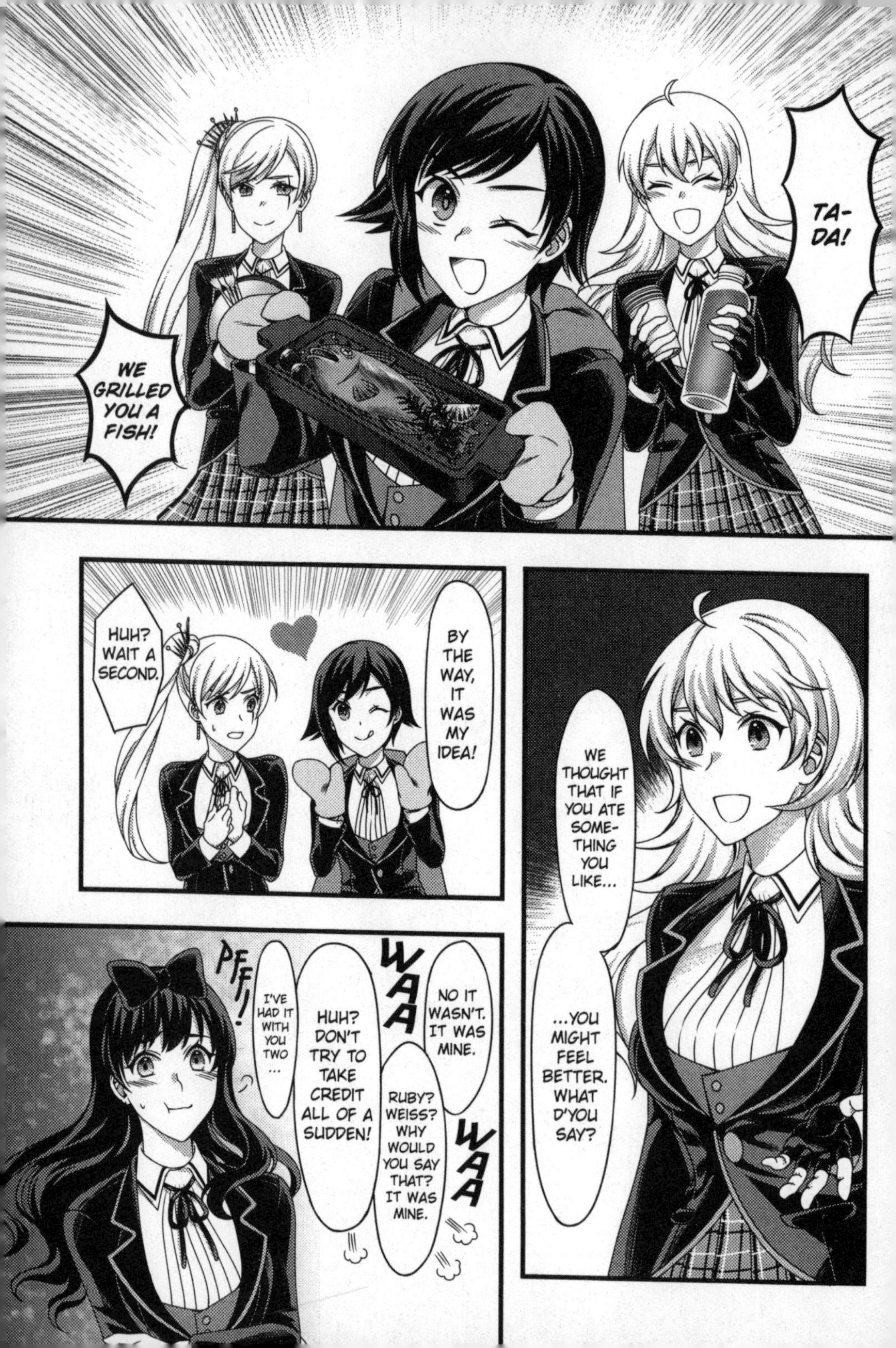
TA-DA!
WE GRILLED YOU A FISH!
WE THOUGHT THAT IF YOU ATE SOME-THING YOU LIKE...
...YOU MIGHT FEEL BETTER. WHAT D'YOU SAY?
BY THE WAY, IT WAS MY IDEA!
HUH? WAIT A SECOND.
NO IT WASN'T. IT WAS MINE.
WAA
RUBY? WEISS? WHY WOULD YOU SAY THAT? IT WAS MINE.
WAA
HUH? DON'T TRY TO TAKE CREDIT ALL OF A SUDDEN!
I'VE HAD IT WITH YOU TWO...
PFF!

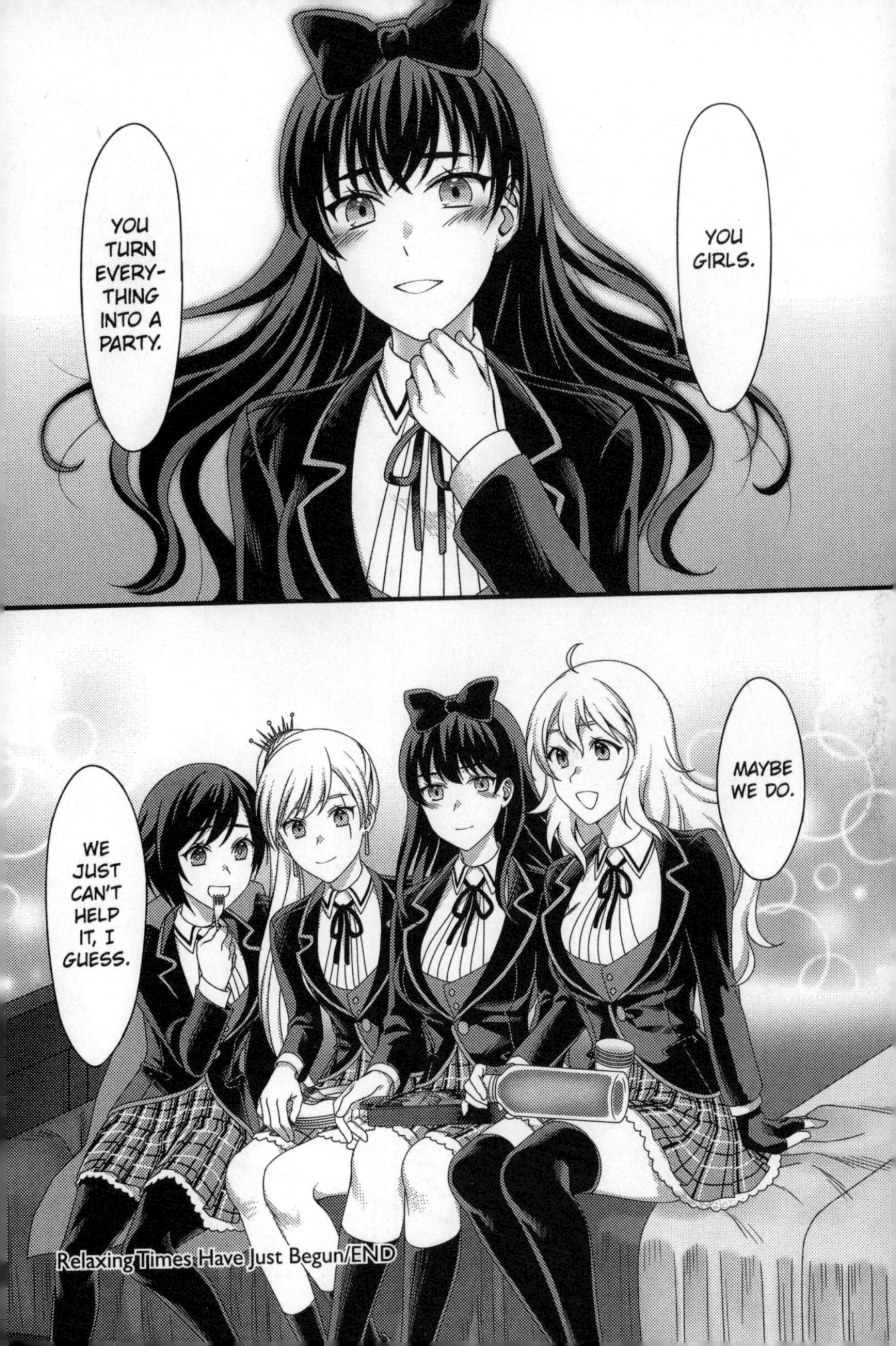
YOU GIRLS.
YOU TURN EVERY-THING INTO A PARTY.
MAYBE WE DO.
WE JUST CAN'T HELP IT, I GUESS.
Relaxing Times Have Just Begun/END

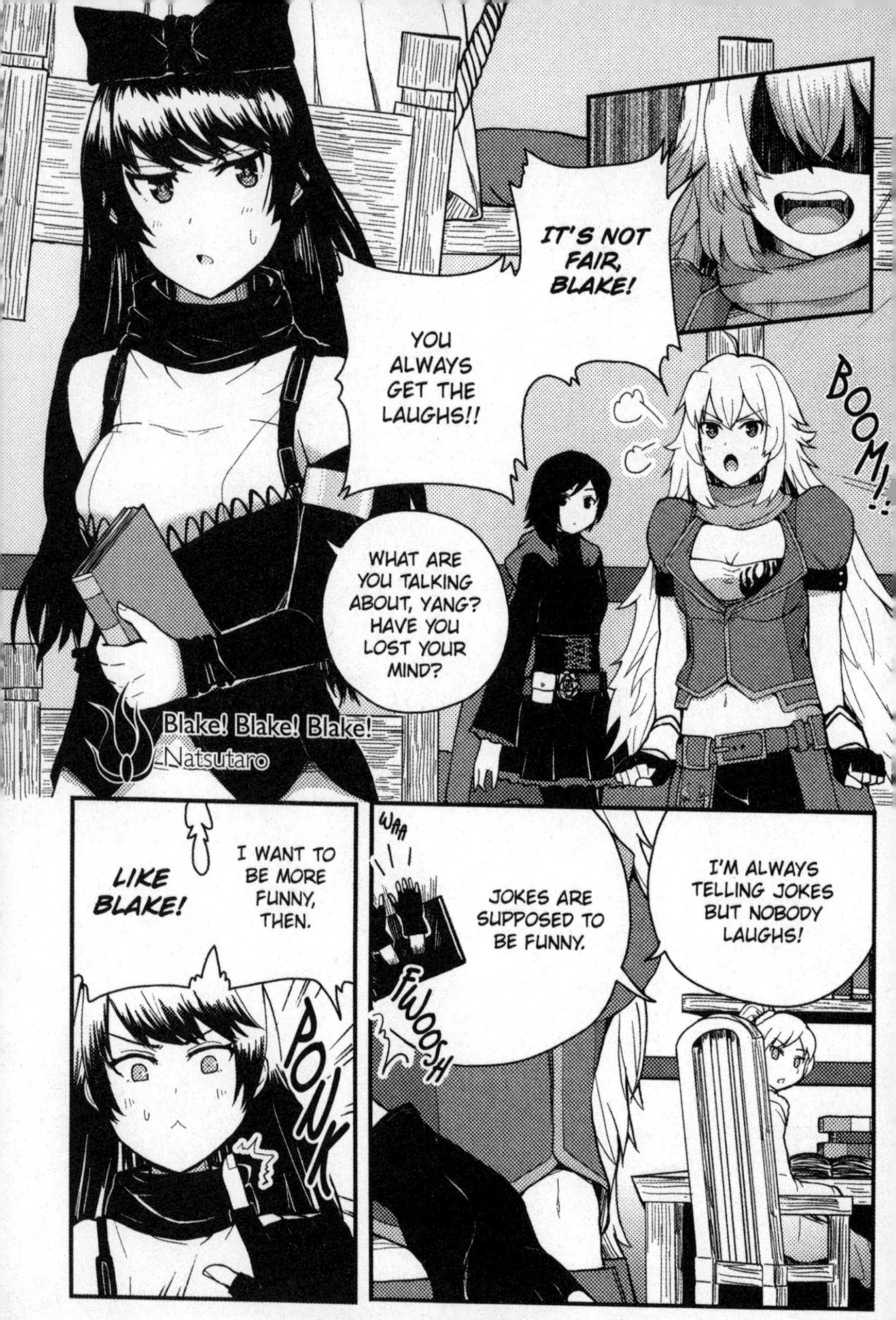
IT'S NOT FAIR, BLAKE!
YOU ALWAYS GET THE LAUGHS!!
BOOM!!
WHAT ARE YOU TALKING ABOUT, YANG? HAVE YOU LOST YOUR MIND?
Blake! Blake! Blake!
Natsutaro
I'M ALWAYS TELLING JOKES BUT NOBODY LAUGHS!
JOKES ARE SUPPOSED TO BE FUNNY.
WAA
FWOOSH
I WANT TO BE MORE FUNNY, THEN.
LIKE BLAKE!
POINK

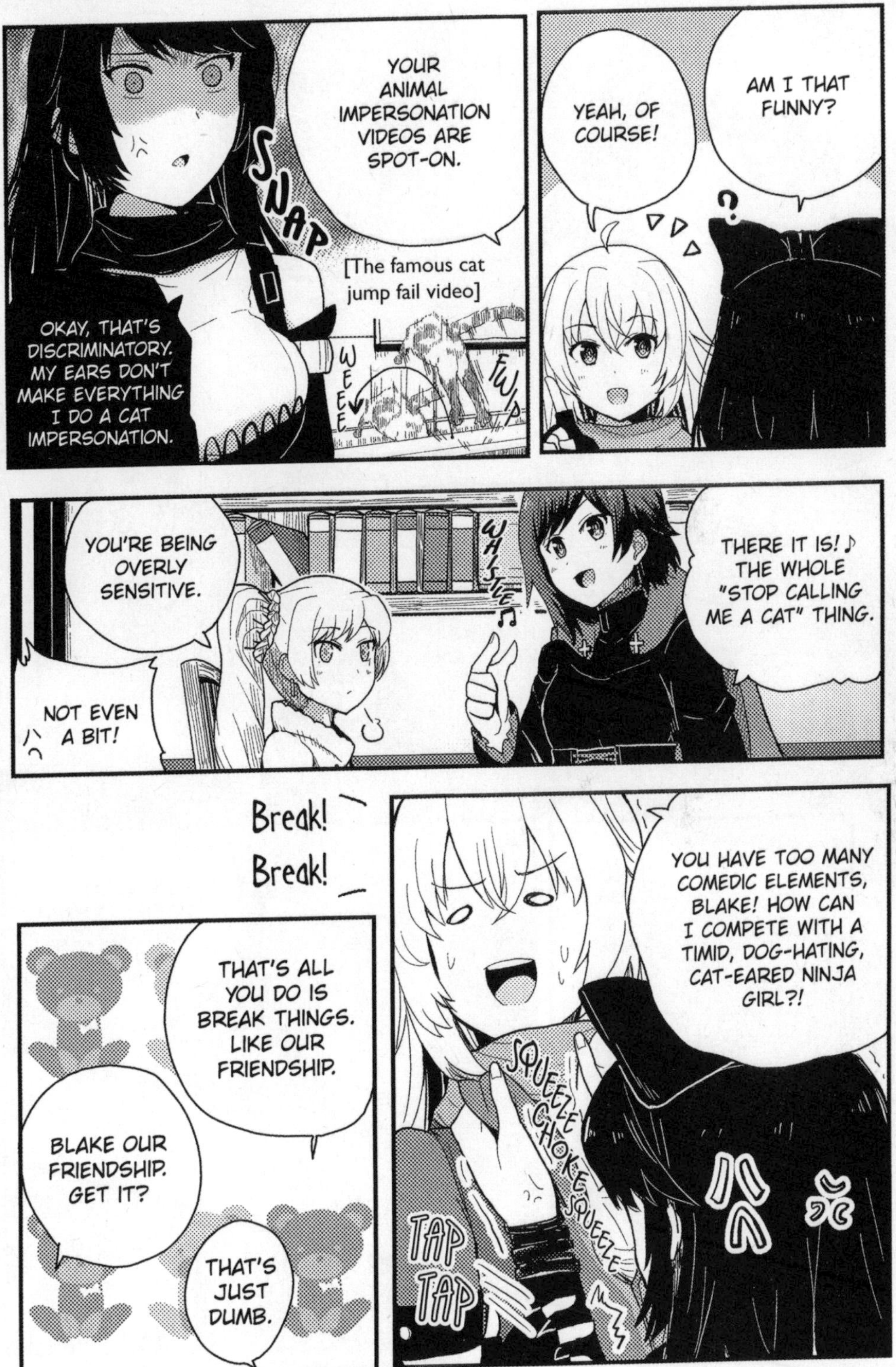
AM I THAT FUNNY?
YEAH, OF COURSE!
YOUR ANIMAL IMPERSONATION VIDEOS ARE SPOT-ON.
SNAP
[The famous cat jump fail video]
FWIP
WEEE
OKAY, THAT'S DISCRIMINATORY. MY EARS DON'T MAKE EVERYTHING I DO A CAT IMPERSONATION.
THERE IT IS!♪ THE WHOLE "STOP CALLING ME A CAT" THING.
WHISTLE
YOU'RE BEING OVERLY SENSITIVE.
NOT EVEN A BIT!
YOU HAVE TOO MANY COMEDIC ELEMENTS, BLAKE! HOW CAN I COMPETE WITH A TIMID, DOG-HATING, CAT-EARED NINJA GIRL?!
SQUEEZE CHOKE SQUEEZE
TAP TAP
Break!
Break!
THAT'S ALL YOU DO IS BREAK THINGS. LIKE OUR FRIENDSHIP.
BLAKE OUR FRIENDSHIP. GET IT?
THAT'S JUST DUMB.

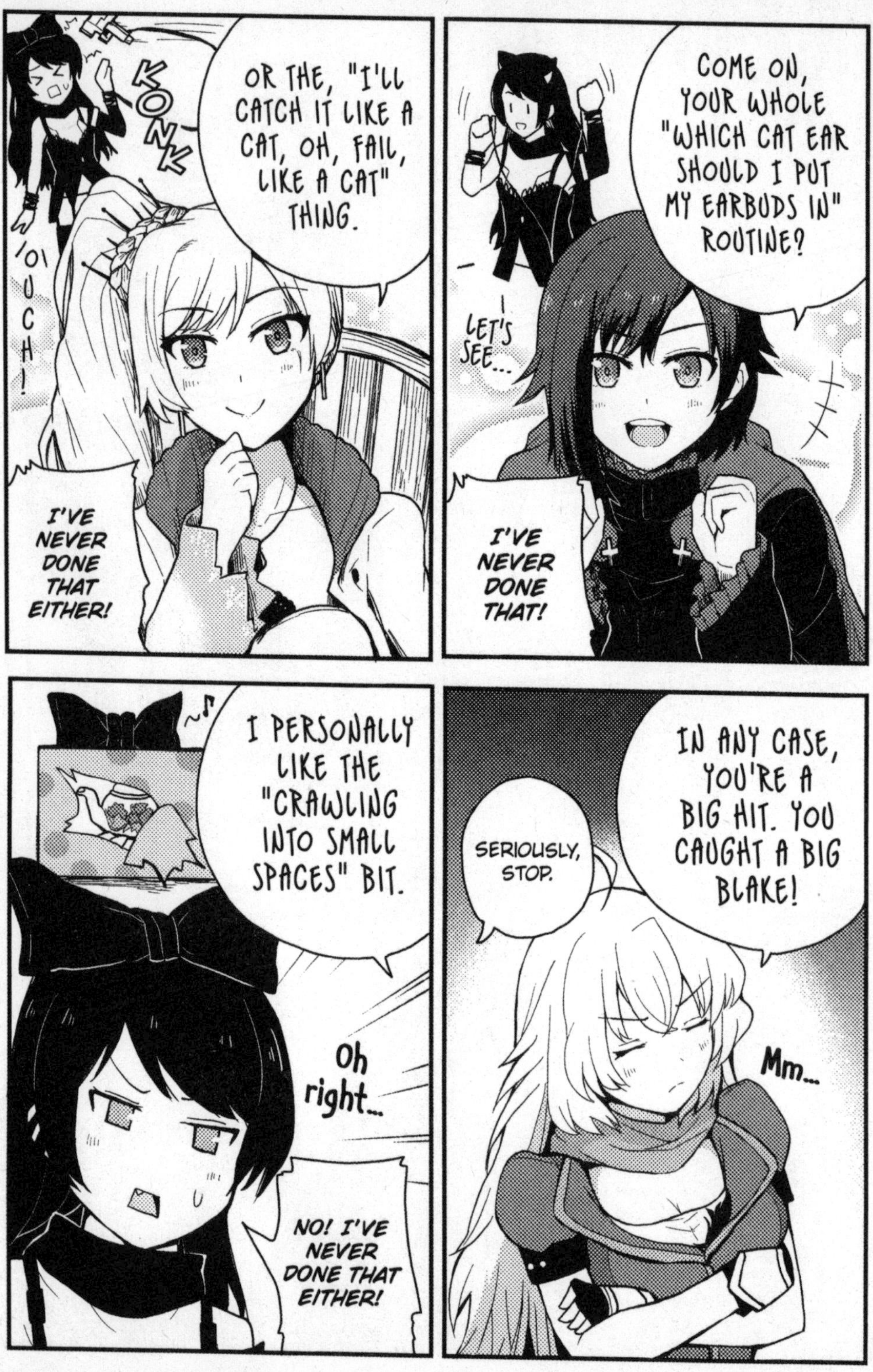
COME ON, YOUR WHOLE "WHICH CAT EAR SHOULD I PUT MY EARBUDS IN" ROUTINE?
LET'S SEE...
I'VE NEVER DONE THAT!
KONK
OR THE, "I'LL CATCH IT LIKE A CAT, OH, FAIL, LIKE A CAT" THING.
OUCH!
I'VE NEVER DONE THAT EITHER!
IN ANY CASE, YOU'RE A BIG HIT. YOU CAUGHT A BIG BLAKE!
SERIOUSLY, STOP.
Mm...
I PERSONALLY LIKE THE "CRAWLING INTO SMALL SPACES" BIT.
Oh right...
NO! I'VE NEVER DONE THAT EITHER!

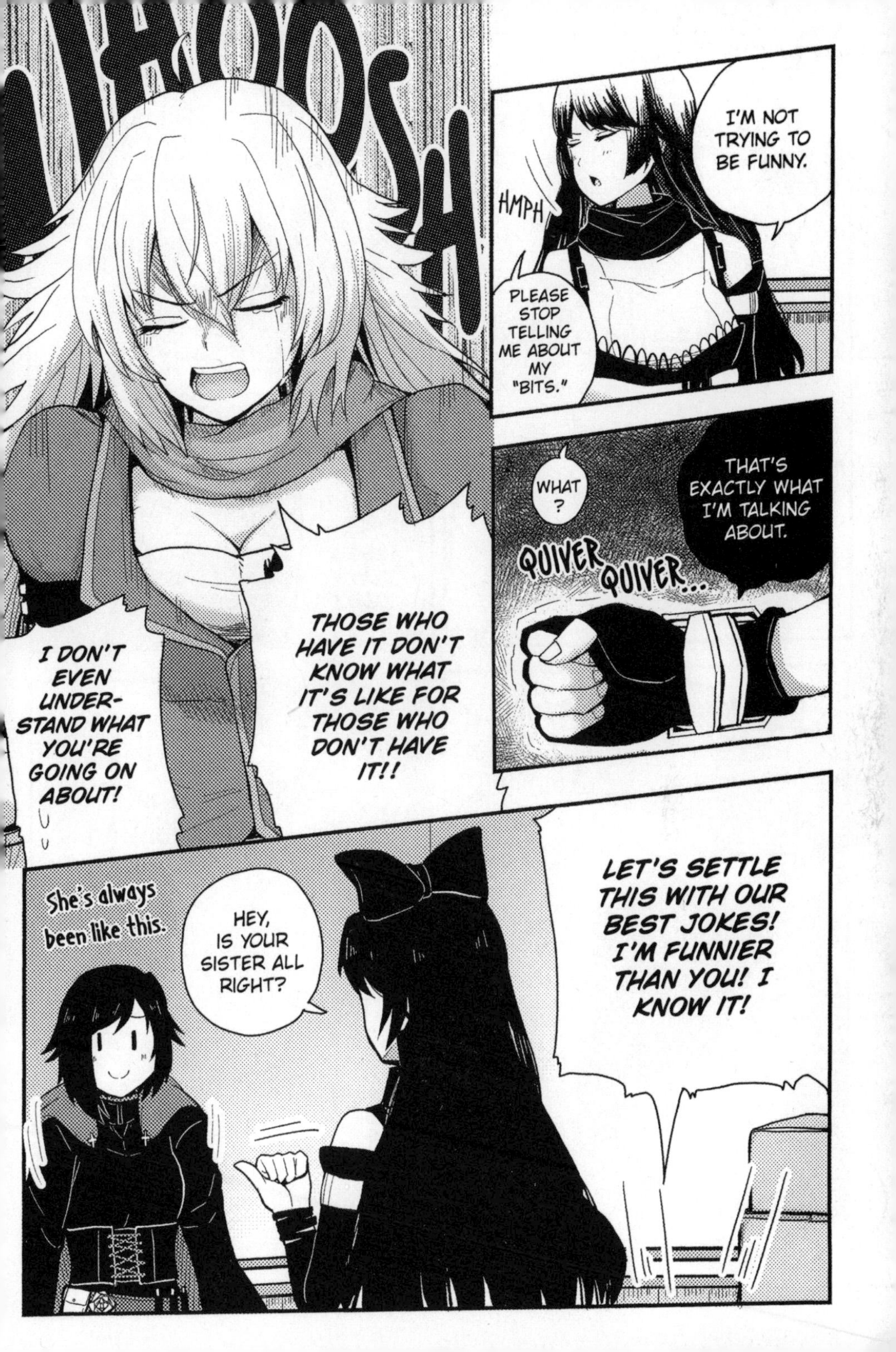
I'M NOT TRYING TO BE FUNNY.
HMPH
PLEASE STOP TELLING ME ABOUT MY "BITS."
THAT'S EXACTLY WHAT I'M TALKING ABOUT.
WHAT?
QUIVER QUIVER...
WHOOSH
THOSE WHO HAVE IT DON'T KNOW WHAT IT'S LIKE FOR THOSE WHO DON'T HAVE IT!!
I DON'T EVEN UNDER-STAND WHAT YOU'RE GOING ON ABOUT!
LET'S SETTLE THIS WITH OUR BEST JOKES! I'M FUNNIER THAN YOU! I KNOW IT!
HEY, IS YOUR SISTER ALL RIGHT?
She's always been like this.

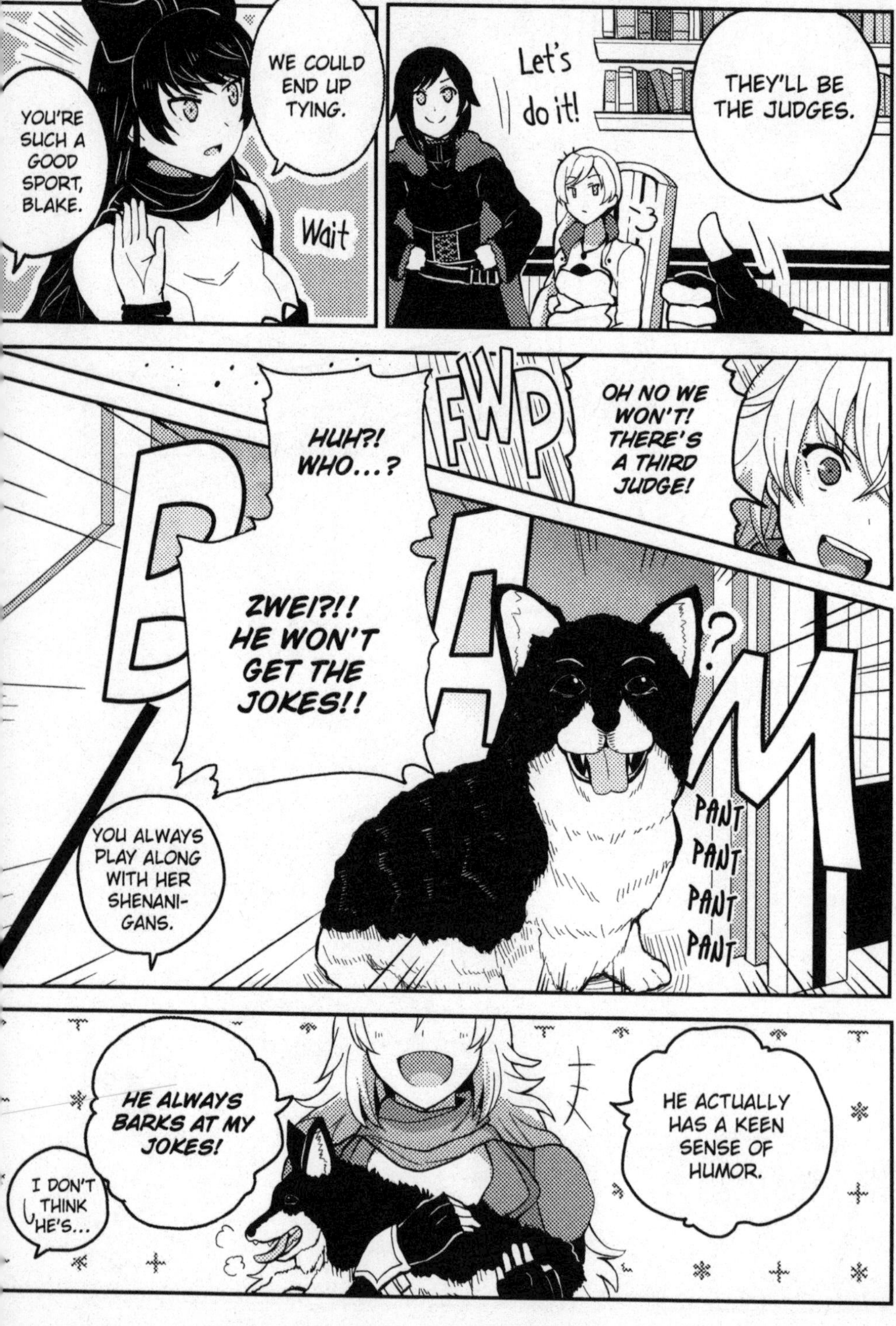
THEY'LL BE THE JUDGES.
Let's do it!
WE COULD END UP TYING.
Wait
YOU'RE SUCH A GOOD SPORT, BLAKE.
OH NO WE WON'T! THERE'S A THIRD JUDGE!
FWP
HUH?! WHO...?
BAM
ZWEI?!! HE WON'T GET THE JOKES!!
?
PANT PANT PANT PANT
YOU ALWAYS PLAY ALONG WITH HER SHENANI-GANS.
HE ACTUALLY HAS A KEEN SENSE OF HUMOR.
HE ALWAYS BARKS AT MY JOKES!
I DON'T THINK HE'S...

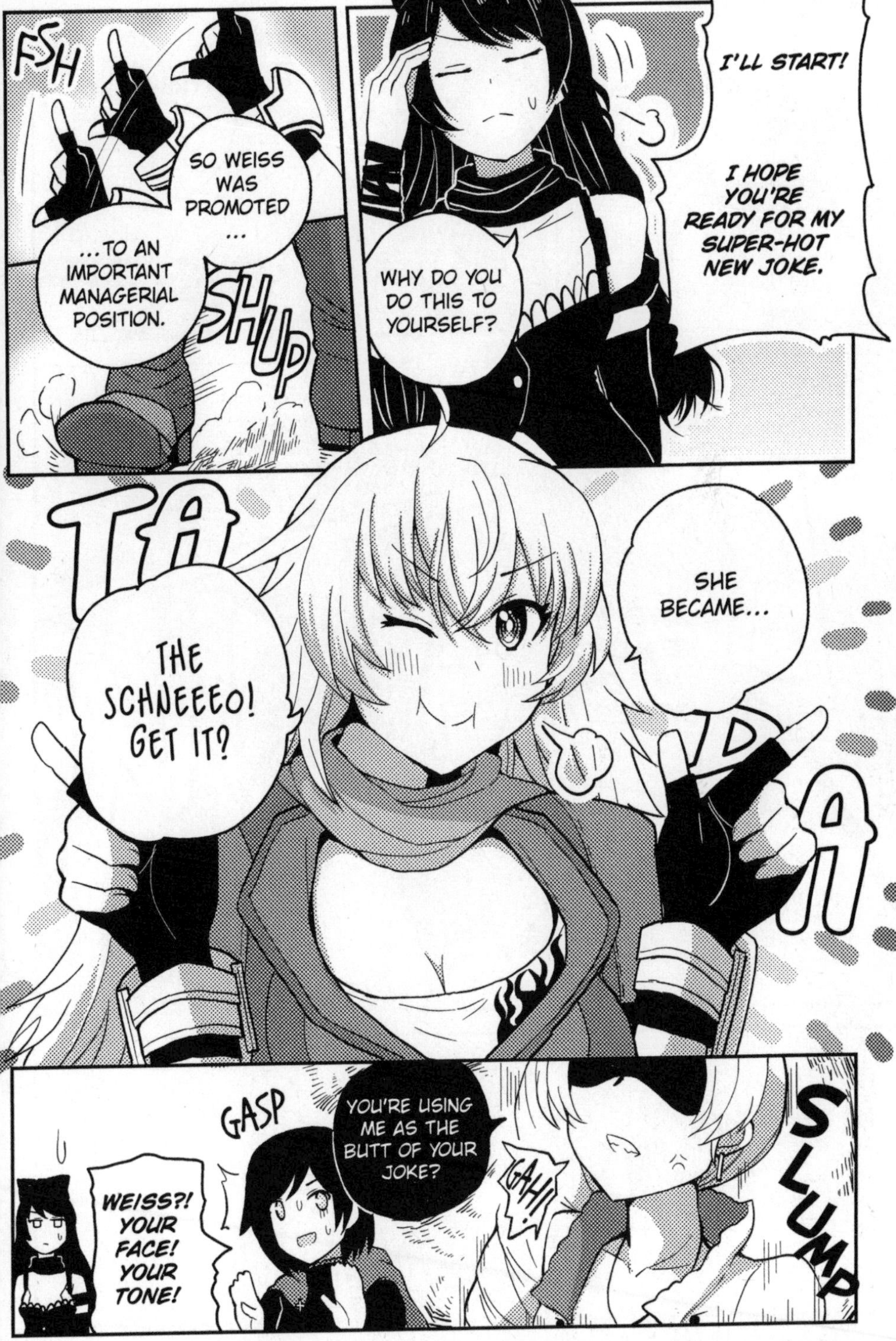
I'LL START!
I HOPE YOU'RE READY FOR MY SUPER-HOT NEW JOKE.
WHY DO YOU DO THIS TO YOURSELF?
FSH
SO WEISS WAS PROMOTED ...
...TO AN IMPORTANT MANAGERIAL POSITION.
SHUP
SHE BECAME...
THE SCHNEEEO! GET IT?
TA
DA
SLUMP
GAH!
YOU'RE USING ME AS THE BUTT OF YOUR JOKE?
GASP
WEISS?! YOUR FACE! YOUR TONE!

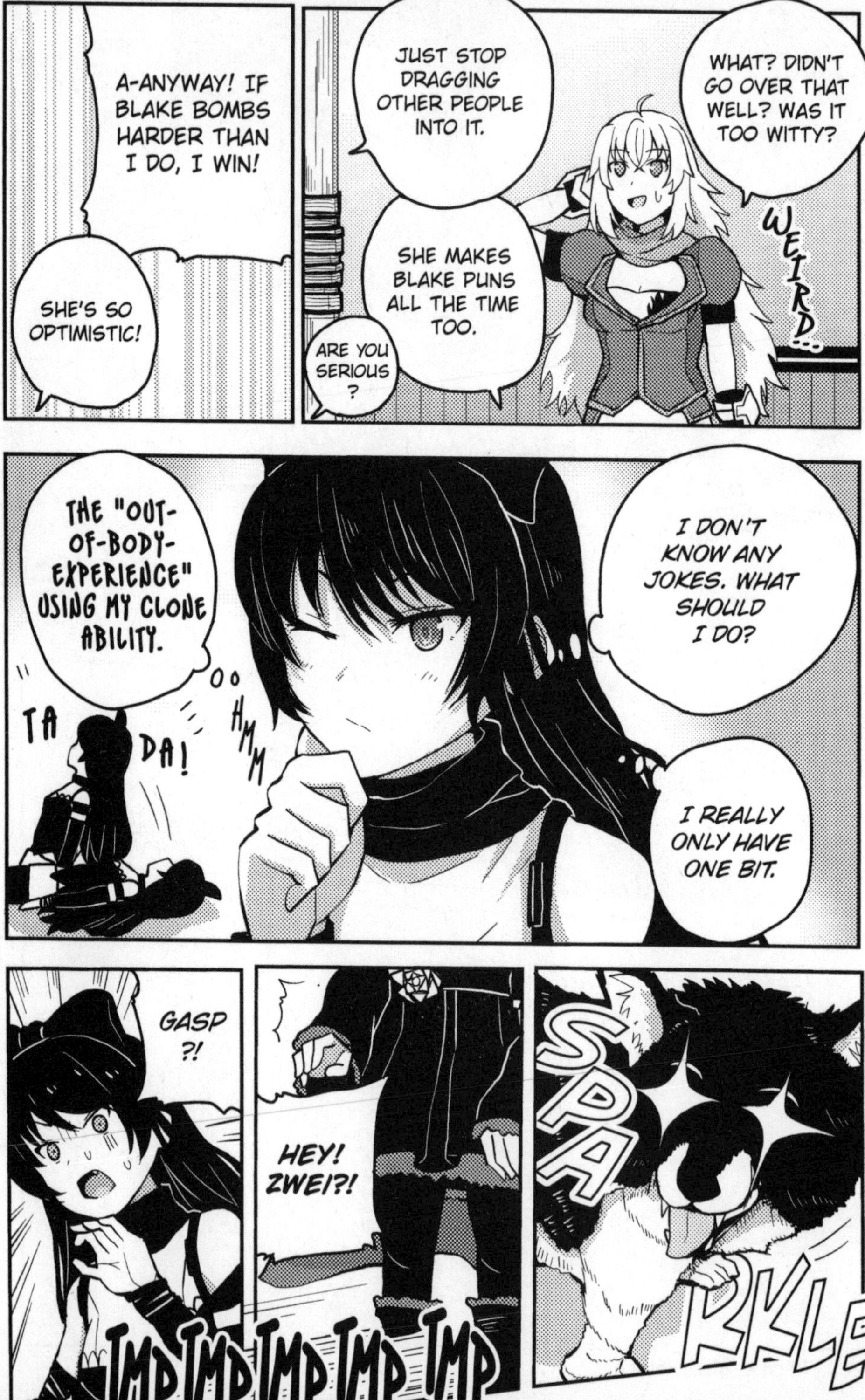
WHAT? DIDN'T GO OVER THAT WELL? WAS IT TOO WITTY?
WEIRD...
JUST STOP DRAGGING OTHER PEOPLE INTO IT.
SHE MAKES BLAKE PUNS ALL THE TIME TOO.
ARE YOU SERIOUS?
A-ANYWAY! IF BLAKE BOMBS HARDER THAN I DO, I WIN!
SHE'S SO OPTIMISTIC!
I DON'T KNOW ANY JOKES. WHAT SHOULD I DO?
I REALLY ONLY HAVE ONE BIT.
HMM
THE "OUT-OF-BODY-EXPERIENCE" USING MY CLONE ABILITY.
OO
TA DA!
SPARKLE
HEY! ZWEI?!
TMP TMP TMP TMP TMP
GASP ?!

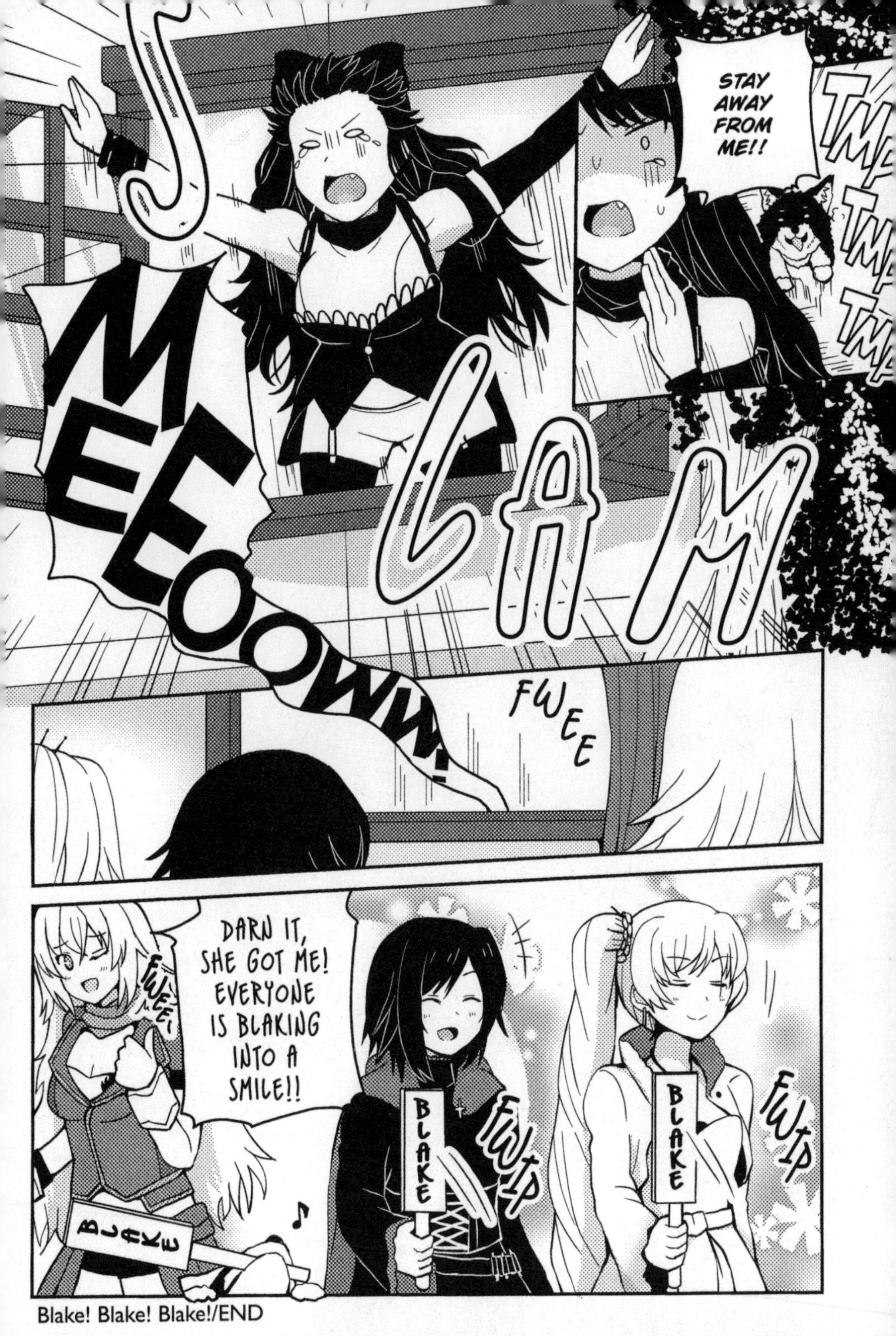
STAY AWAY FROM ME!!
TMP TMP TMP
MEEOOWW!
LAM
FWEE
FWIP
BLAKE
FWIP
BLAKE
DARN IT, SHE GOT ME! EVERYONE IS BLAKING INTO A SMILE!!
FWEE!
BLAKE

Blake! Blake! Blake!/END

RWBY
OFFICIAL MANGA ANTHOLOGY
Volume 3

From Shadows

A Break for Two

Mochiyama

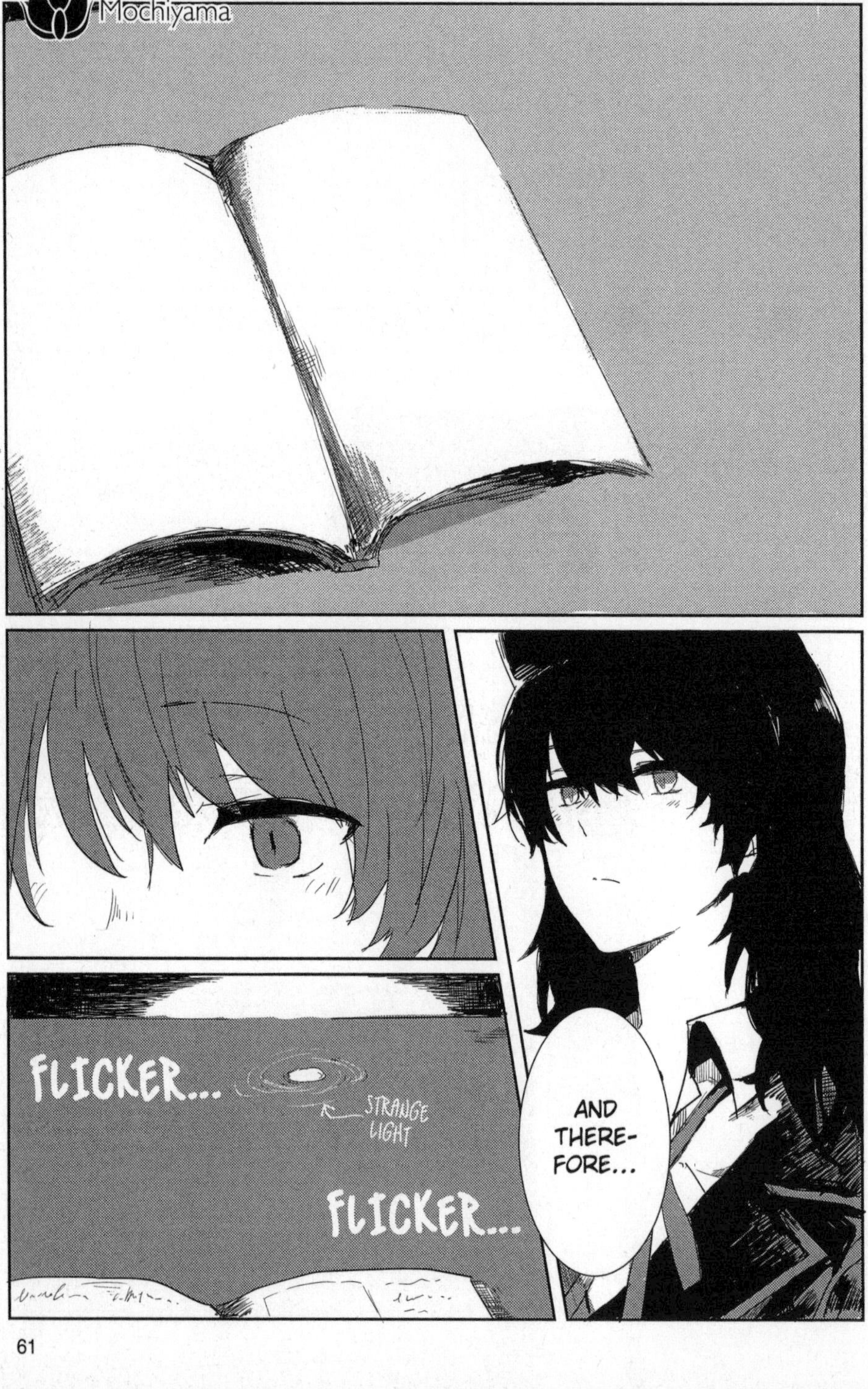
AND THERE-
FORE...
FLICKER...
STRANGE LIGHT
FLICKER...

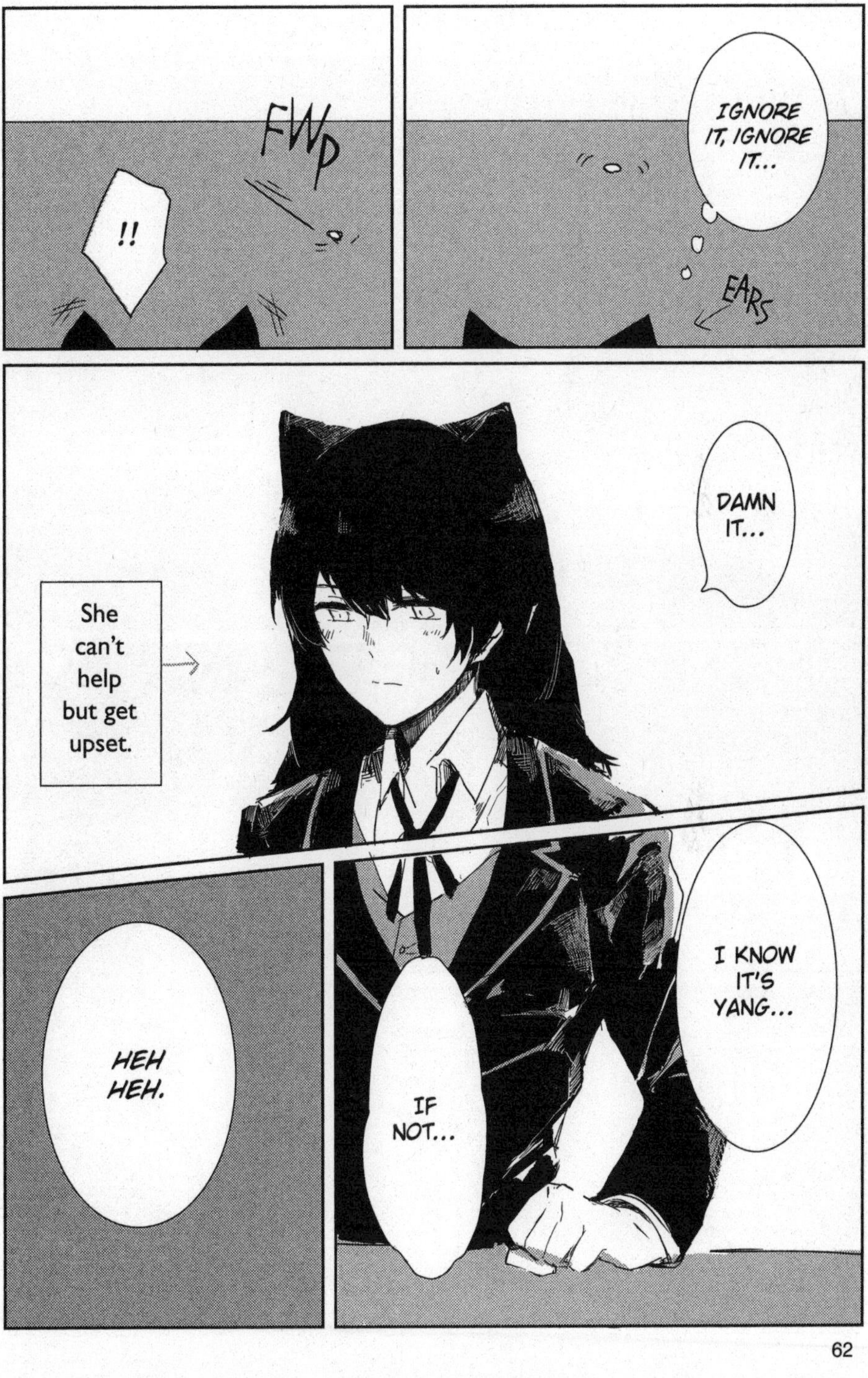
IGNORE IT, IGNORE IT...
EARS
FWP
!!
DAMN IT...
She can't help but get upset.
I KNOW IT'S YANG...
IF NOT...
HEH HEH.

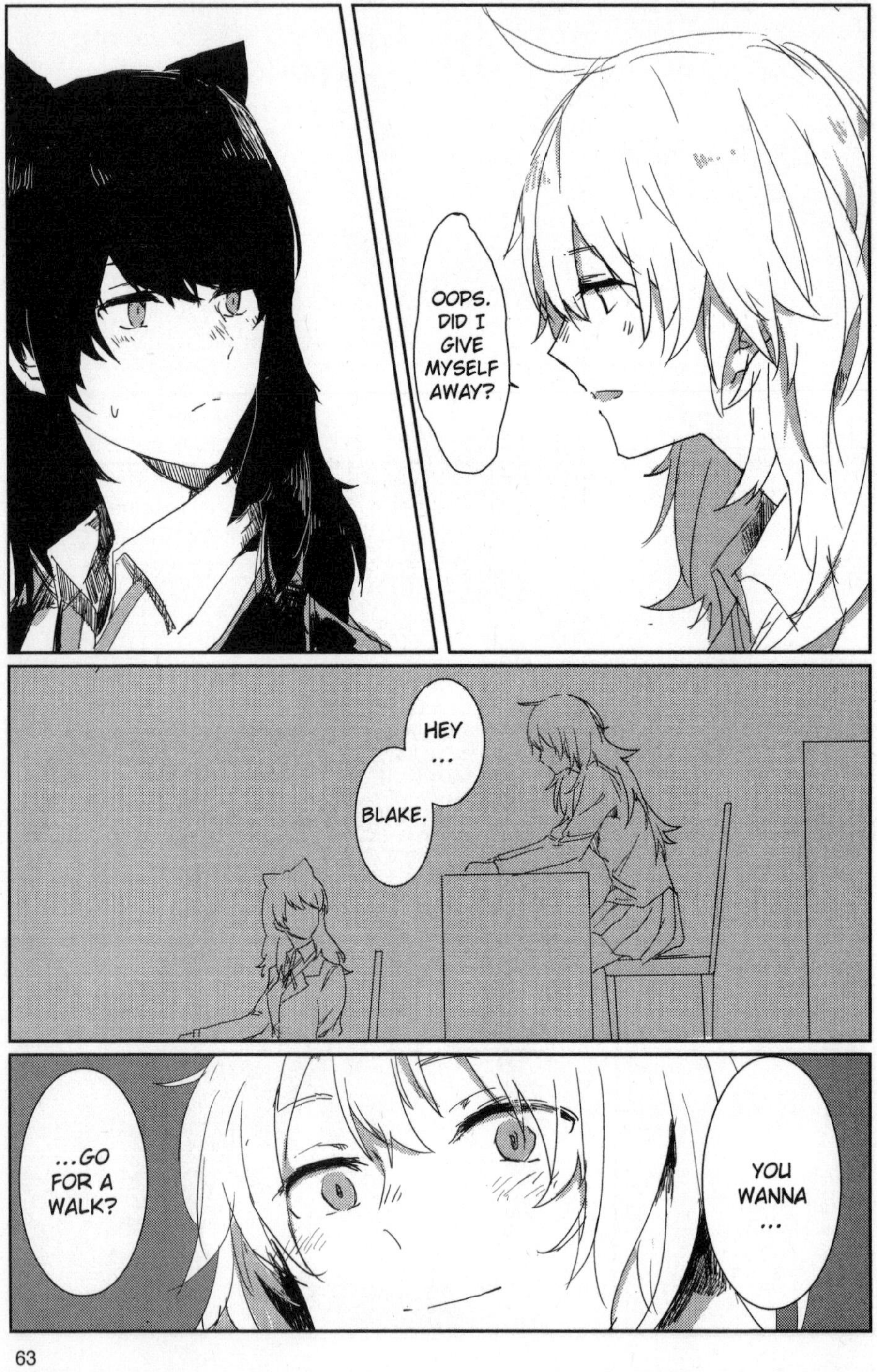
OOPS. DID I GIVE MYSELF AWAY?
HEY ...
BLAKE.
YOU WANNA ...
...GO FOR A WALK?

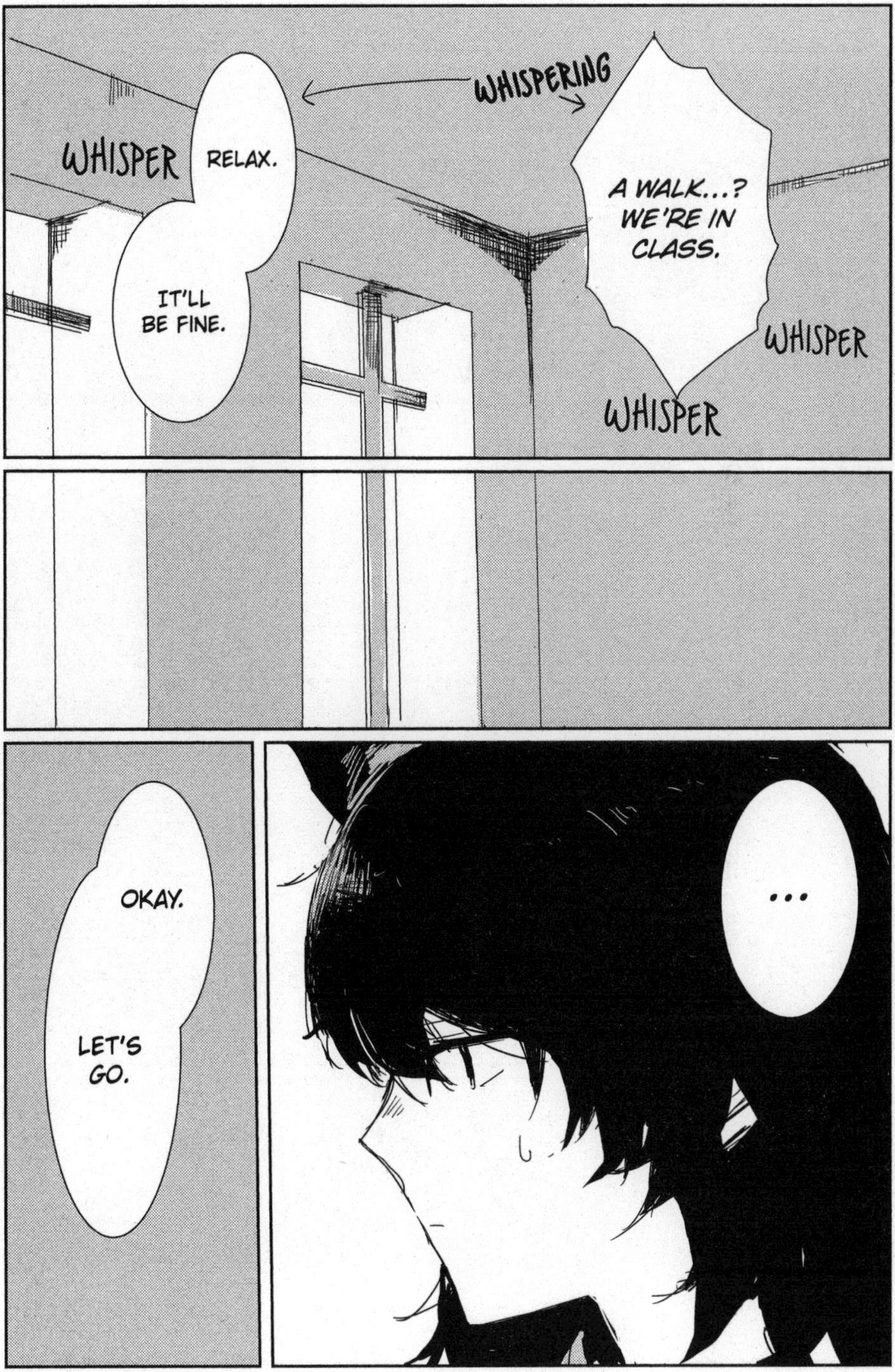
WHISPERING
A WALK...? WE'RE IN CLASS.
WHISPER
WHISPER
RELAX.
IT'LL BE FINE.
WHISPER
...
OKAY.
LET'S GO.

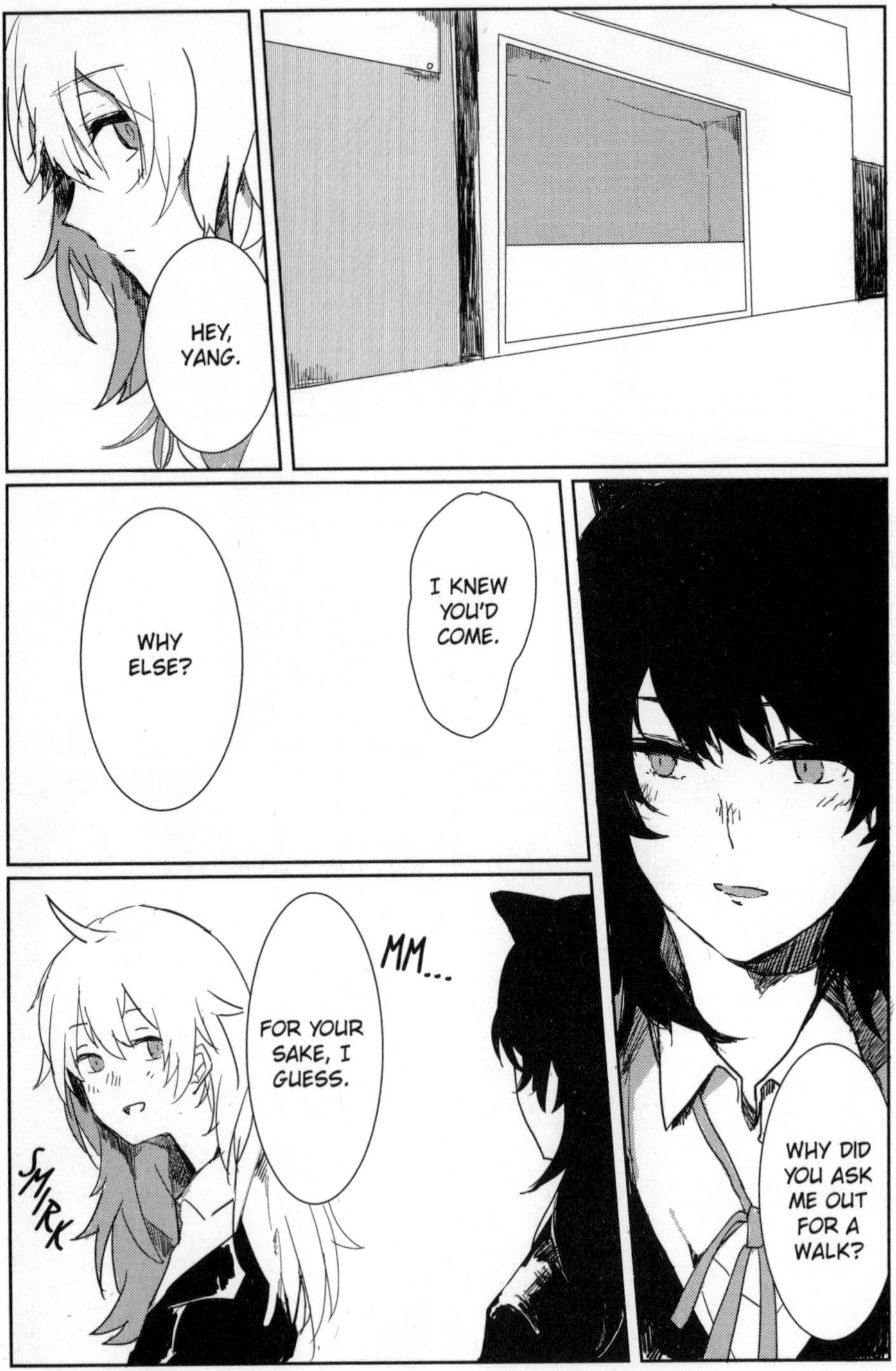
HEY, YANG.
WHY DID YOU ASK ME OUT FOR A WALK?
I KNEW YOU'D COME.
WHY ELSE?
MM...
FOR YOUR SAKE, I GUESS.
SMIRK

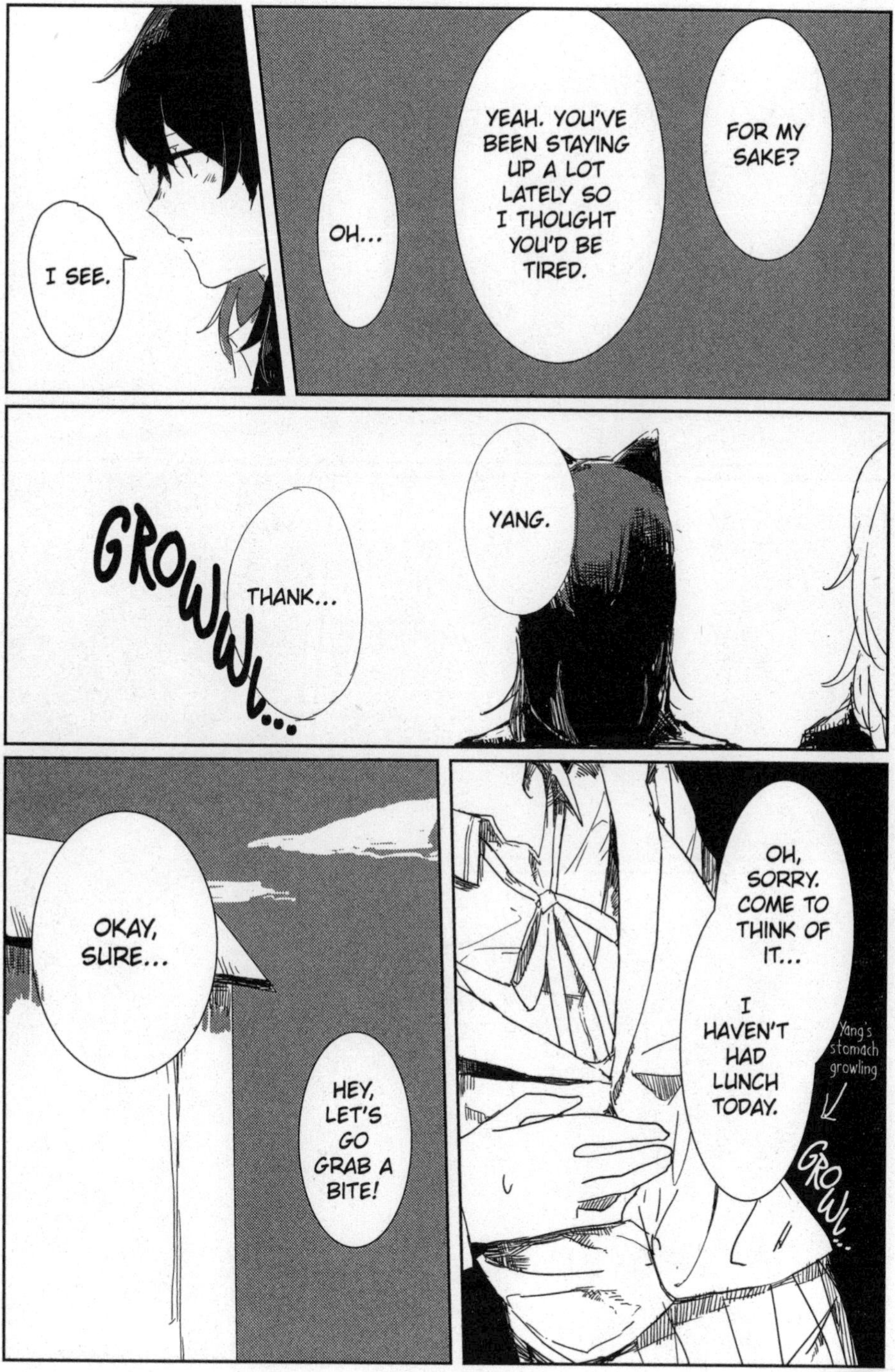
FOR MY SAKE?
YEAH. YOU'VE BEEN STAYING UP A LOT LATELY SO I THOUGHT YOU'D BE TIRED.
OH...
I SEE.
YANG.
THANK...
GROWWL...
OH, SORRY. COME TO THINK OF IT...
I HAVEN'T HAD LUNCH TODAY.
Yang's stomach growling
GROWL...
OKAY, SURE...
HEY, LET'S GO GRAB A BITE!

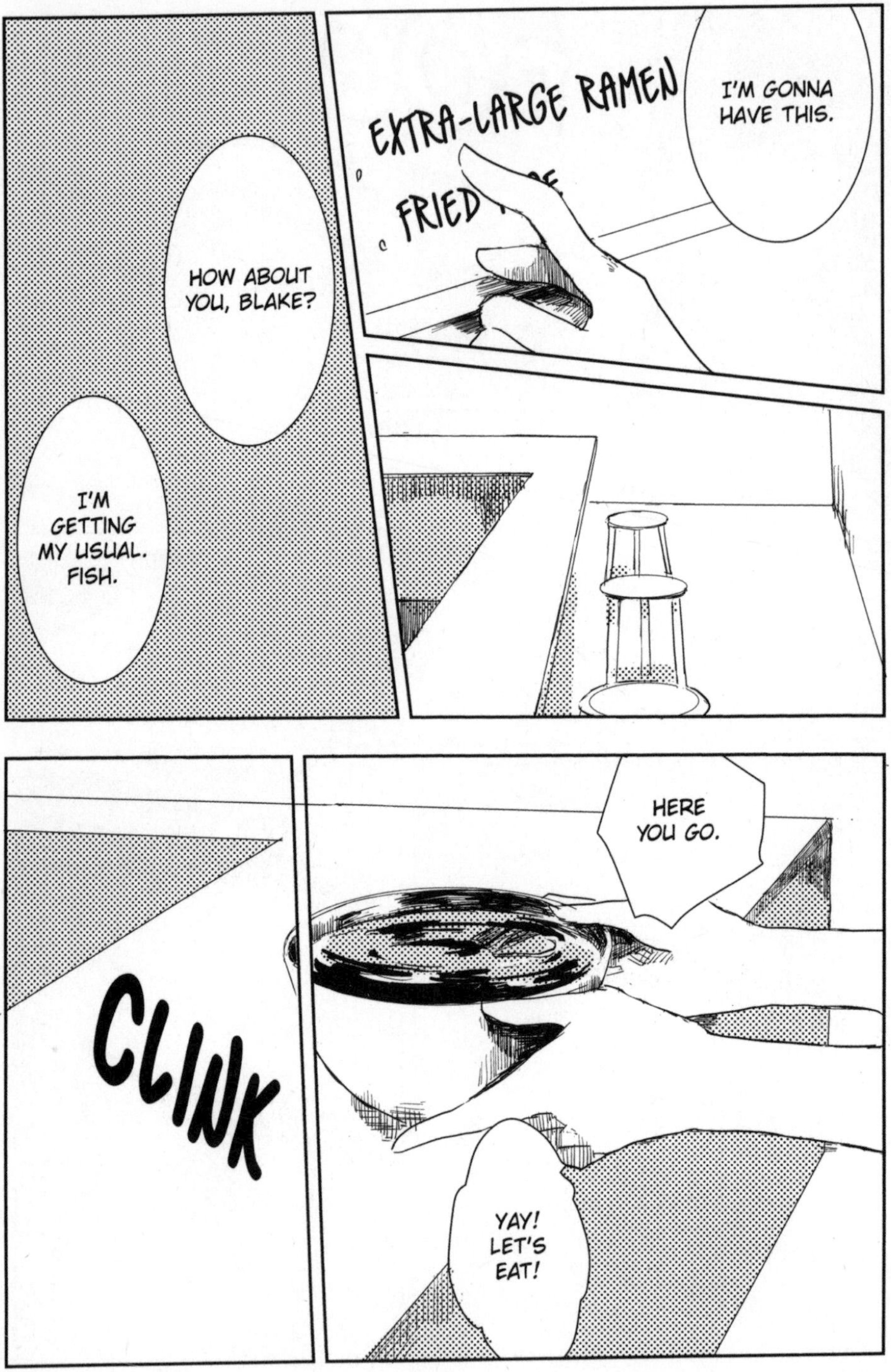
I'M GONNA HAVE THIS.
EXTRA-LARGE RAMEN
FRIED
HOW ABOUT YOU, BLAKE?
I'M GETTING MY USUAL. FISH.
HERE YOU GO.
YAY! LET'S EAT!
CLINK

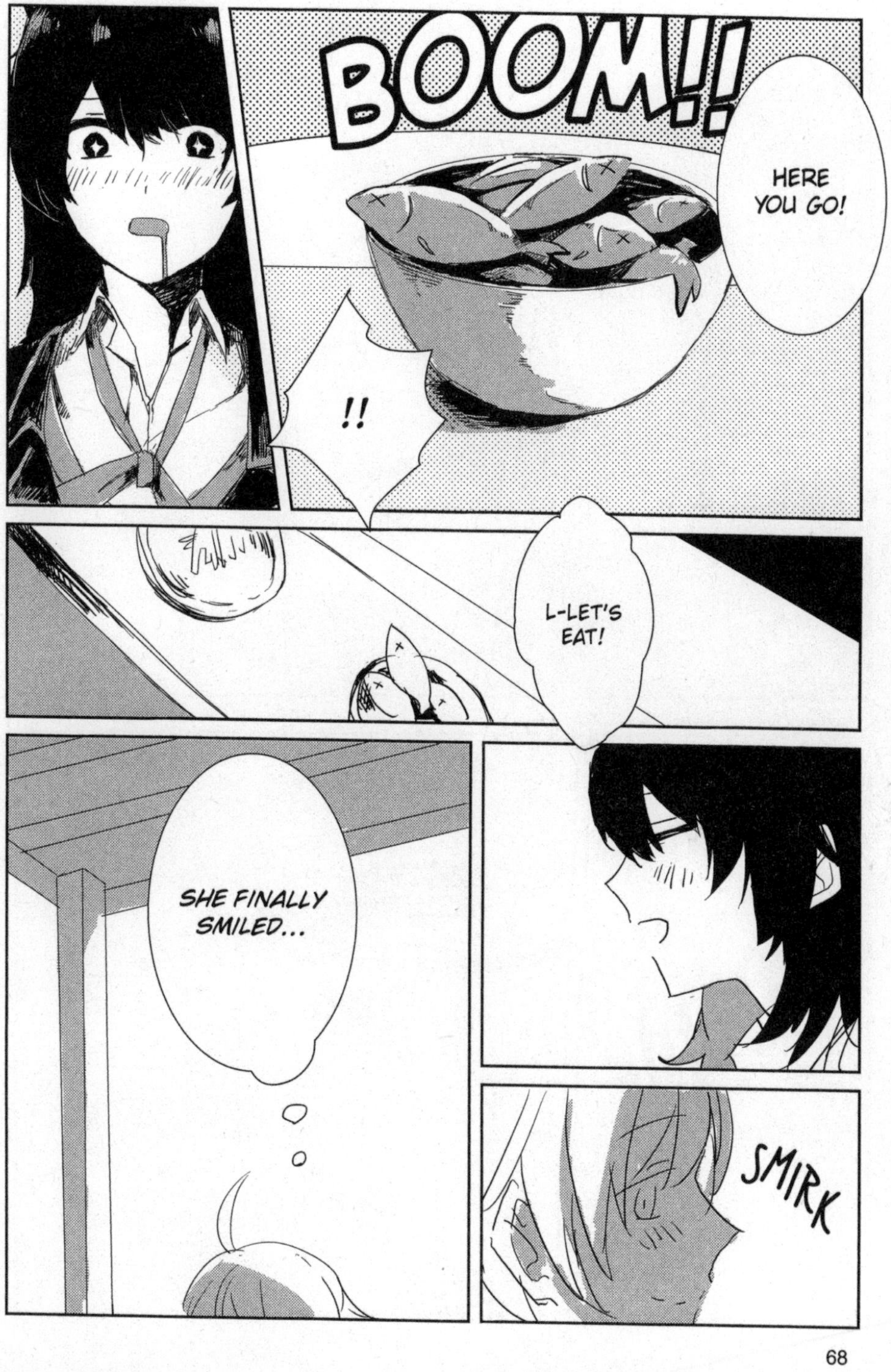
HERE YOU GO!
BOOM!!
!!
L-LET'S EAT!
SMIRK
SHE FINALLY SMILED...

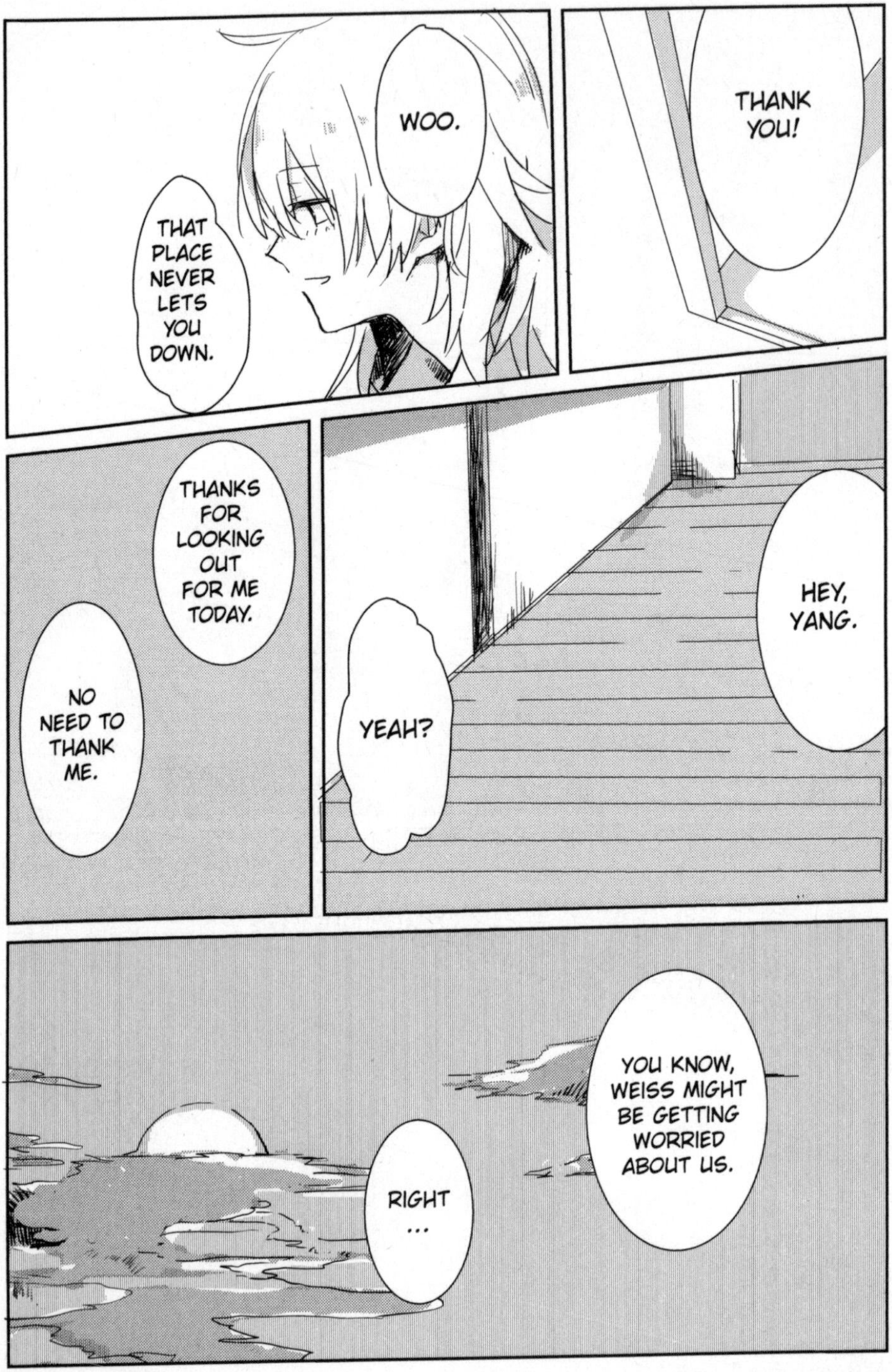
THANK YOU!
WOO.
THAT PLACE NEVER LETS YOU DOWN.
HEY, YANG.
YEAH?
THANKS FOR LOOKING OUT FOR ME TODAY.
NO NEED TO THANK ME.
YOU KNOW, WEISS MIGHT BE GETTING WORRIED ABOUT US.
RIGHT ...

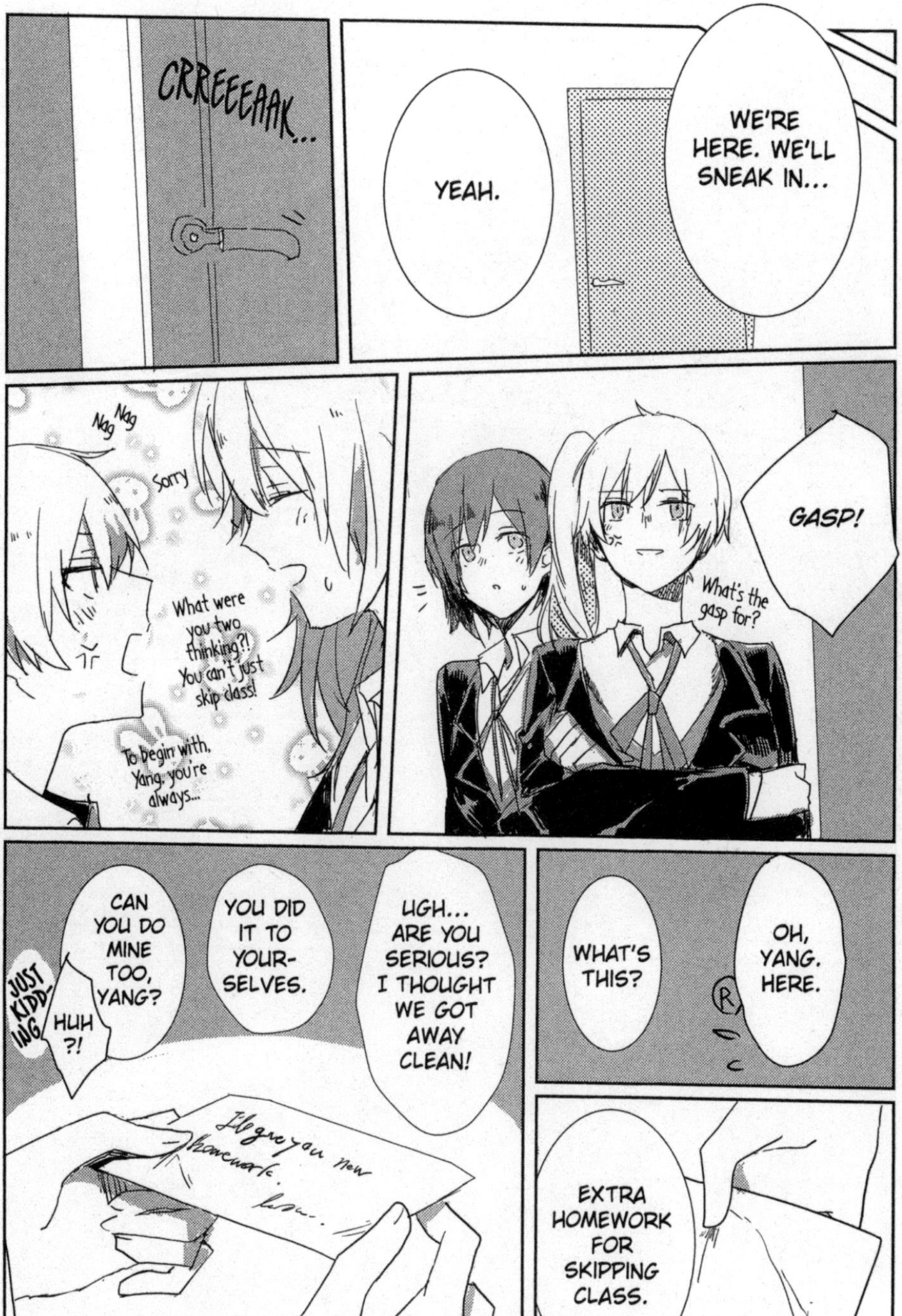
WE'RE HERE. WE'LL SNEAK IN...
YEAH.
CRREEEAAK...
GASP!
What's the gasp for?
Nag Nag
Sorry
What were you two thinking?! You can't just skip class!
To begin with, Yang, you're always...
OH, YANG. HERE.
WHAT'S THIS?
EXTRA HOMEWORK FOR SKIPPING CLASS.
UGH... ARE YOU SERIOUS? I THOUGHT WE GOT AWAY CLEAN!
YOU DID IT TO YOUR-SELVES.
CAN YOU DO MINE TOO, YANG?
HUH?!
JUST KIDD-ING
I'll give you new homework.

A Break for Two/END

Beacon Days (Blake)

mojojoj

This Is Who Blake Is

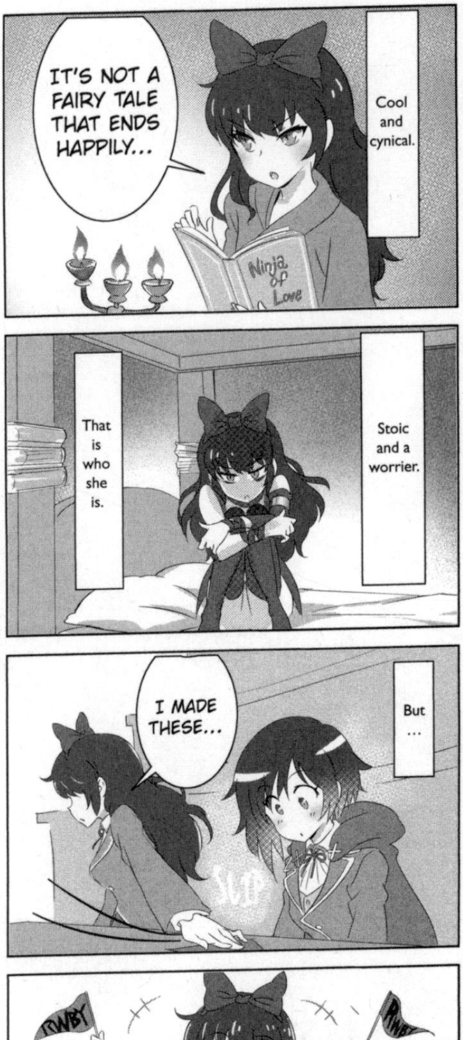
Cool and cynical.
IT'S NOT A FAIRY TALE THAT ENDS HAPPILY...
Ninja of Love
Stoic and a worrier.
That is who she is.
But ...
I MADE THESE...
RWBY
RWBY
She's playful at heart.

Reason for Leaving

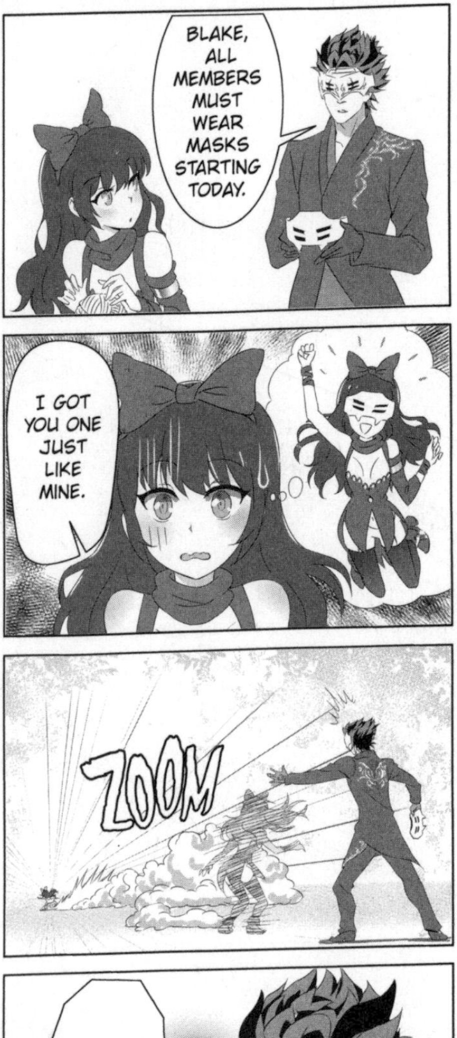
BLAKE, ALL MEMBERS MUST WEAR MASKS STARTING TODAY.
I GOT YOU ONE JUST LIKE MINE.
ZOOM
I'M GLAD SHE'S SO HAPPY...

Find Blake!

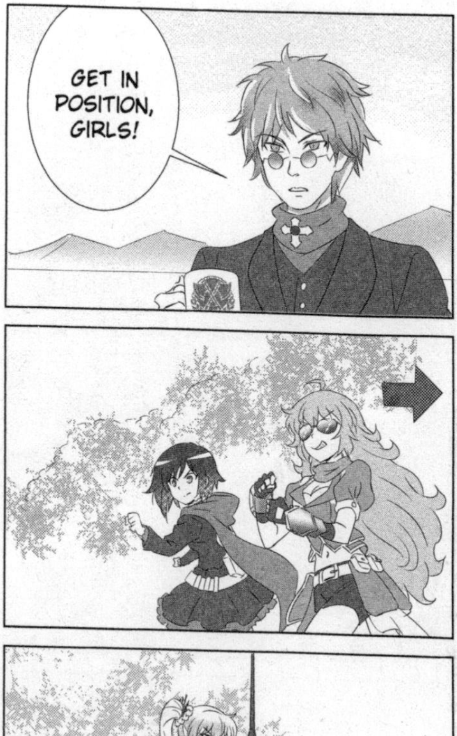
GET IN POSITION, GIRLS!

Landing Strategy

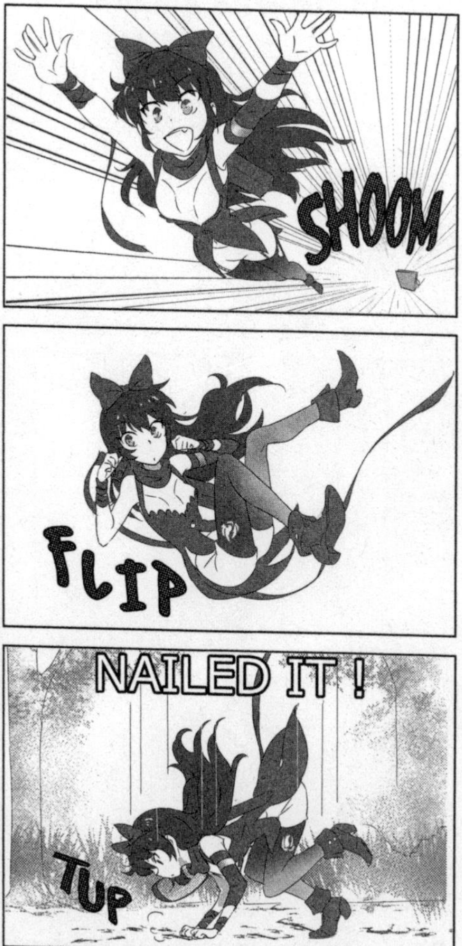
SHOOM
FLIP
NAILED IT !
TUP
THAT'S HOW YOU LAND, RIGHT?
NO.

Personal Space

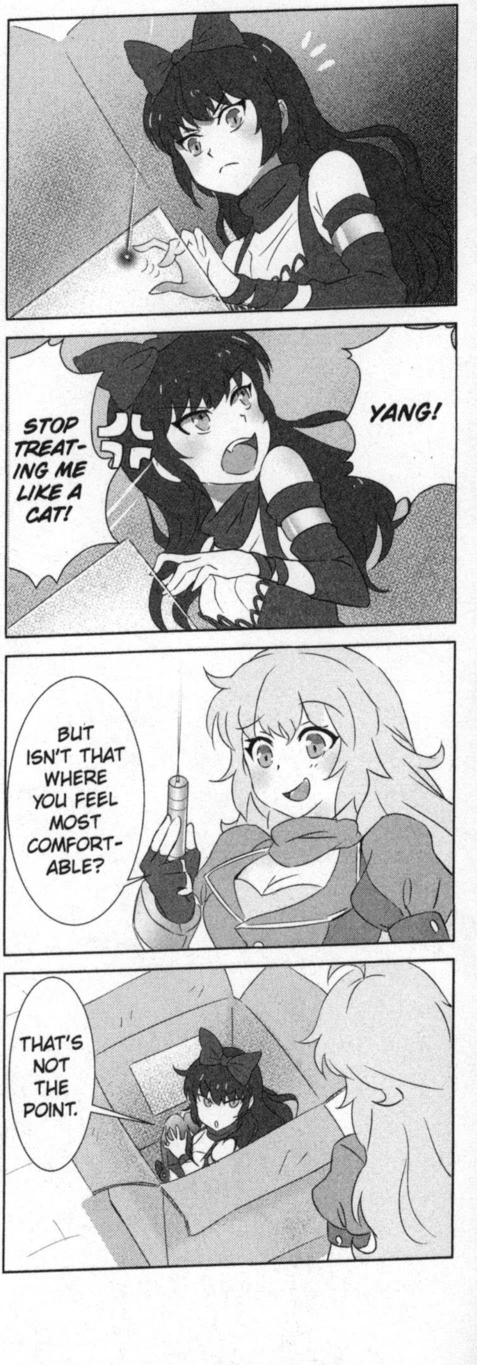
YANG!
STOP TREATING ME LIKE A CAT!
BUT ISN'T THAT WHERE YOU FEEL MOST COMFORTABLE?
THAT'S NOT THE POINT.

Playing Dead

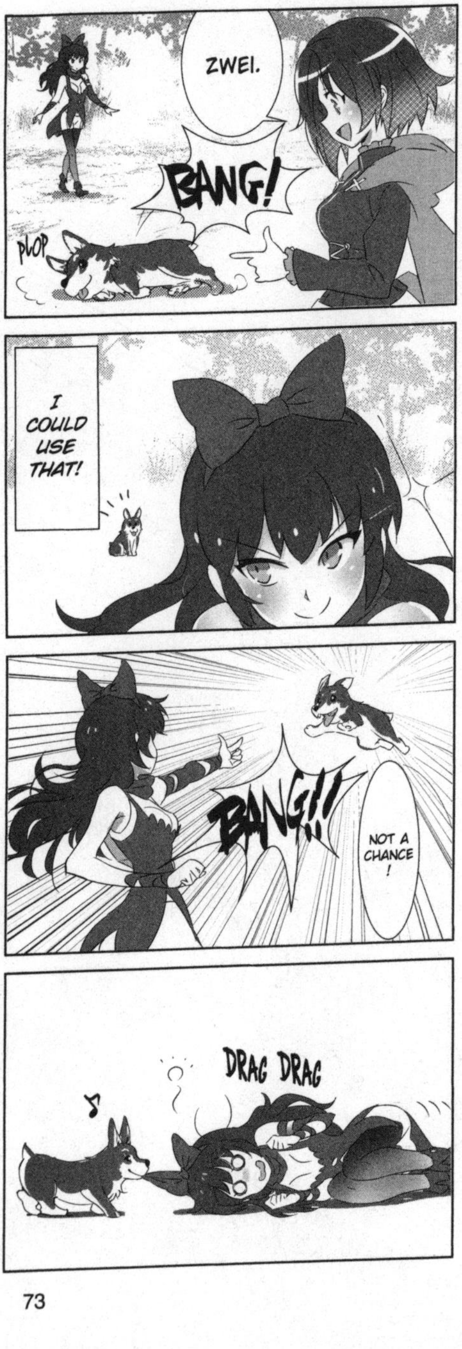
ZWEI.
BANG!
PLOP
I COULD USE THAT!
BANG!!
NOT A CHANCE!
DRAG DRAG

Cast-Off

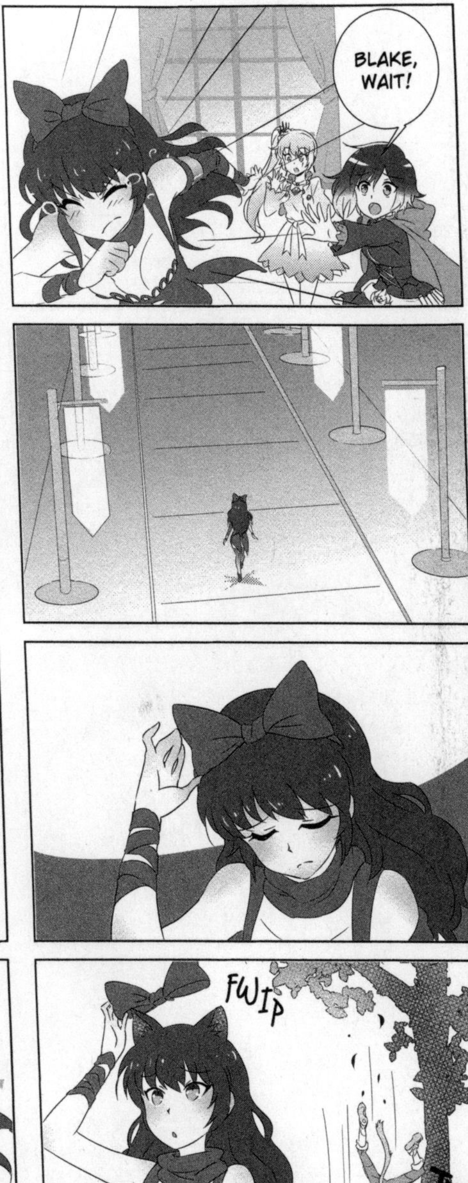
BLAKE, WAIT!
FWIP
THUD

Smell of the Ocean

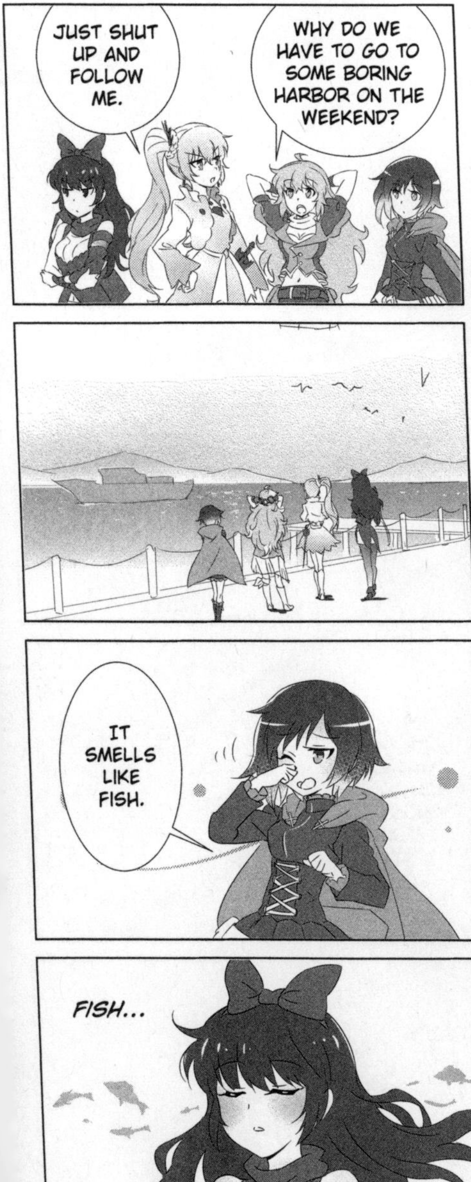
WHY DO WE HAVE TO GO TO SOME BORING HARBOR ON THE WEEKEND?
JUST SHUT UP AND FOLLOW ME.
IT SMELLS LIKE FISH.
FISH...

Beacon Days (Blake)/END

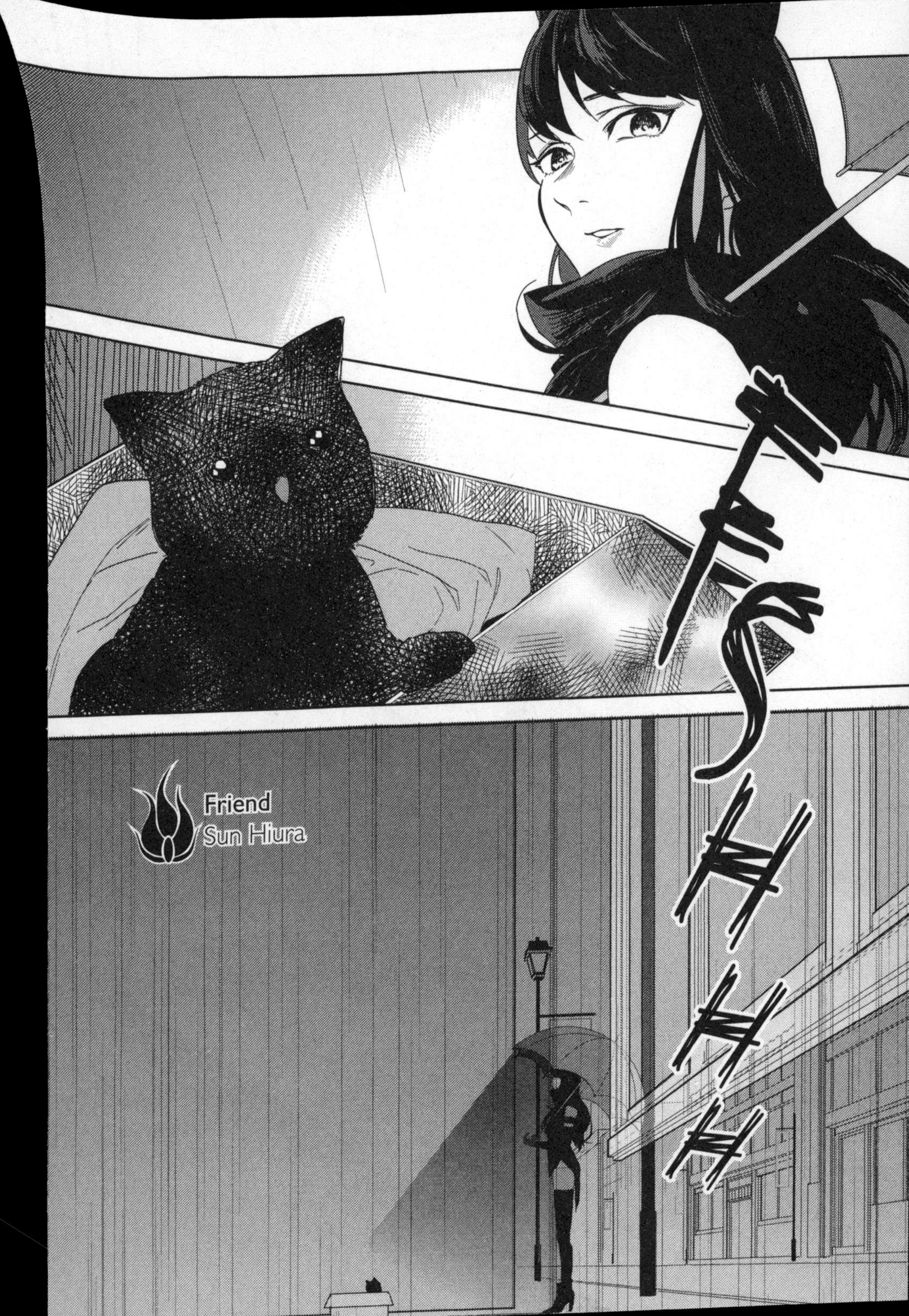
FSHHH
Friend
Sun Hiura

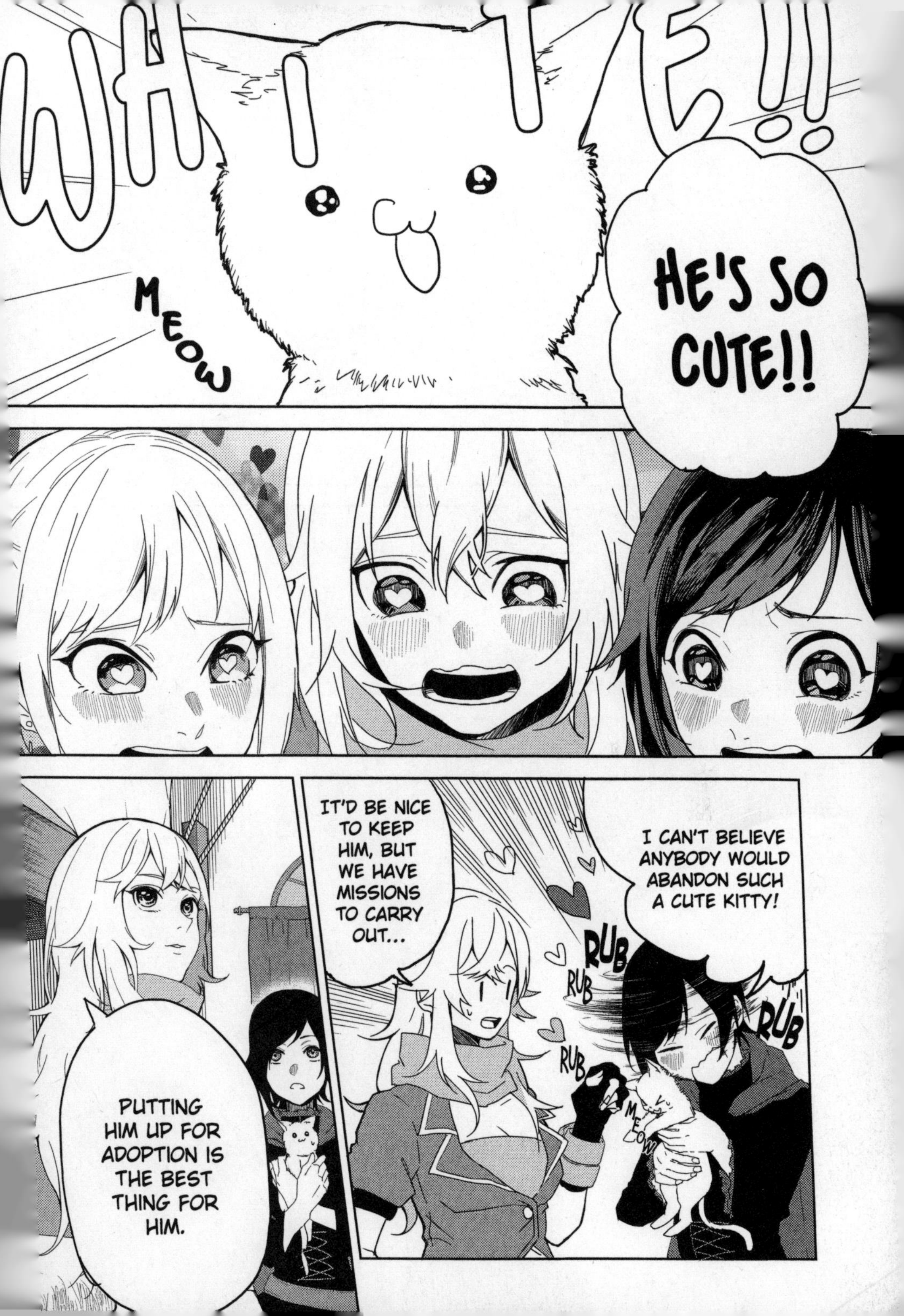
WHITE!!
HE'S SO CUTE!!
MEOW
I CAN'T BELIEVE ANYBODY WOULD ABANDON SUCH A CUTE KITTY!
IT'D BE NICE TO KEEP HIM, BUT WE HAVE MISSIONS TO CARRY OUT...
RUB
RUB
RUB
RUB
MEOW
PUTTING HIM UP FOR ADOPTION IS THE BEST THING FOR HIM.

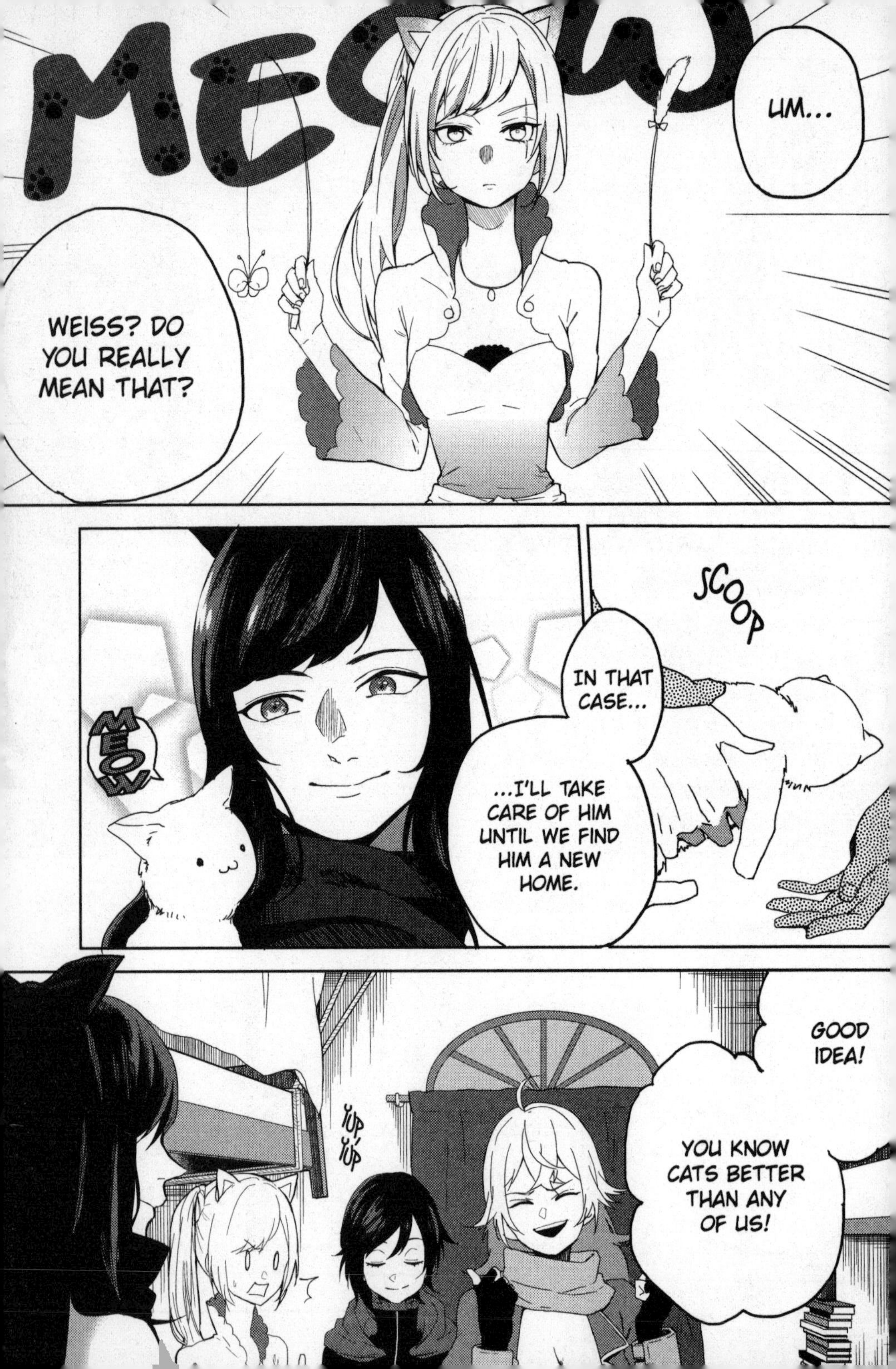
UM...
MEOW
WEISS? DO YOU REALLY MEAN THAT?
SCOOP
IN THAT CASE...
...I'LL TAKE CARE OF HIM UNTIL WE FIND HIM A NEW HOME.
MEOW
GOOD IDEA!
YOU KNOW CATS BETTER THAN ANY OF US!
YUP, YUP

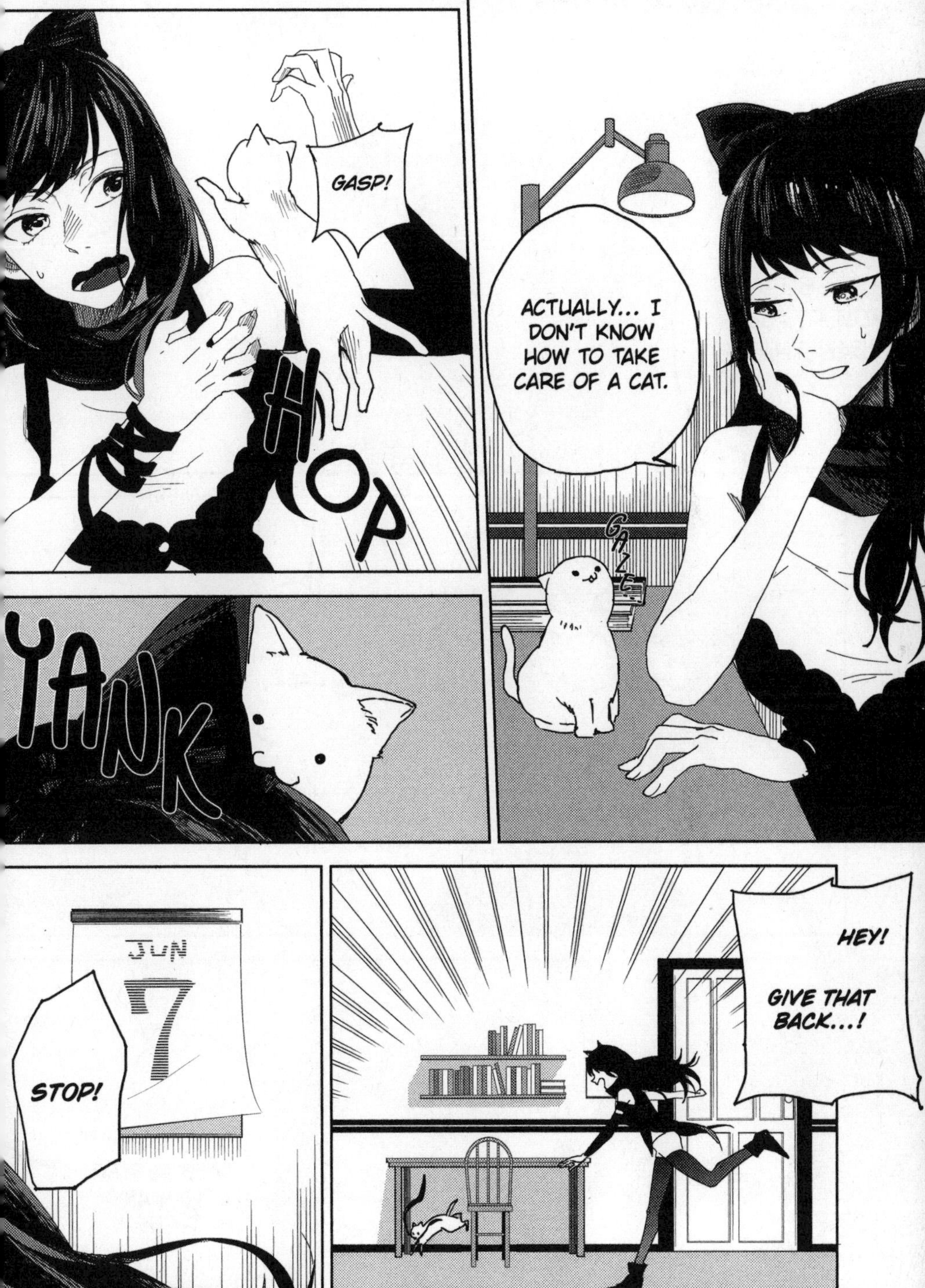
ACTUALLY... I DON'T KNOW HOW TO TAKE CARE OF A CAT.
GAZE
GASP!
HOP
YANK
HEY!
GIVE THAT BACK...!
STOP!
JUN
7

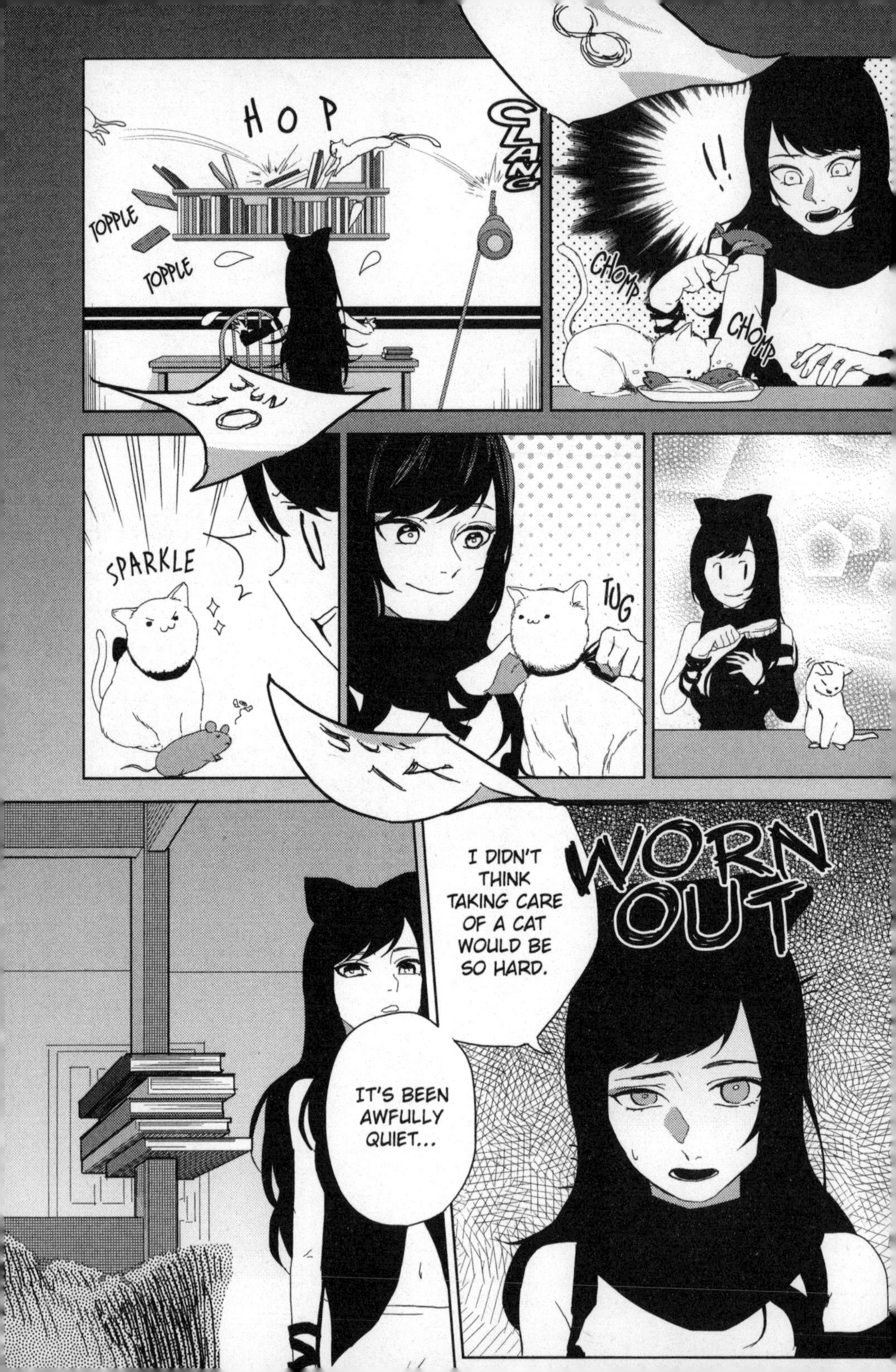
!!
CHOMP
CHOMP
CLANG
HOP
TOPPLE
TOPPLE
JUN 10
TUG
SPARKLE
WORN OUT
I DIDN'T THINK TAKING CARE OF A CAT WOULD BE SO HARD.
IT'S BEEN AWFULLY QUIET...

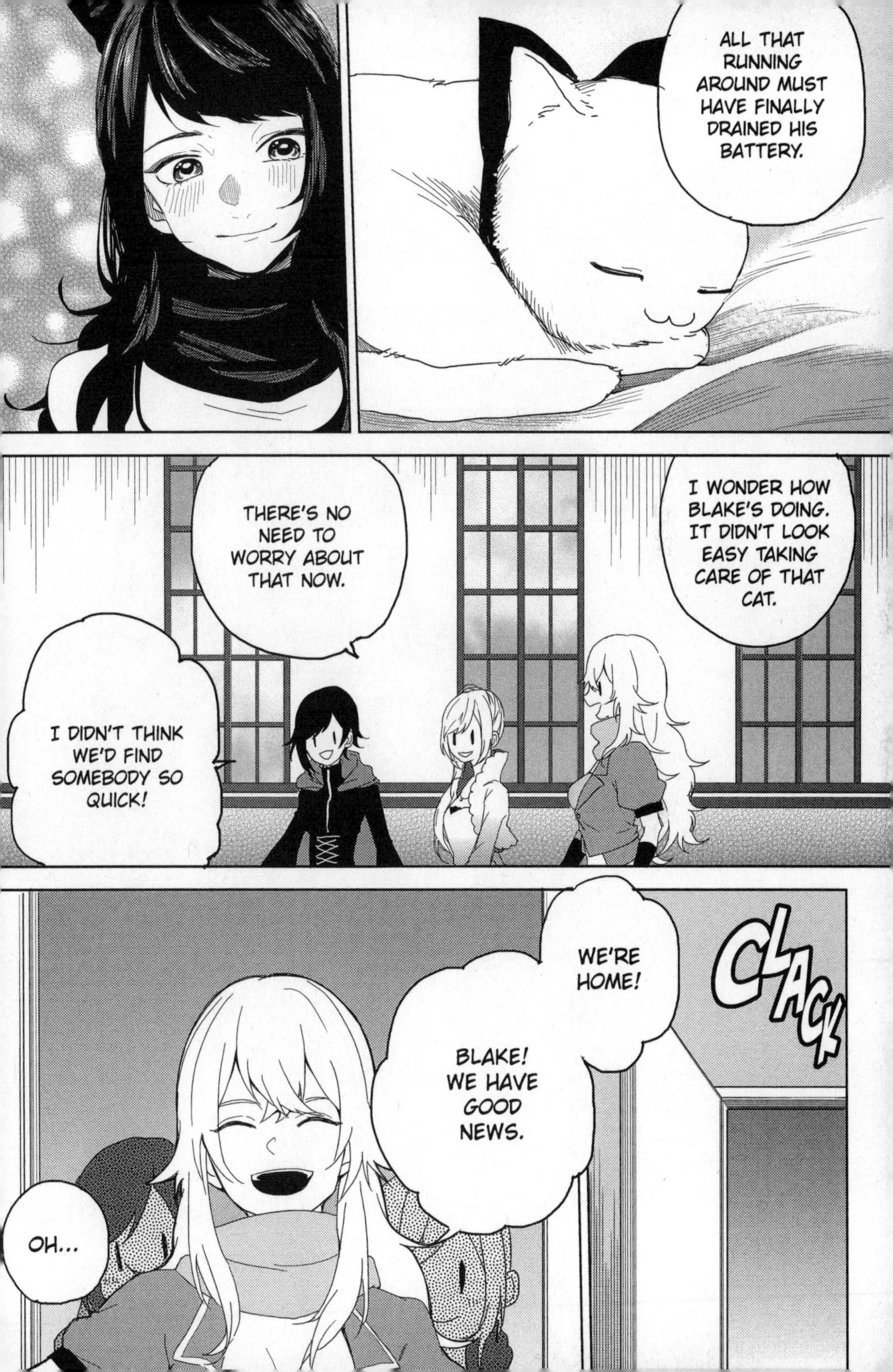
ALL THAT RUNNING AROUND MUST HAVE FINALLY DRAINED HIS BATTERY.
I WONDER HOW BLAKE'S DOING. IT DIDN'T LOOK EASY TAKING CARE OF THAT CAT.
THERE'S NO NEED TO WORRY ABOUT THAT NOW.
I DIDN'T THINK WE'D FIND SOMEBODY SO QUICK!
CLACK
WE'RE HOME!
BLAKE! WE HAVE GOOD NEWS.
OH...

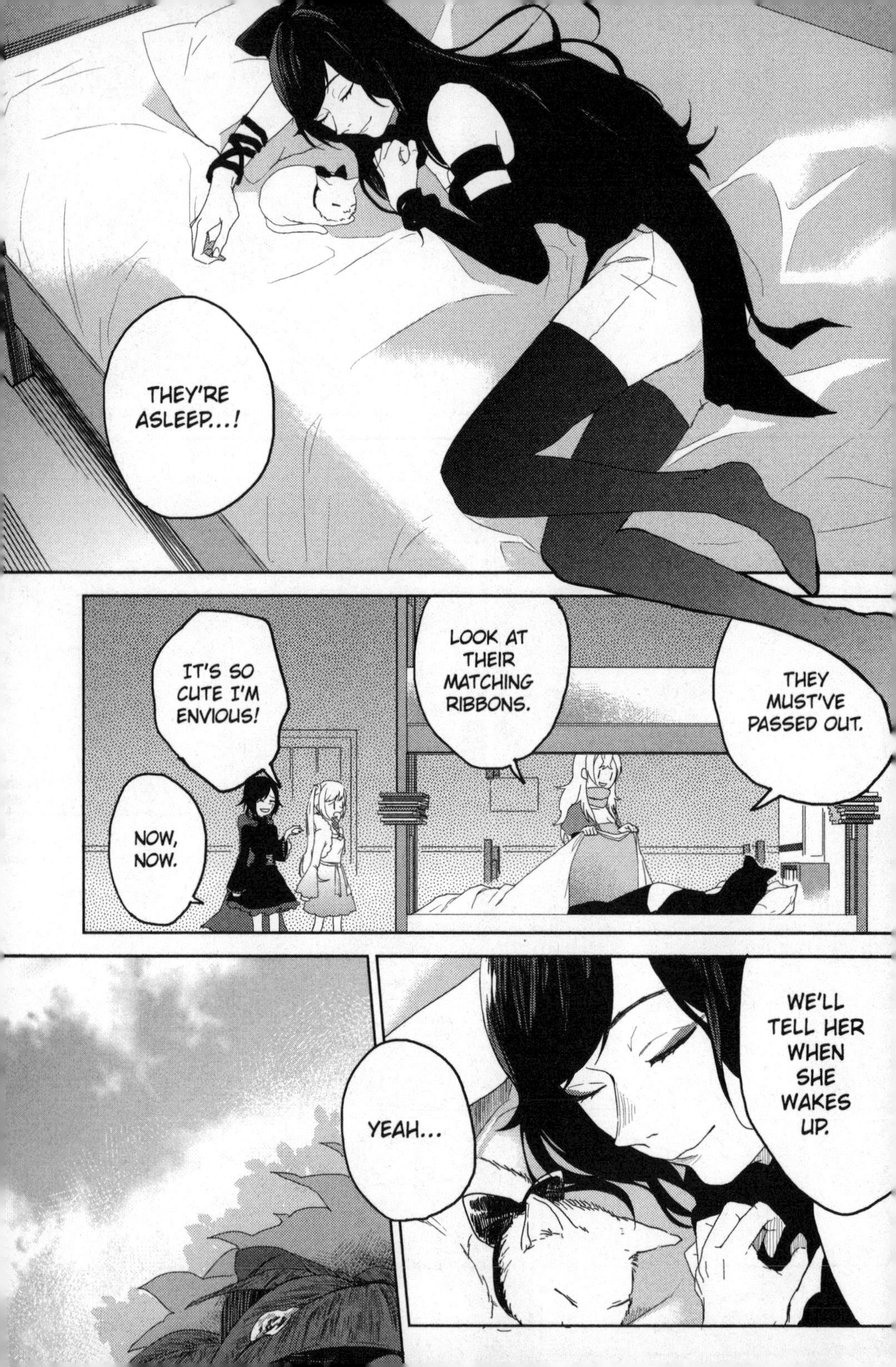
THEY'RE ASLEEP...!
THEY MUST'VE PASSED OUT.
LOOK AT THEIR MATCHING RIBBONS.
IT'S SO CUTE I'M ENVIOUS!
NOW, NOW.
WE'LL TELL HER WHEN SHE WAKES UP.
YEAH...

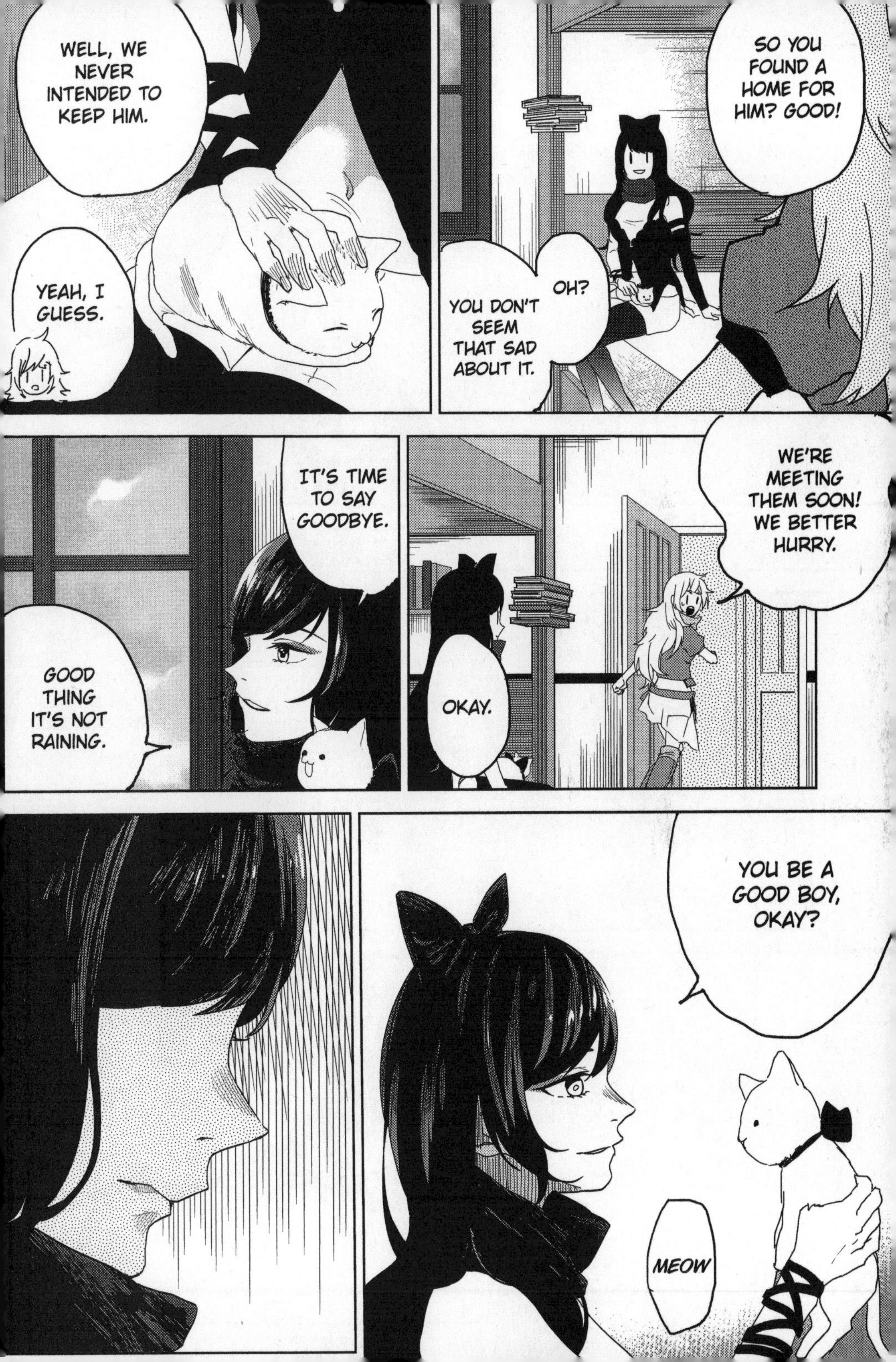
SO YOU FOUND A HOME FOR HIM? GOOD!
OH? YOU DON'T SEEM THAT SAD ABOUT IT.
WELL, WE NEVER INTENDED TO KEEP HIM.
YEAH, I GUESS.
WE'RE MEETING THEM SOON! WE BETTER HURRY.
OKAY.
IT'S TIME TO SAY GOODBYE.
GOOD THING IT'S NOT RAINING.
YOU BE A GOOD BOY, OKAY?
MEOW

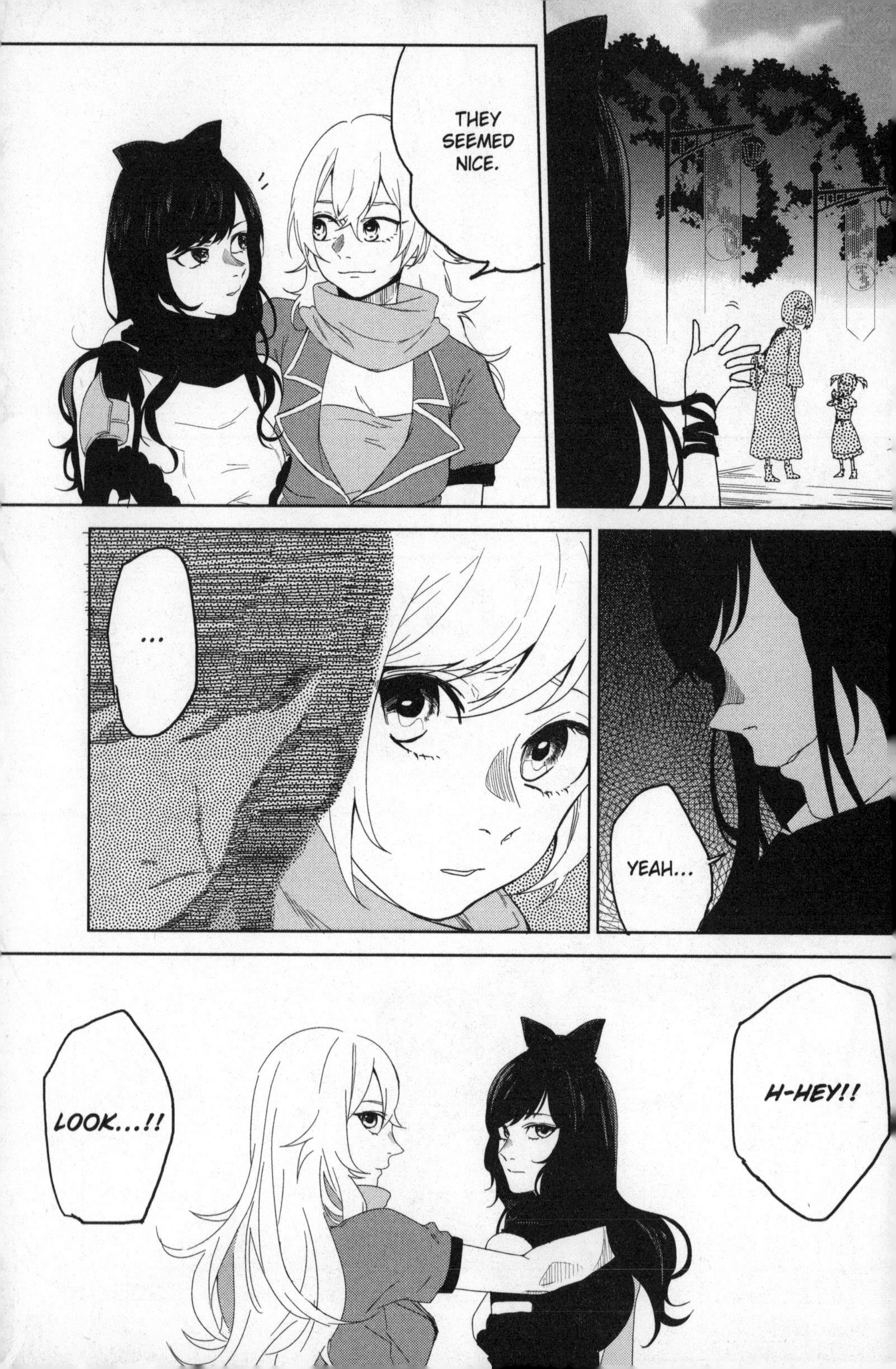
THEY SEEMED NICE.
YEAH...
...
H-HEY!!
LOOK...!!

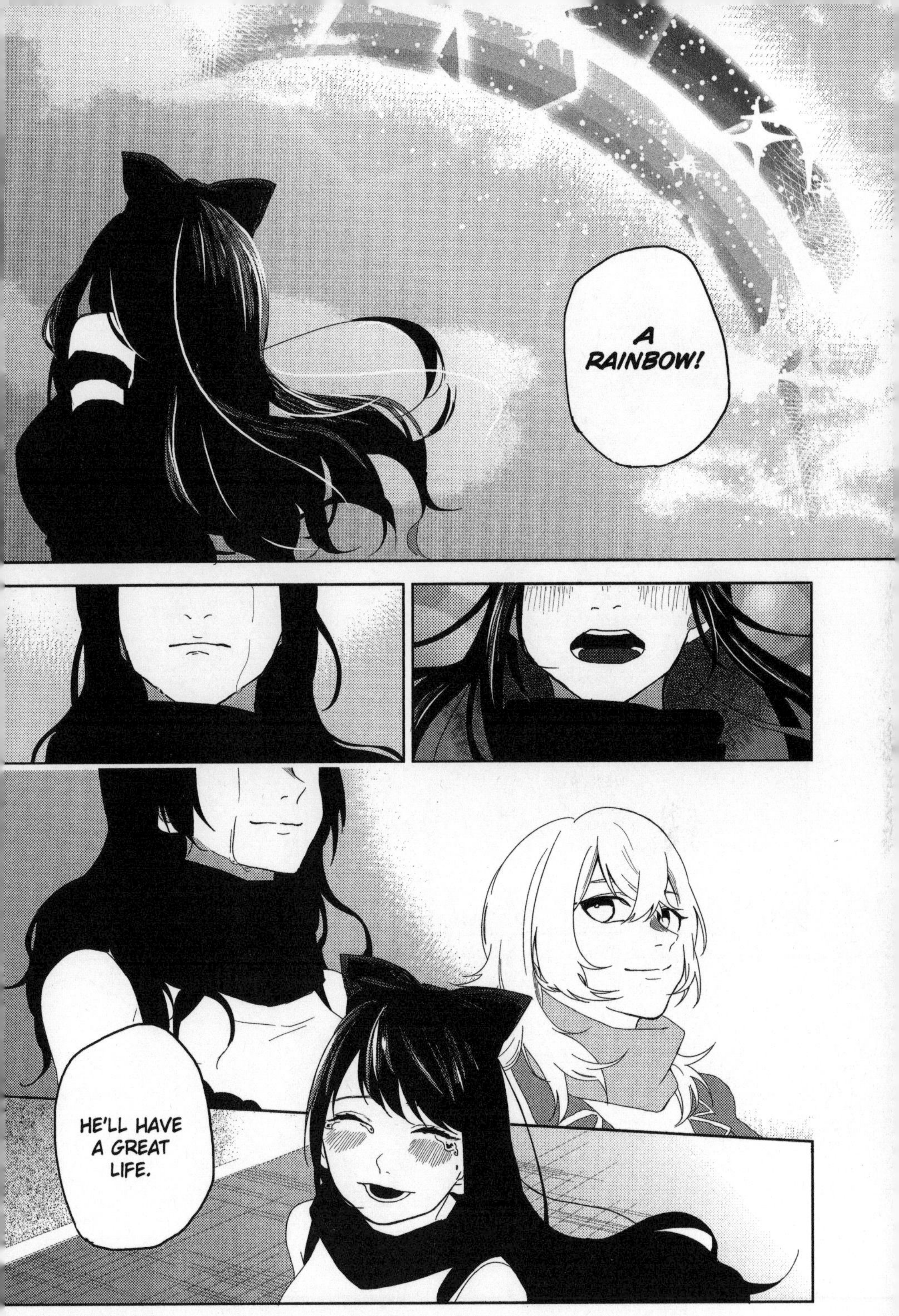
A RAINBOW!
HE'LL HAVE A GREAT LIFE.

Friend/END

RWBY

OFFICIAL MANGA ANTHOLOGY

Volume 3

From Shadows

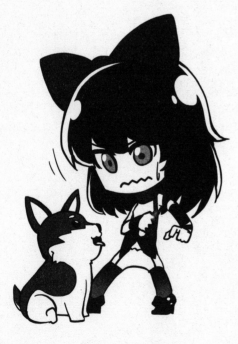

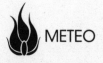

RWBY
OFFICIAL MANGA ANTHOLOGY
Volume 3

From Shadows

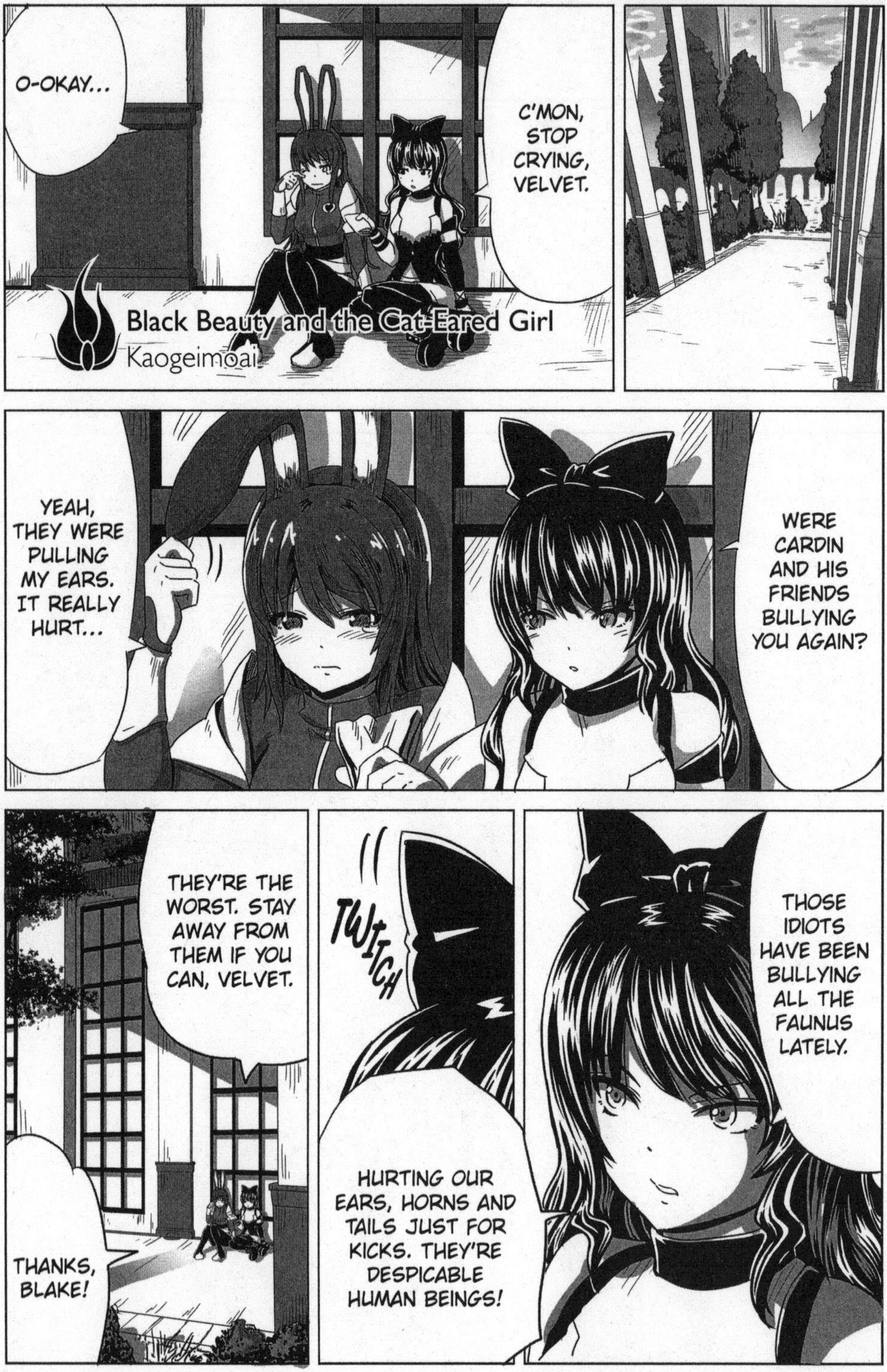

C'MON, STOP CRYING, VELVET.
O-OKAY...
Black Beauty and the Cat-Eared Girl
Kaogeimoai
WERE CARDIN AND HIS FRIENDS BULLYING YOU AGAIN?
YEAH, THEY WERE PULLING MY EARS. IT REALLY HURT...
THOSE IDIOTS HAVE BEEN BULLYING ALL THE FAUNUS LATELY.
HURTING OUR EARS, HORNS AND TAILS JUST FOR KICKS. THEY'RE DESPICABLE HUMAN BEINGS!
TWITCH
THEY'RE THE WORST. STAY AWAY FROM THEM IF YOU CAN, VELVET.
THANKS, BLAKE!

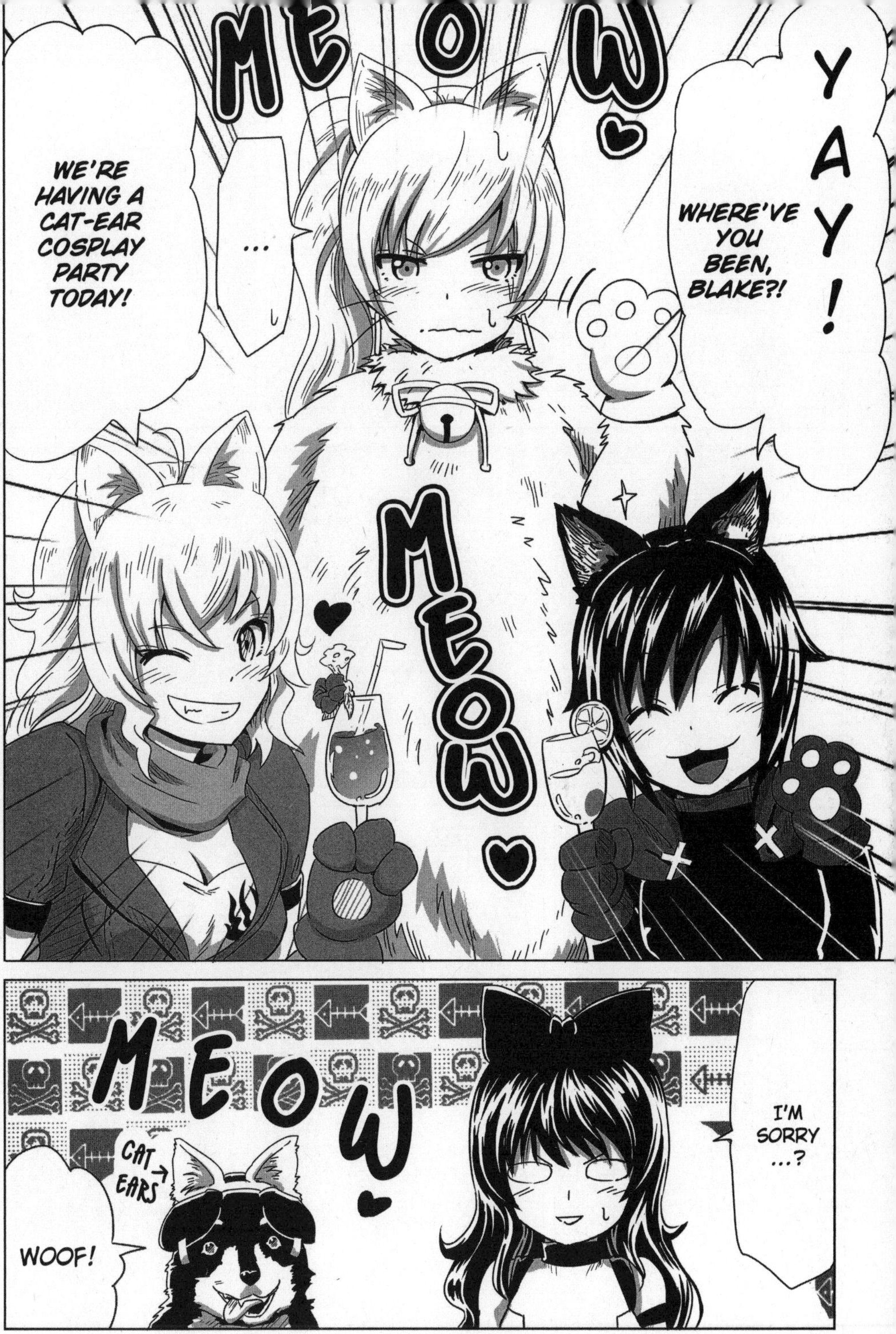
YAY!
WHERE'VE YOU BEEN, BLAKE?!
MEOW
MEOW
...
WE'RE HAVING A CAT-EAR COSPLAY PARTY TODAY!
I'M SORRY ...?
MEOW
CAT EARS
WOOF!

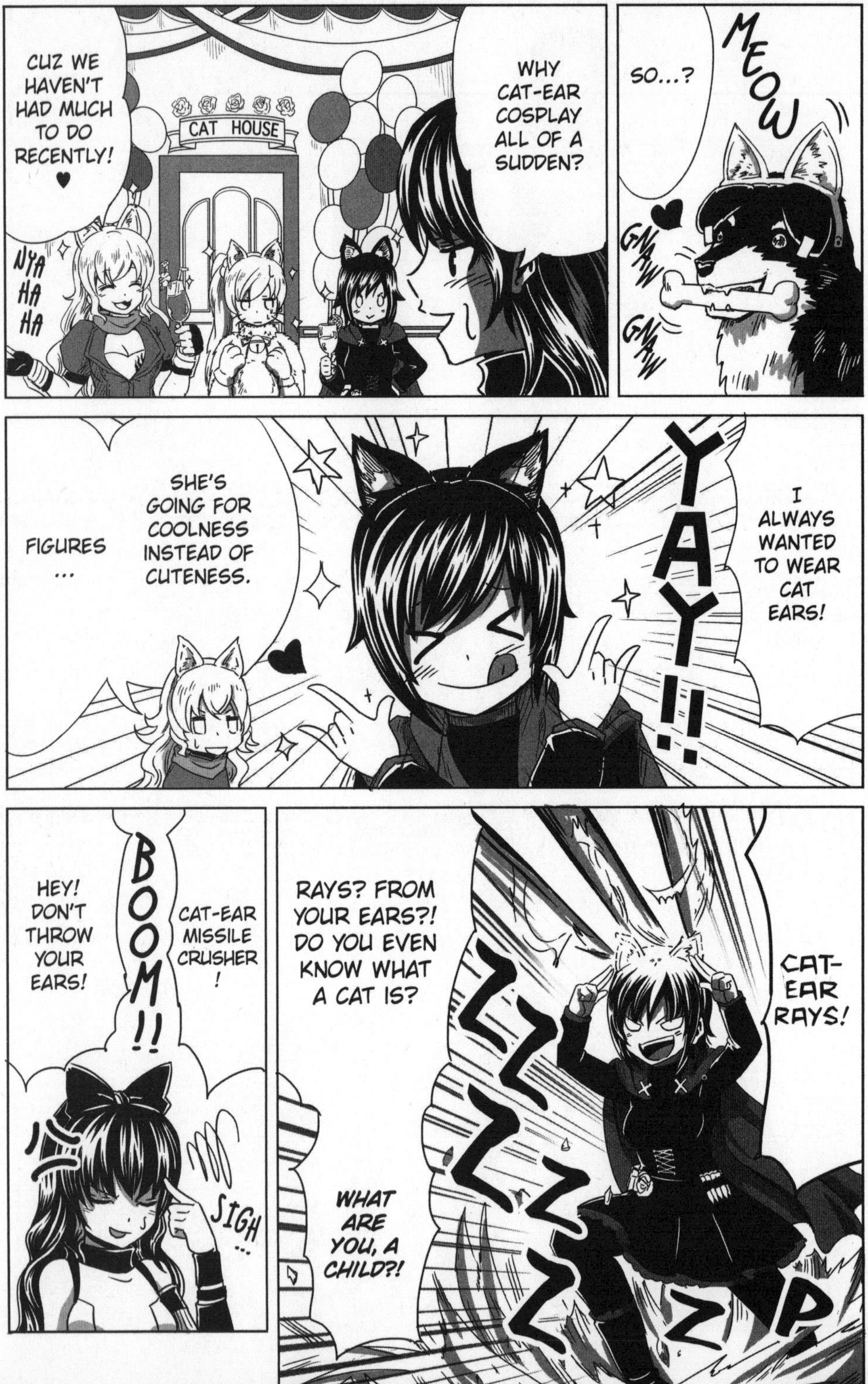
SO...?
MEOW
GNAW
GNAW
WHY CAT-EAR COSPLAY ALL OF A SUDDEN?
CUZ WE HAVEN'T HAD MUCH TO DO RECENTLY! ♥
CAT HOUSE
NYA HA HA
I ALWAYS WANTED TO WEAR CAT EARS!
YAY!!
SHE'S GOING FOR COOLNESS INSTEAD OF CUTENESS.
FIGURES ...
CAT-EAR RAYS!
ZZZZZZZP
RAYS? FROM YOUR EARS?! DO YOU EVEN KNOW WHAT A CAT IS?
WHAT ARE YOU, A CHILD?!
CAT-EAR MISSILE CRUSHER!
BOOM!!
HEY! DON'T THROW YOUR EARS!
SIGH...

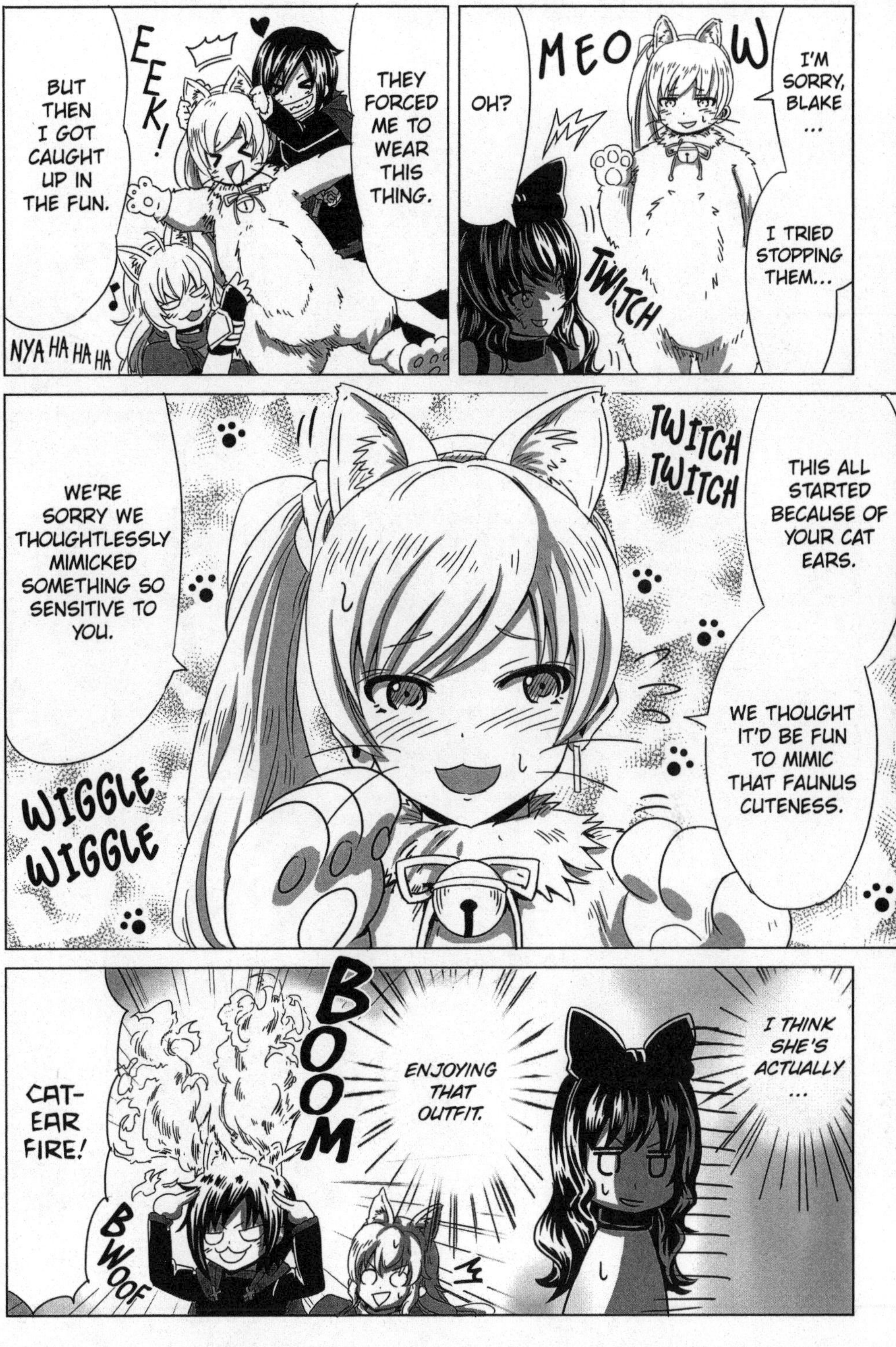
I'M SORRY, BLAKE ...
MEOW
OH?
I TRIED STOPPING THEM...
TWITCH
THEY FORCED ME TO WEAR THIS THING.
EEK!
BUT THEN I GOT CAUGHT UP IN THE FUN.
NYA HA HA HA
THIS ALL STARTED BECAUSE OF YOUR CAT EARS.
TWITCH TWITCH
WE THOUGHT IT'D BE FUN TO MIMIC THAT FAUNUS CUTENESS.
WE'RE SORRY WE THOUGHTLESSLY MIMICKED SOMETHING SO SENSITIVE TO YOU.
WIGGLE WIGGLE
I THINK SHE'S ACTUALLY ...
ENJOYING THAT OUTFIT.
BOOM
CAT-EAR FIRE!
BWOOF

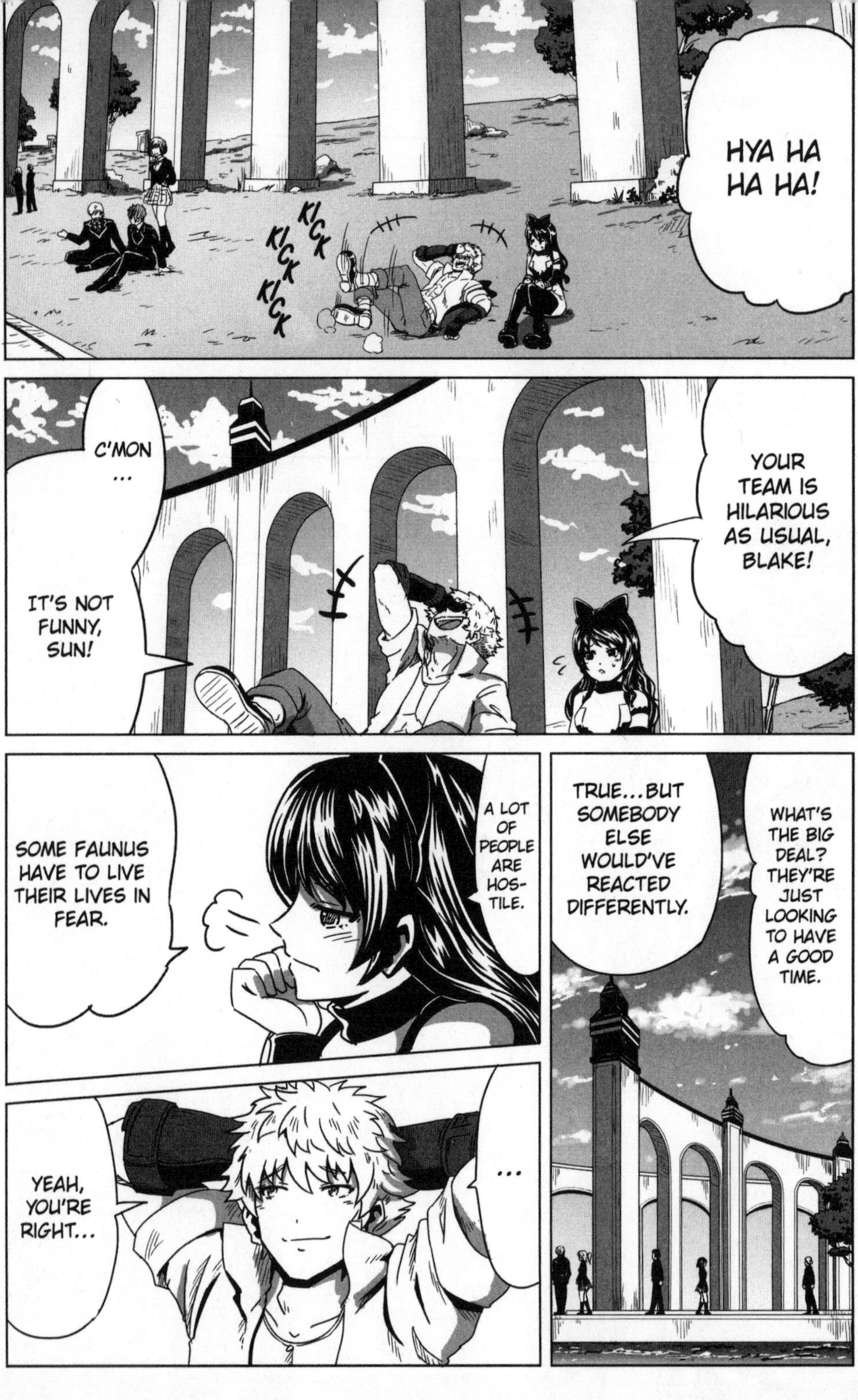
HYA HA HA HA!
KICK KICK KICK
YOUR TEAM IS HILARIOUS AS USUAL, BLAKE!
C'MON...
IT'S NOT FUNNY, SUN!
WHAT'S THE BIG DEAL? THEY'RE JUST LOOKING TO HAVE A GOOD TIME.
TRUE...BUT SOMEBODY ELSE WOULD'VE REACTED DIFFERENTLY.
A LOT OF PEOPLE ARE HOS-TILE.
SOME FAUNUS HAVE TO LIVE THEIR LIVES IN FEAR.
...
YEAH, YOU'RE RIGHT...

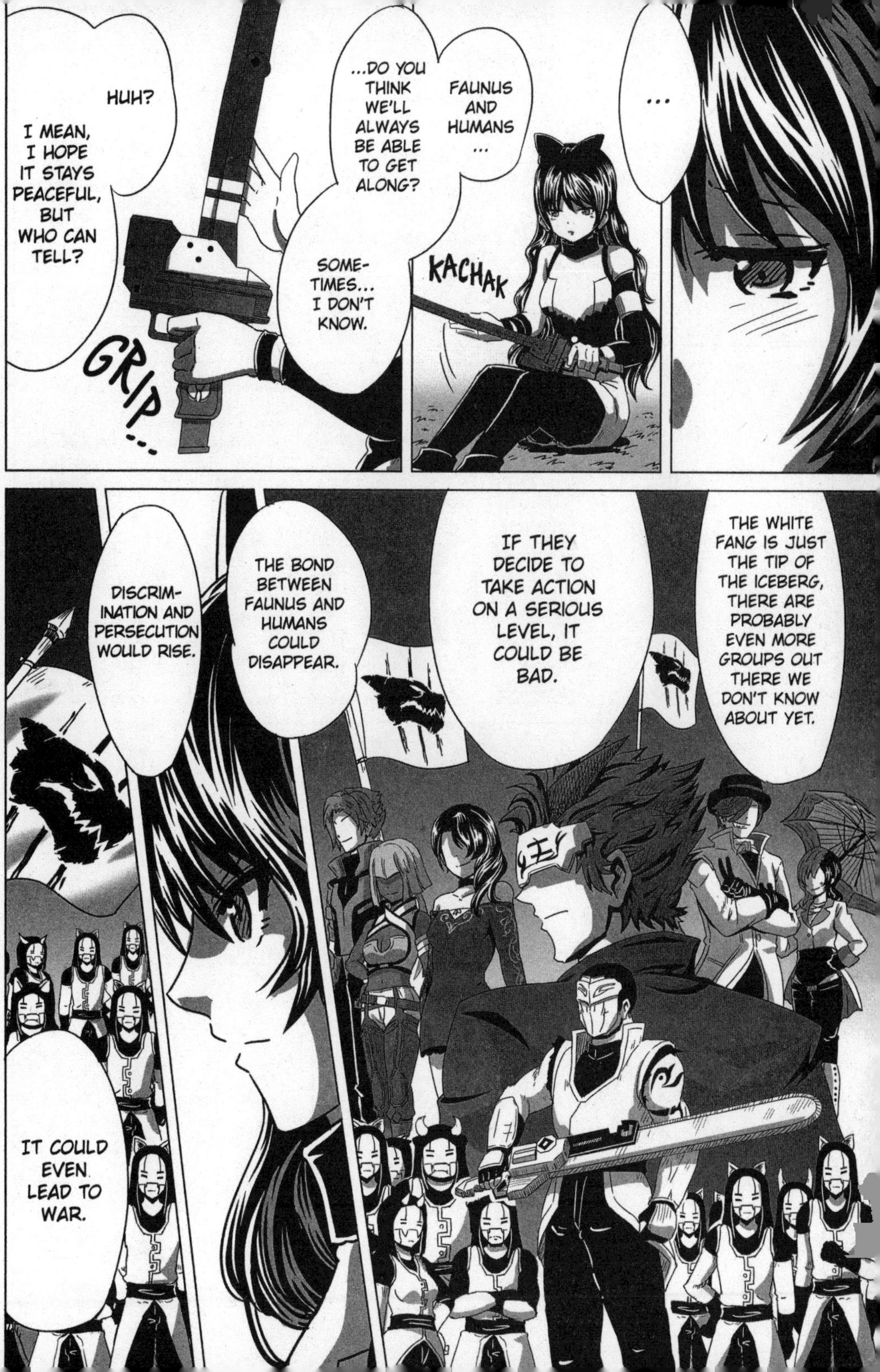
...
FAUNUS AND HUMANS ...
...DO YOU THINK WE'LL ALWAYS BE ABLE TO GET ALONG?
KACHAK
HUH?
I MEAN, I HOPE IT STAYS PEACEFUL, BUT WHO CAN TELL?
SOME-TIMES... I DON'T KNOW.
GRIP...
THE WHITE FANG IS JUST THE TIP OF THE ICEBERG, THERE ARE PROBABLY EVEN MORE GROUPS OUT THERE WE DON'T KNOW ABOUT YET.
IF THEY DECIDE TO TAKE ACTION ON A SERIOUS LEVEL, IT COULD BE BAD.
THE BOND BETWEEN FAUNUS AND HUMANS COULD DISAPPEAR.
DISCRIM-INATION AND PERSECUTION WOULD RISE.
IT COULD EVEN LEAD TO WAR.

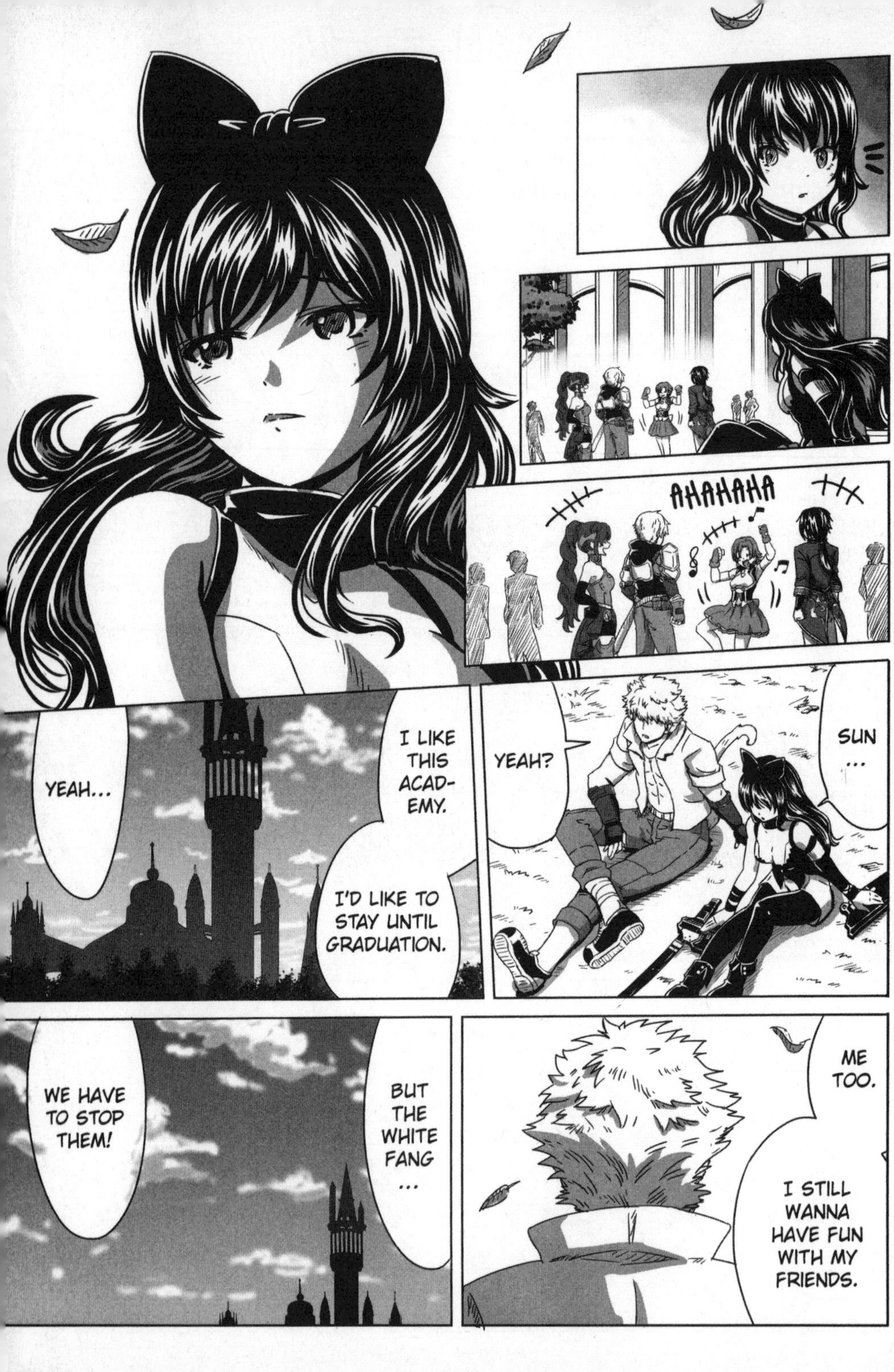
AHAHAHA
SUN ...
YEAH?
I LIKE THIS ACADEMY.
I'D LIKE TO STAY UNTIL GRADUATION.
YEAH...
ME TOO.
I STILL WANNA HAVE FUN WITH MY FRIENDS.
BUT THE WHITE FANG ...
WE HAVE TO STOP THEM!

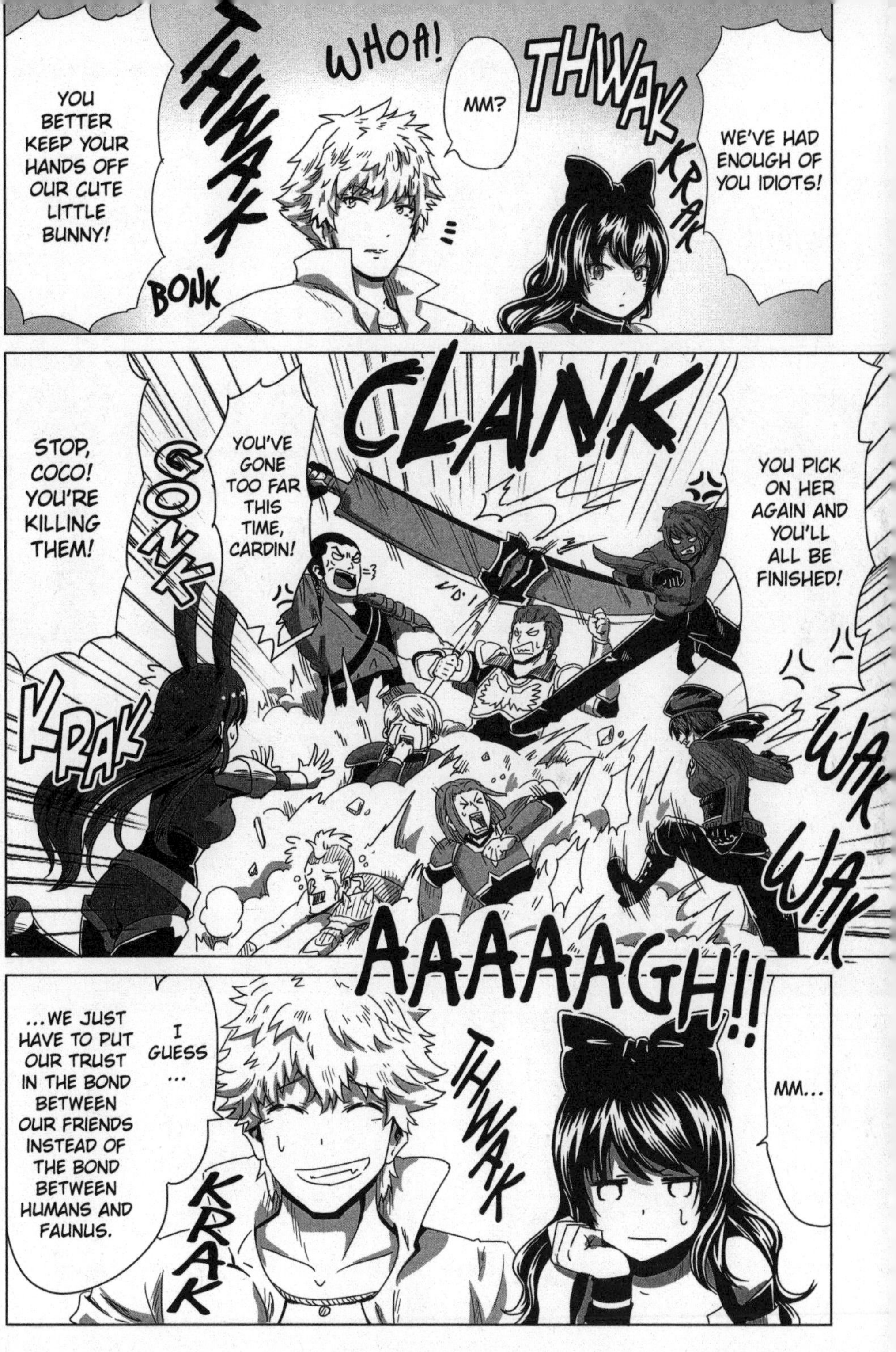
WE'VE HAD ENOUGH OF YOU IDIOTS!
THWAK
KRAK
MM?
WHOA!
THWAK
YOU BETTER KEEP YOUR HANDS OFF OUR CUTE LITTLE BUNNY!
BONK
YOU PICK ON HER AGAIN AND YOU'LL ALL BE FINISHED!
CLANK
YOU'VE GONE TOO FAR THIS TIME, CARDIN!
GONK
STOP, COCO! YOU'RE KILLING THEM!
WAK
WAK
KRAK
AAAAAGH!!
MM...
THWAK
KRAK
I GUESS...
...WE JUST HAVE TO PUT OUR TRUST IN THE BOND BETWEEN OUR FRIENDS INSTEAD OF THE BOND BETWEEN HUMANS AND FAUNUS.

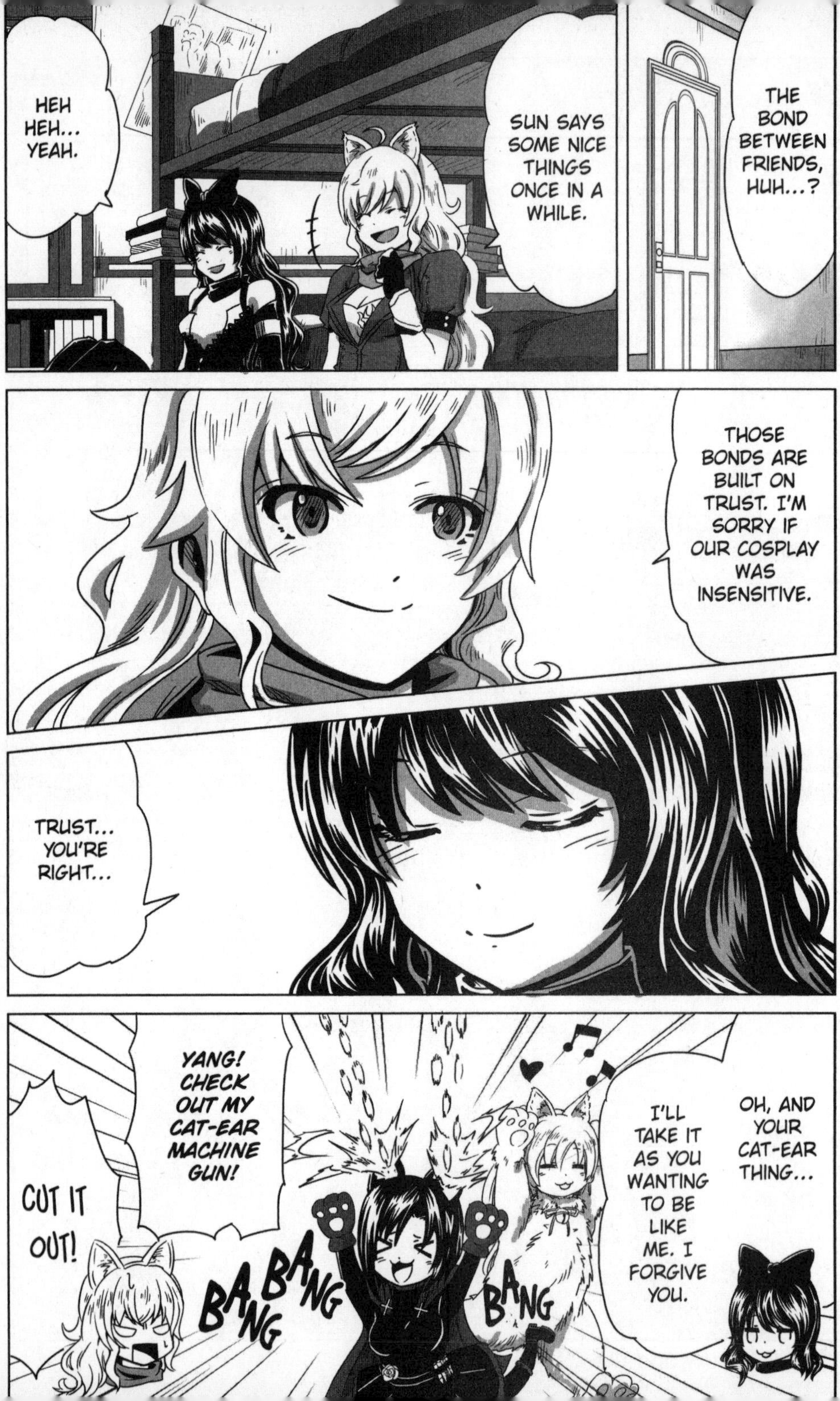
THE BOND BETWEEN FRIENDS, HUH...?
SUN SAYS SOME NICE THINGS ONCE IN A WHILE.
HEH HEH... YEAH.
THOSE BONDS ARE BUILT ON TRUST. I'M SORRY IF OUR COSPLAY WAS INSENSITIVE.
TRUST... YOU'RE RIGHT...
OH, AND YOUR CAT-EAR THING...
I'LL TAKE IT AS YOU WANTING TO BE LIKE ME. I FORGIVE YOU.
BANG
YANG! CHECK OUT MY CAT-EAR MACHINE GUN!
BANG
BANG
CUT IT OUT!

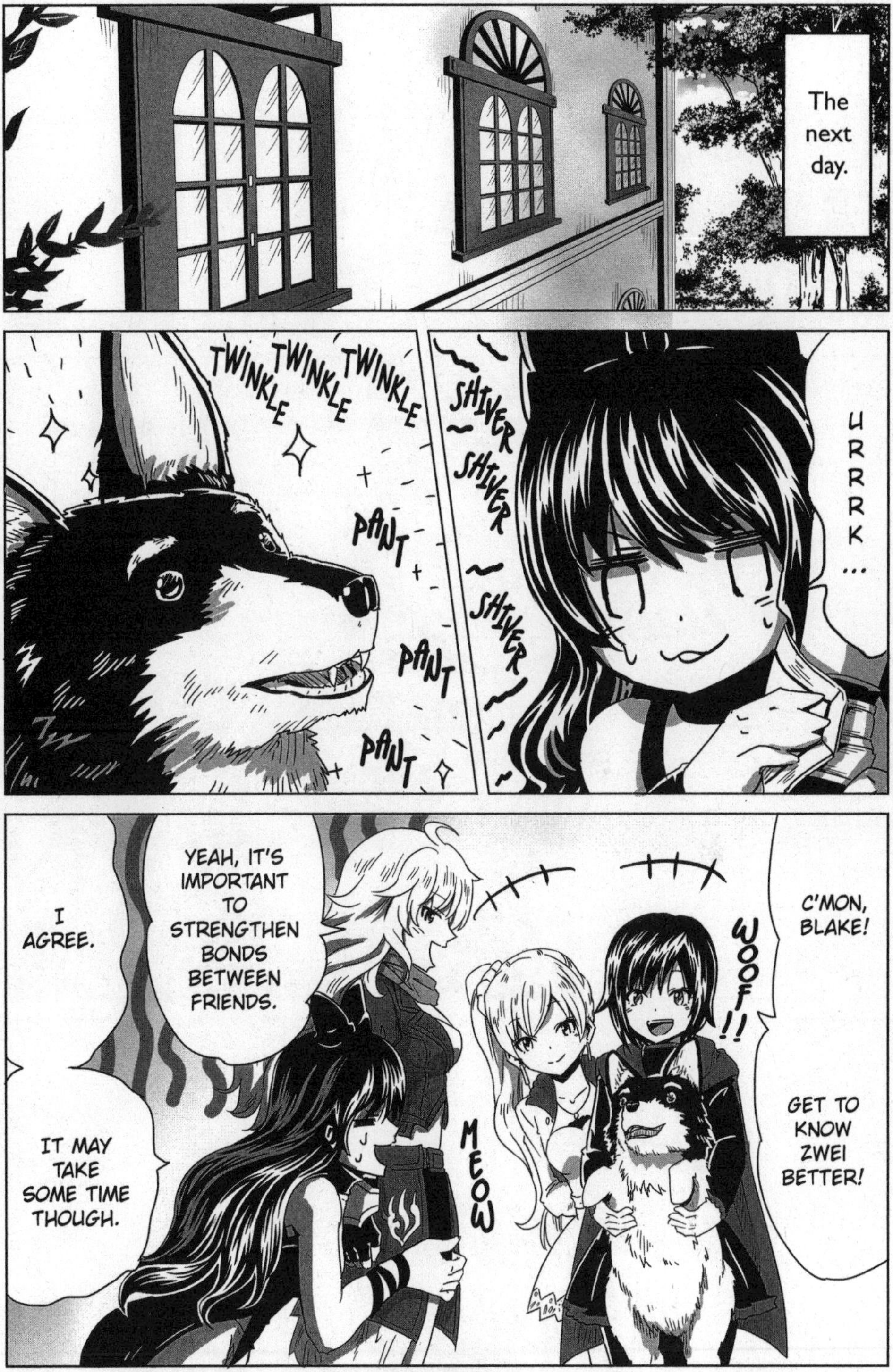
The next day.
URRRK...
SHIVER SHIVER SHIVER
TWINKLE TWINKLE
PANT PANT PANT
C'MON, BLAKE!
GET TO KNOW ZWEI BETTER!
WOOF!!
MEOW
YEAH, IT'S IMPORTANT TO STRENGTHEN BONDS BETWEEN FRIENDS.
I AGREE.
IT MAY TAKE SOME TIME THOUGH.

Black Beauty and the Cat-Eared Girl/END

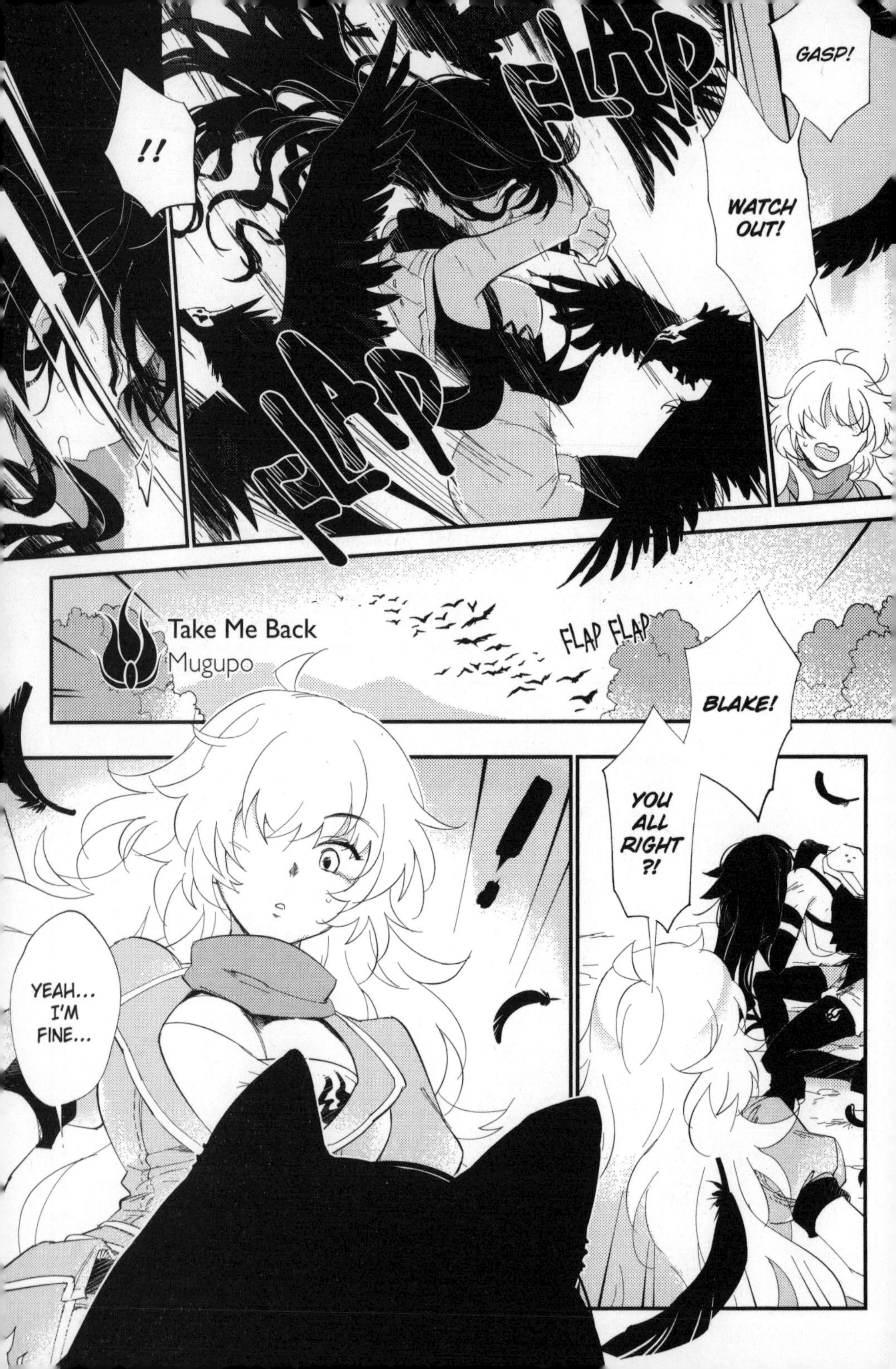
GASP!
WATCH OUT!
FLAP
FLAP
!!
BLAKE!
FLAP FLAP
Take Me Back
Mugupo
YOU ALL RIGHT ?!
!
YEAH... I'M FINE...

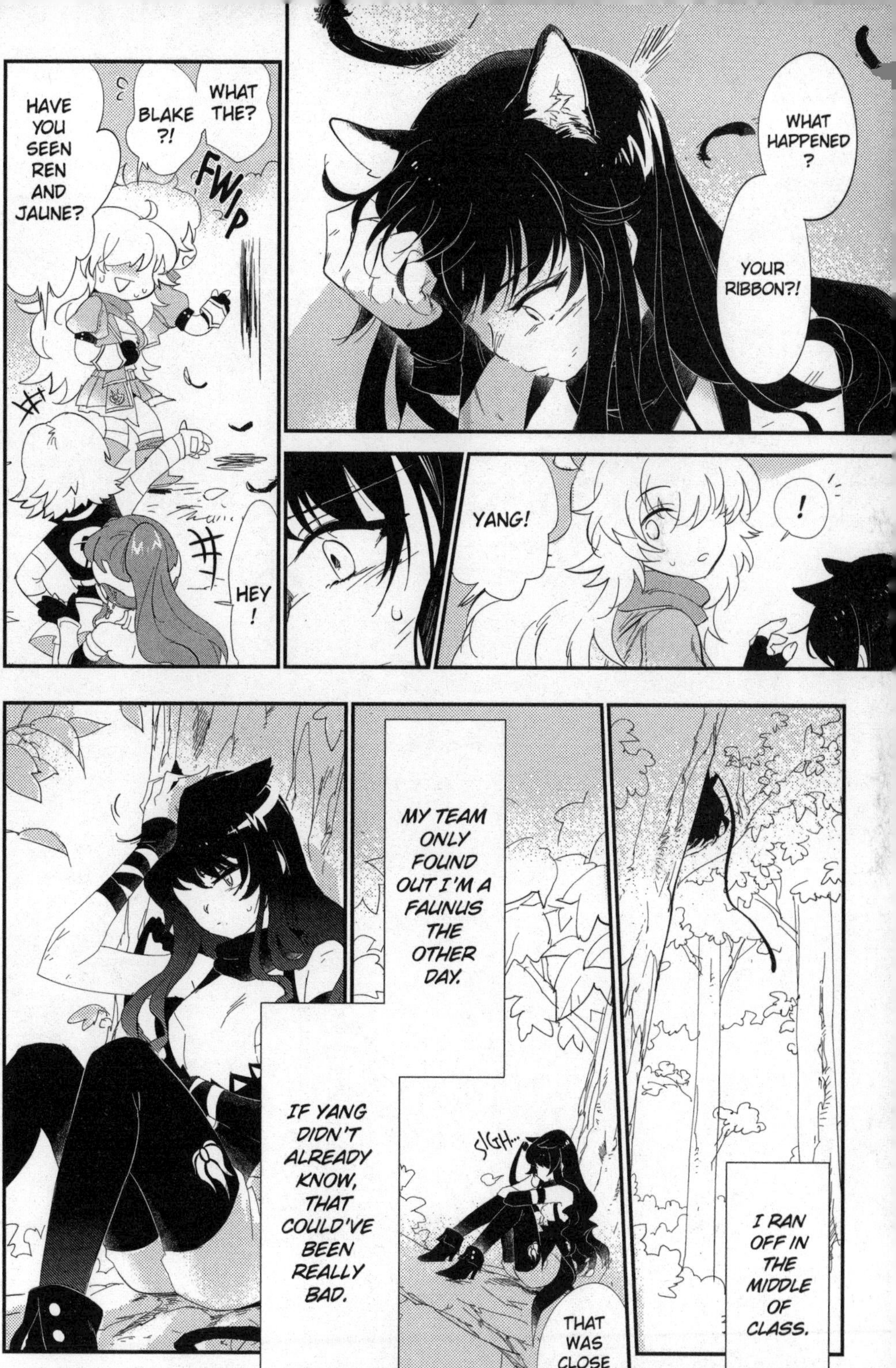
WHAT HAPPENED?
YOUR RIBBON?!
!
YANG!
WHAT THE?
BLAKE?!
HAVE YOU SEEN REN AND JAUNE?
FWIP
HEY!
I RAN OFF IN THE MIDDLE OF CLASS.
SIGH...
THAT WAS CLOSE...
MY TEAM ONLY FOUND OUT I'M A FAUNUS THE OTHER DAY.
IF YANG DIDN'T ALREADY KNOW, THAT COULD'VE BEEN REALLY BAD.

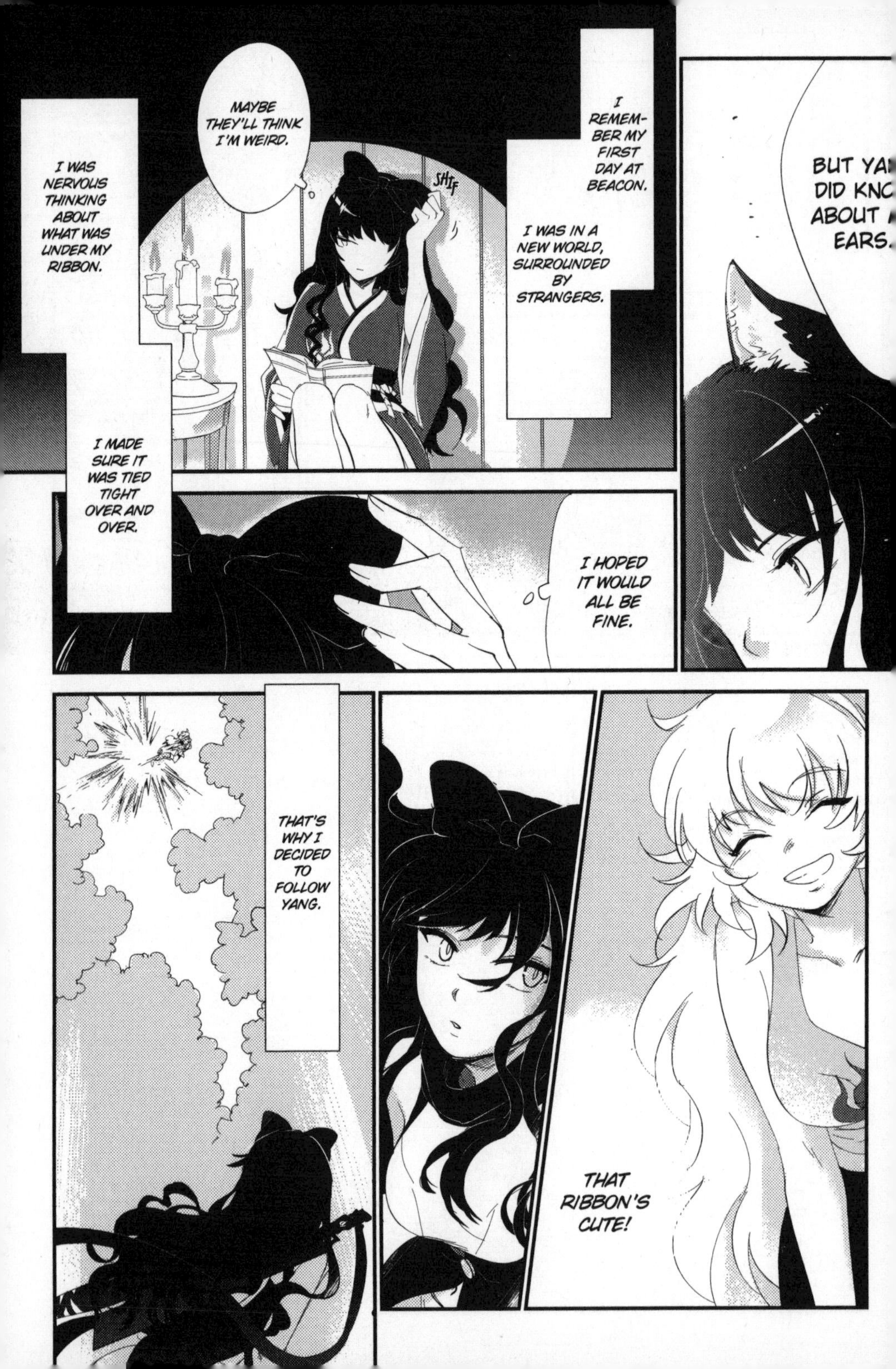

BUT YA DID KNO ABOUT EARS.
I REMEMBER MY FIRST DAY AT BEACON.
I WAS IN A NEW WORLD, SURROUNDED BY STRANGERS.
MAYBE THEY'LL THINK I'M WEIRD.
SHIF
I WAS NERVOUS THINKING ABOUT WHAT WAS UNDER MY RIBBON.
I MADE SURE IT WAS TIED TIGHT OVER AND OVER.
I HOPED IT WOULD ALL BE FINE.
THAT RIBBON'S CUTE!
THAT'S WHY I DECIDED TO FOLLOW YANG.

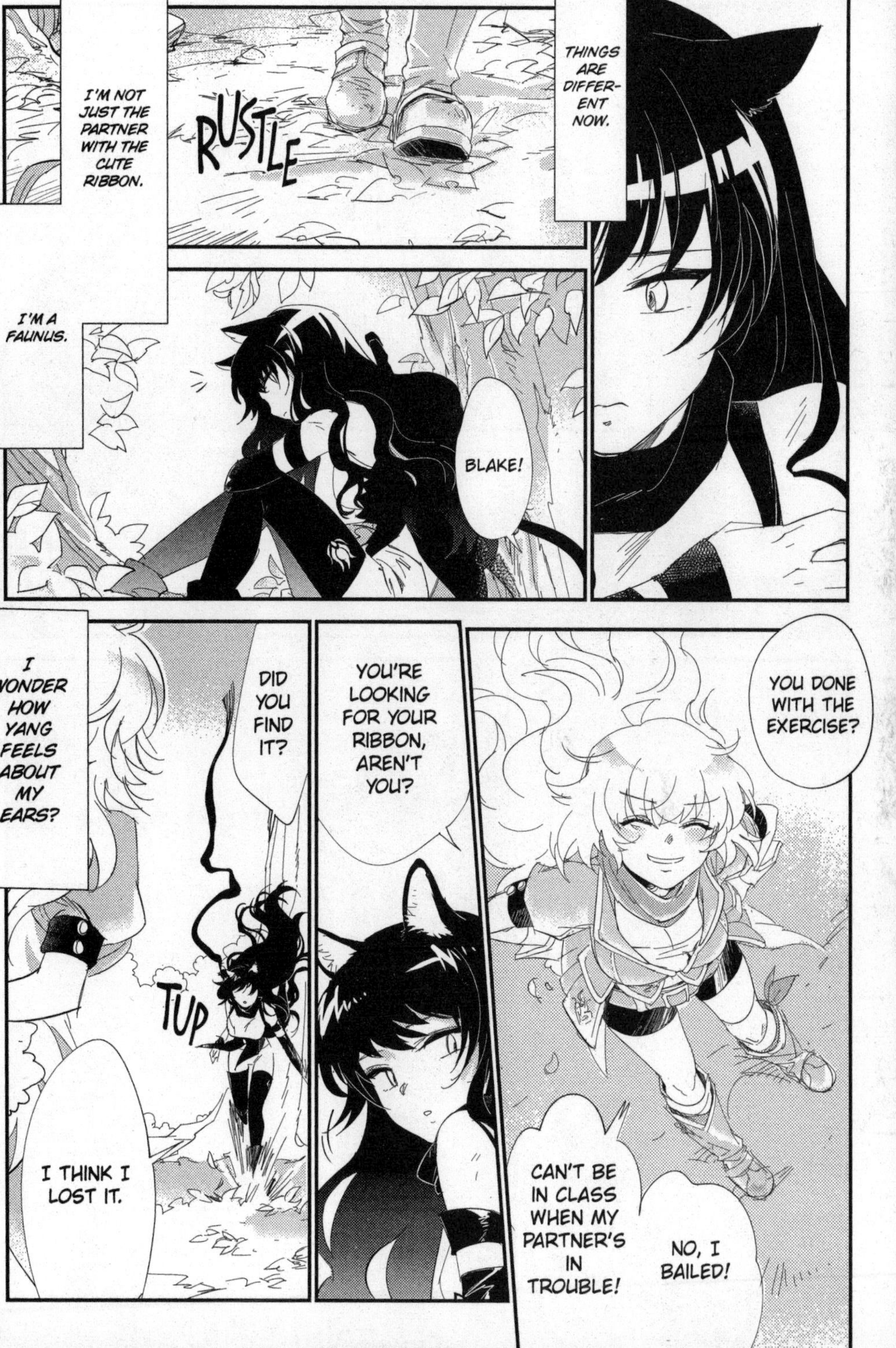
THINGS ARE DIFFER-ENT NOW.
I'M NOT JUST THE PARTNER WITH THE CUTE RIBBON.
RUSTLE
I'M A FAUNUS.
BLAKE!
YOU DONE WITH THE EXERCISE?
NO, I BAILED!
CAN'T BE IN CLASS WHEN MY PARTNER'S IN TROUBLE!
YOU'RE LOOKING FOR YOUR RIBBON, AREN'T YOU?
DID YOU FIND IT?
I WONDER HOW YANG FEELS ABOUT MY EARS?
TUP
I THINK I LOST IT.

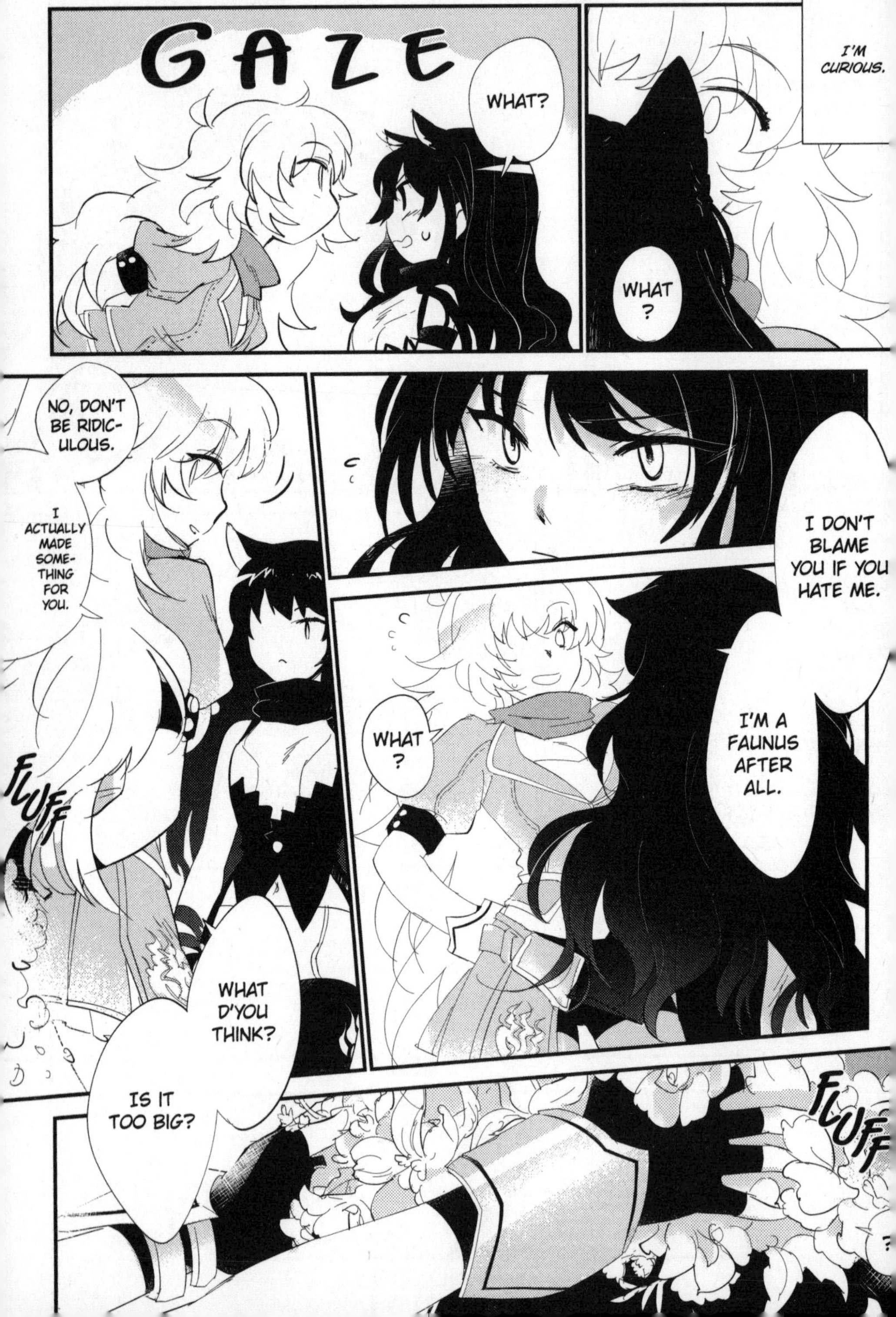
I'M CURIOUS.
WHAT ?
GAZE
WHAT?
I DON'T BLAME YOU IF YOU HATE ME.
I'M A FAUNUS AFTER ALL.
WHAT ?
NO, DON'T BE RIDICULOUS.
I ACTUALLY MADE SOMETHING FOR YOU.
FLUFF
FLUFF
?
WHAT D'YOU THINK?
IS IT TOO BIG?

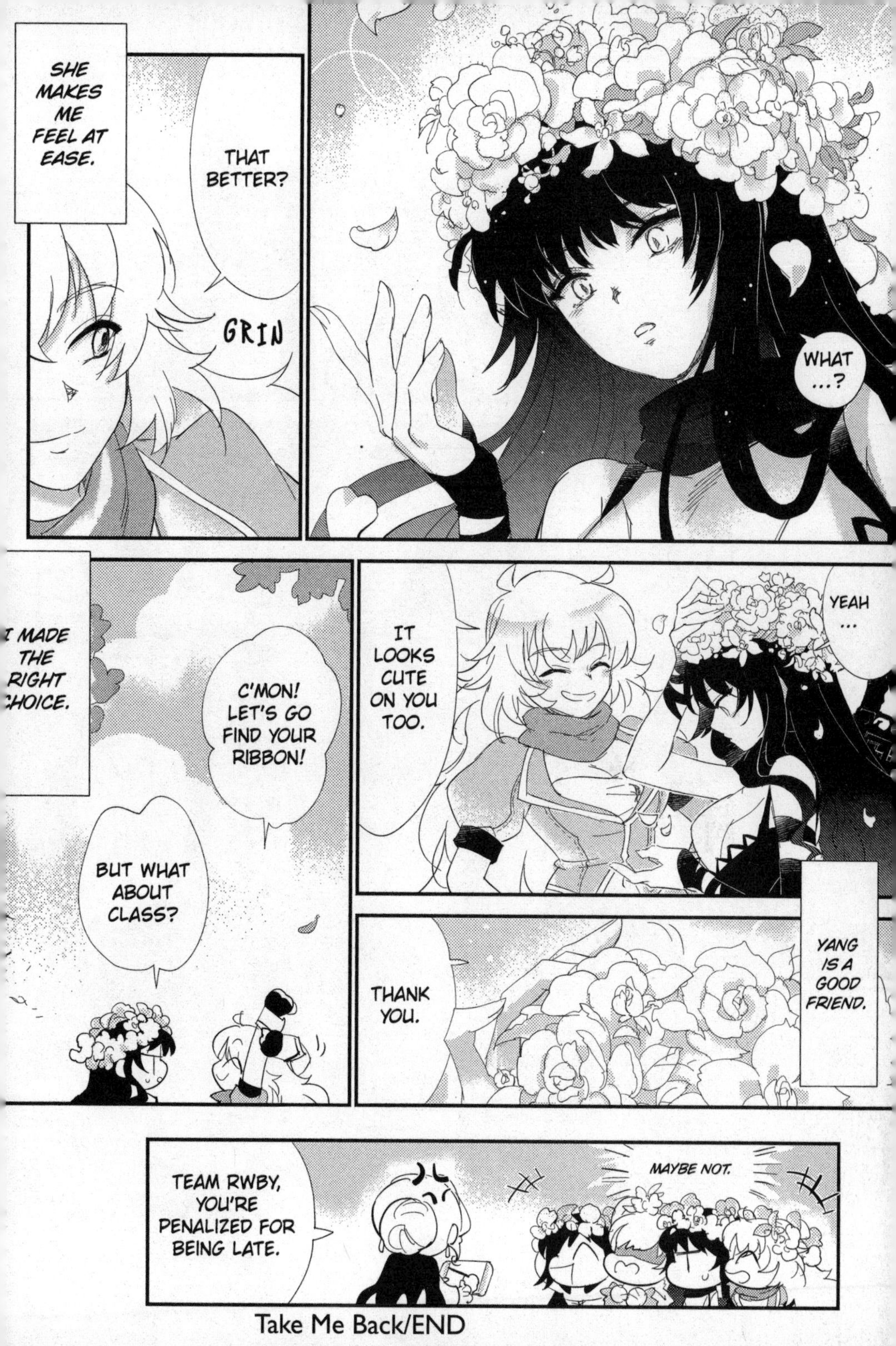
WHAT ...?
THAT BETTER?
GRIN
SHE MAKES ME FEEL AT EASE.
YEAH ...
IT LOOKS CUTE ON YOU TOO.
YANG IS A GOOD FRIEND.
THANK YOU.
C'MON! LET'S GO FIND YOUR RIBBON!
I MADE THE RIGHT CHOICE.
BUT WHAT ABOUT CLASS?
MAYBE NOT.
TEAM RWBY, YOU'RE PENALIZED FOR BEING LATE.

Take Me Back/END

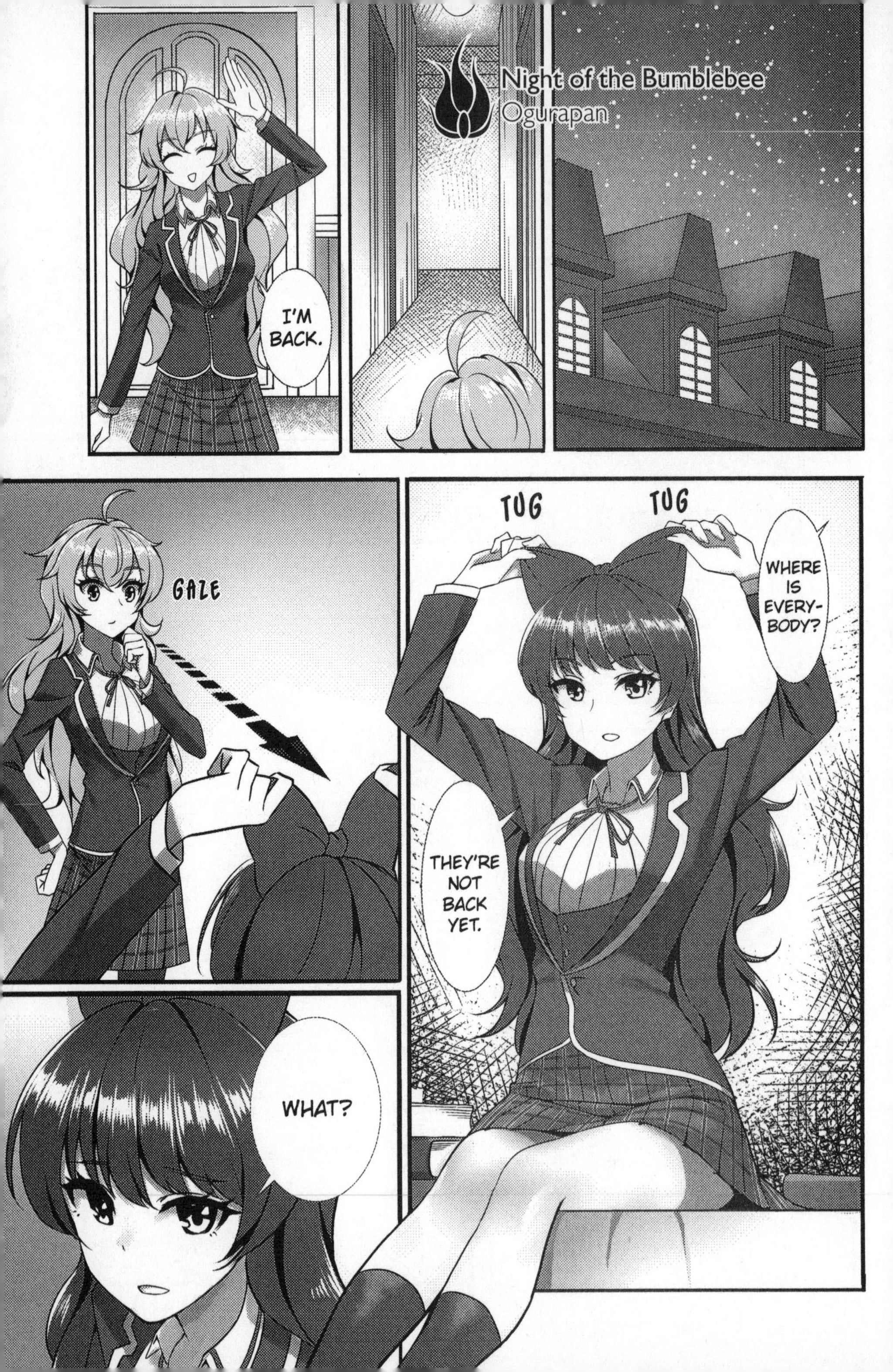
Night of the Bumblebee
Ogurapan
I'M BACK.
TUG
TUG
WHERE IS EVERY-BODY?
THEY'RE NOT BACK YET.
GAZE
WHAT?

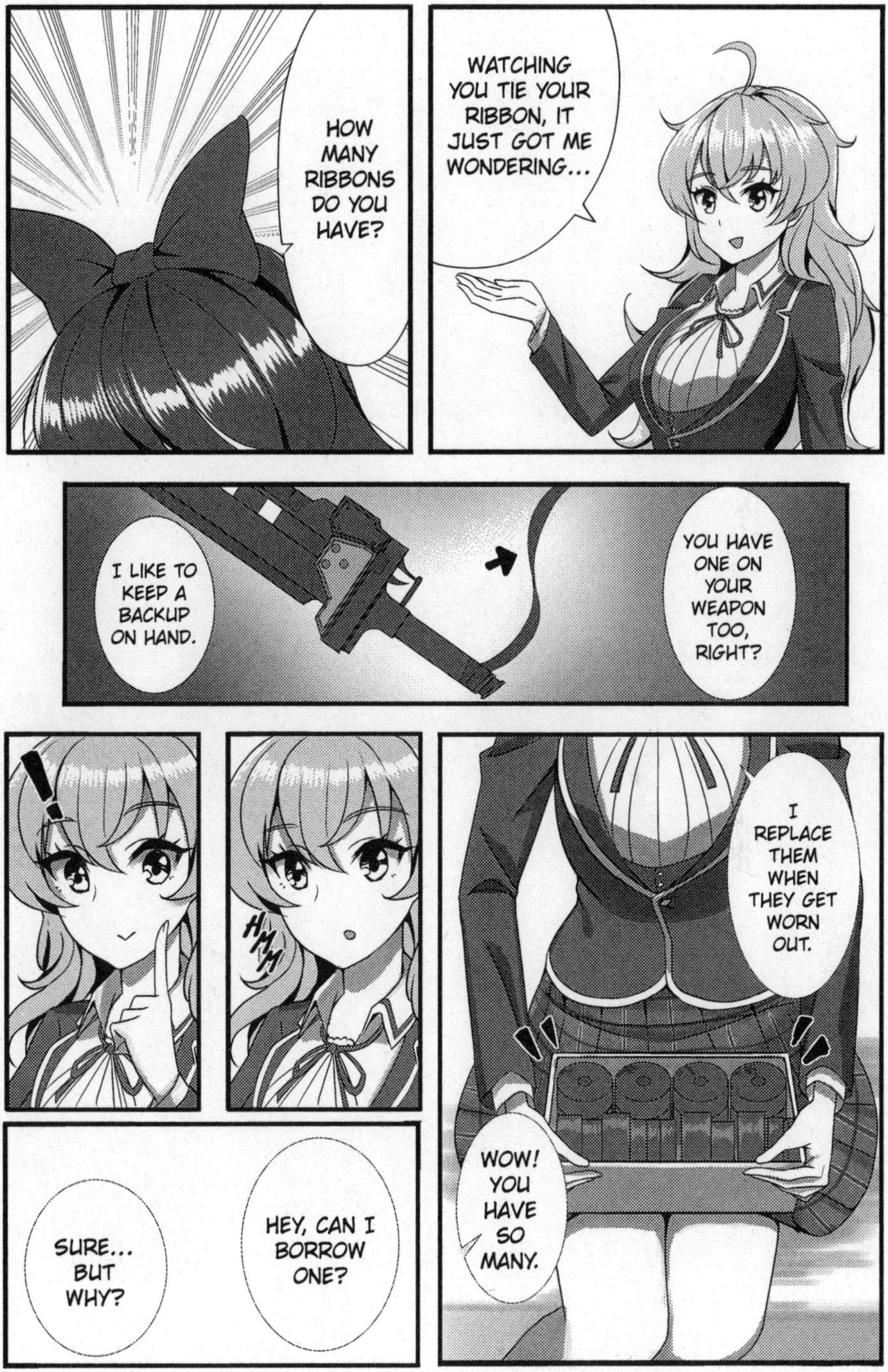
WATCHING YOU TIE YOUR RIBBON, IT JUST GOT ME WONDERING...
HOW MANY RIBBONS DO YOU HAVE?
YOU HAVE ONE ON YOUR WEAPON TOO, RIGHT?
I LIKE TO KEEP A BACKUP ON HAND.
I REPLACE THEM WHEN THEY GET WORN OUT.
WOW! YOU HAVE SO MANY.
HMM
!
HEY, CAN I BORROW ONE?
SURE... BUT WHY?

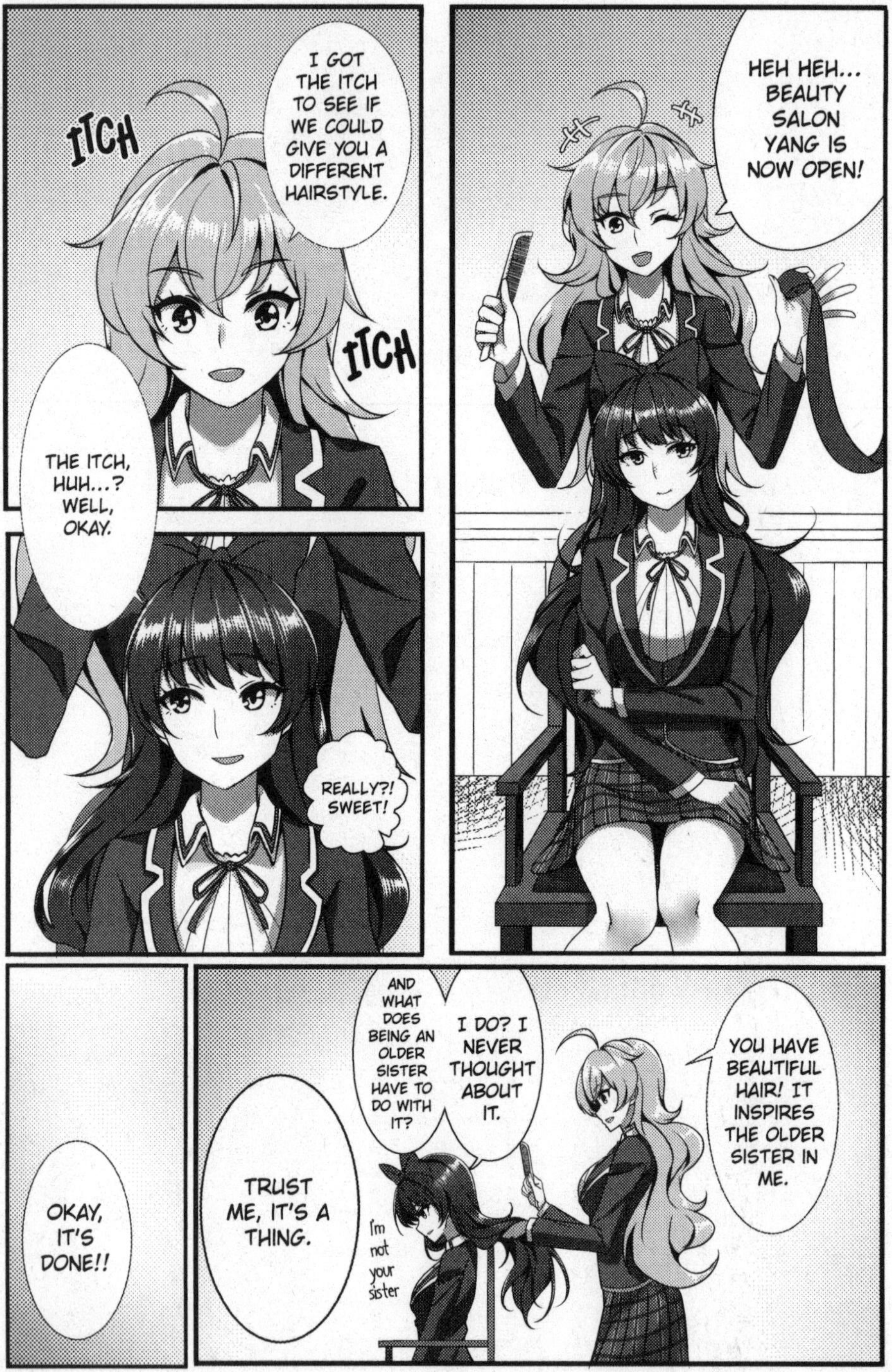
HEH HEH... BEAUTY SALON YANG IS NOW OPEN!
ITCH
I GOT THE ITCH TO SEE IF WE COULD GIVE YOU A DIFFERENT HAIRSTYLE.
ITCH
THE ITCH, HUH...? WELL, OKAY.
REALLY?! SWEET!
YOU HAVE BEAUTIFUL HAIR! IT INSPIRES THE OLDER SISTER IN ME.
I DO? I NEVER THOUGHT ABOUT IT.
AND WHAT DOES BEING AN OLDER SISTER HAVE TO DO WITH IT?
TRUST ME, IT'S A THING.
I'm not your sister
OKAY, IT'S DONE!!

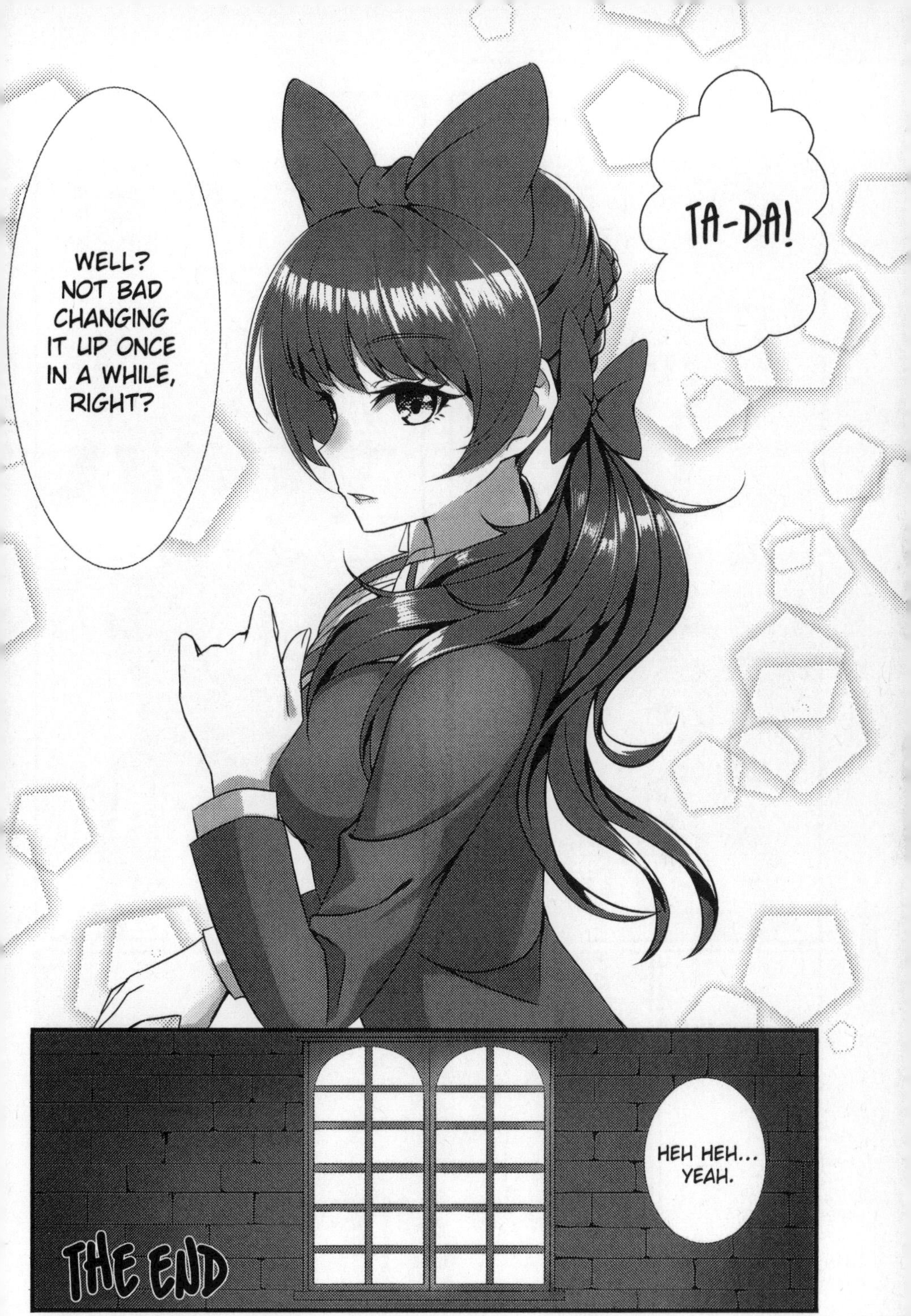
TA-DA!
WELL? NOT BAD CHANGING IT UP ONCE IN A WHILE, RIGHT?
HEH HEH... YEAH.
THE END

Night of the Bumblebee/END

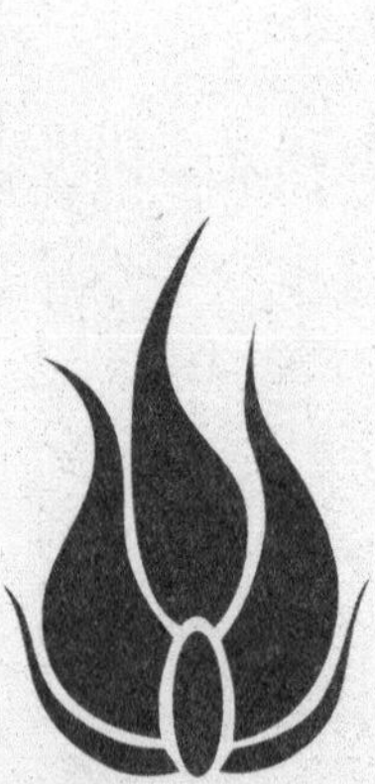

RWBY
OFFICIAL MANGA ANTHOLOGY
Volume 3

From Shadows

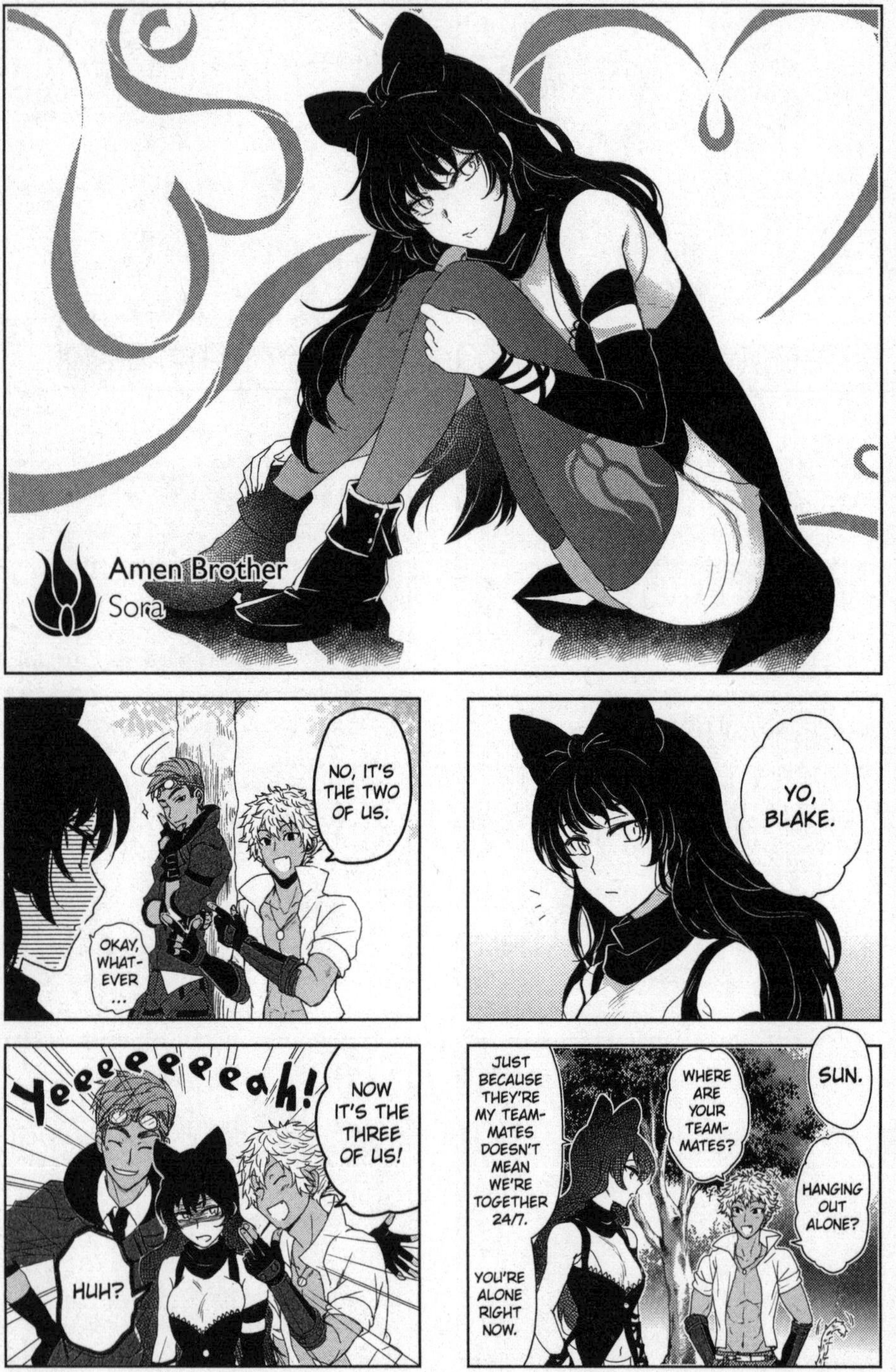
Amen Brother
Sora
YO, BLAKE.
SUN.
HANGING OUT ALONE?
WHERE ARE YOUR TEAM-MATES?
JUST BECAUSE THEY'RE MY TEAM-MATES DOESN'T MEAN WE'RE TOGETHER 24/7.
YOU'RE ALONE RIGHT NOW.
NO, IT'S THE TWO OF US.
OKAY, WHATEVER...
NOW IT'S THE THREE OF US!
Yeeeeeeeah!
HUH?

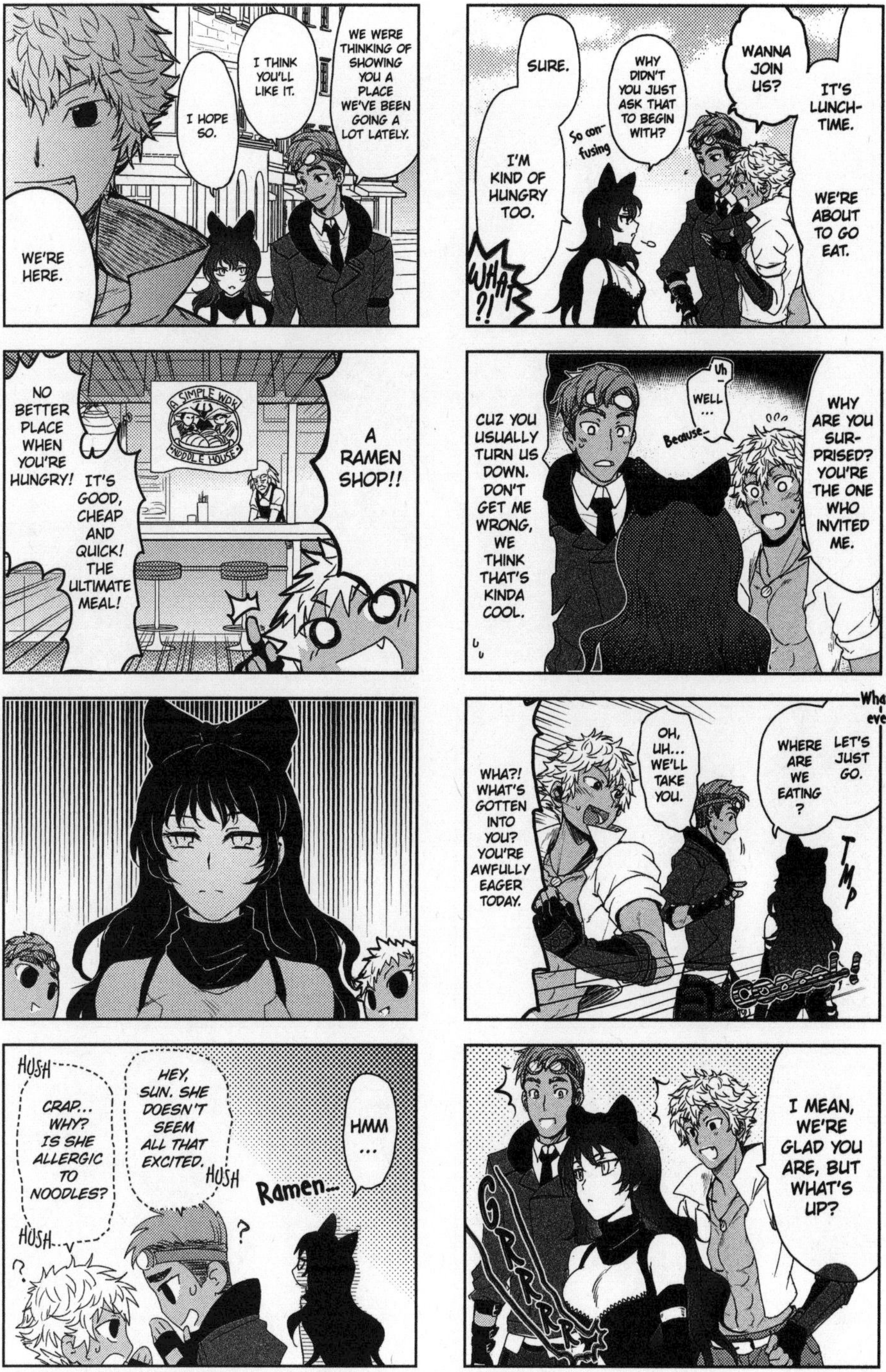
WANNA JOIN US?
IT'S LUNCH-TIME.
WE'RE ABOUT TO GO EAT.
WHY DIDN'T YOU JUST ASK THAT TO BEGIN WITH?
So con-fusing
SURE.
I'M KIND OF HUNGRY TOO.
WHAT?!
WHY ARE YOU SUR-PRISED? YOU'RE THE ONE WHO INVITED ME.
Uh-WELL...
Because...
CUZ YOU USUALLY TURN US DOWN. DON'T GET ME WRONG, WE THINK THAT'S KINDA COOL.
What-ever
LET'S JUST GO.
WHERE ARE WE EATING?
TMP
OH, UH... WE'LL TAKE YOU.
WHAT?! WHAT'S GOTTEN INTO YOU? YOU'RE AWFULLY EAGER TODAY.
I MEAN, WE'RE GLAD YOU ARE, BUT WHAT'S UP?
GRRRRR
WE WERE THINKING OF SHOWING YOU A PLACE WE'VE BEEN GOING A LOT LATELY.
I THINK YOU'LL LIKE IT.
I HOPE SO.
WE'RE HERE.
A RAMEN SHOP!!
A SIMPLE WOK NOODLE HOUSE
NO BETTER PLACE WHEN YOU'RE HUNGRY!
IT'S GOOD, CHEAP AND QUICK! THE ULTIMATE MEAL!
HMM...
Ramen...
HEY, SUN. SHE DOESN'T SEEM ALL THAT EXCITED.
HUSH
CRAP... WHY? IS SHE ALLERGIC TO NOODLES?
HUSH
HUSH

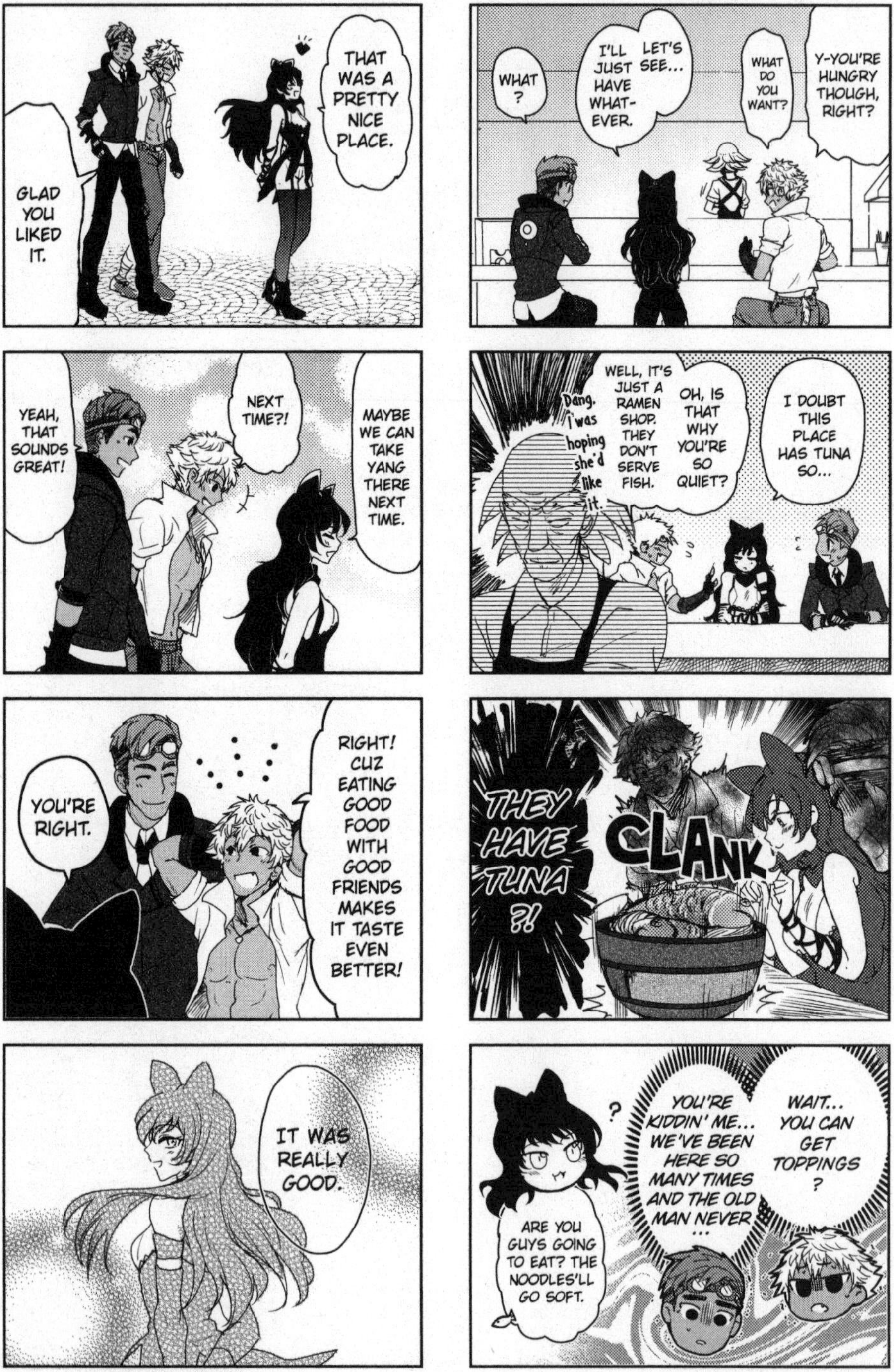
Y-YOU'RE HUNGRY THOUGH, RIGHT?
WHAT DO YOU WANT?
LET'S SEE...
I'LL JUST HAVE WHAT-EVER.
WHAT ?
I DOUBT THIS PLACE HAS TUNA SO...
OH, IS THAT WHY YOU'RE SO QUIET?
WELL, IT'S JUST A RAMEN SHOP. THEY DON'T SERVE FISH.
Dang. I was hoping she'd like it.
CLANK
THEY HAVE TUNA ?!
WAIT... YOU CAN GET TOPPINGS ?
YOU'RE KIDDIN' ME... WE'VE BEEN HERE SO MANY TIMES AND THE OLD MAN NEVER ...
ARE YOU GUYS GOING TO EAT? THE NOODLES'LL GO SOFT.
THAT WAS A PRETTY NICE PLACE.
GLAD YOU LIKED IT.
MAYBE WE CAN TAKE YANG THERE NEXT TIME.
NEXT TIME?!
YEAH, THAT SOUNDS GREAT!
RIGHT! CUZ EATING GOOD FOOD WITH GOOD FRIENDS MAKES IT TASTE EVEN BETTER!
YOU'RE RIGHT.
IT WAS REALLY GOOD.

Amen Brother/END

RWBY
OFFICIAL MANGA ANTHOLOGY
Volume 3

From Shadows

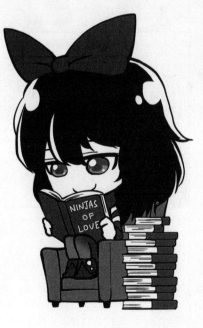

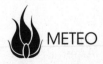

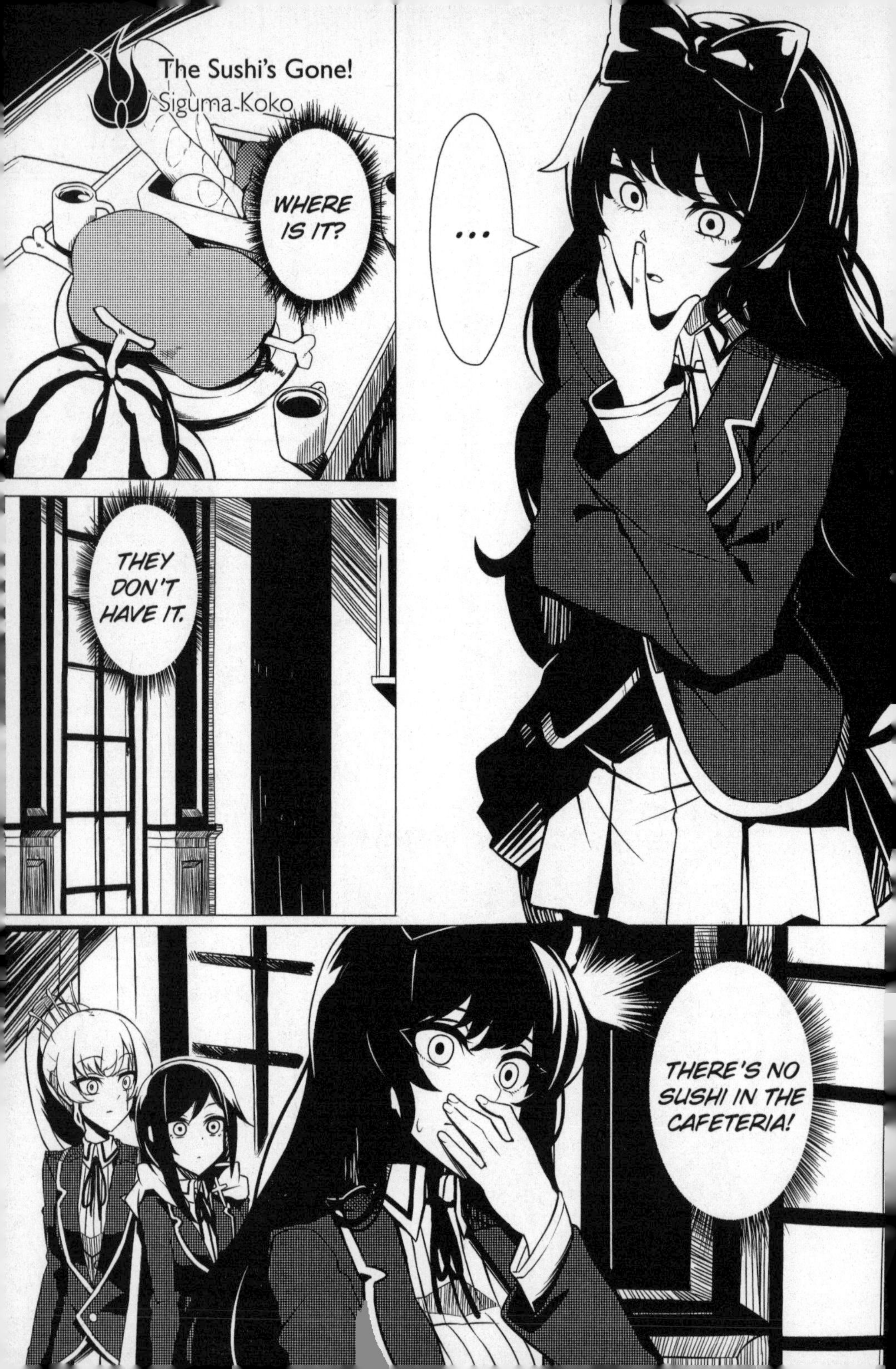
...
The Sushi's Gone!
Siguma Koko
WHERE IS IT?
THEY DON'T HAVE IT.
THERE'S NO SUSHI IN THE CAFETERIA!

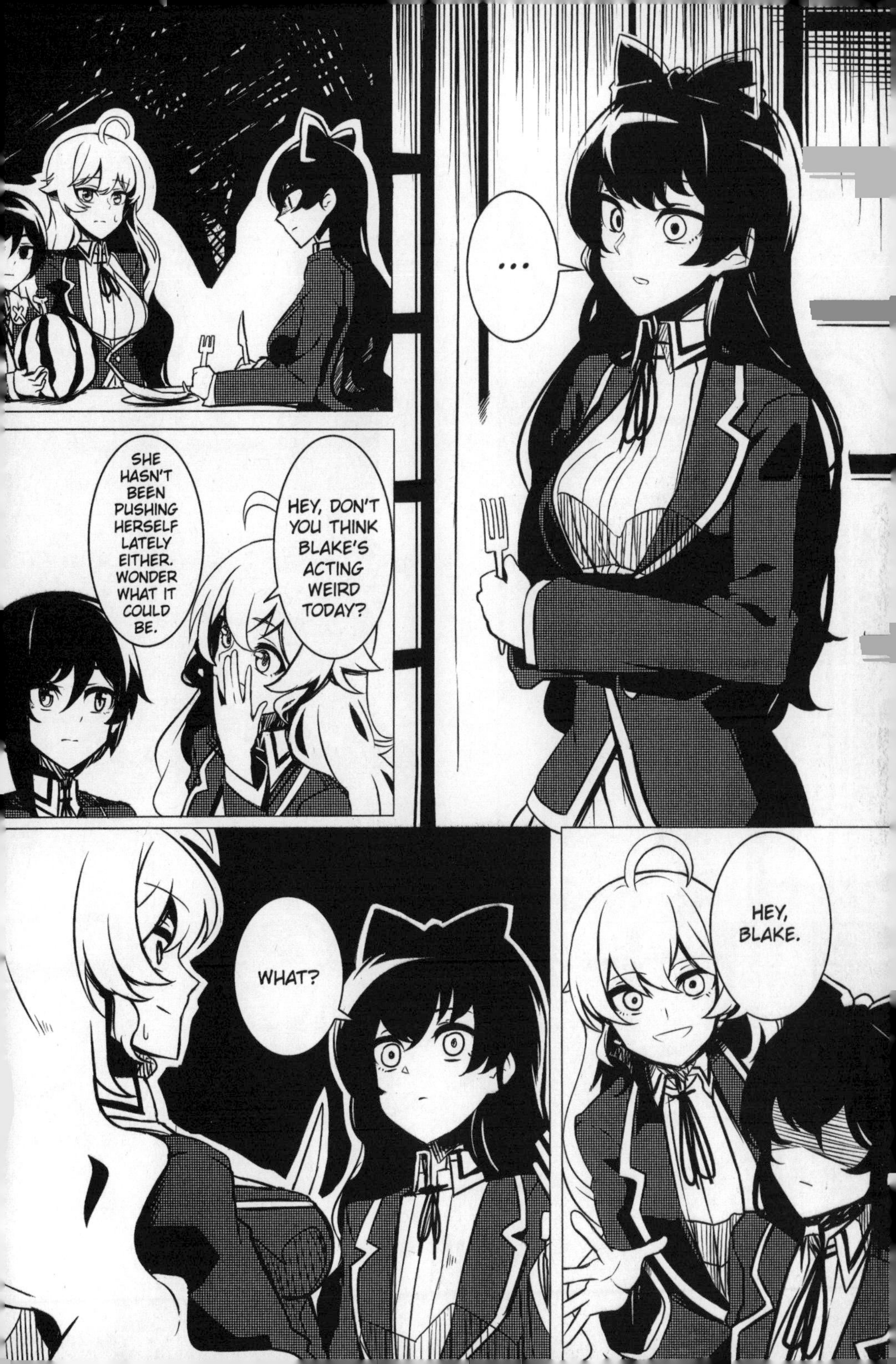
...
HEY, DON'T YOU THINK BLAKE'S ACTING WEIRD TODAY?
SHE HASN'T BEEN PUSHING HERSELF LATELY EITHER. WONDER WHAT IT COULD BE.
HEY, BLAKE.
WHAT?

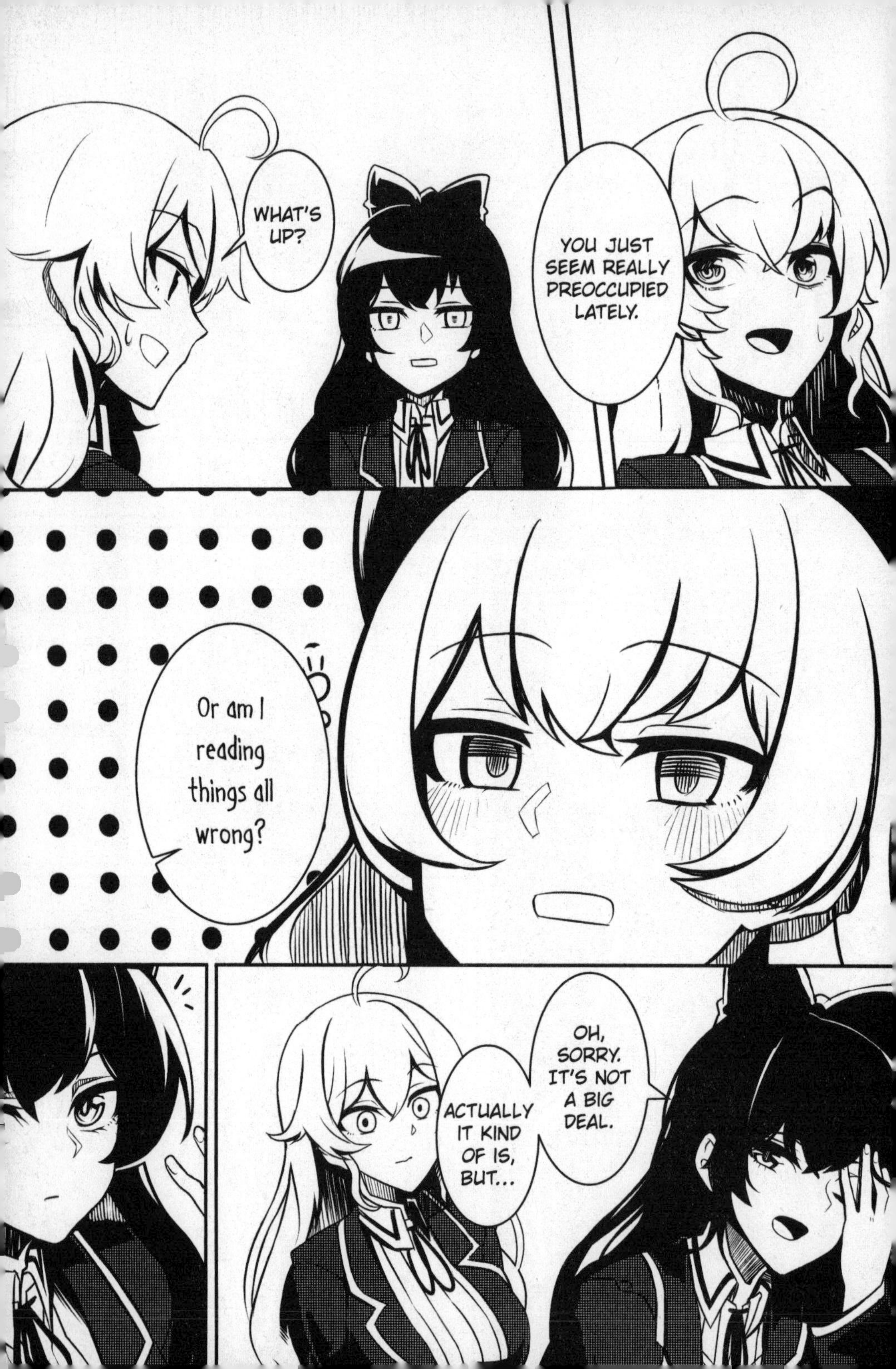
YOU JUST SEEM REALLY PREOCCUPIED LATELY.
WHAT'S UP?
Or am I reading things all wrong?
OH, SORRY. IT'S NOT A BIG DEAL.
ACTUALLY IT KIND OF IS, BUT...

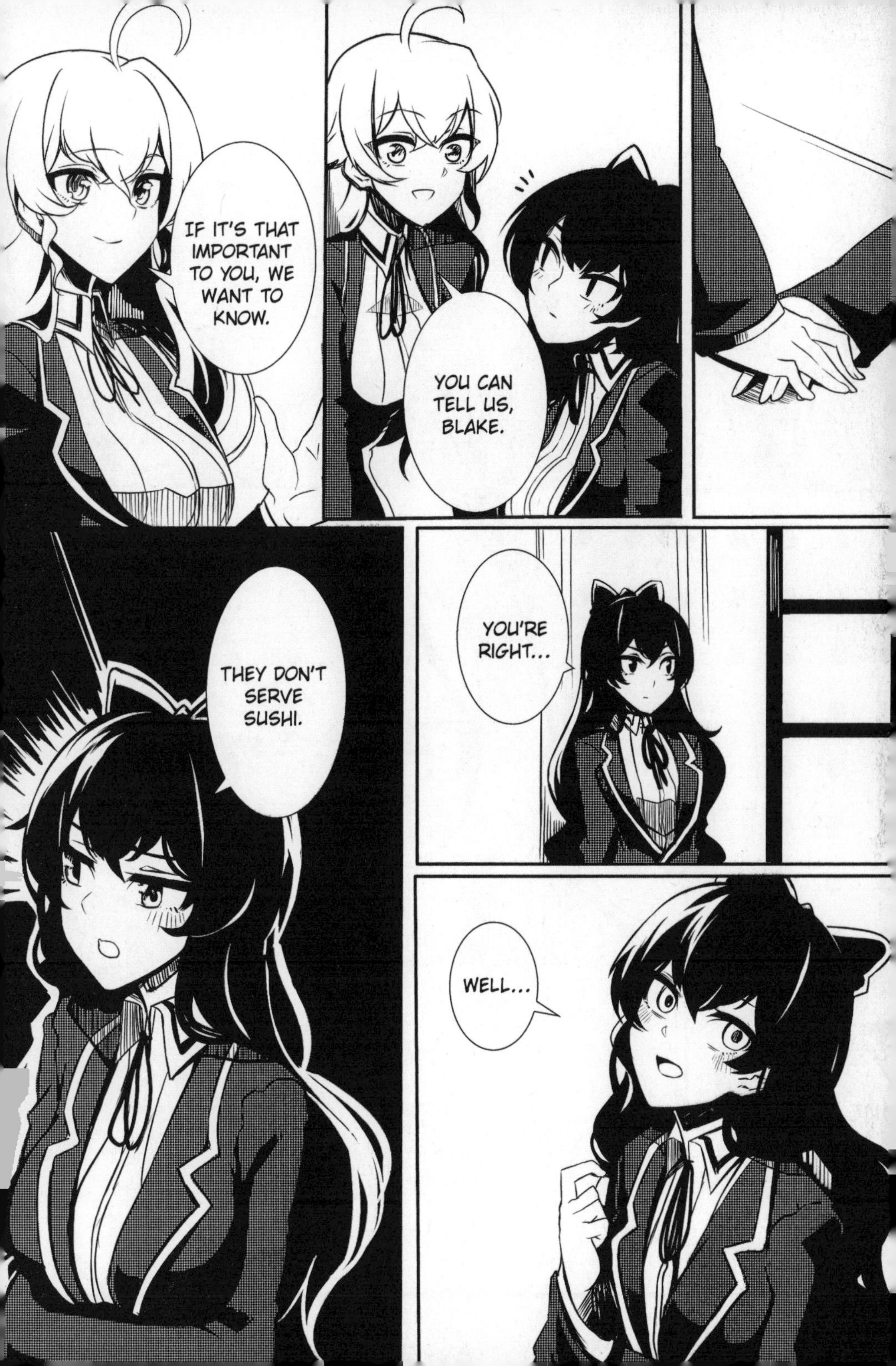
YOU CAN TELL US, BLAKE.
IF IT'S THAT IMPORTANT TO YOU, WE WANT TO KNOW.
YOU'RE RIGHT...
WELL...
THEY DON'T SERVE SUSHI.

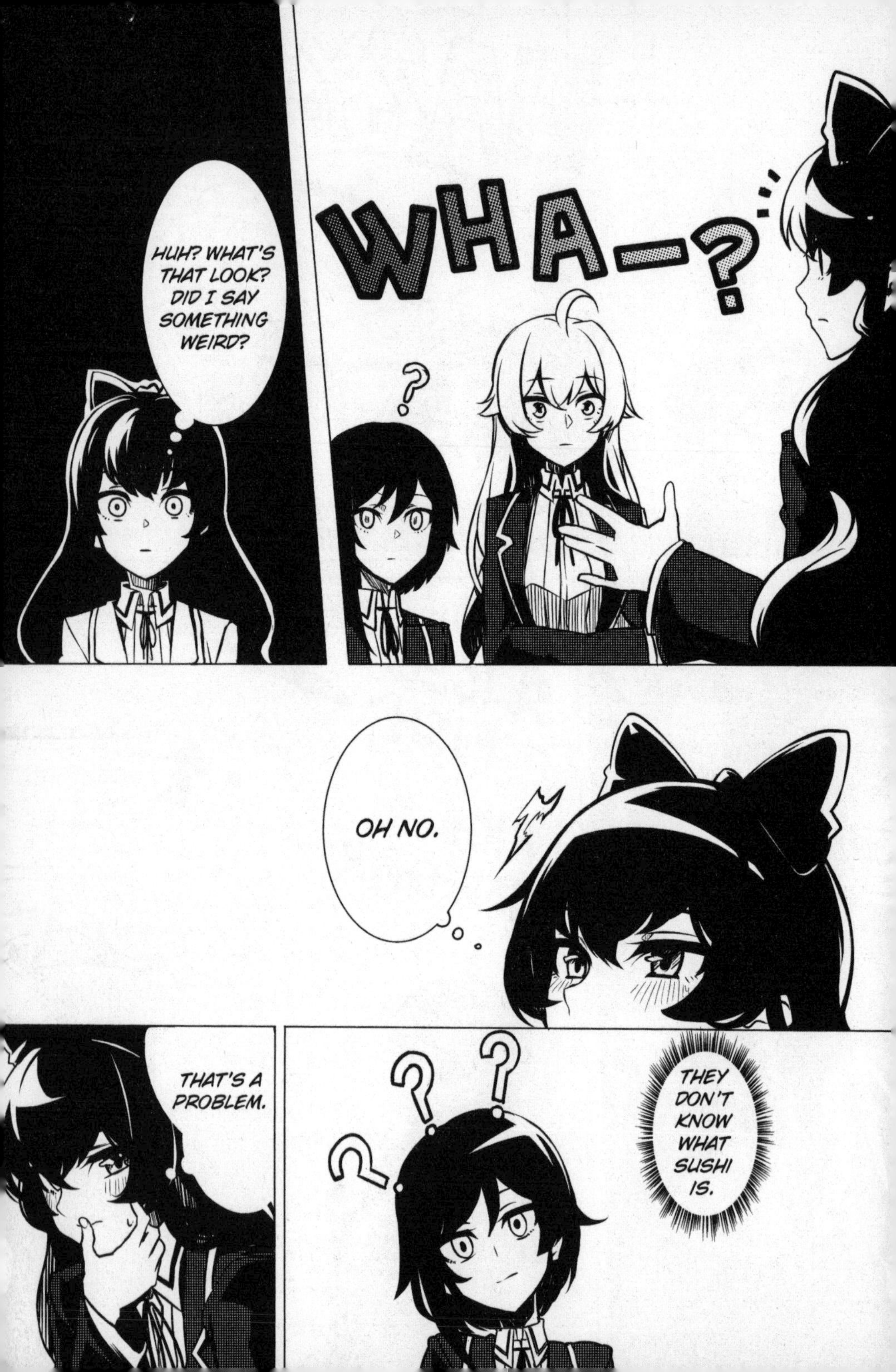
WHA-?
HUH? WHAT'S THAT LOOK? DID I SAY SOMETHING WEIRD?
OH NO.
THEY DON'T KNOW WHAT SUSHI IS.
THAT'S A PROBLEM.

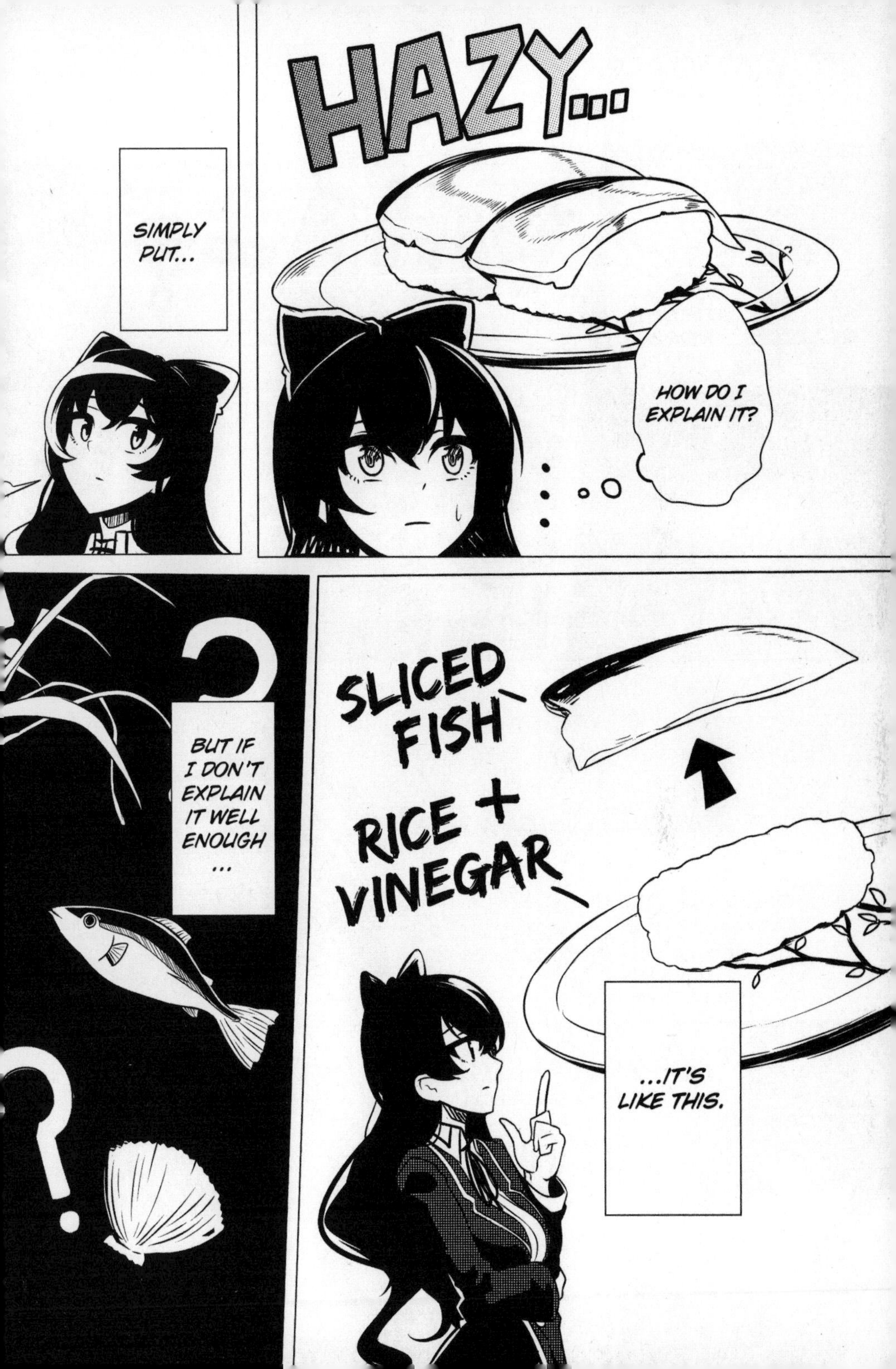
HAZY...
HOW DO I EXPLAIN IT?
SIMPLY PUT...
SLICED FISH
RICE + VINEGAR
...IT'S LIKE THIS.
BUT IF I DON'T EXPLAIN IT WELL ENOUGH ...

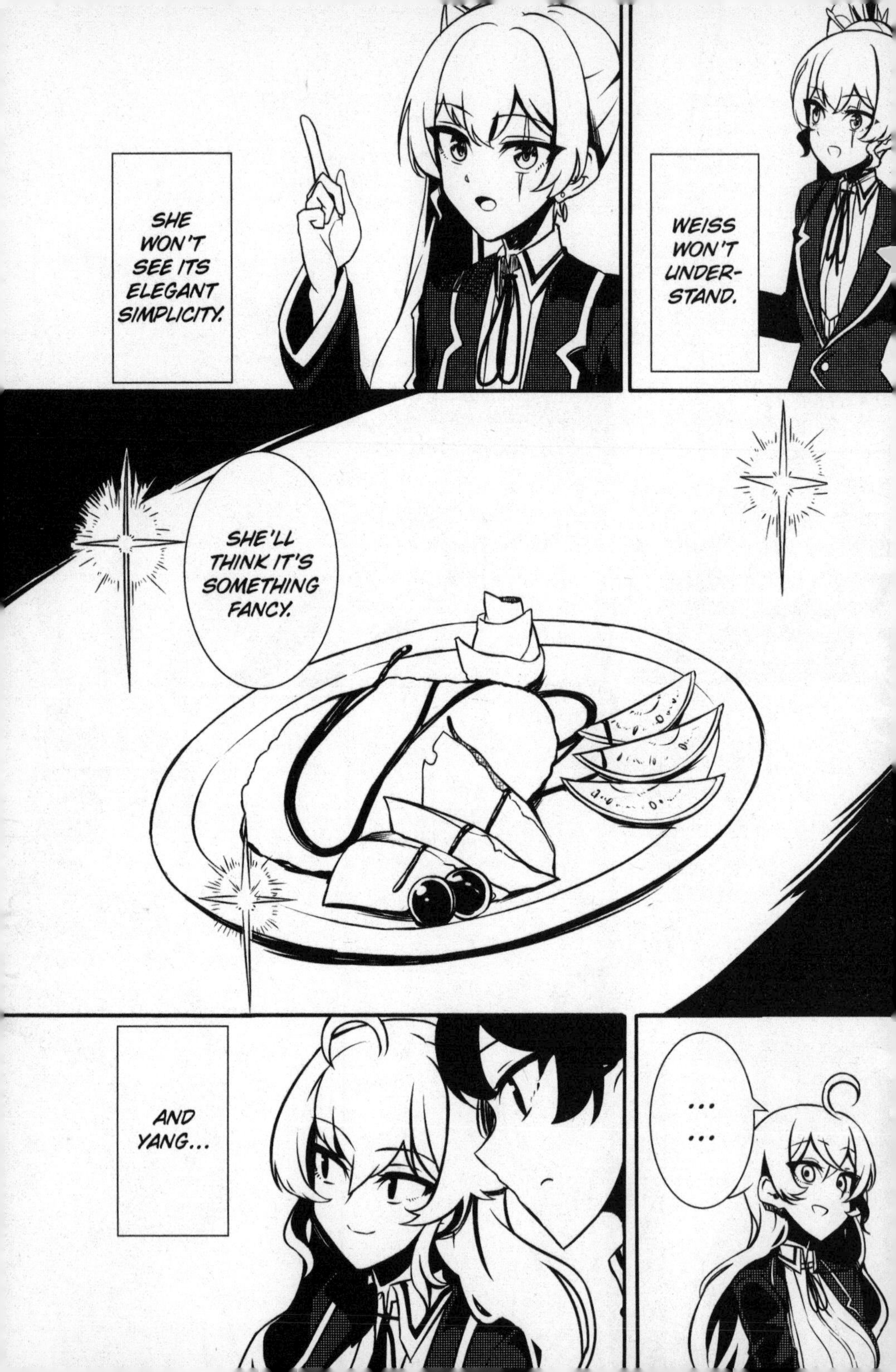
WEISS WON'T UNDER-STAND.
SHE WON'T SEE ITS ELEGANT SIMPLICITY.
SHE'LL THINK IT'S SOMETHING FANCY.
... ...
AND YANG...

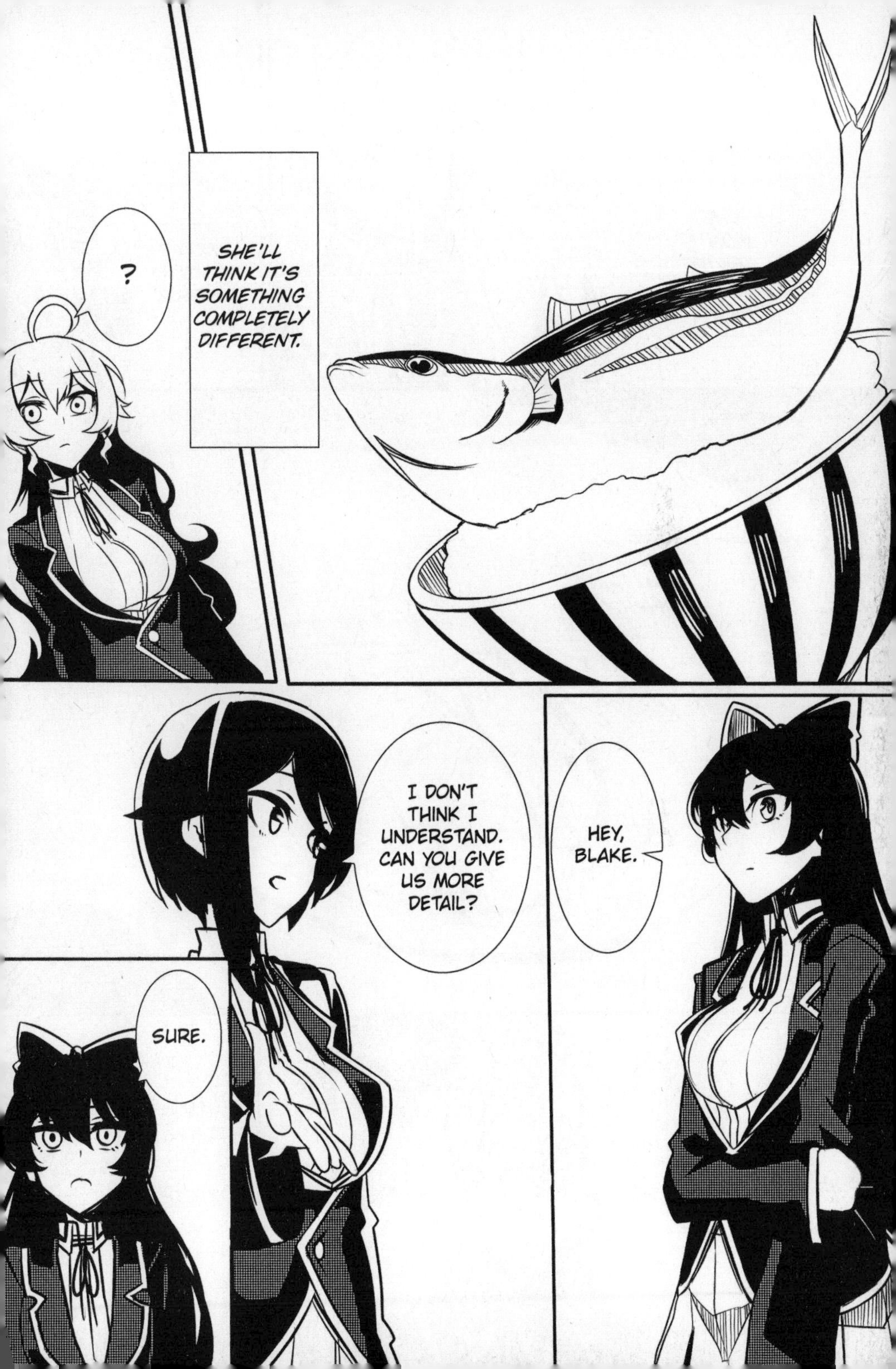
SHE'LL THINK IT'S SOMETHING COMPLETELY DIFFERENT.
?
HEY, BLAKE.
I DON'T THINK I UNDERSTAND. CAN YOU GIVE US MORE DETAIL?
SURE.

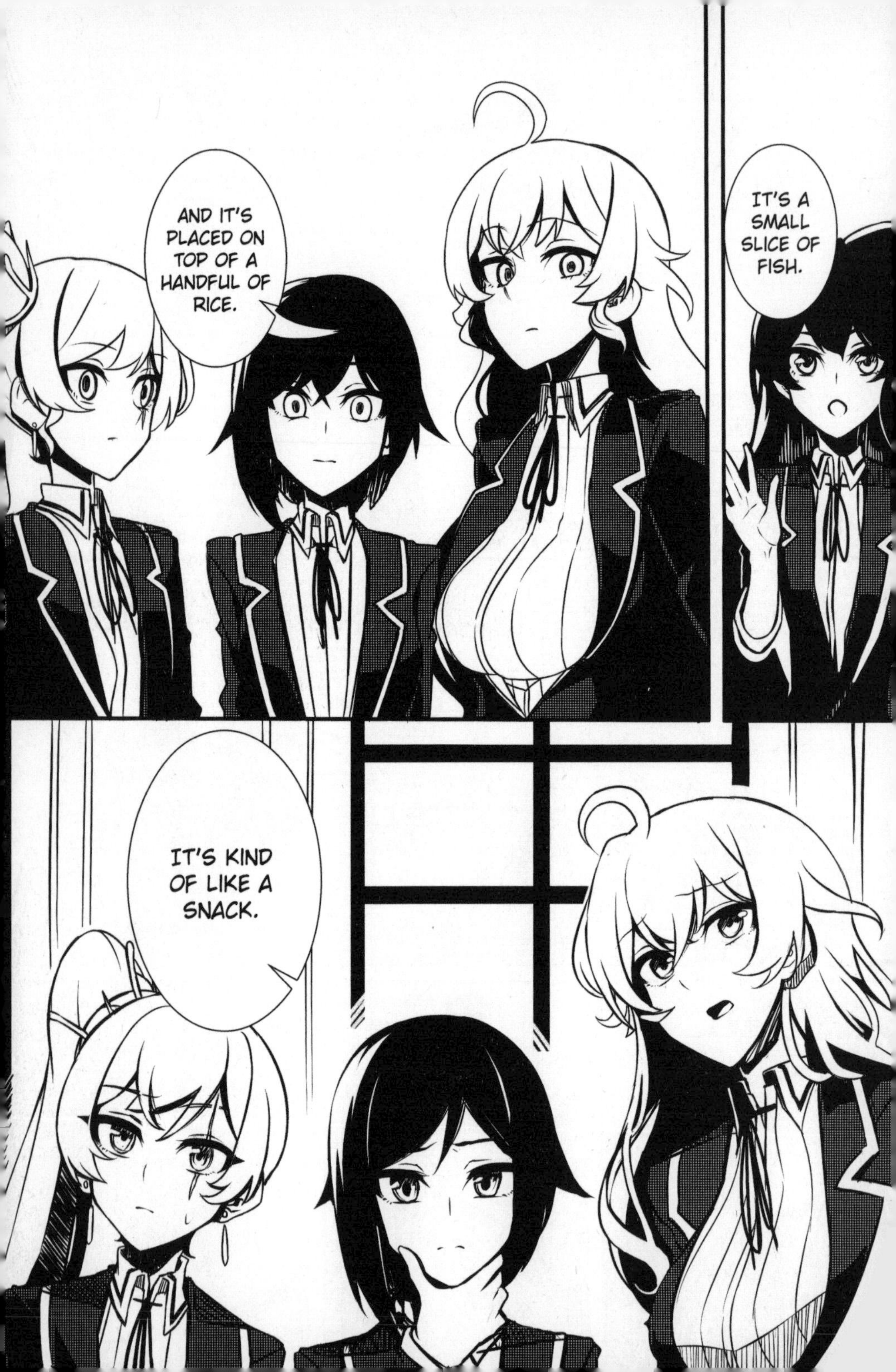
IT'S A SMALL SLICE OF FISH.
AND IT'S PLACED ON TOP OF A HANDFUL OF RICE.
IT'S KIND OF LIKE A SNACK.

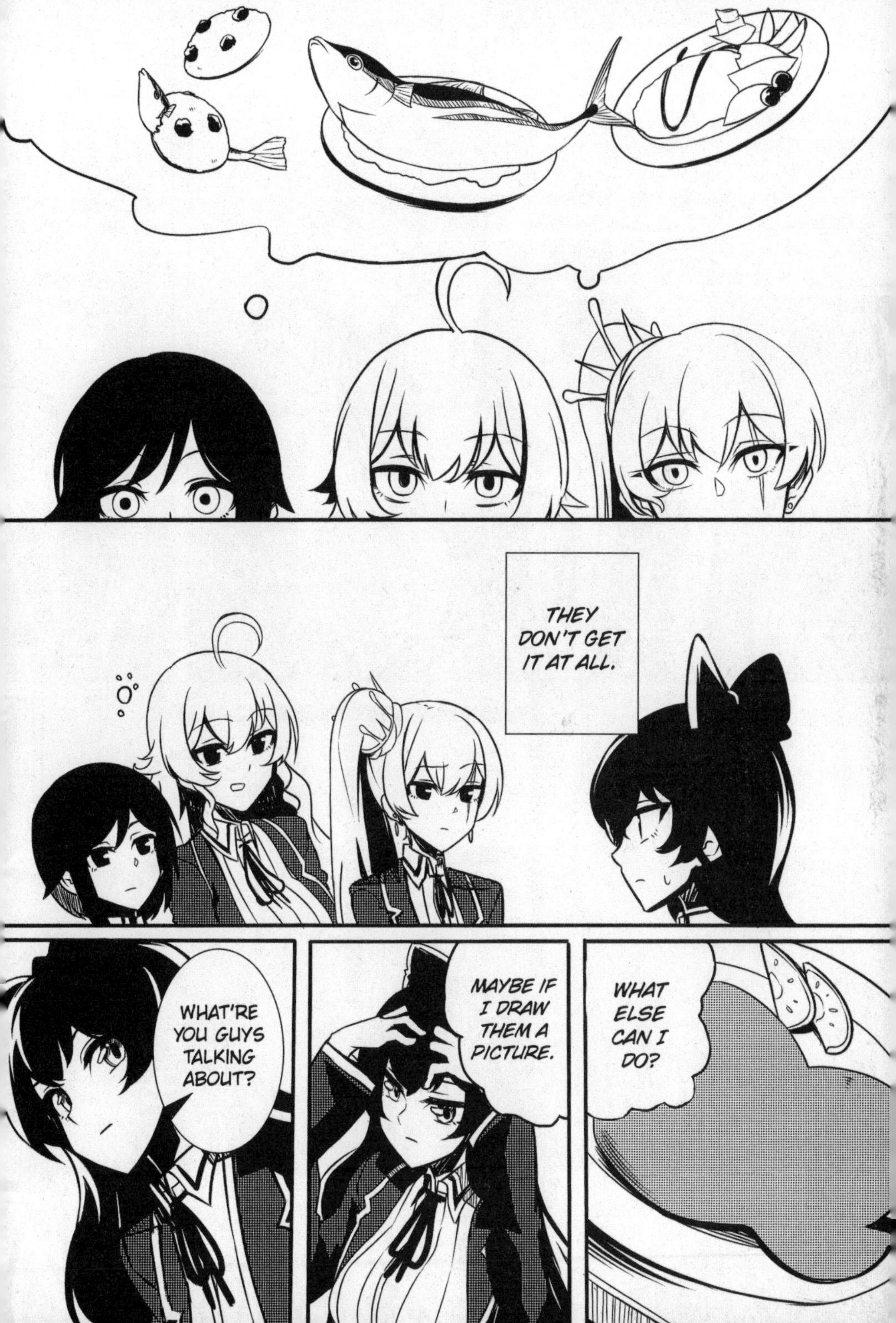
THEY DON'T GET IT AT ALL.
WHAT ELSE CAN I DO?
MAYBE IF I DRAW THEM A PICTURE.
WHAT'RE YOU GUYS TALKING ABOUT?

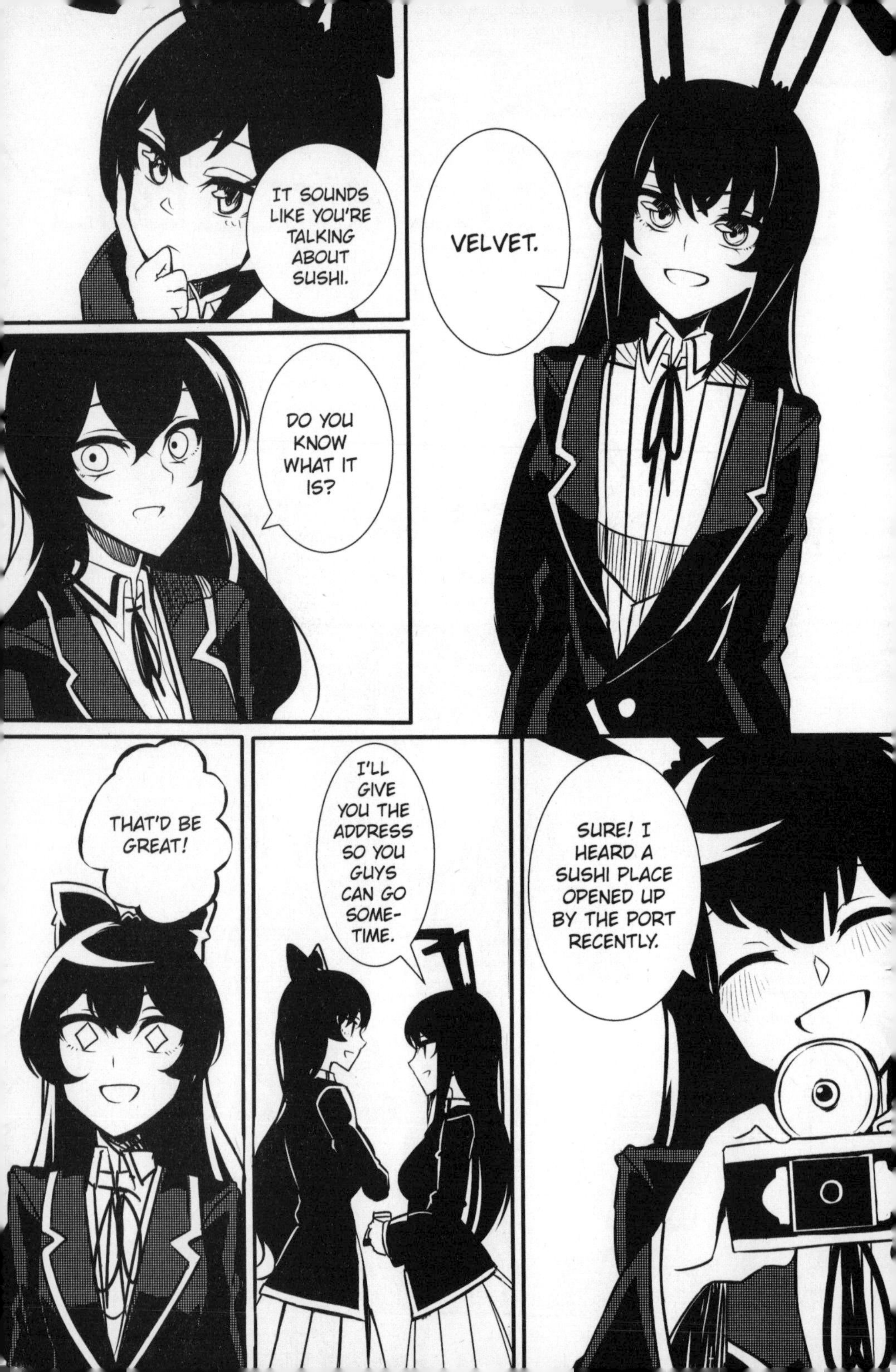
VELVET.
IT SOUNDS LIKE YOU'RE TALKING ABOUT SUSHI.
DO YOU KNOW WHAT IT IS?
SURE! I HEARD A SUSHI PLACE OPENED UP BY THE PORT RECENTLY.
I'LL GIVE YOU THE ADDRESS SO YOU GUYS CAN GO SOME-TIME.
THAT'D BE GREAT!

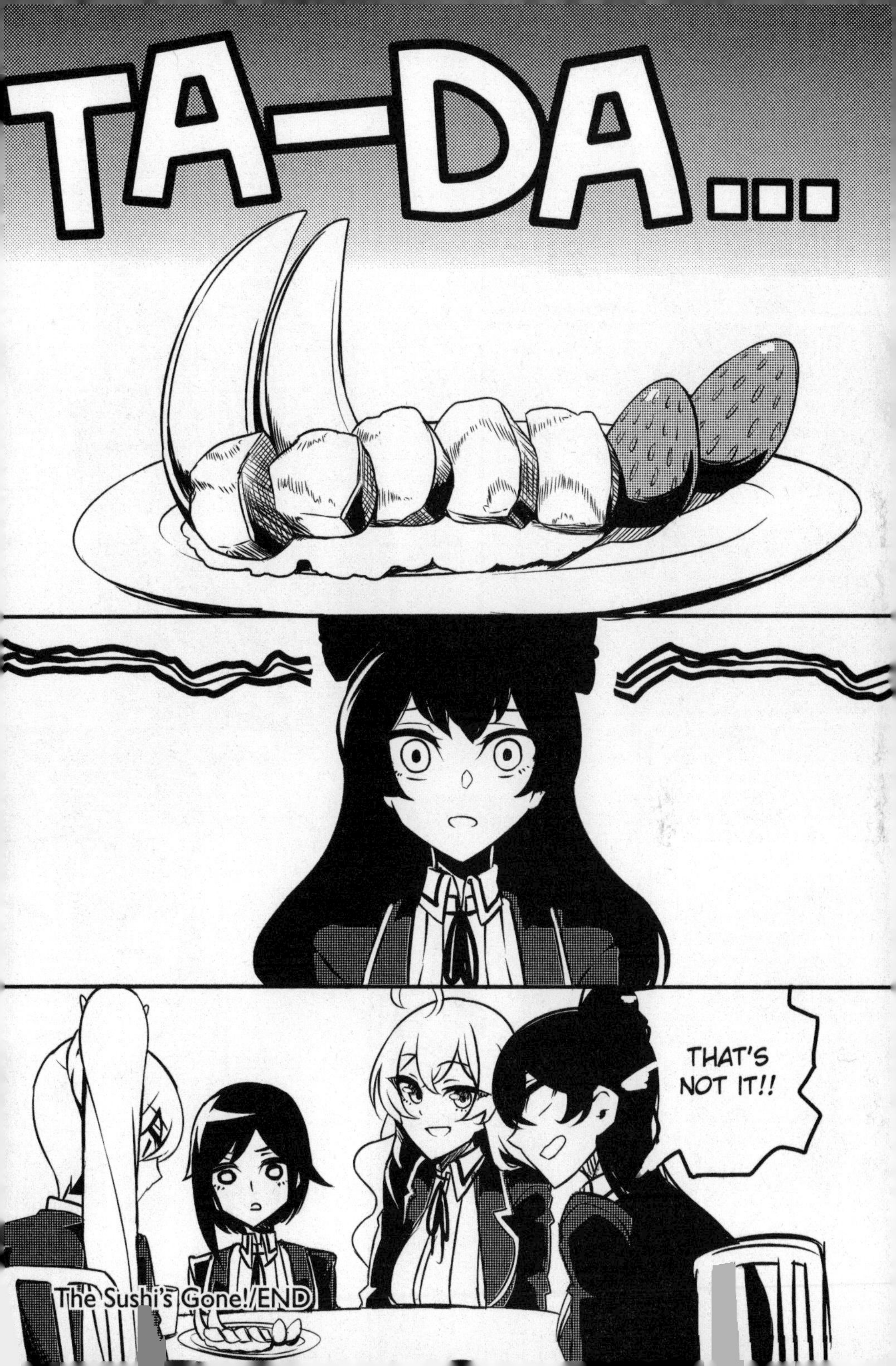
TA-DA...
THAT'S NOT IT!!
The Sushi's Gone!/END

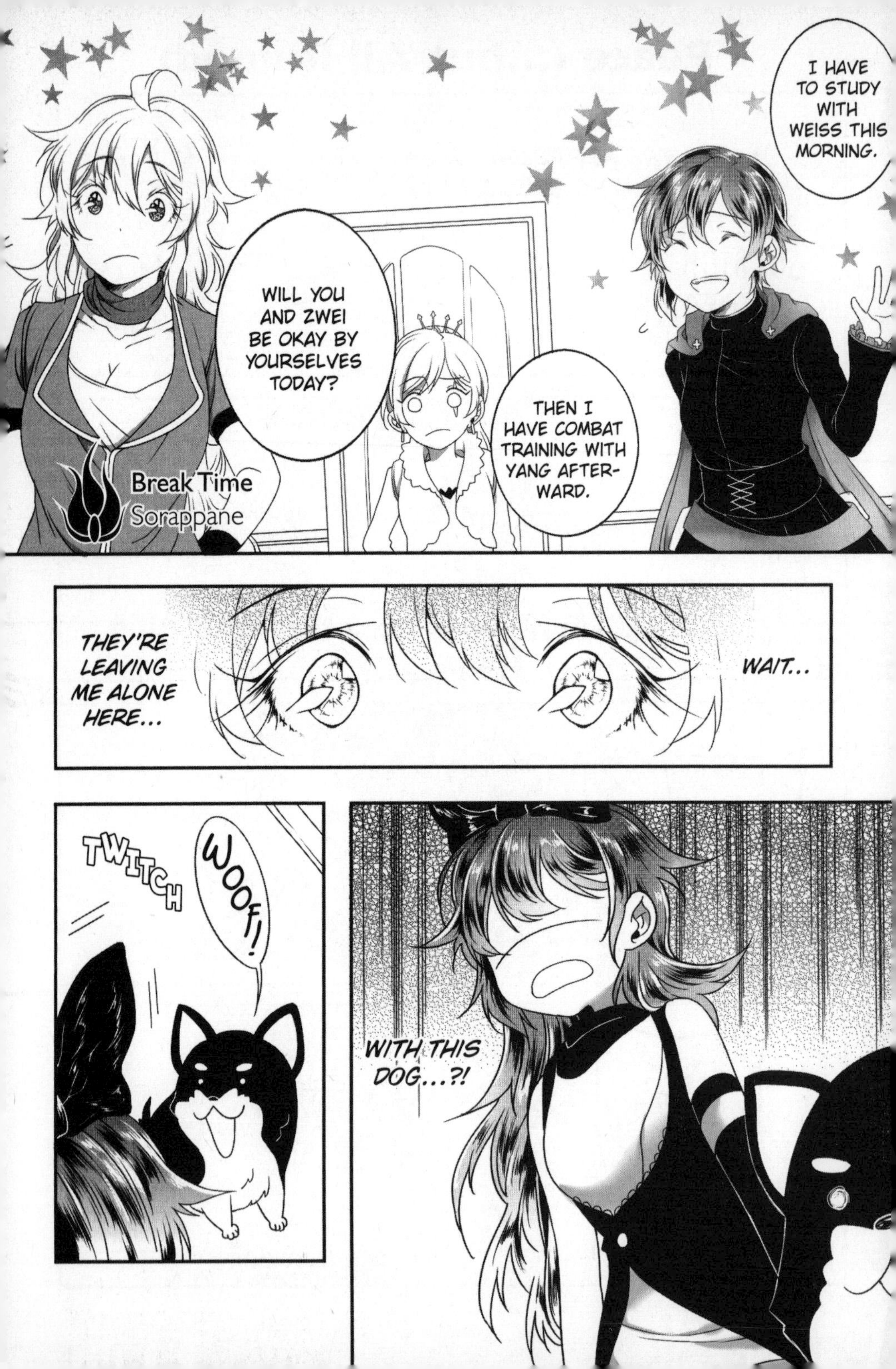
I HAVE TO STUDY WITH WEISS THIS MORNING.
THEN I HAVE COMBAT TRAINING WITH YANG AFTER-WARD.
WILL YOU AND ZWEI BE OKAY BY YOURSELVES TODAY?
Break Time
Sorappane
WAIT...
THEY'RE LEAVING ME ALONE HERE...
WITH THIS DOG...?!
WOOF!!
TWITCH

Peace (...but All Ruined)

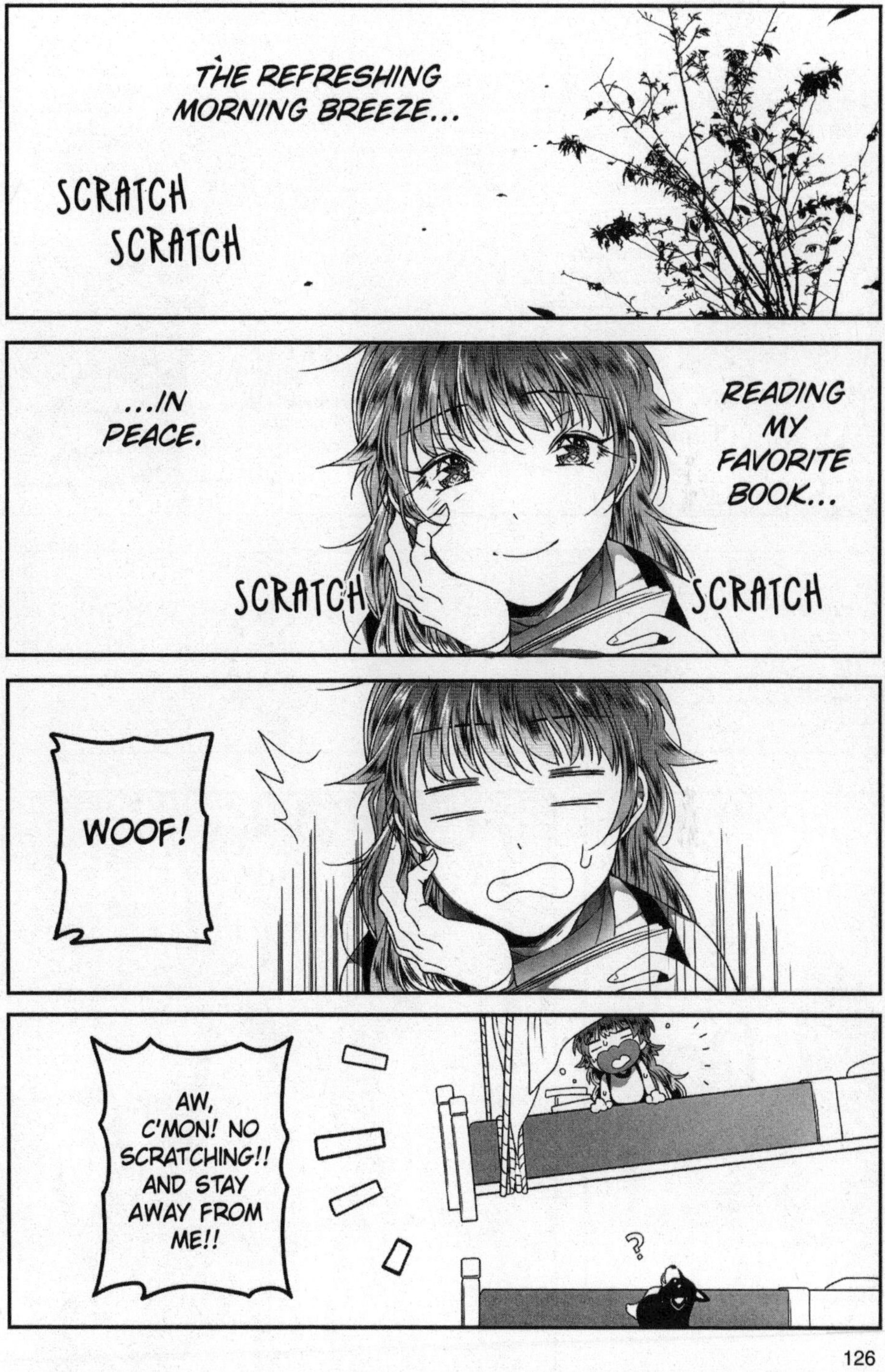
THE REFRESHING MORNING BREEZE...
SCRATCH SCRATCH
READING MY FAVORITE BOOK...
...IN PEACE.
SCRATCH
SCRATCH
WOOF!
AW, C'MON! NO SCRATCHING!! AND STAY AWAY FROM ME!!
?

Ignorance

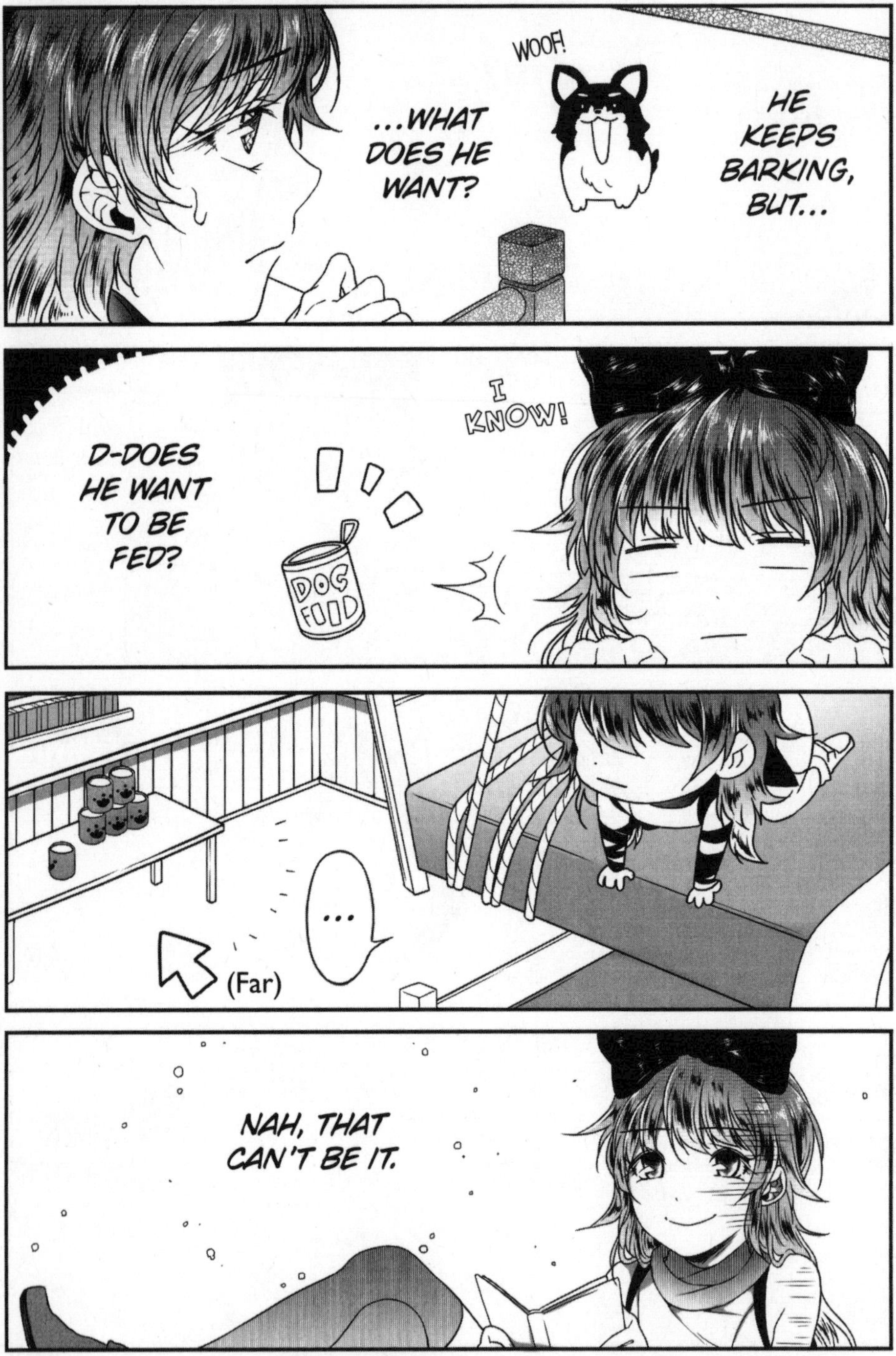

WOOF!
HE KEEPS BARKING, BUT...
...WHAT DOES HE WANT?
I KNOW!
D-DOES HE WANT TO BE FED?
DOG FOOD
...
(Far)
NAH, THAT CAN'T BE IT.

Trust

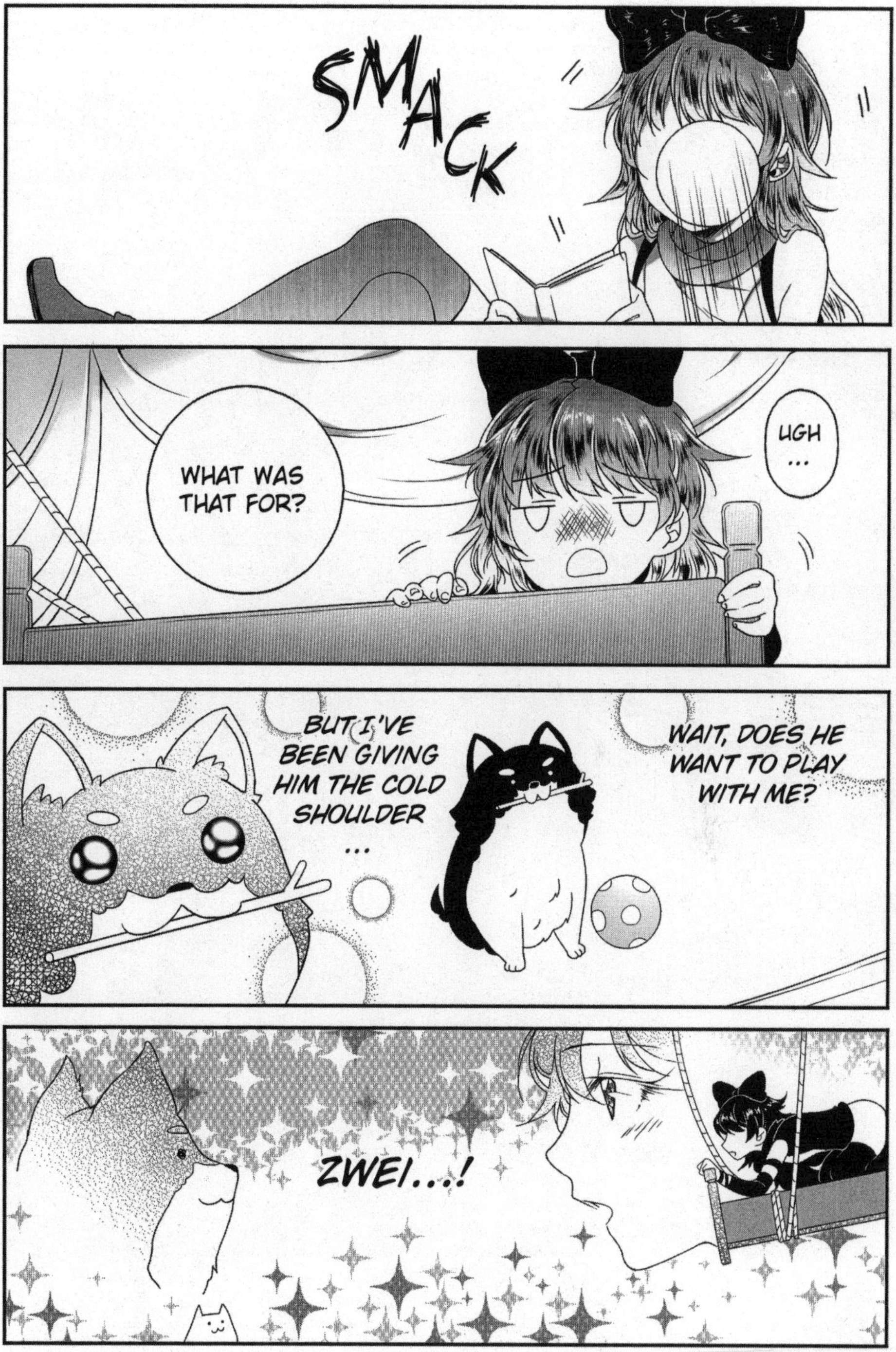
SMACK
UGH ...
WHAT WAS THAT FOR?
WAIT, DOES HE WANT TO PLAY WITH ME?
BUT I'VE BEEN GIVING HIM THE COLD SHOULDER ...
ZWEI...!

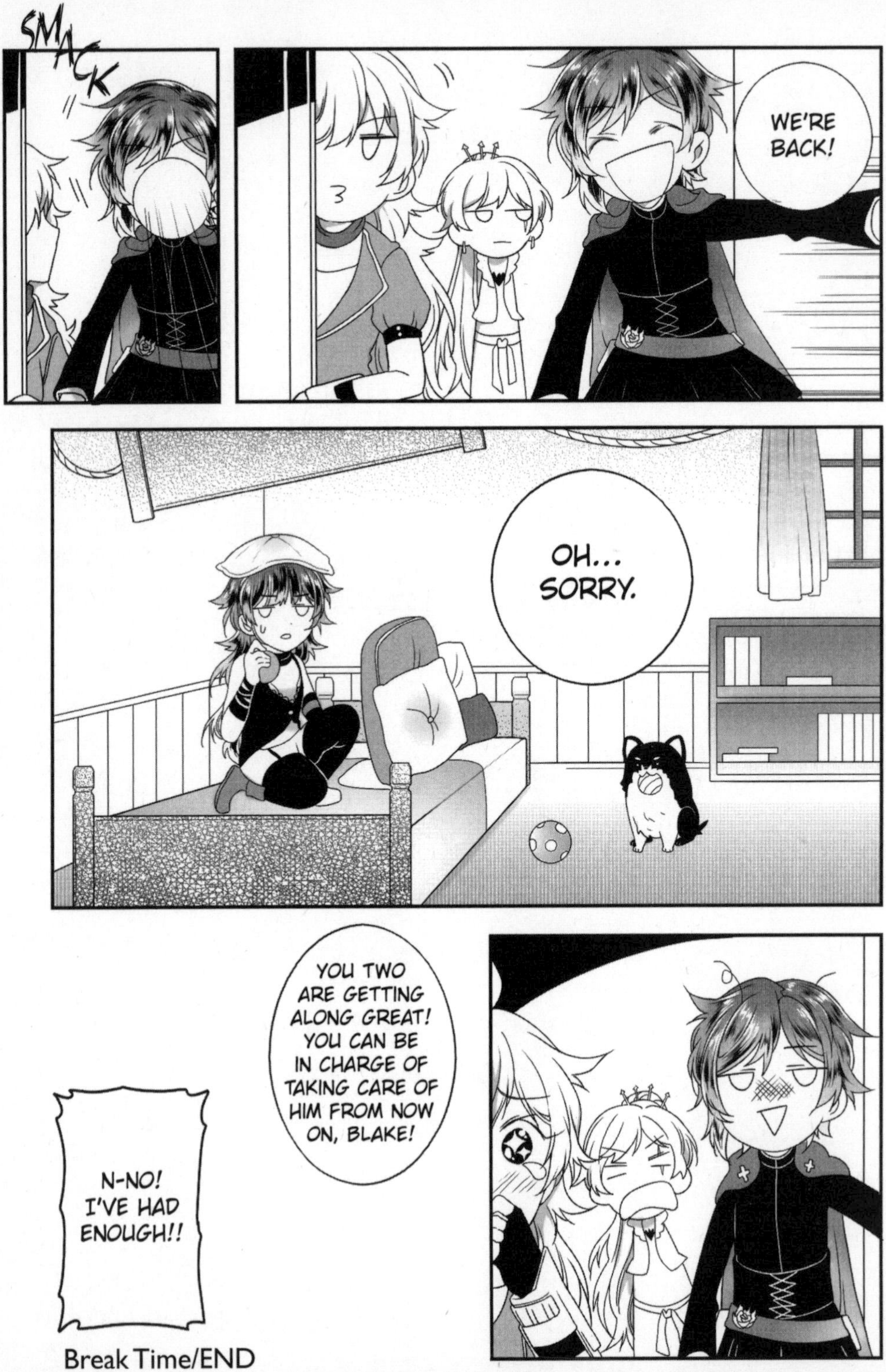
WE'RE BACK!
SMACK
OH... SORRY.
YOU TWO ARE GETTING ALONG GREAT! YOU CAN BE IN CHARGE OF TAKING CARE OF HIM FROM NOW ON, BLAKE!
N-NO! I'VE HAD ENOUGH!!

Break Time/END

RWBY
OFFICIAL MANGA ANTHOLOGY
Volume 3

From Shadows

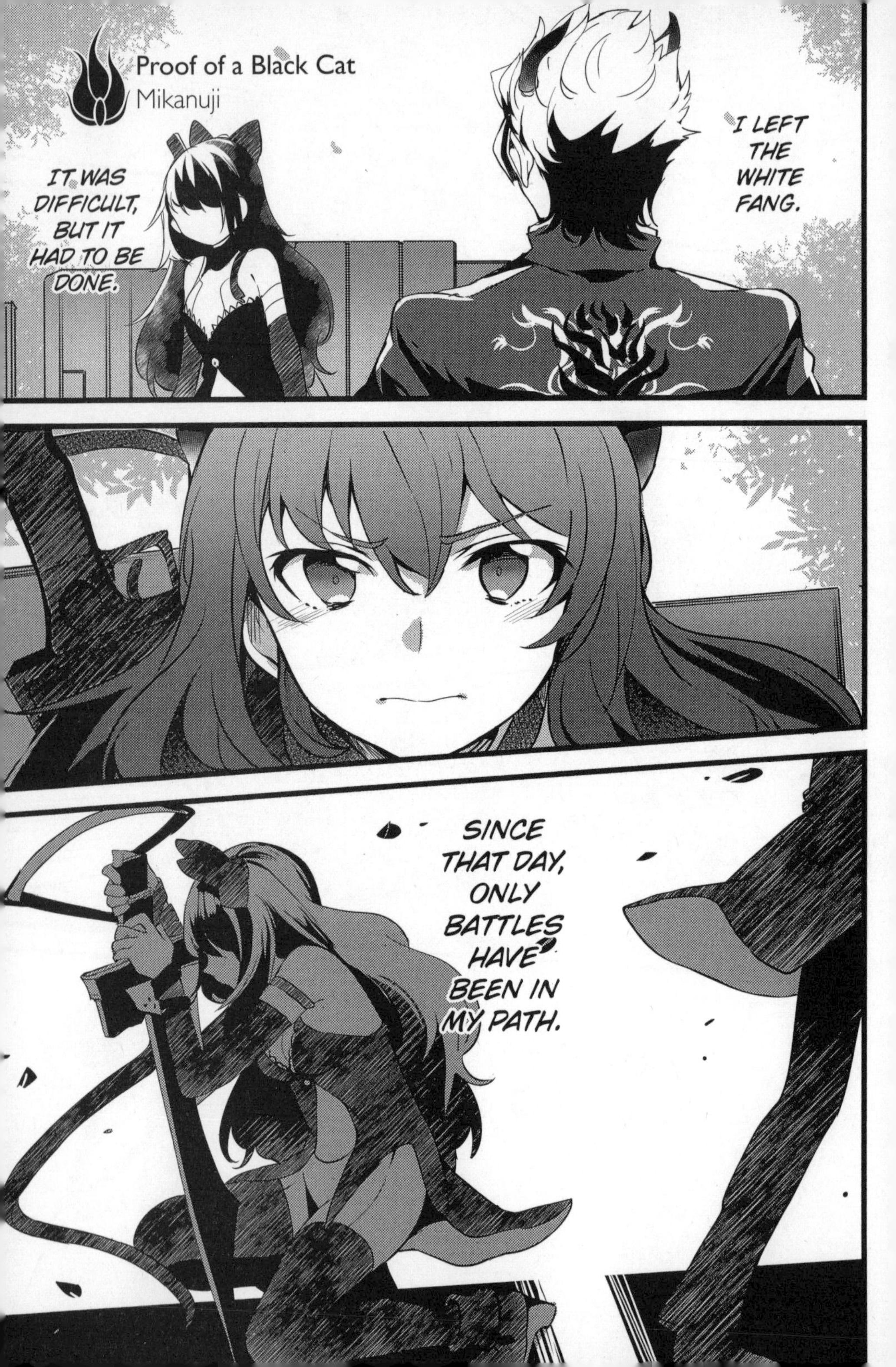
Proof of a Black Cat
Mikanuji
I LEFT THE WHITE FANG.
IT WAS DIFFICULT, BUT IT HAD TO BE DONE.
SINCE THAT DAY, ONLY BATTLES HAVE BEEN IN MY PATH.

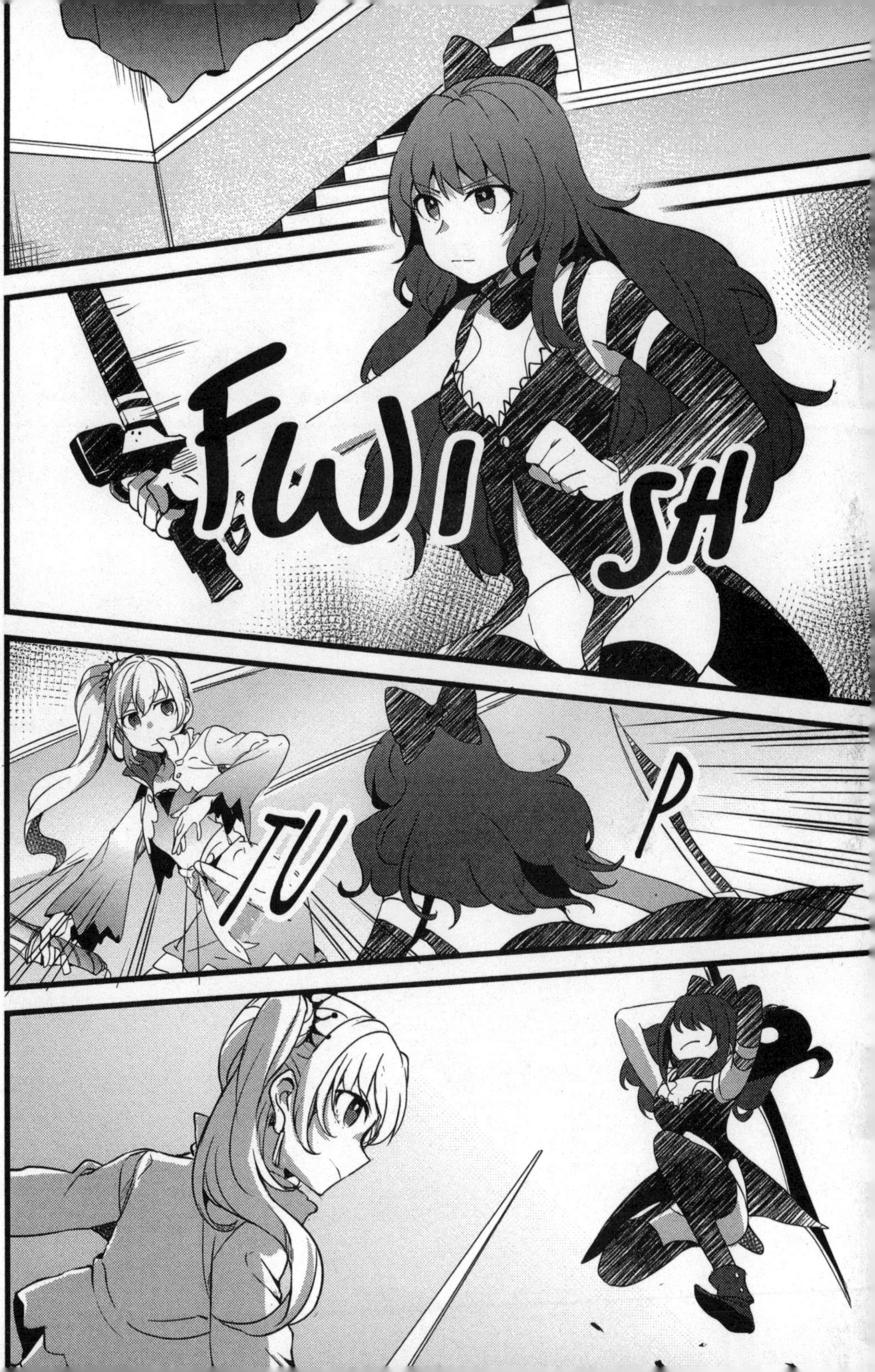
FWI SH
TU P

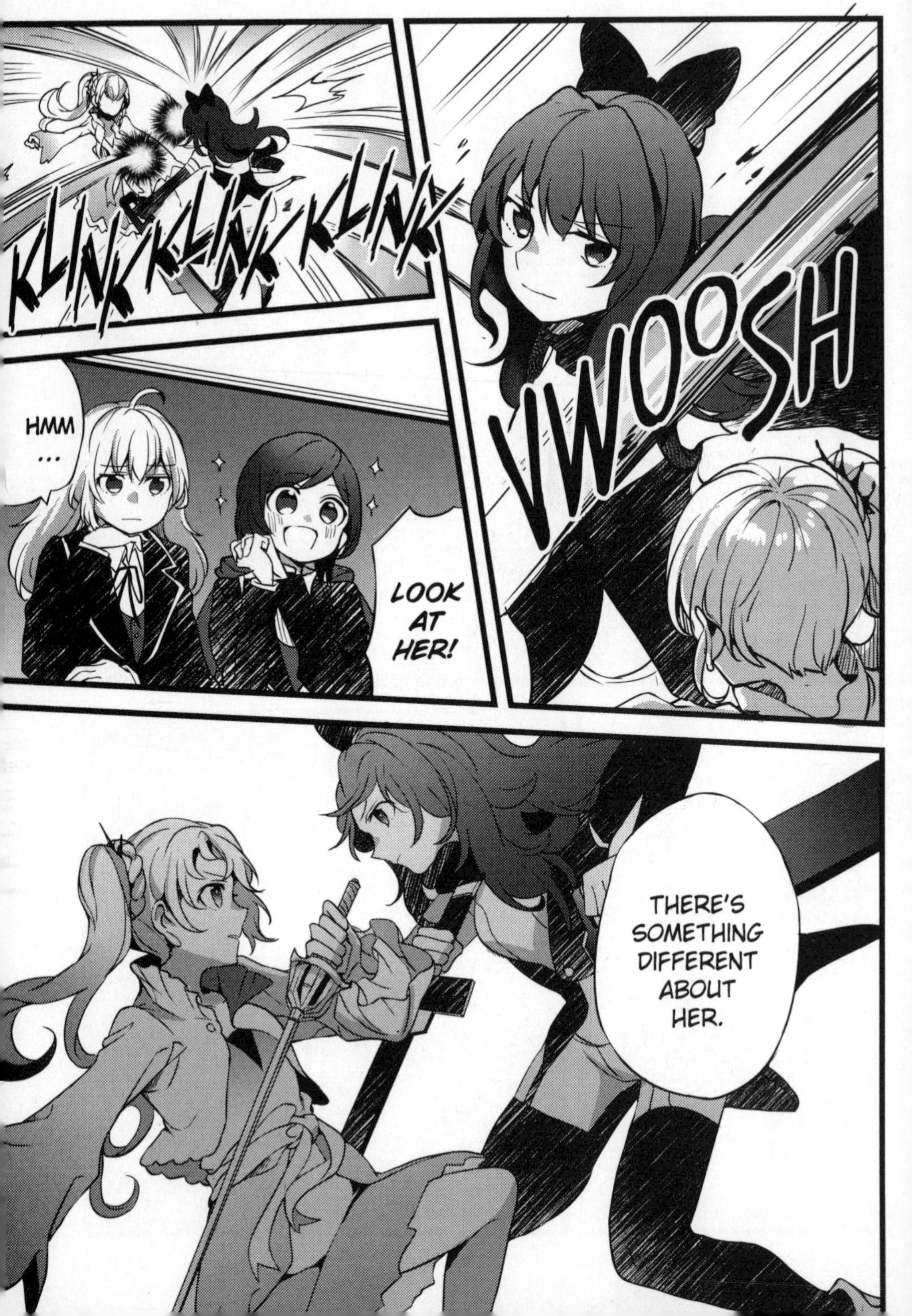
VWOOSH
KLINK KLINK KLINK
LOOK AT HER!
HMM ...
THERE'S SOMETHING DIFFERENT ABOUT HER.

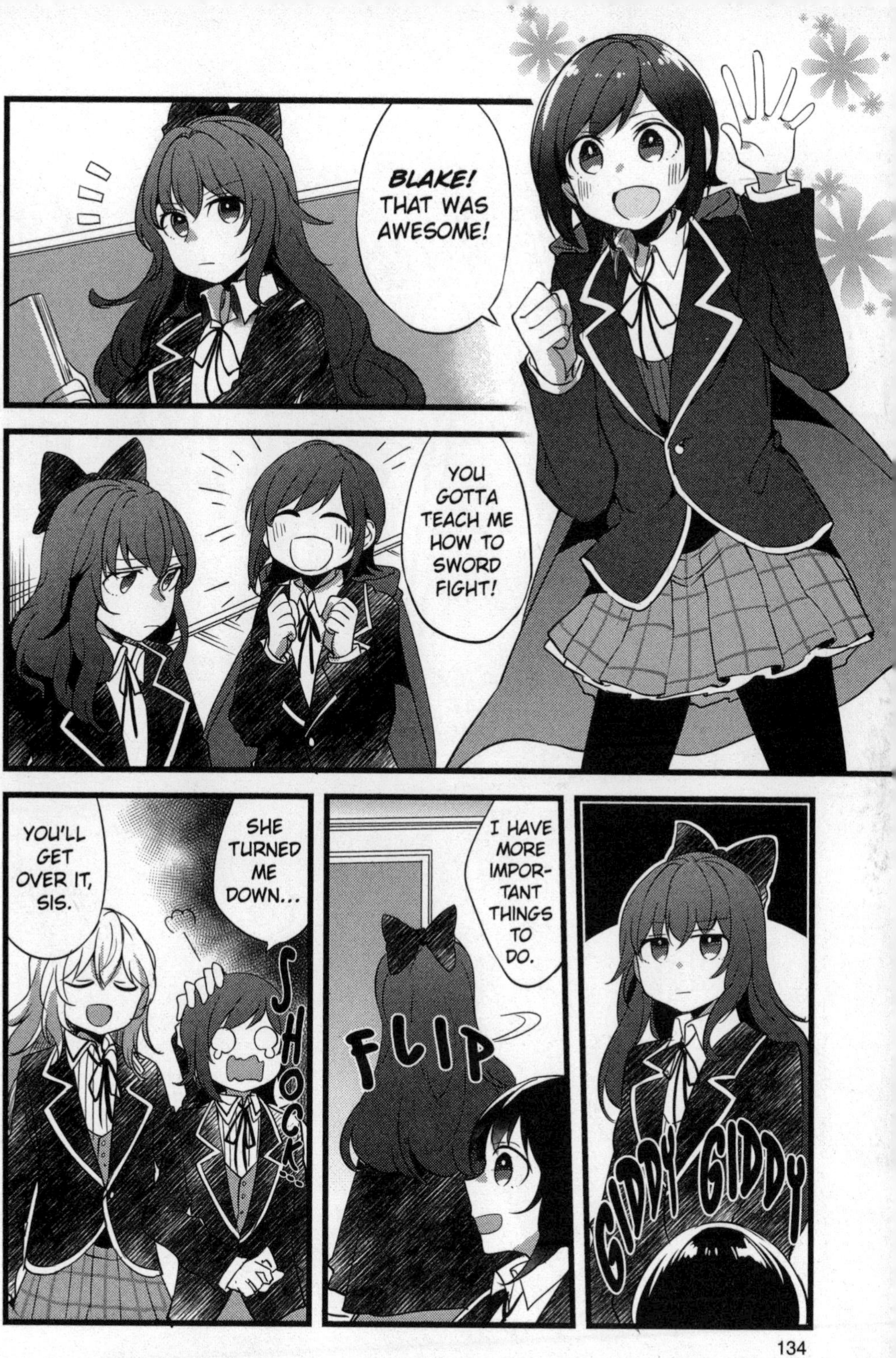
BLAKE! THAT WAS AWESOME!
YOU GOTTA TEACH ME HOW TO SWORD FIGHT!
GIDDY GIDDY
I HAVE MORE IMPOR-TANT THINGS TO DO.
FLIP
SHE TURNED ME DOWN...
YOU'LL GET OVER IT, SIS.
SHOCK

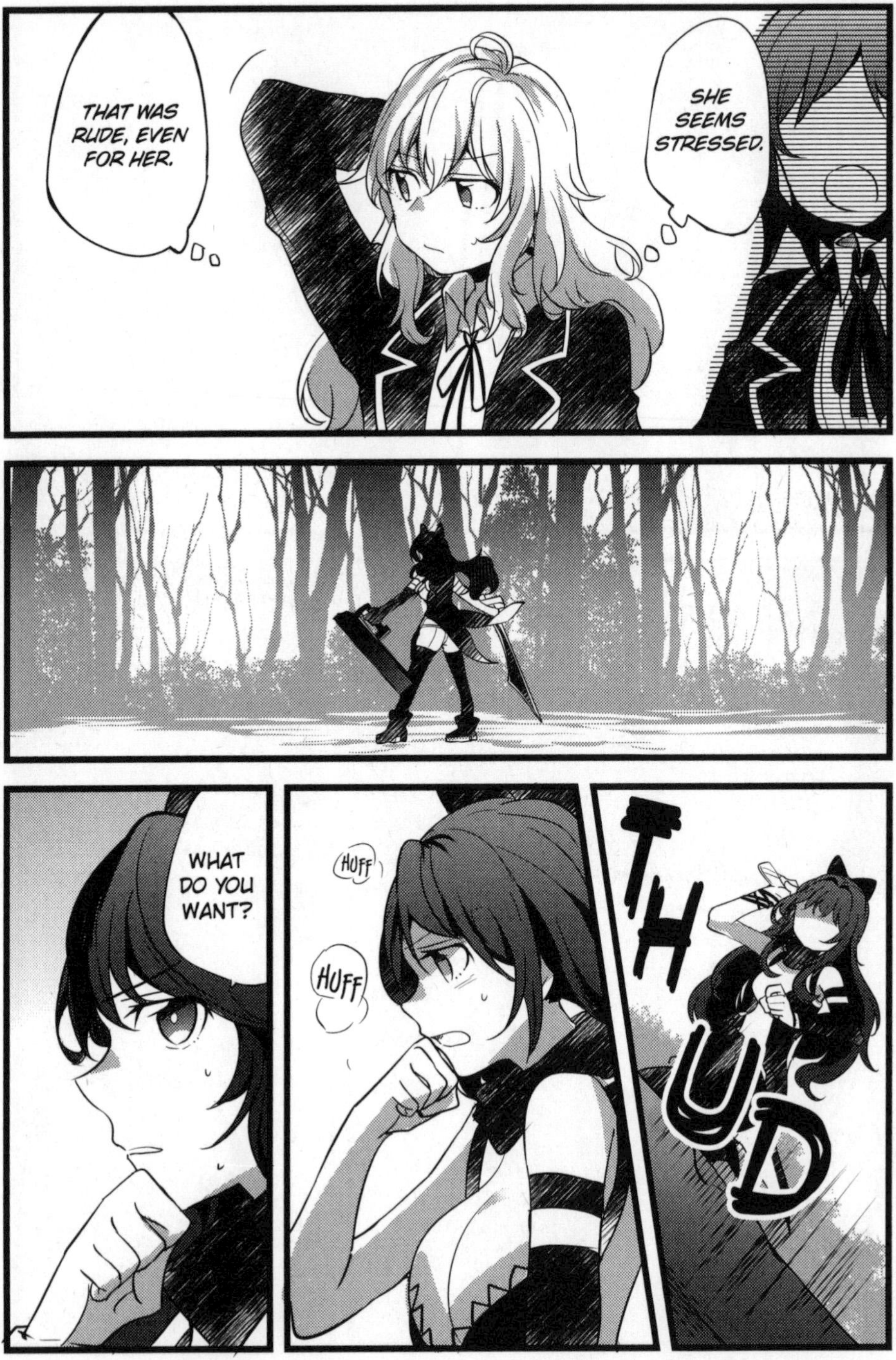
SHE SEEMS STRESSED.
THAT WAS RUDE, EVEN FOR HER.
THUD
HUFF
HUFF
WHAT DO YOU WANT?

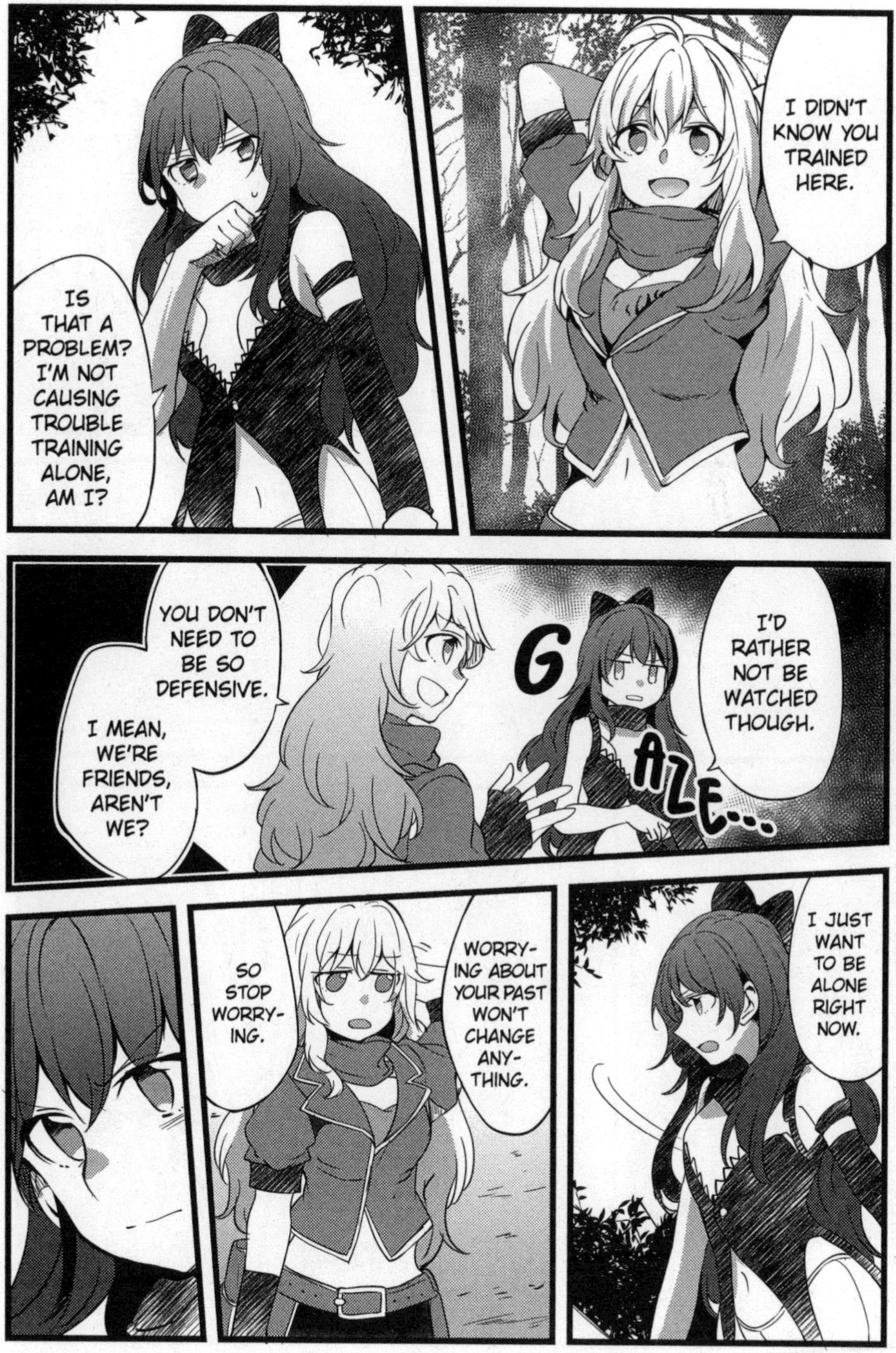
I DIDN'T KNOW YOU TRAINED HERE.
IS THAT A PROBLEM? I'M NOT CAUSING TROUBLE TRAINING ALONE, AM I?
I'D RATHER NOT BE WATCHED THOUGH.
GAZE...
YOU DON'T NEED TO BE SO DEFENSIVE.
I MEAN, WE'RE FRIENDS, AREN'T WE?
I JUST WANT TO BE ALONE RIGHT NOW.
WORRY-ING ABOUT YOUR PAST WON'T CHANGE ANY-THING.
SO STOP WORRY-ING.

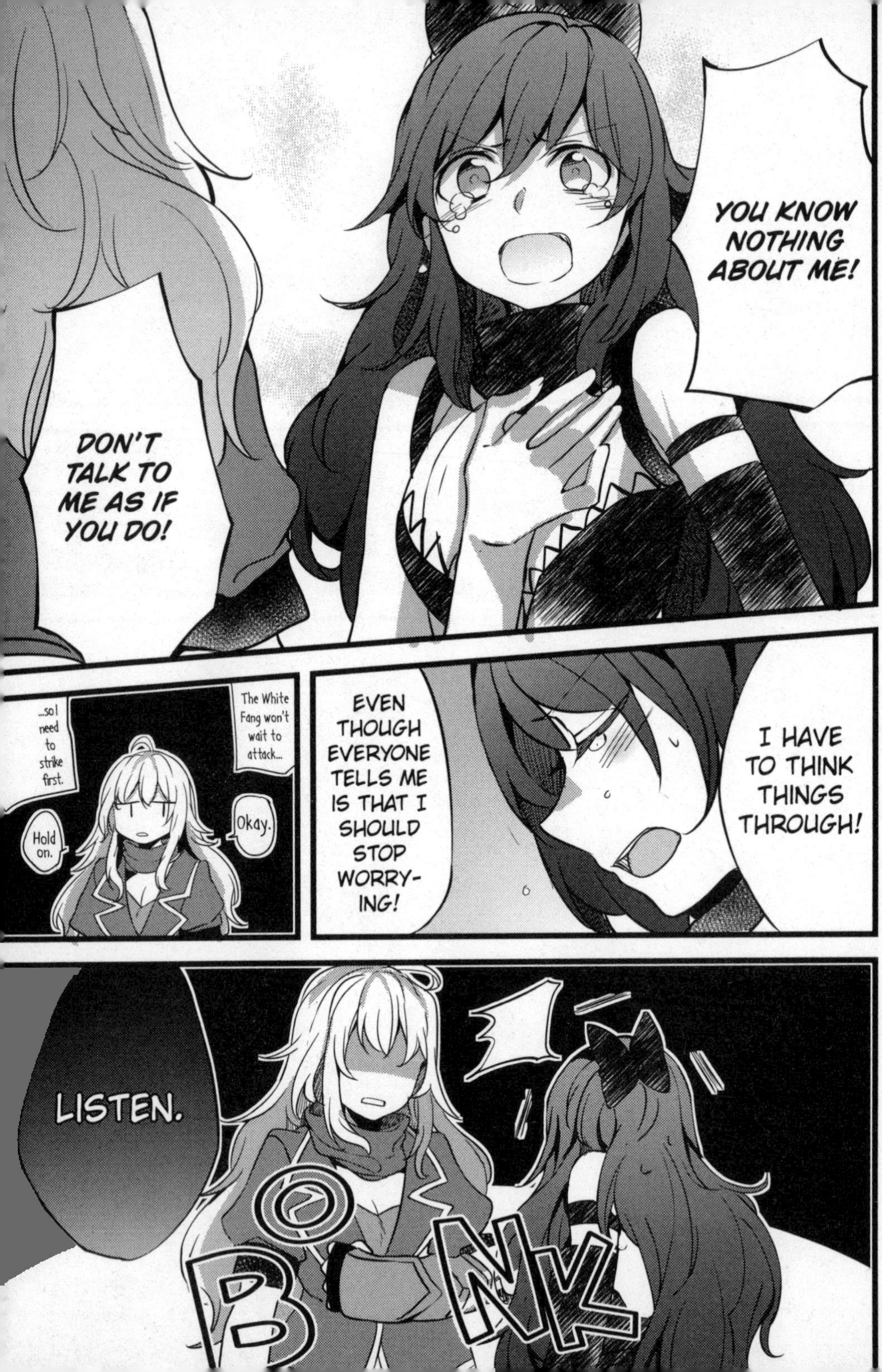
YOU KNOW NOTHING ABOUT ME!
DON'T TALK TO ME AS IF YOU DO!
I HAVE TO THINK THINGS THROUGH!
EVEN THOUGH EVERYONE TELLS ME IS THAT I SHOULD STOP WORRY-ING!
The White Fang won't wait to attack...
...so I need to strike first.
Okay.
Hold on.
LISTEN.
BONK

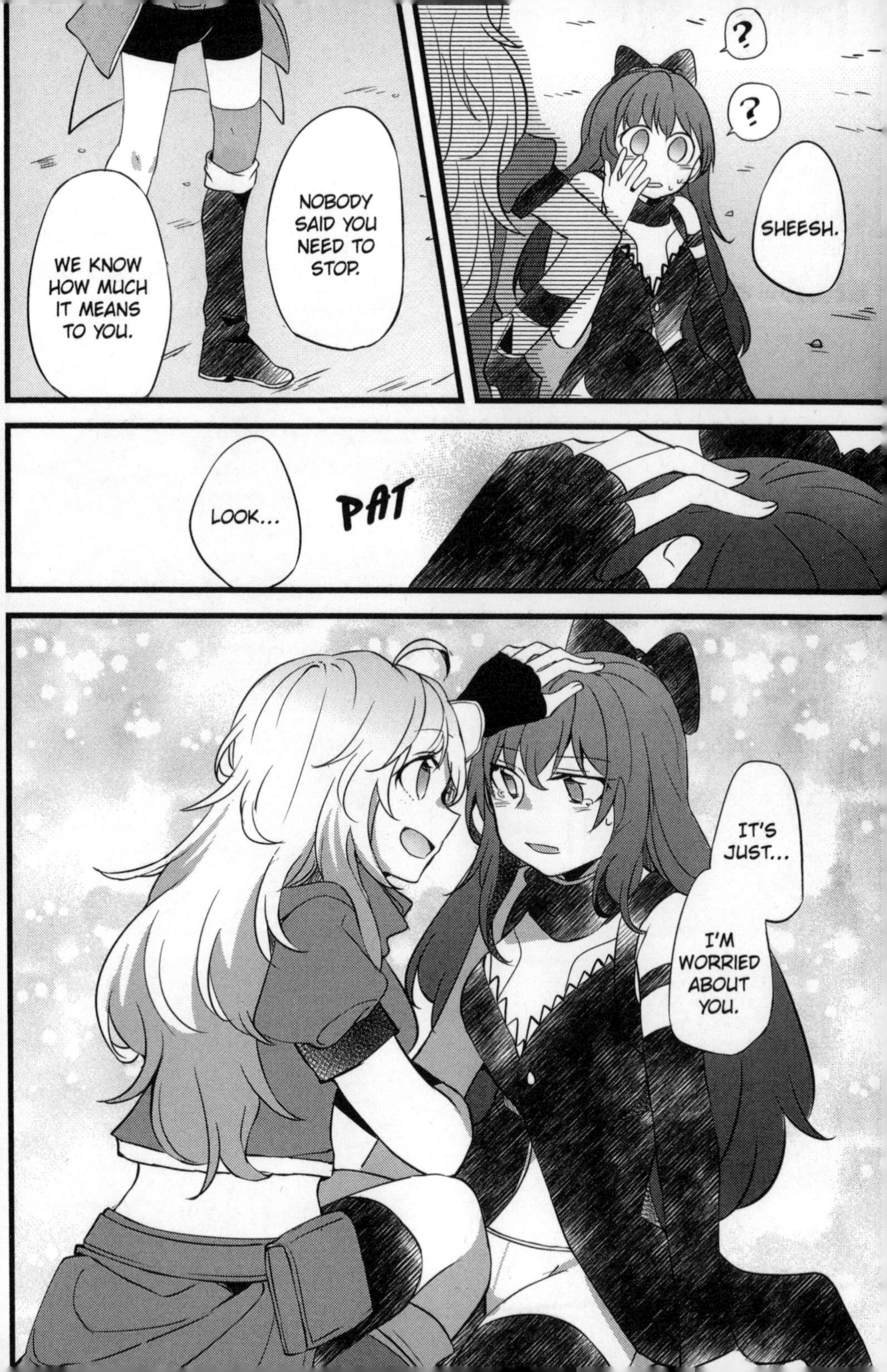
?
?
SHEESH.
NOBODY SAID YOU NEED TO STOP.
WE KNOW HOW MUCH IT MEANS TO YOU.
PAT
LOOK...
IT'S JUST...
I'M WORRIED ABOUT YOU.

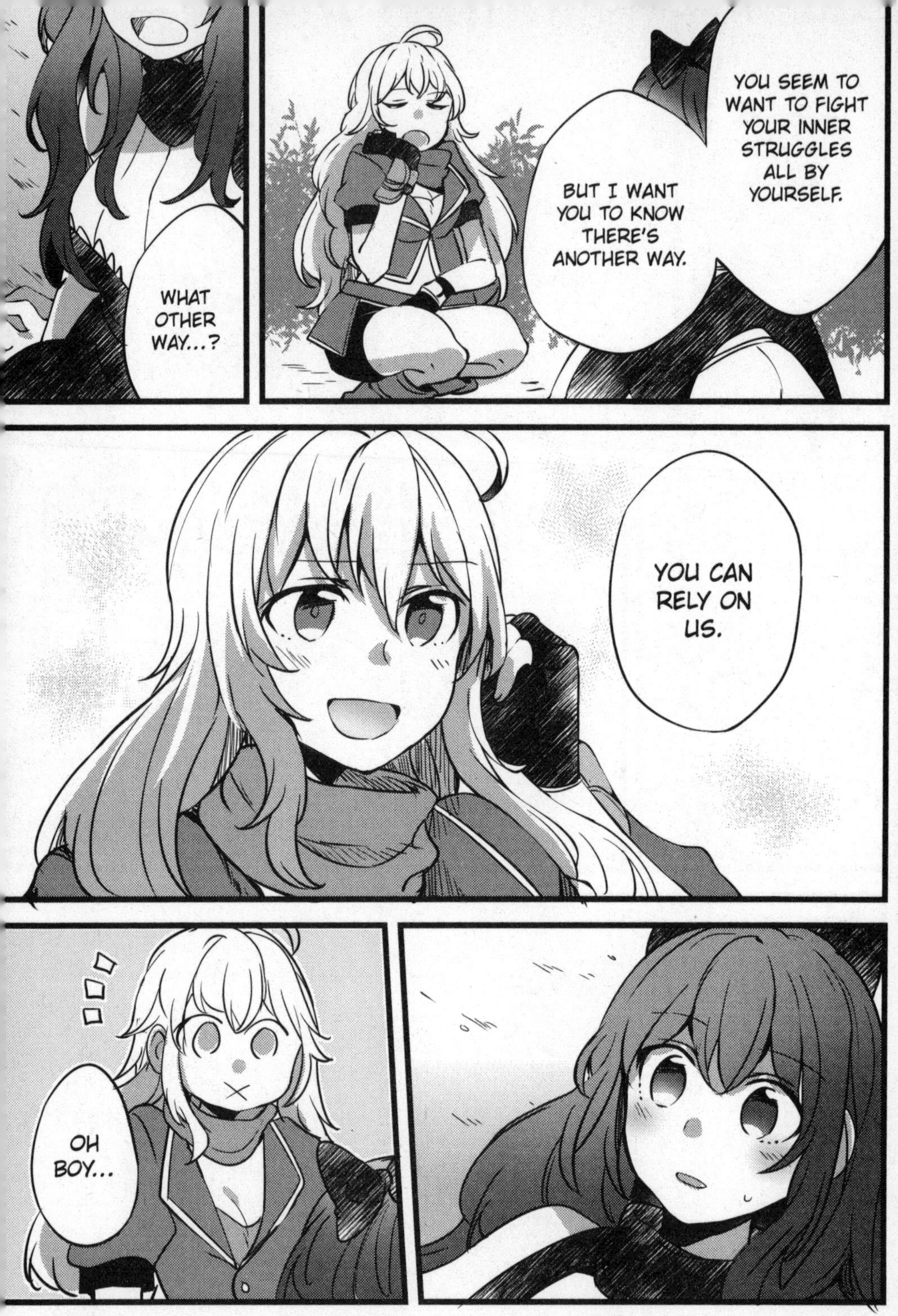
YOU SEEM TO WANT TO FIGHT YOUR INNER STRUGGLES ALL BY YOURSELF.
BUT I WANT YOU TO KNOW THERE'S ANOTHER WAY.
WHAT OTHER WAY...?
YOU CAN RELY ON US.
OH BOY...

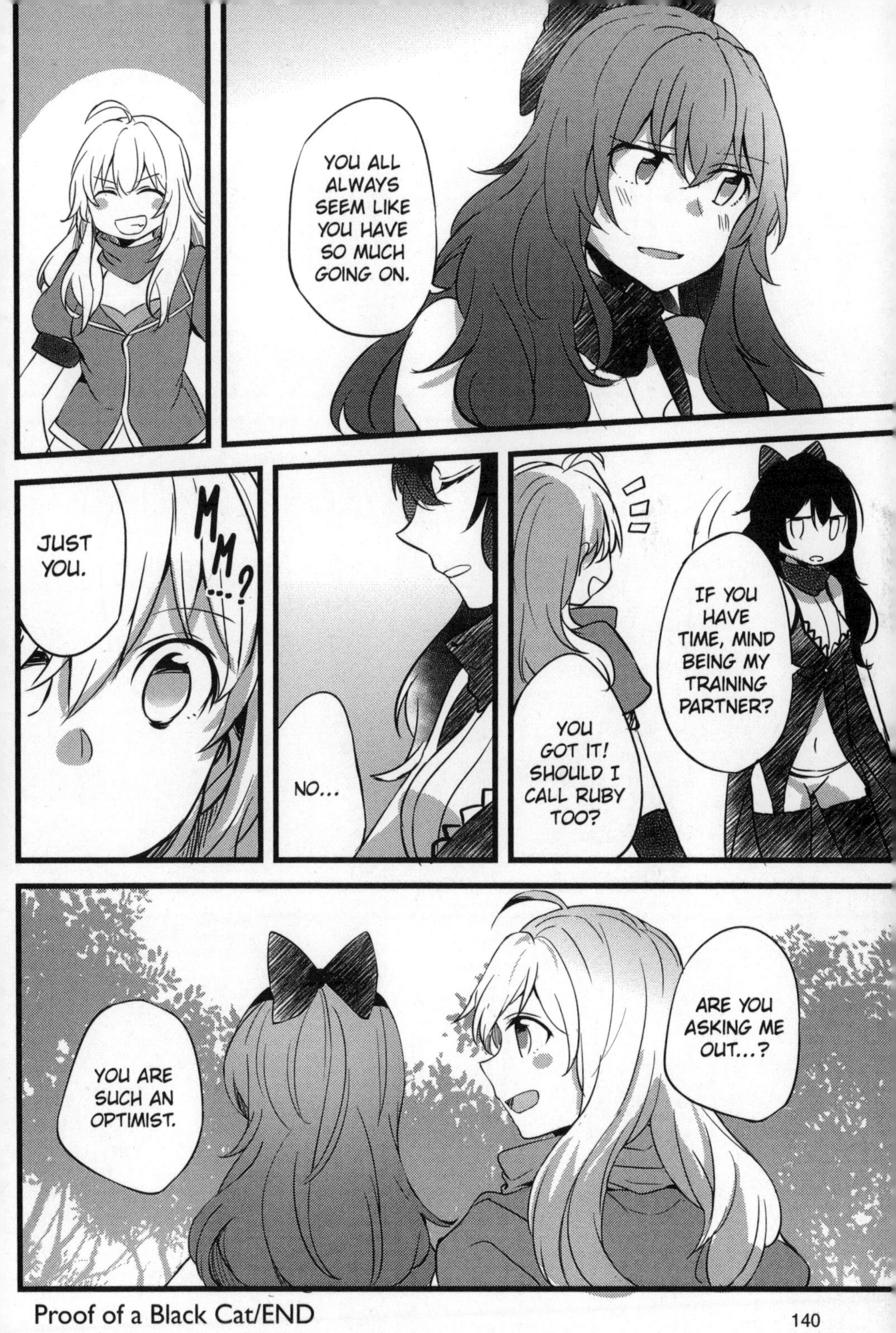
YOU ALL ALWAYS SEEM LIKE YOU HAVE SO MUCH GOING ON.
IF YOU HAVE TIME, MIND BEING MY TRAINING PARTNER?
YOU GOT IT! SHOULD I CALL RUBY TOO?
NO...
MM...?
JUST YOU.
ARE YOU ASKING ME OUT...?
YOU ARE SUCH AN OPTIMIST.

Proof of a Black Cat/END

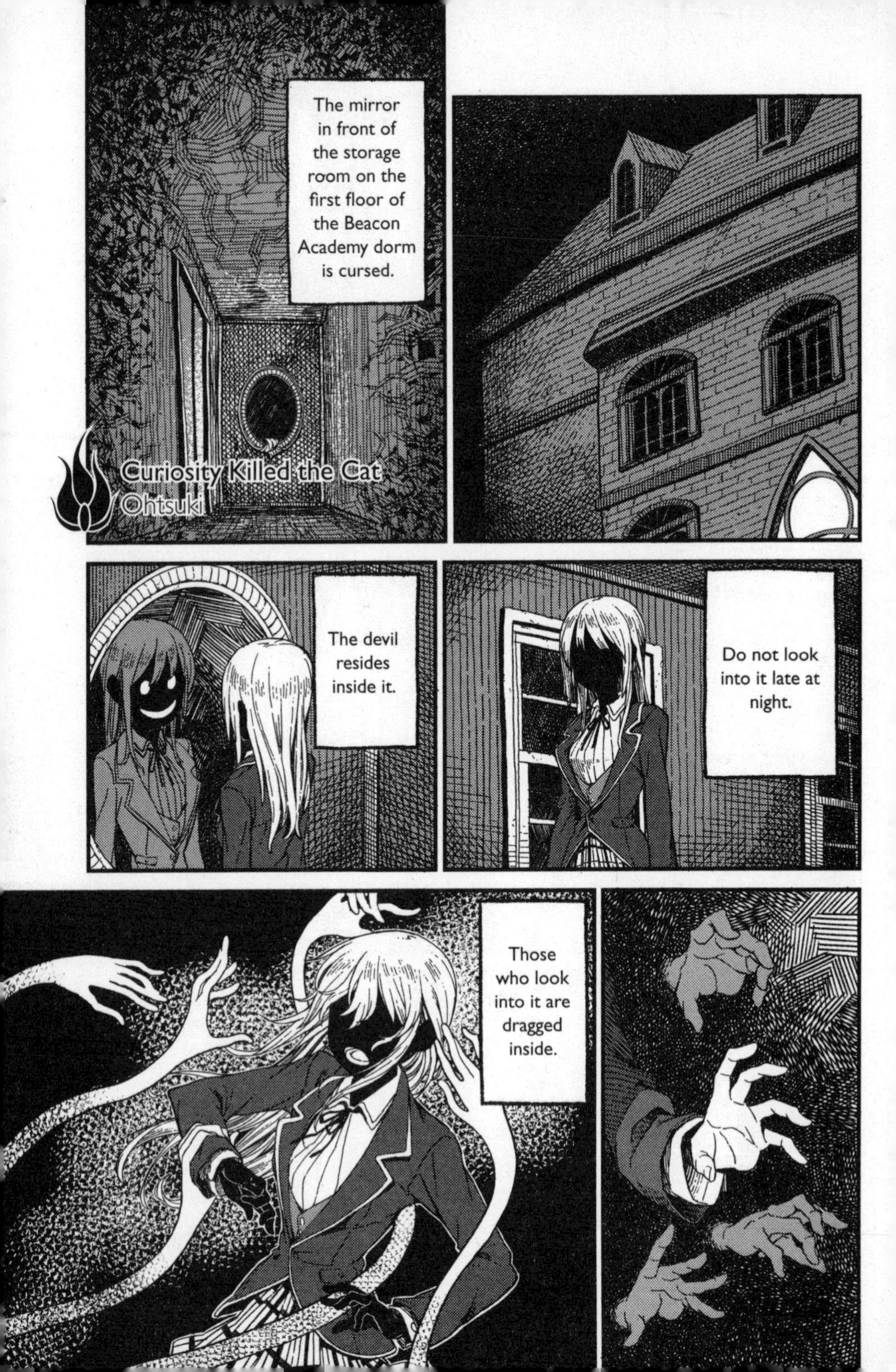
The mirror in front of the storage room on the first floor of the Beacon Academy dorm is cursed.
Curiosity Killed the Cat
Ohtsuki
Do not look into it late at night.
The devil resides inside it.
Those who look into it are dragged inside.

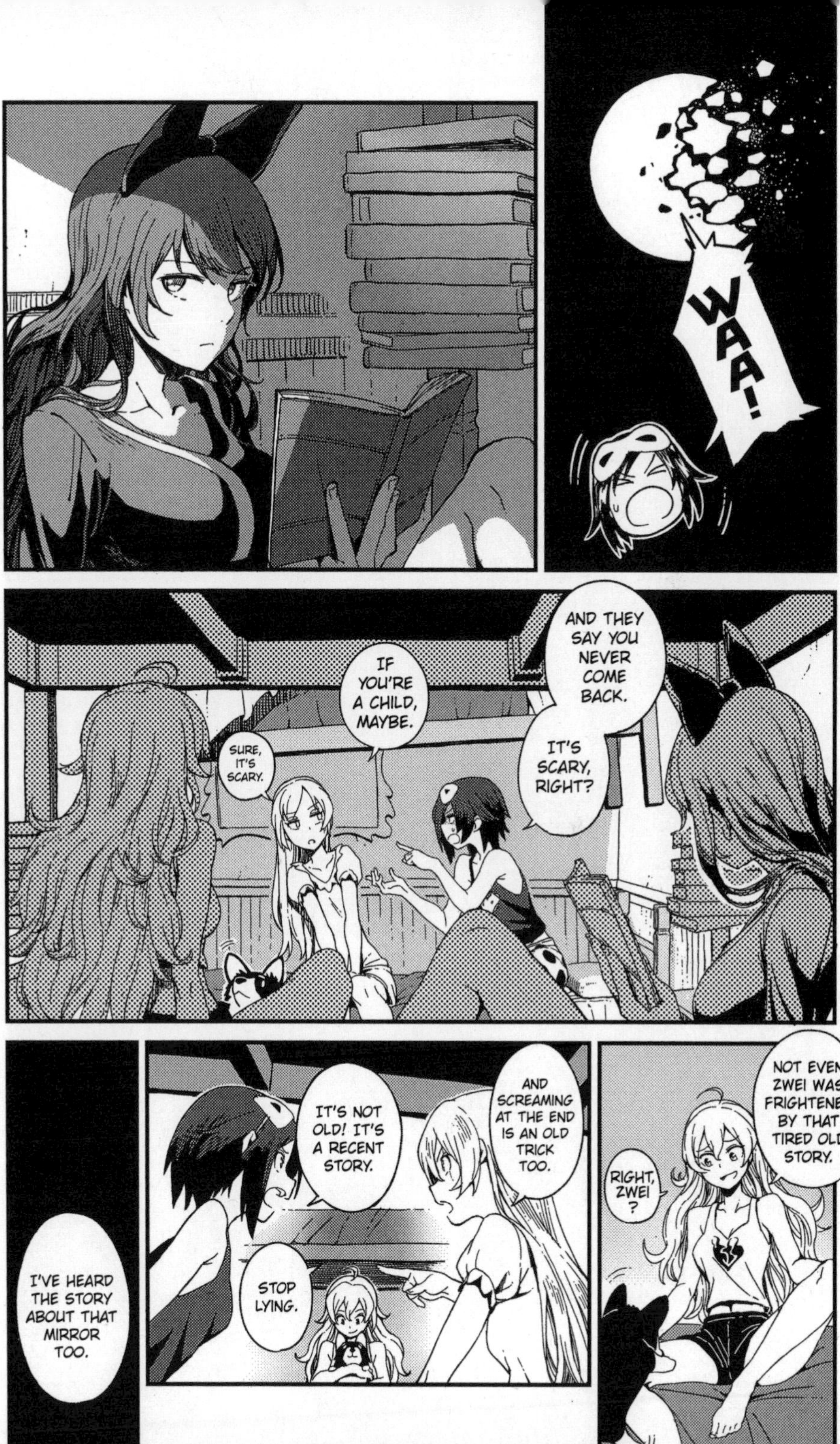
WAA!
AND THEY SAY YOU NEVER COME BACK.
IT'S SCARY, RIGHT?
IF YOU'RE A CHILD, MAYBE.
SURE, IT'S SCARY.
NOT EVEN ZWEI WAS FRIGHTENED BY THAT TIRED OLD STORY.
RIGHT, ZWEI?
AND SCREAMING AT THE END IS AN OLD TRICK TOO.
IT'S NOT OLD! IT'S A RECENT STORY.
STOP LYING.
I'VE HEARD THE STORY ABOUT THAT MIRROR TOO.

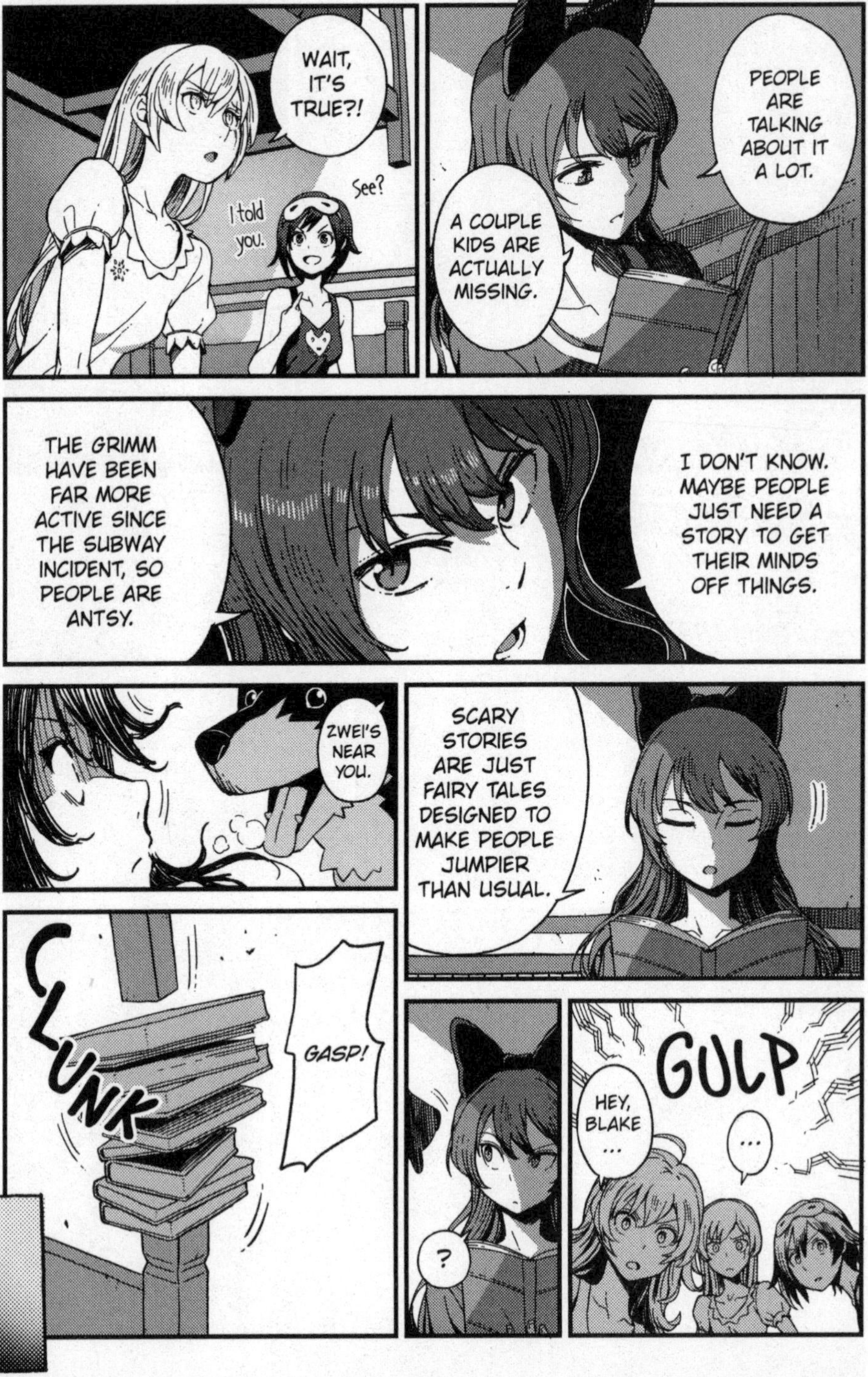
PEOPLE ARE TALKING ABOUT IT A LOT.
A COUPLE KIDS ARE ACTUALLY MISSING.
WAIT, IT'S TRUE?!
See?
I told you.
I DON'T KNOW. MAYBE PEOPLE JUST NEED A STORY TO GET THEIR MINDS OFF THINGS.
THE GRIMM HAVE BEEN FAR MORE ACTIVE SINCE THE SUBWAY INCIDENT, SO PEOPLE ARE ANTSY.
SCARY STORIES ARE JUST FAIRY TALES DESIGNED TO MAKE PEOPLE JUMPIER THAN USUAL.
ZWEI'S NEAR YOU.
GULP
HEY, BLAKE ...
...
?
CLUNK
GASP!

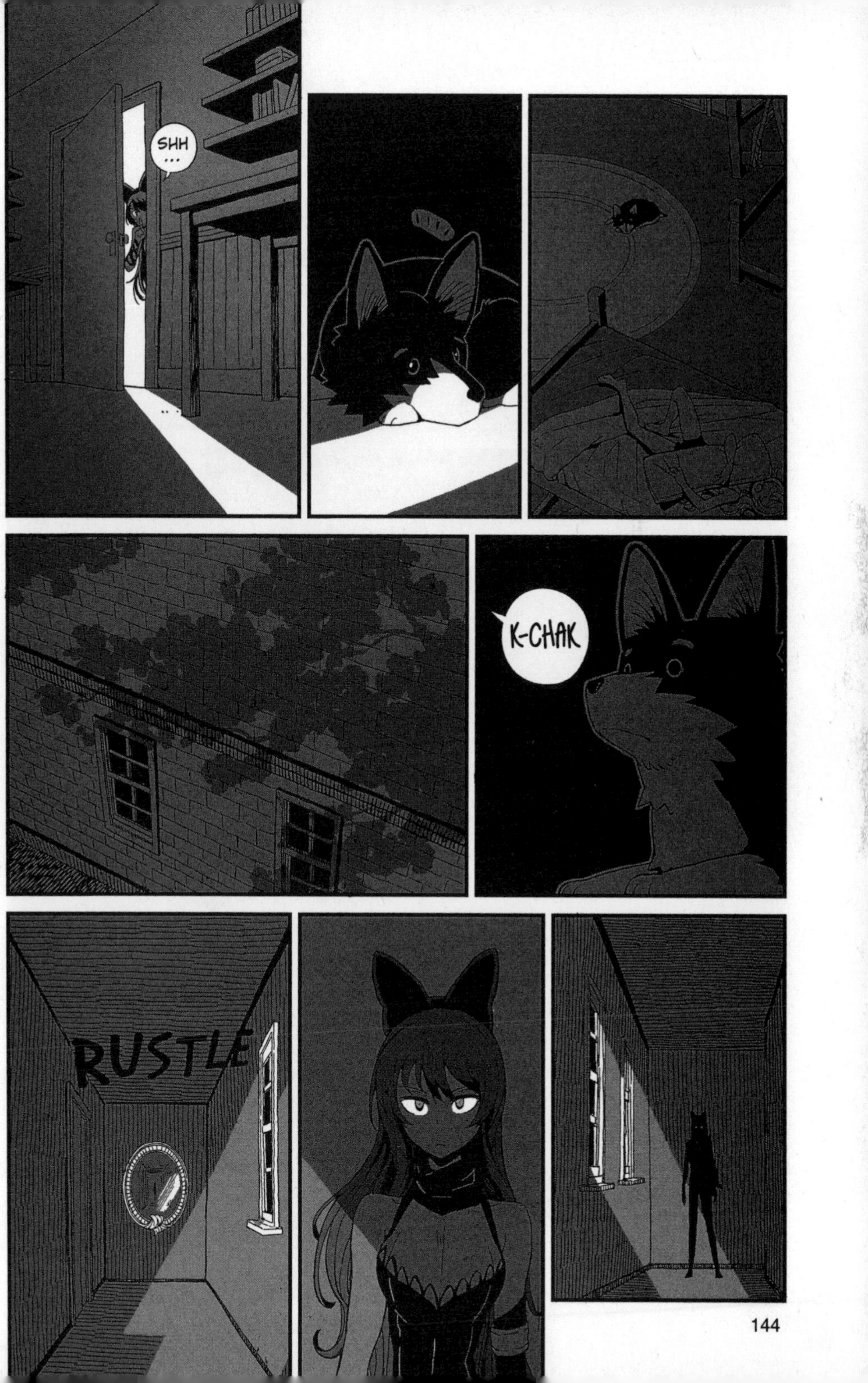
SHH...
K-CHAK
RUSTLE

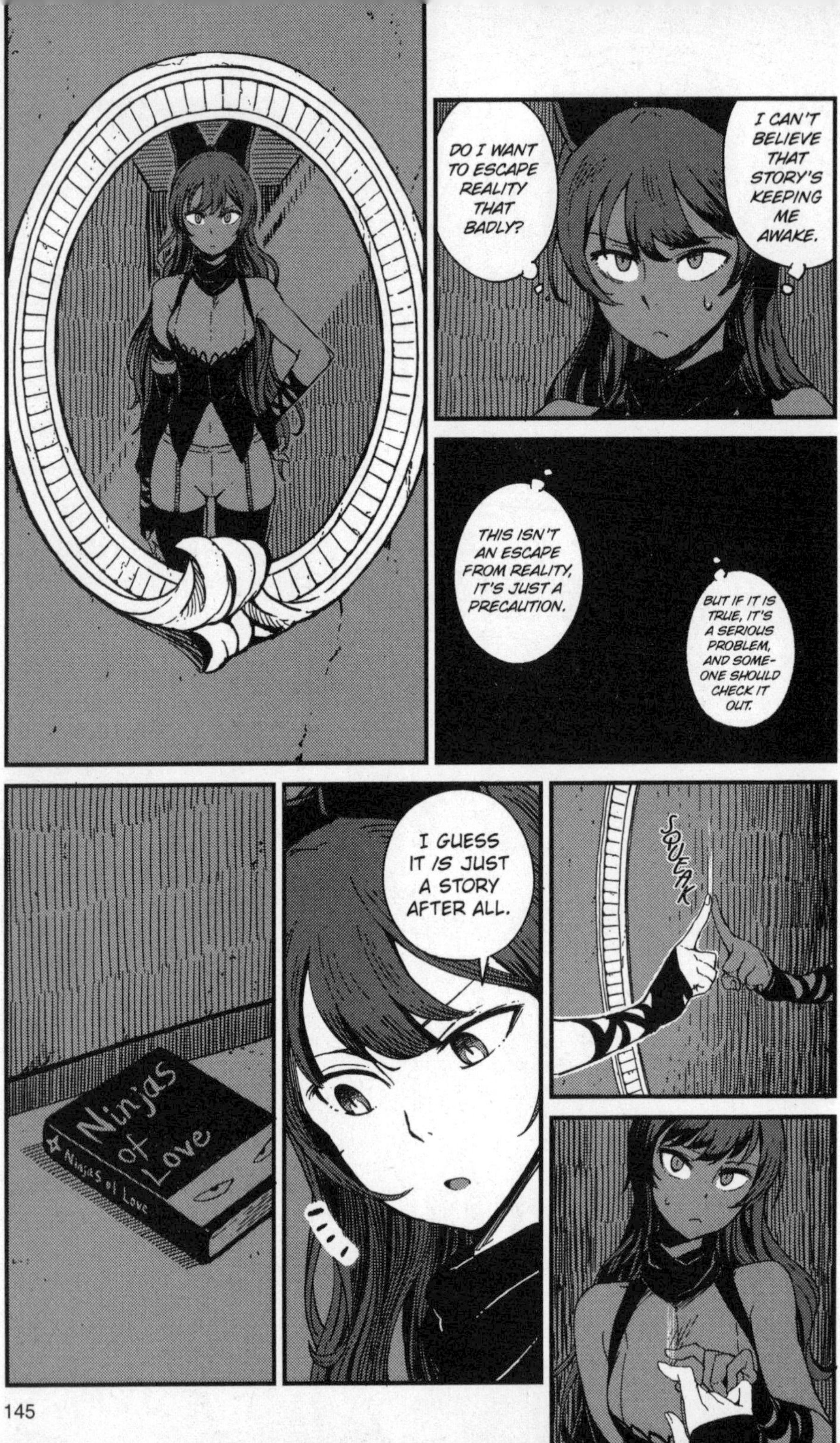
I CAN'T BELIEVE THAT STORY'S KEEPING ME AWAKE.
DO I WANT TO ESCAPE REALITY THAT BADLY?
THIS ISN'T AN ESCAPE FROM REALITY, IT'S JUST A PRECAUTION.
BUT IF IT IS TRUE, IT'S A SERIOUS PROBLEM, AND SOME-ONE SHOULD CHECK IT OUT.
SQUEAK
I GUESS IT IS JUST A STORY AFTER ALL.
Ninjas of Love
Ninjas of Love

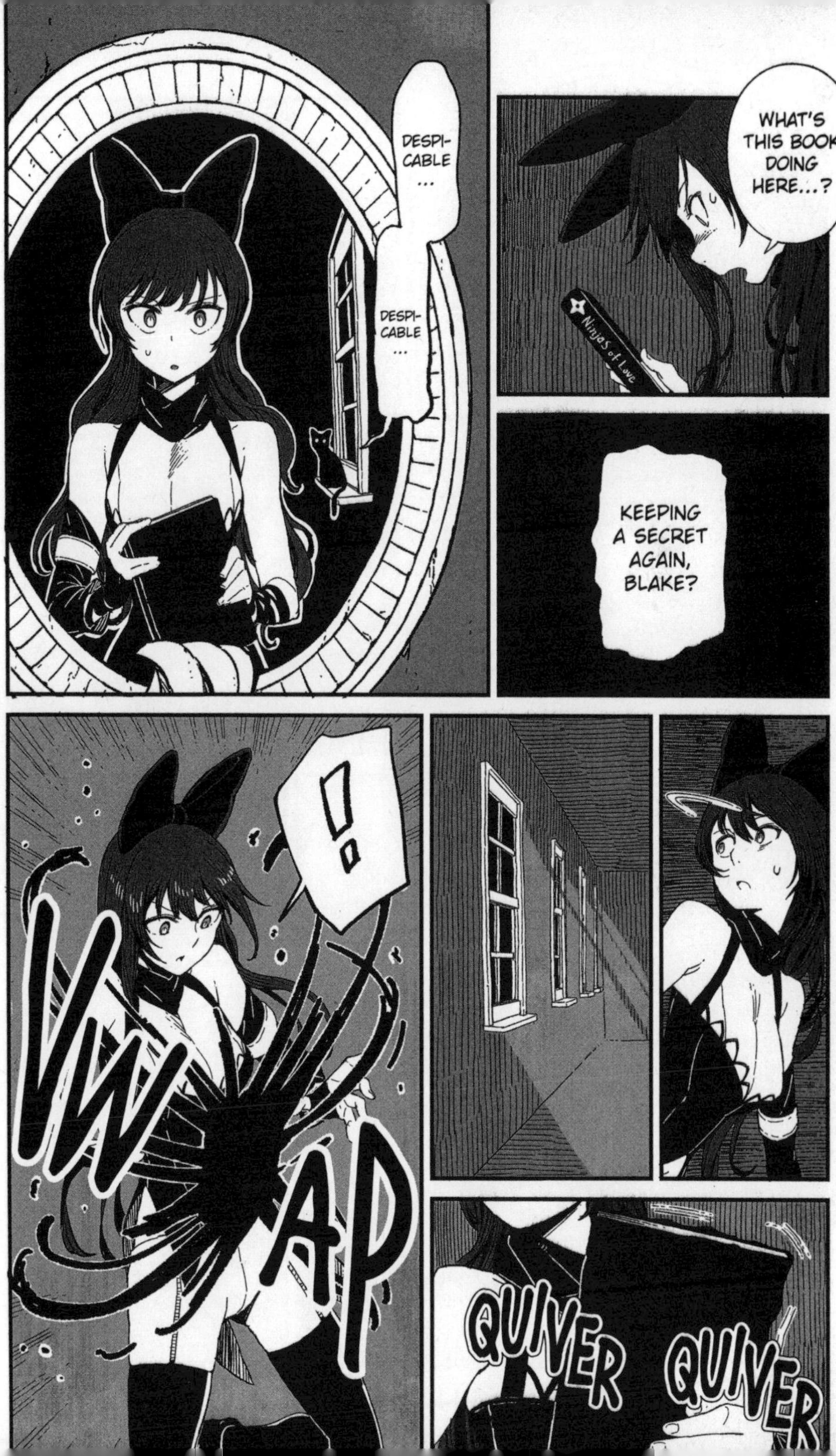
WHAT'S THIS BOOK DOING HERE...?
Ninjas of Love
KEEPING A SECRET AGAIN, BLAKE?
DESPI-CABLE...
DESPI-CABLE...
QUIVER QUIVER
!?
WAP

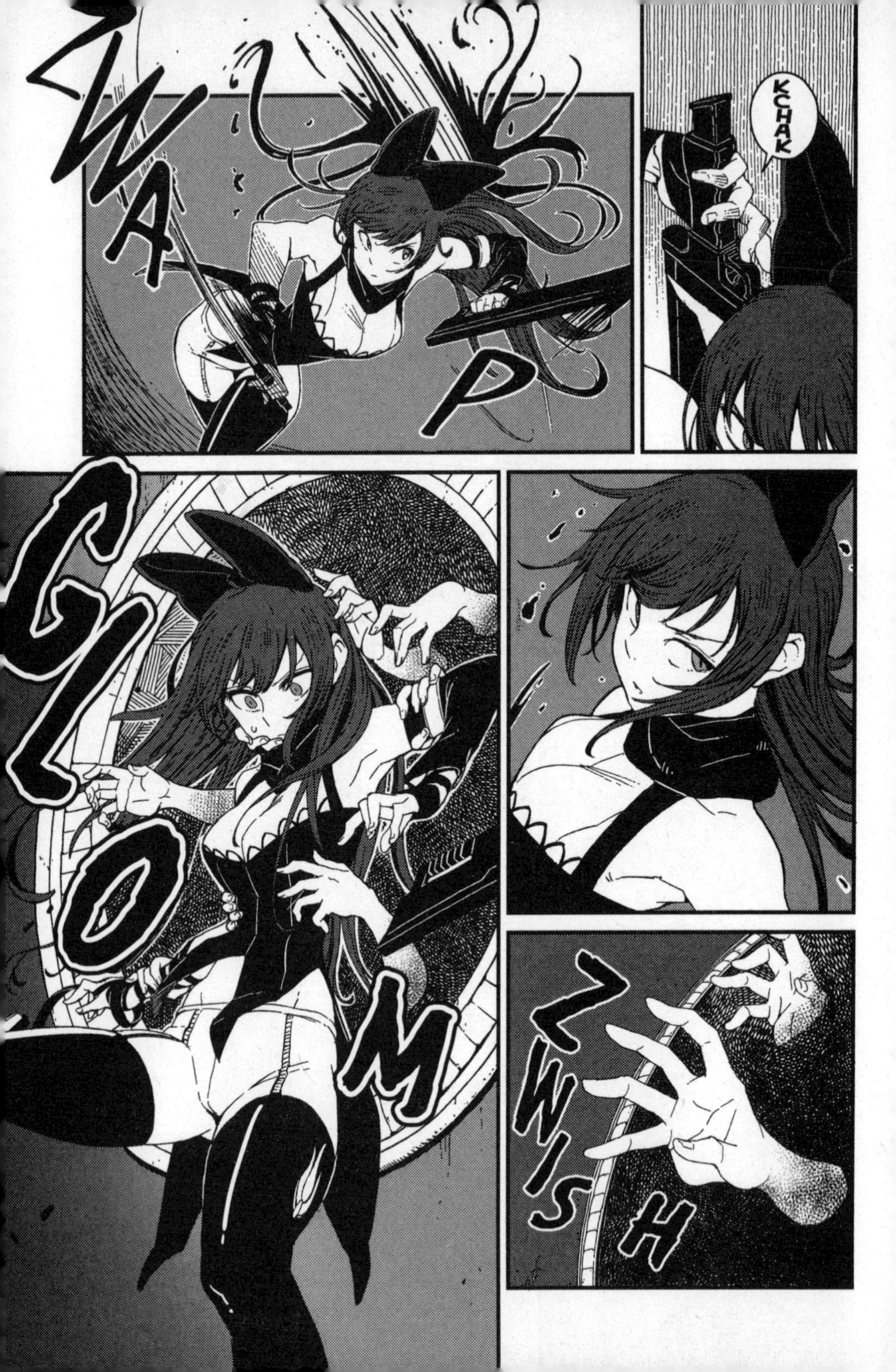
KCHAK
ZWAP
ZWISH
GLOM

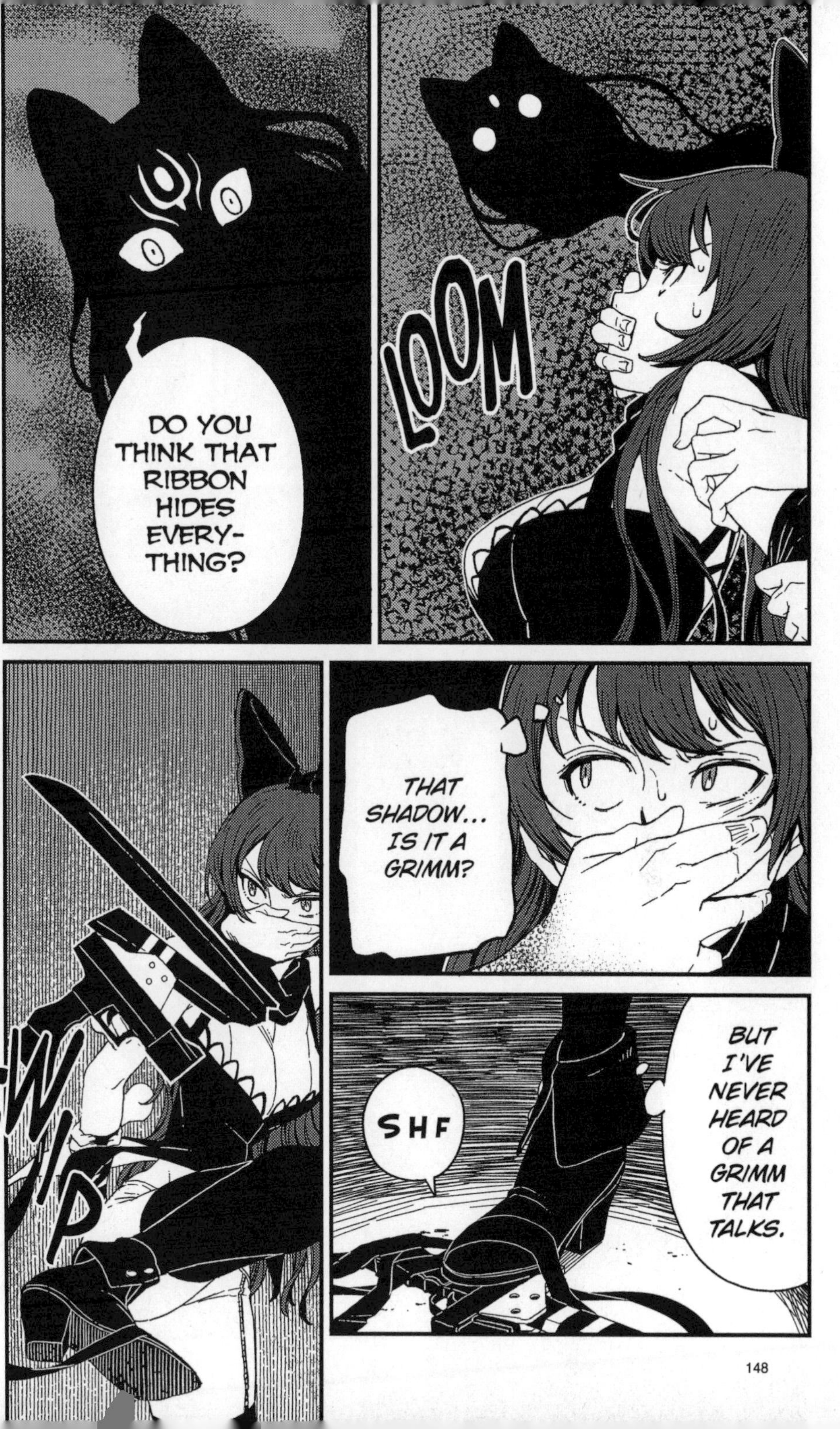
LOOM
DO YOU THINK THAT RIBBON HIDES EVERY-THING?
THAT SHADOW... IS IT A GRIMM?
BUT I'VE NEVER HEARD OF A GRIMM THAT TALKS.
SHF
FWIP

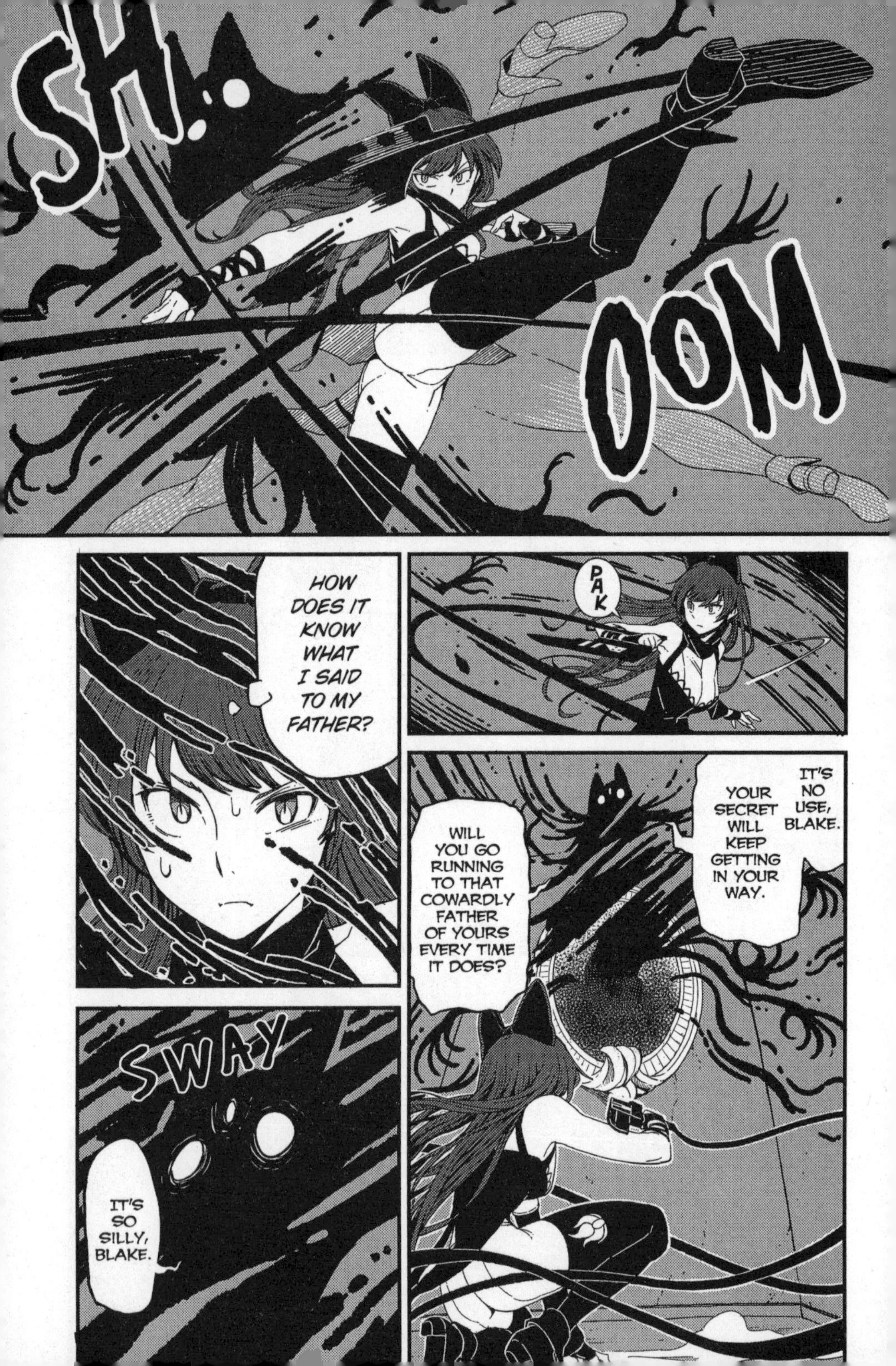

SH
OOM
PAK
HOW DOES IT KNOW WHAT I SAID TO MY FATHER?
IT'S NO USE, BLAKE.
YOUR SECRET WILL KEEP GETTING IN YOUR WAY.
WILL YOU GO RUNNING TO THAT COWARDLY FATHER OF YOURS EVERY TIME IT DOES?
SWAY
IT'S SO SILLY, BLAKE.

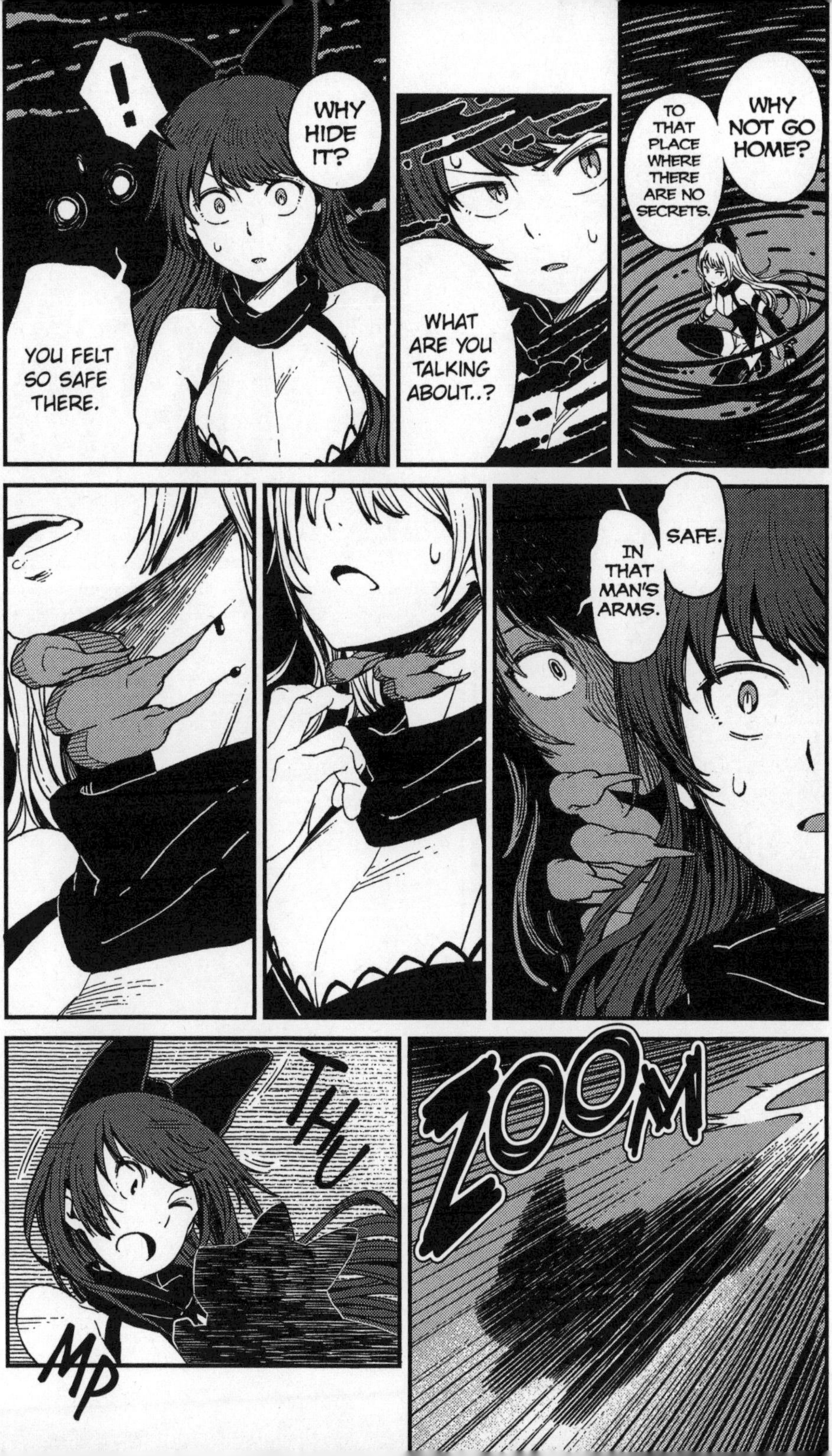
WHY NOT GO HOME?
TO THAT PLACE WHERE THERE ARE NO SECRETS.
WHAT ARE YOU TALKING ABOUT..?
!
WHY HIDE IT?
YOU FELT SO SAFE THERE.
SAFE.
IN THAT MAN'S ARMS.
ZOOM
THUMP

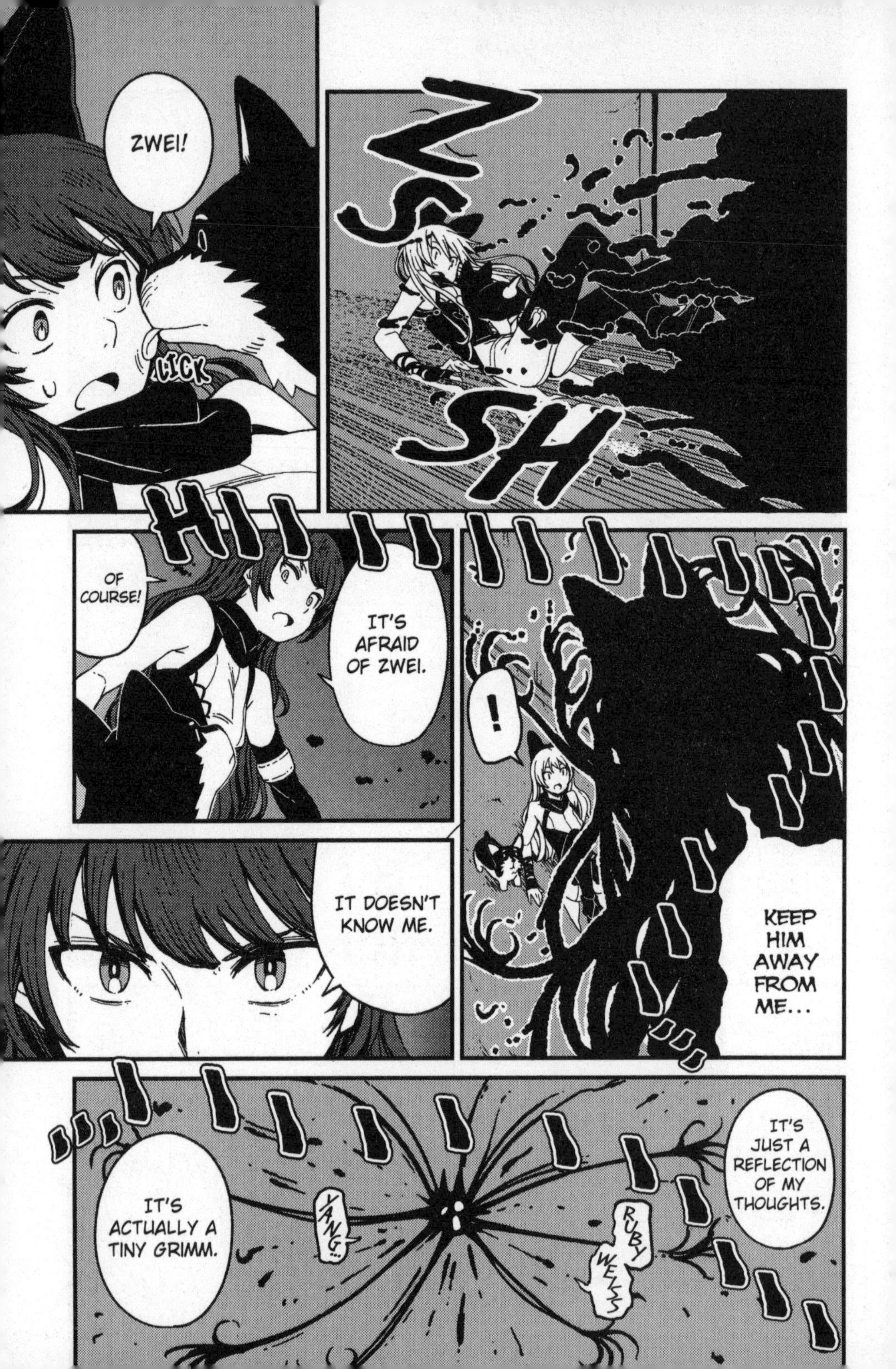
ZSSSH
ZWEI!
LICK
HIIIIIIIIIIIIIII
!
KEEP HIM AWAY FROM ME...
OF COURSE!
IT'S AFRAID OF ZWEI.
IT DOESN'T KNOW ME.
IT'S JUST A REFLECTION OF MY THOUGHTS.
RUBY
WEISS
YANG...
IT'S ACTUALLY A TINY GRIMM.

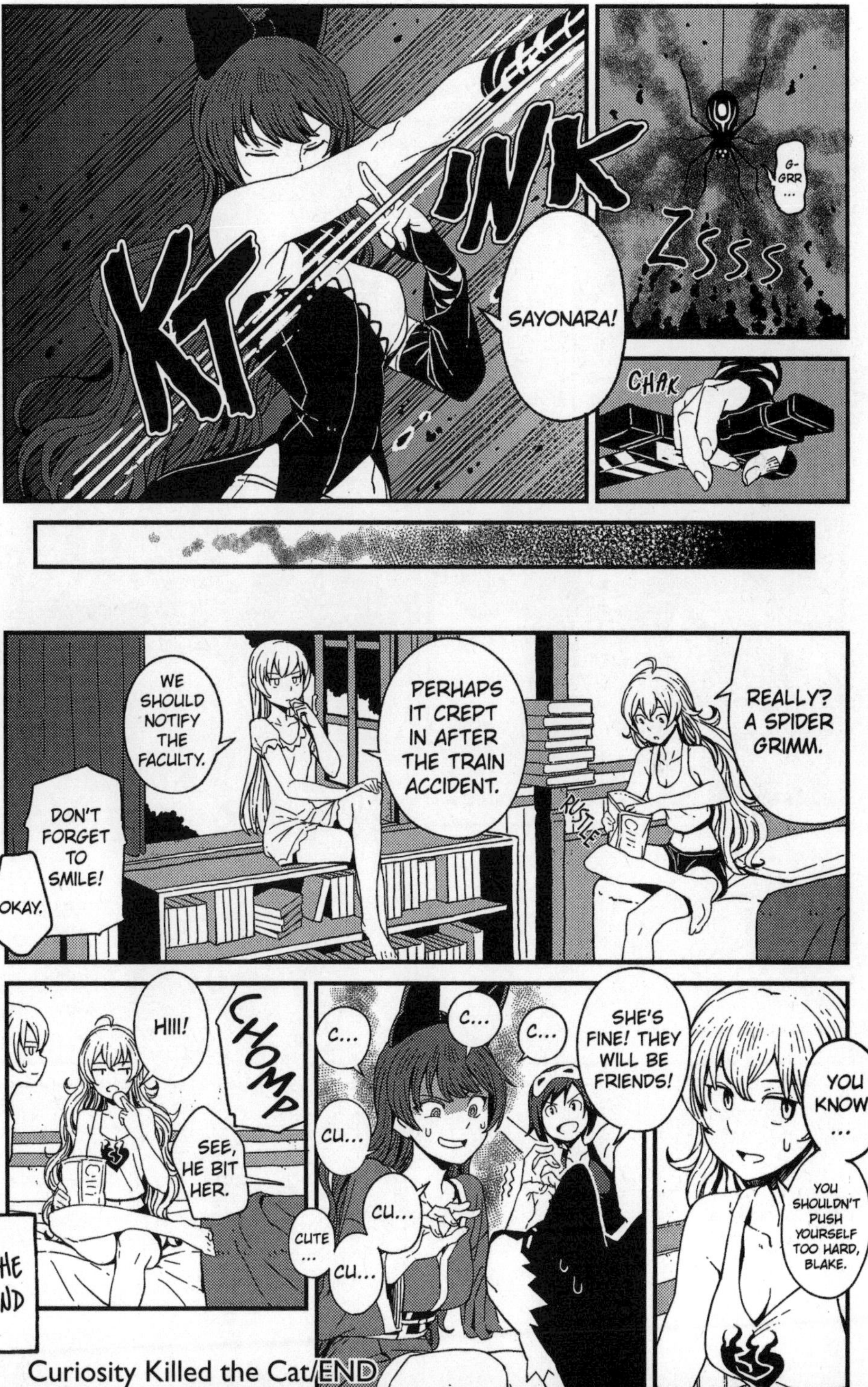
G-GRR...
ZSSS
CHAK
KTINK
SAYONARA!
REALLY? A SPIDER GRIMM.
RUSTLE
PERHAPS IT CREPT IN AFTER THE TRAIN ACCIDENT.
WE SHOULD NOTIFY THE FACULTY.
DON'T FORGET TO SMILE!
OKAY.
YOU KNOW...
YOU SHOULDN'T PUSH YOURSELF TOO HARD, BLAKE.
SHE'S FINE! THEY WILL BE FRIENDS!
C...
C...
C...
CU...
CU...
CUTE...
CU...
CHOMP
HIII!
SEE, HE BIT HER.
THE END

Curiosity Killed the Cat/END

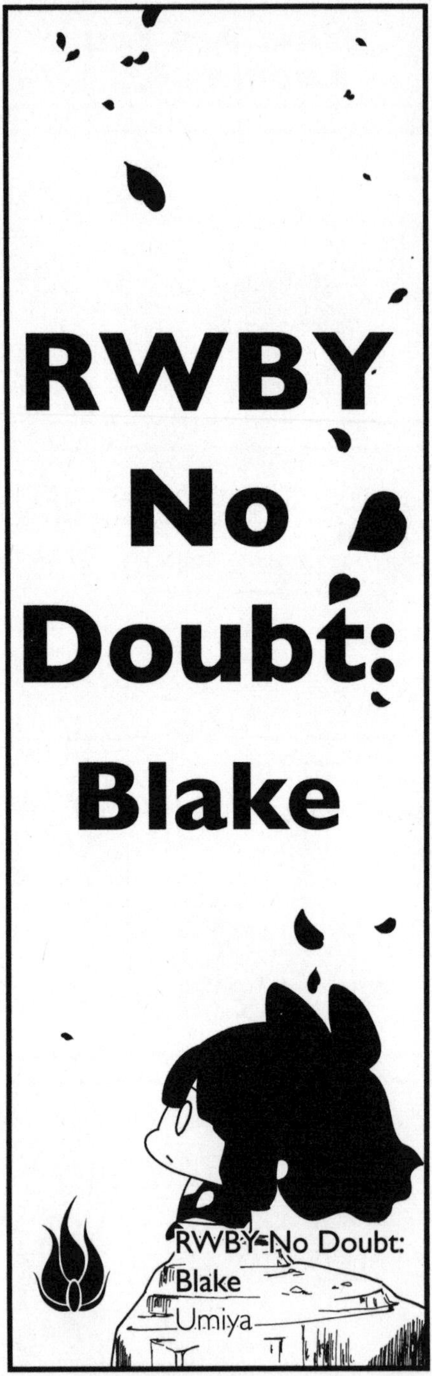
RWBY
No
Doubt:
Blake
RWBY No Doubt:
Blake
Umiya

Help Me

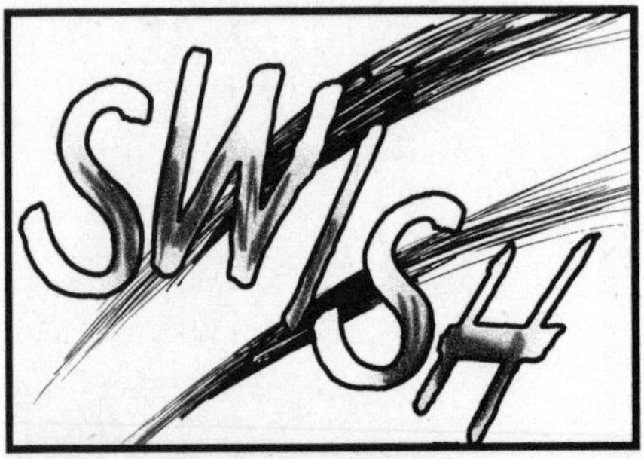
SWISH

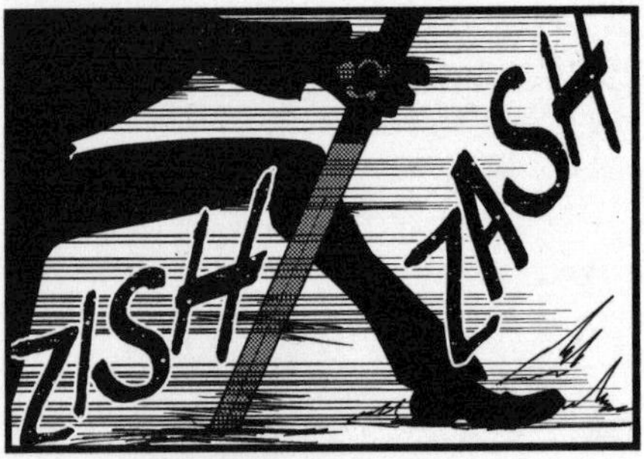
ZASH
ZISH

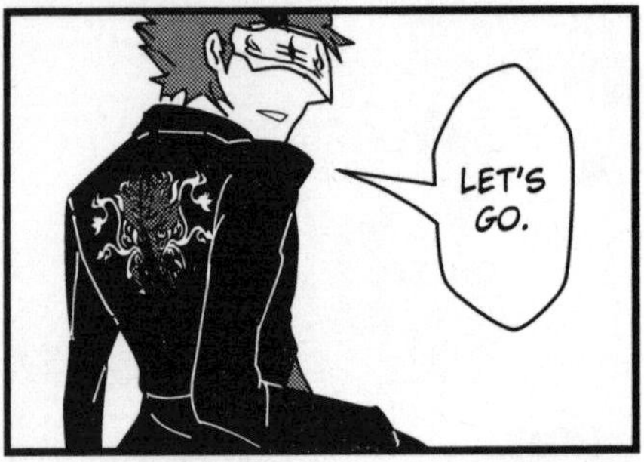
LET'S GO.

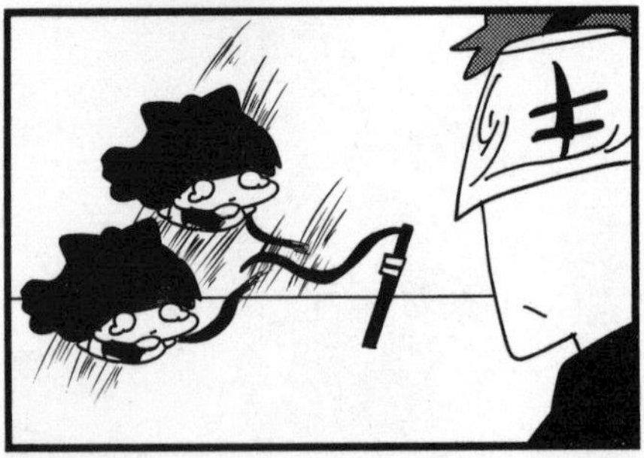

Clones

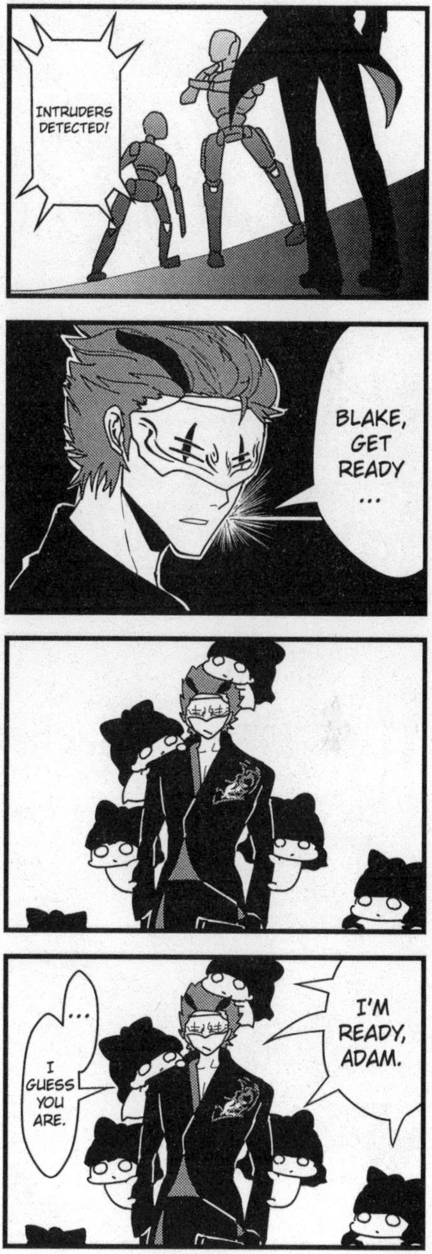
INTRUDERS DETECTED!
BLAKE, GET READY ...
I'M READY, ADAM.
...
I GUESS YOU ARE.

What Are You Looking At?

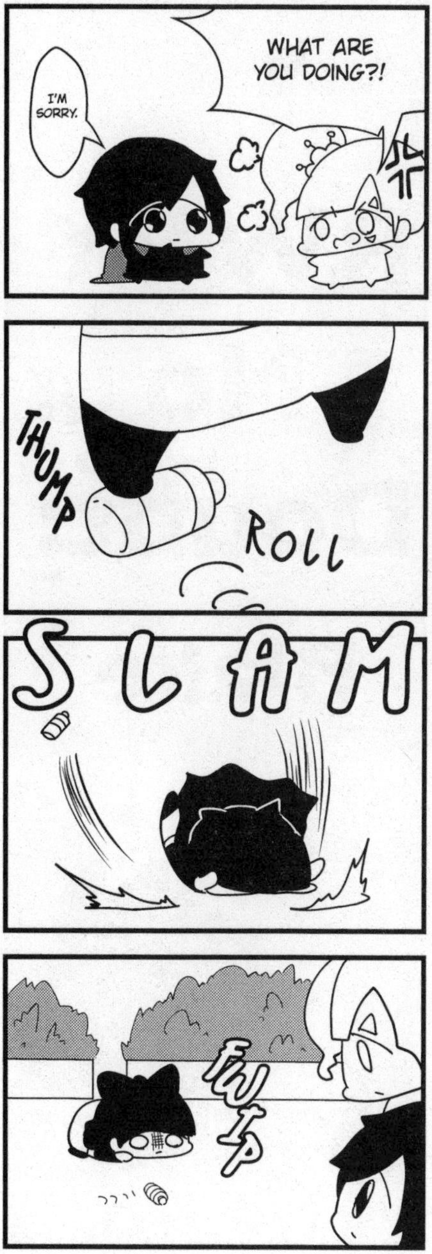
WHAT ARE YOU DOING?!
I'M SORRY.
THUMP
ROLL
SLAM
FWIP

Let's Dance

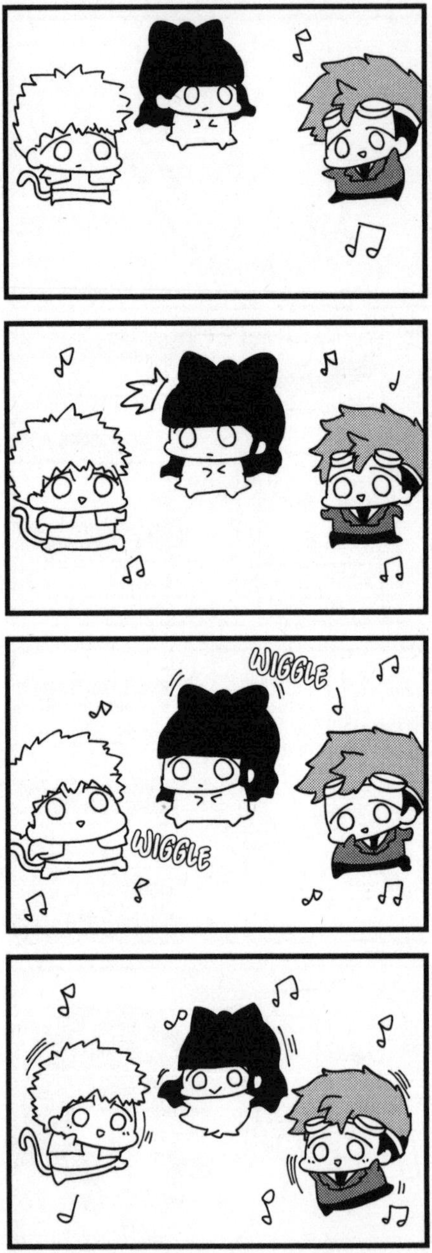
WIGGLE
WIGGLE

Blake Teaser

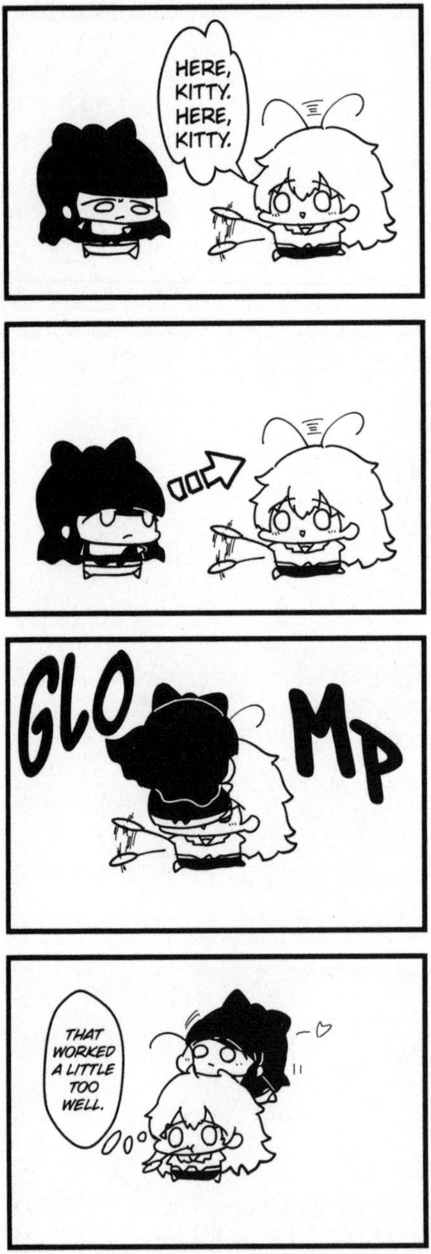
HERE, KITTY. HERE, KITTY.
GLOMP
THAT WORKED A LITTLE TOO WELL.

Love Fish

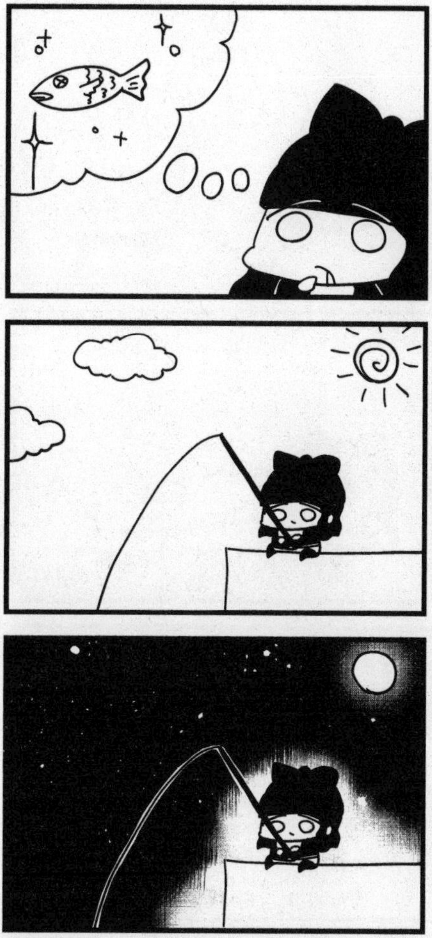
SPLASH
FOUND YOU!

Yang Challenge!

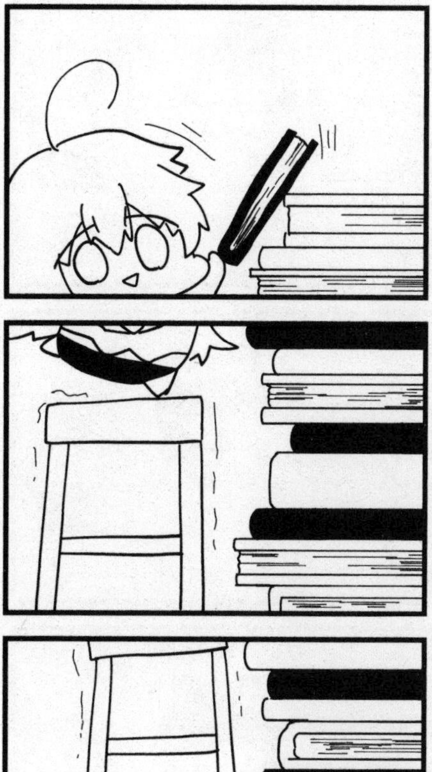
SHE'S SO HEAVY ...

RWBY No Doubt: Blake/END

RWBY
OFFICIAL MANGA ANTHOLOGY
Volume 3

From Shadows

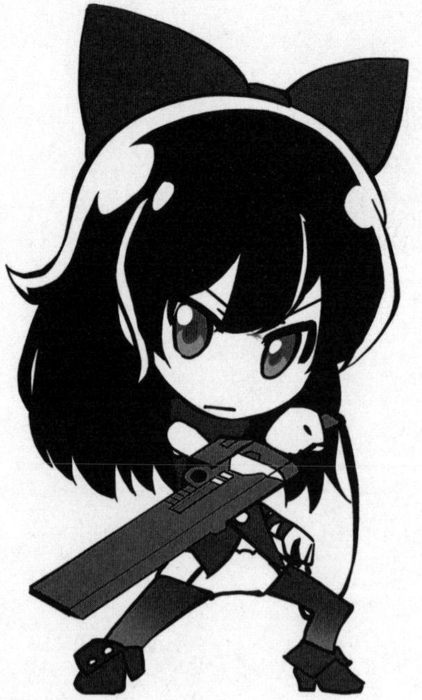

METEO

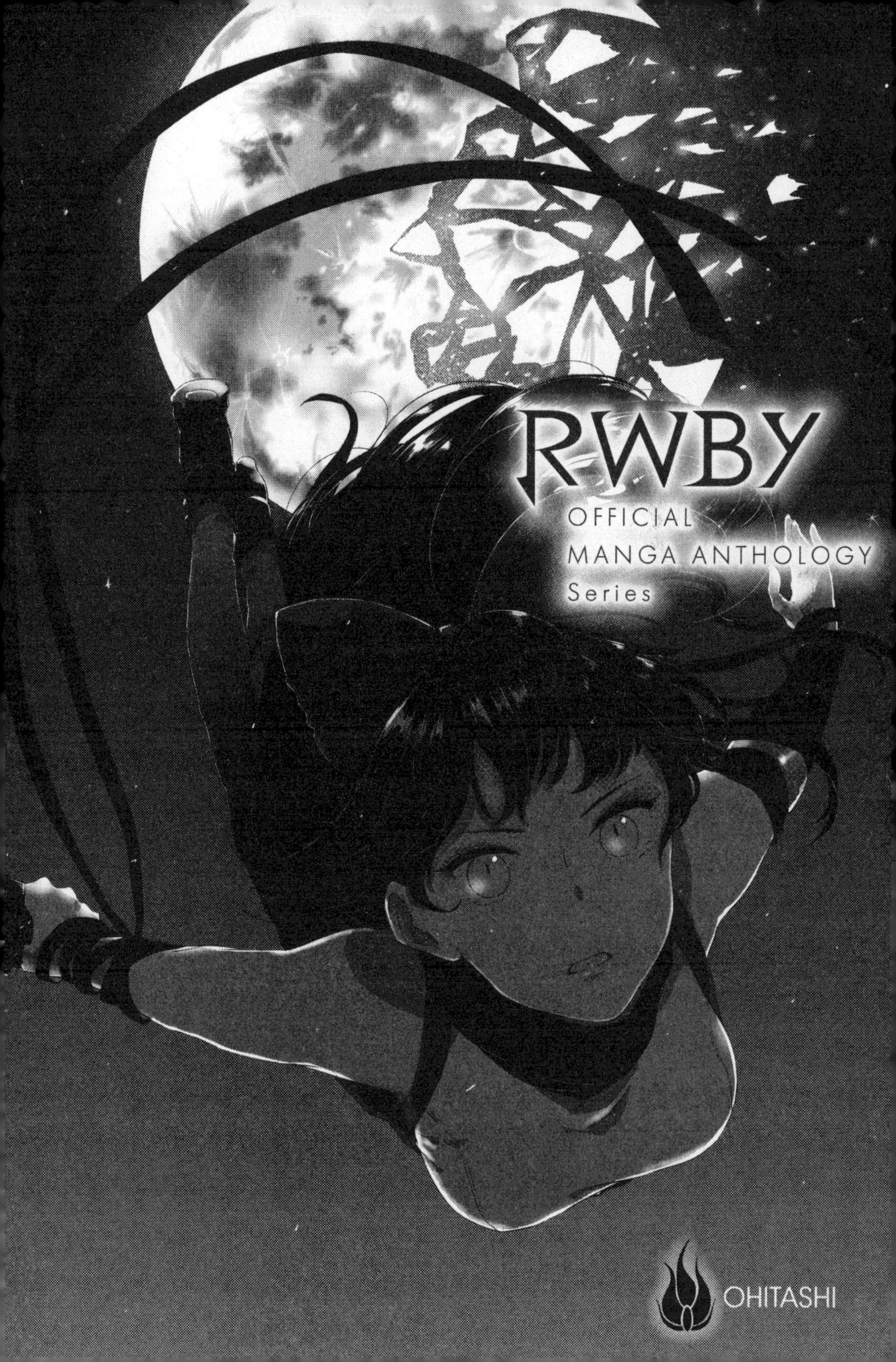
RWBY
OFFICIAL
MANGA ANTHOLOGY
Series
OHITASHI

We *RWBY* fans love you, Monty!

Thank you for continuing *RWBY* and providing
a magical experience for us, Rooster Teeth!

Messages From Illustrators & Mangaka

Illustrations & Manga

SOME TIME PASSED IN BETWEEN DUE TO BLAKE'S DISAPPEARANCE (?), BUT BLAKE IS DOING JUST FINE.
HI, EVERYONE. MOJOJOJ HERE.
THANK YOU FOR PURCHASING *RWBY* ANTHOLOGY VOLUME 3.
THIS TIME, I HAD THE HONOR OF DRAWING A COLOR ILLUSTRATION.
I HOPE YOU ENJOY IT AS WELL AS MY FOUR PANEL COMIC STRIPS.

MUGUPO
FOR ALLOWING ME TO BE A PART OF THIS...
TO ALL THE READERS...
TO ALL THOSE THAT PURCHASED IT...
THANK YOU!
SPECIAL THANKS TO ROOKIE, KUROTA, AND WAKANABE

Illustrations

Blake may seem aloof, but she can be friendly. That's what's so cute about her.
I want to touch her ears...
NINJA
ryuga

I love the contrast between the voracious Blake and cool Blake.

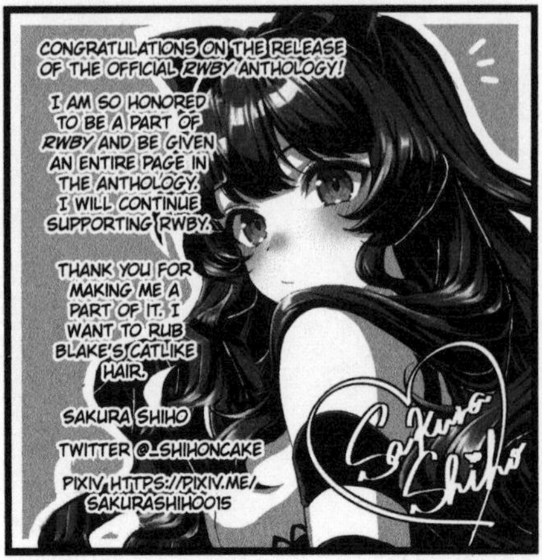
CONGRATULATIONS ON THE RELEASE OF THE OFFICIAL RWBY ANTHOLOGY!
I AM SO HONORED TO BE A PART OF RWBY AND BE GIVEN AN ENTIRE PAGE IN THE ANTHOLOGY. I WILL CONTINUE SUPPORTING RWBY.
THANK YOU FOR MAKING ME A PART OF IT. I WANT TO RUB BLAKE'S CATLIKE HAIR.
SAKURA SHIHO
TWITTER @_SHIHONCAKE
PIXIV HTTPS://PIXIV.ME/SAKURASHIHO015
Sakura Shiho

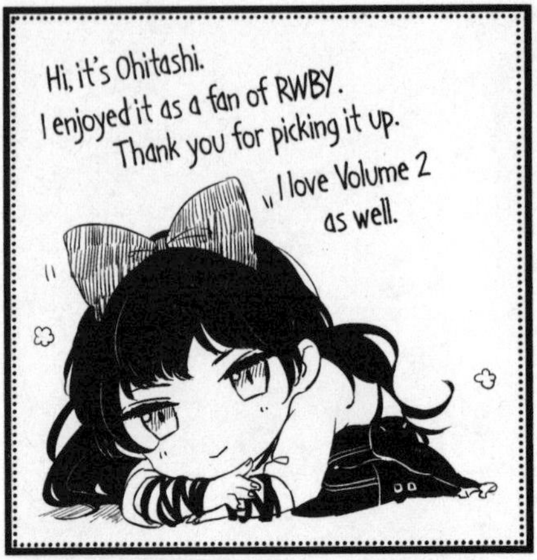
Hi, it's Ohitashi.
I enjoyed it as a fan of RWBY.
Thank you for picking it up.
I love Volume 2 as well.

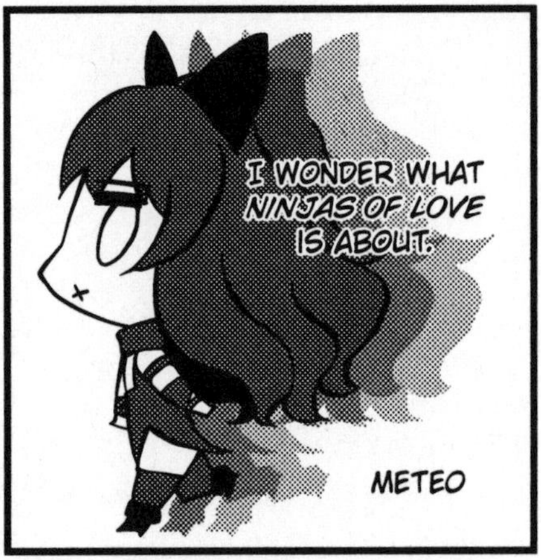
I WONDER WHAT NINJAS OF LOVE IS ABOUT.
METEO

← Manga

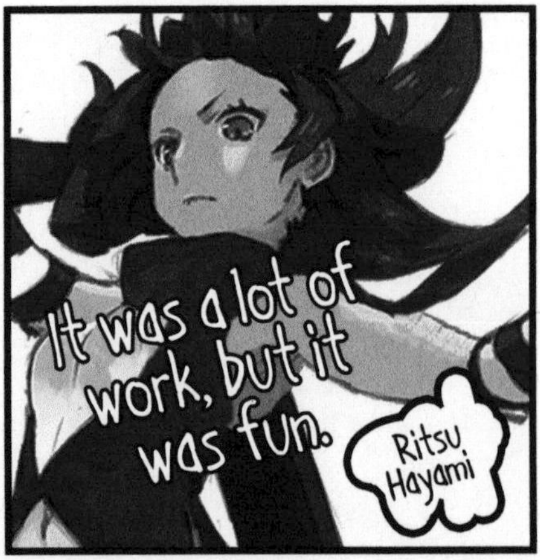
It was a lot of work, but it was fun.
Ritsu Hayami

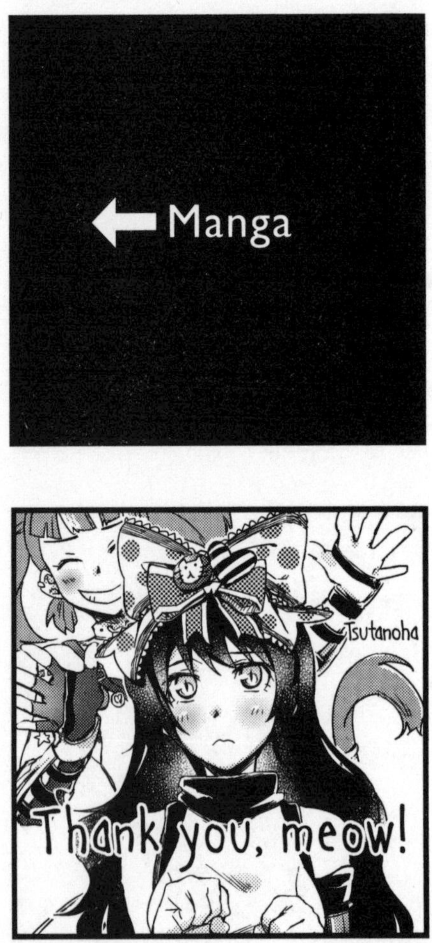
Tsutanoha
Thank you, meow!

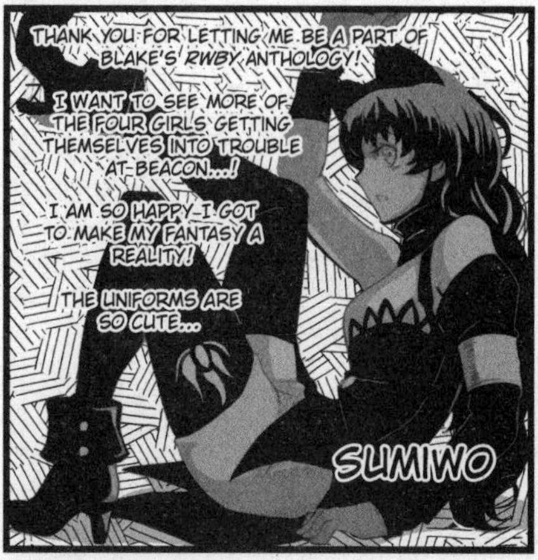
THANK YOU FOR LETTING ME BE A PART OF BLAKE'S RWBY ANTHOLOGY!
I WANT TO SEE MORE OF THE FOUR GIRLS GETTING THEMSELVES INTO TROUBLE AT BEACON...!
I AM SO HAPPY I GOT TO MAKE MY FANTASY A REALITY!
THE UNIFORMS ARE SO CUTE...
SUMIWO

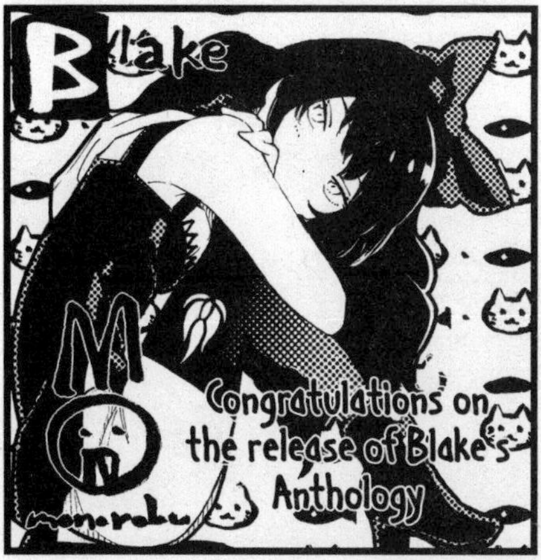
Blake
Congratulations on the release of Blake's Anthology
monorobu

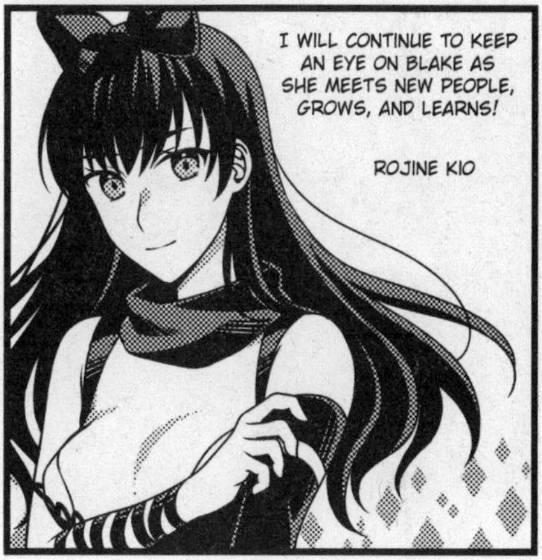
I WILL CONTINUE TO KEEP AN EYE ON BLAKE AS SHE MEETS NEW PEOPLE, GROWS, AND LEARNS!
ROJINE KIO

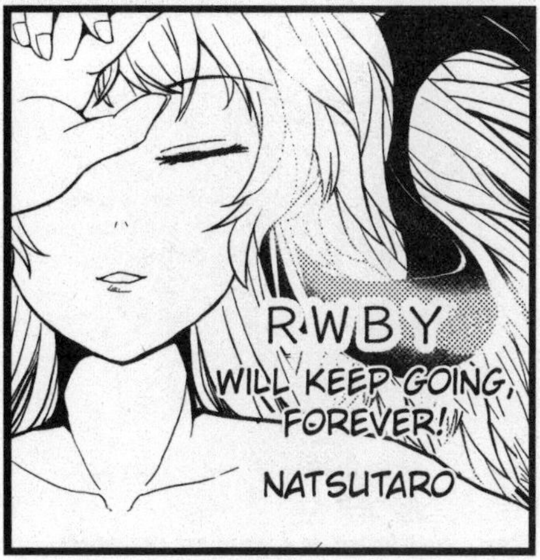
RWBY
WILL KEEP GOING, FOREVER!
NATSUTARO

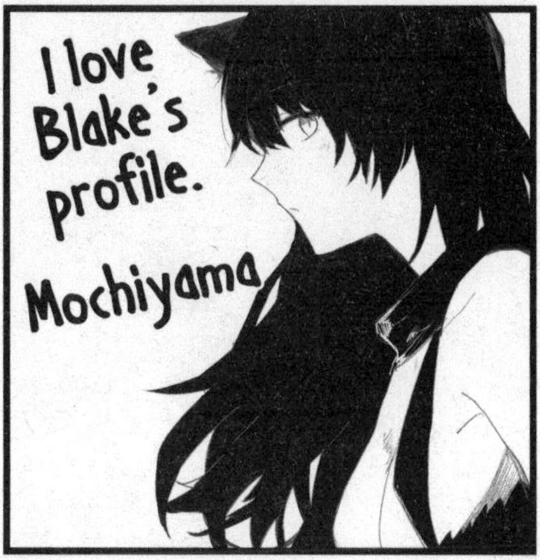
I love Blake's profile.
Mochiyama

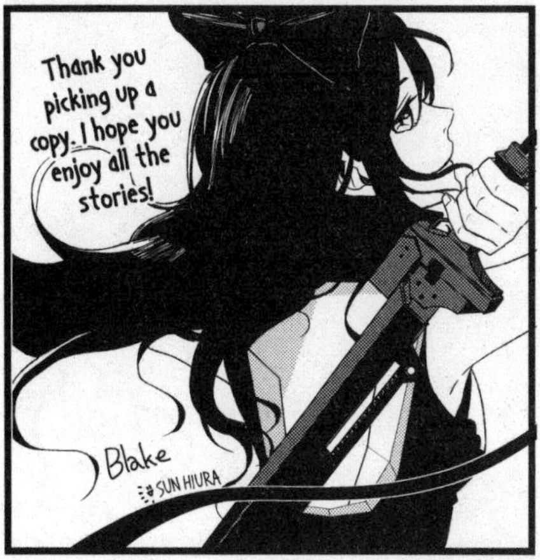
Thank you picking up a copy. I hope you enjoy all the stories!
Blake
SUN HIURA

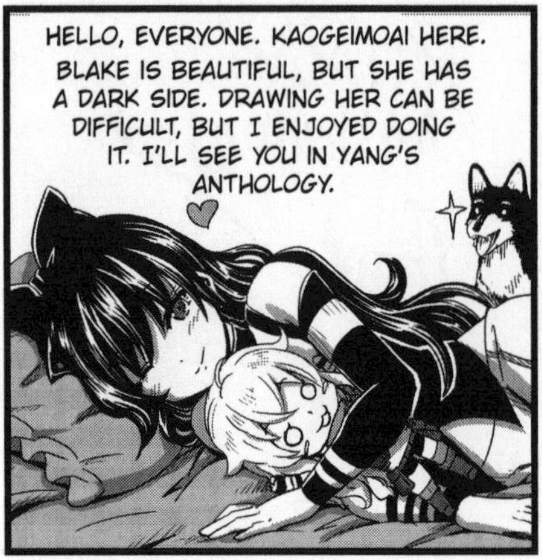
HELLO, EVERYONE. KAOGEIMOAI HERE. BLAKE IS BEAUTIFUL, BUT SHE HAS A DARK SIDE. DRAWING HER CAN BE DIFFICULT, BUT I ENJOYED DOING IT. I'LL SEE YOU IN YANG'S ANTHOLOGY.

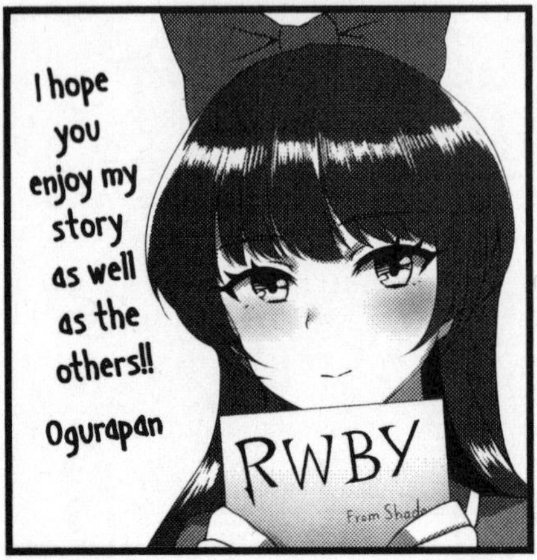
I hope you enjoy my story as well as the others!!
Ogurapan
RWBY

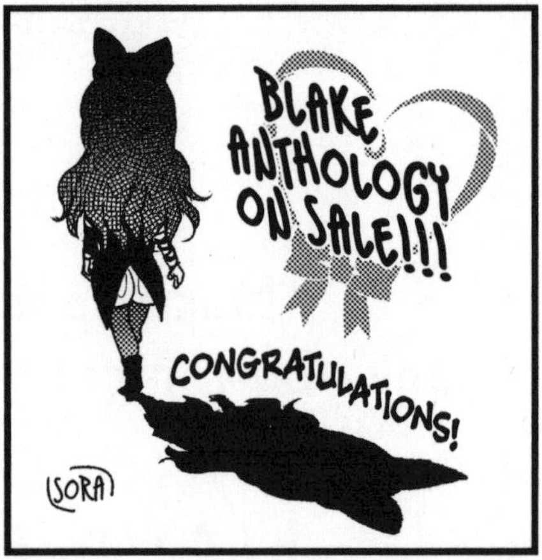
BLAKE ANTHOLOGY ON SALE!!!
CONGRATULATIONS!
SORA

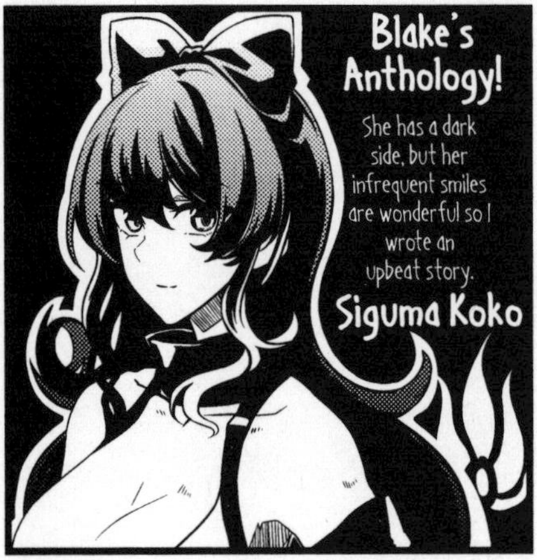
Blake's Anthology!
She has a dark side, but her infrequent smiles are wonderful so I wrote an upbeat story.
Siguma Koko

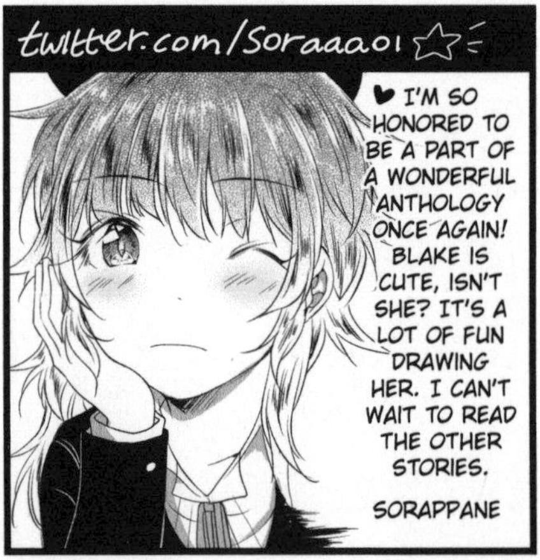
twitter.com/soraaa01
I'M SO HONORED TO BE A PART OF A WONDERFUL ANTHOLOGY ONCE AGAIN! BLAKE IS CUTE, ISN'T SHE? IT'S A LOT OF FUN DRAWING HER. I CAN'T WAIT TO READ THE OTHER STORIES.
SORAPPANE

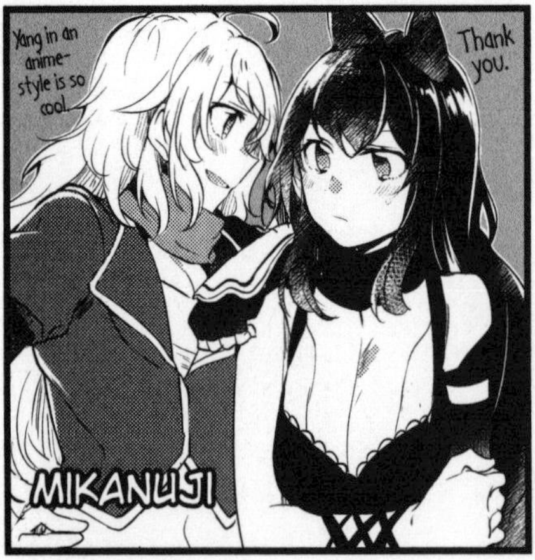
Thank you.
Yang in an anime-style is so cool.
MIKANUJI

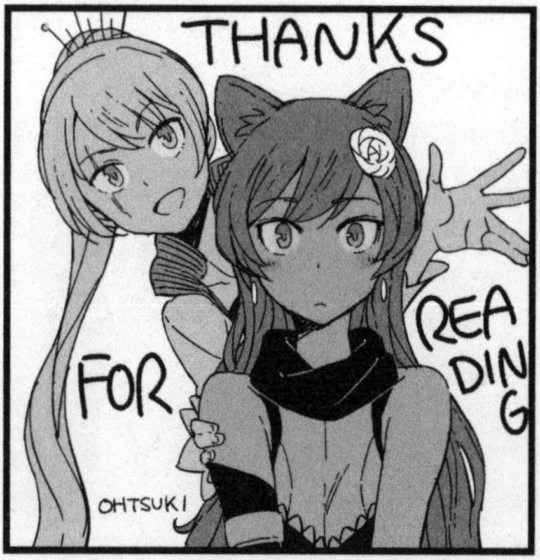
THANKS
FOR
REA
DIN
G
OHTSUKI

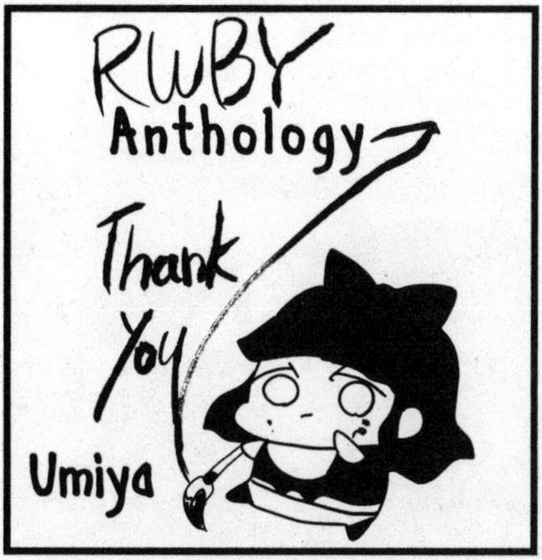
RWBY
Anthology
Thank
You
Umiya

Much appreciated.
Thank you for getting this anthology.

HAVE FUN!

About Blake

Ein Lee

In *RWBY*, Blake is a character with an air of mystery. Thanks to this quality, despite her deceptively simple character design, she quickly left a strong impression on me. I went through a process of trial and error to come up with the design of her outfit. She started off wearing knee-high lace-up boots, a wide skirt, and a catlike hair band, but I eventually settled on her current covert assassin look.

All of Team RWBY's individual weapons are cool and stylish, but I think Blake's particularly stands out. Like Blake's character, her weapon is mysterious and seems like it can do anything. To be honest, I'm not quite sure how it works myself.

I love drawing her flowing hair and ribbon. The real mystery of her character design is how they don't get tangled up with everything all the time!

If you'll notice, the cover illustration here uses only sparse black coloring. This time I created most of the shadows by using deep purple and shades of turquoise. Deeper colors like navy blue, deep purple, or even deep red can sometimes create richer, darker shadows.

Just like Ruby and Weiss' rough sketches, Blake's illustration is designed to be paired with Yang's image. I feel that I was able to express a calm stillness with her character. I have to say, this cover art is definitely my favorite of the four!

Hello Lovelies!

I'm so very excited to be part of the adventure that is *RWBY* and I'm pleased to have you along with me! Because of you, we've been able to tell the fascinating stories of those who live in the world of Remnant, from the students at Beacon Academy to the Faunus of Menagerie.

We've come a long way since 2013, when *RWBY*'s first episode aired, and it's since expanded with Chibi, Grimm Eclipse, billboards, toys, and now a manga! It's been an absolute whirlwind and we couldn't have done it without you. So thank you. Thank you so much.

Will all my little Faunus heart.

Arryn Zech

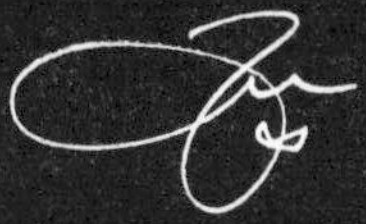

RWBY OFFICIAL MANGA ANTHOLOGY 3

From Shadows

VIZ Signature Edition
Official Manga Anthology Vol. 3
FROM SHADOWS
Based on the Rooster Teeth Series Created by MONTY OUM.

TRANSLATION Joe Yamazaki
ENGLISH ADAPTATION Jason A. Hurley
TOUCH-UP ART AND LETTERING Evan Waldinger
DESIGN Shawn Carrico
EDITOR Joel Enos

COVER ILLUSTRATION Ein Lee/Meteo
ORIGINAL COVER DESIGN Tsuyoshi Kusano

SPECIAL THANKS
Ken Takizawa (Home-sha)
Takanori Inoue (Home-sha)
Misato Kaneko
Yoshihiko Wakanabe (Editor/Planner of RWBY OFFICIAL MANGA ANTHOLOGY)

Printed in the U.S.A.

Published by VIZ Media, LLC
P.O. Box 77010
San Francisco, CA 94107

10 9 8 7 6 5 4 3 2 1
First printing, November 2018

VIZ SIGNATURE
vizsignature.com

VIZ MEDIA
viz.com

ratings.viz.com RATED T TEEN

PARENTAL ADVISORY
RWBY is rated T for Teen and is recommended for ages 13 and up. This volume contains violence and peril.

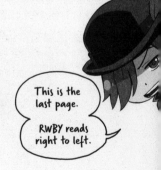

This is the last page.

RWBY reads right to left.